STUDY GUIDE

to accompany

FUNDAMENTAL STATISTICS
for BEHAVIORAL SCIENCES

EIGHTH EDITION

Robert B. McCall

with

Richard E. Sass

WADSWORTH
CENGAGE Learning

Australia • Brazil • Japan • Korea • Mexico • Singapore • Spain • United Kingdom • United States

Study Guide to Accompany: Fundamental Statistics for Behavioral Sciences, Eight Edition
Robert B. McCall, Richard E. Sass

For product information and technology assistance, contact us at
Cengage Learning Customer & Sales Support, 1-800-354-9706

For permission to use material from this text or product,
submit all requests online at **cengage.com/permissions**
Further permissions questions can be emailed to
permissionrequest@cengage.com

ISBN-13: 978-0-534-57781-0

ISBN-10: 0-534-57781-4

Wadsworth
10 Davis Drive
Belmont, CA 94002-3098
USA

Cengage Learning is a leading provider of customized learning solutions with office locations around the globe, including Singapore, the United Kingdom, Australia, Mexico, Brazil, and Japan. Locate your local office at **international.cengage.com/region**

Cengage Learning products are represented in Canada by Nelson Education, Ltd.

For your course and learning solutions, visit **academic.cengage.com**

Purchase any of our products at your local college store or at our preferred online store **www.ichapters.com**

Printed in the United States of America
2 3 4 5 6   19 18 17 16 15

CONTENTS • • • • •

To the student

To the instructor

● ● ● ● ●

to the student

The Study Guide has been prepared to supplement your text, *Fundamental Statistics for Behavioral Sciences,* Eighth Edition. Each chapter of the *Guide* corresponds to a chapter in the text and consists of six sections: concept goals, guide to major concepts, self-test, exercises, answers, and optional instructions for using two computerized statistical packages.

The concept goals are the focal topics of a chapter, arranged in a simple list; be sure you master these topics. The guide to major concepts is a semi-programmed review of the basic vocabulary, concepts, and computational routines presented in the text. It requires you to complete an integrated series of statements that summarize the main points of the chapter. The self-test measures your mastery of the material from the text and guide, and the exercises offer you an opportunity to apply the methods and principles of statistics to actual numerical data. The optional boxes at the end of the chapter provide instructions on how to use two computerized statistical packages, MINITAB, and SPSS, to perform the computations presented in the exercises of the text and *Guide.*

Recommended procedure. My students have found that following certain procedures seems to make this *Study Guide* more valuable. First, *read each text chapter before working on the guide chapter*, which is a review of, not an introduction to, the most important material. After you have read the text chapter, read and complete the guide to major concepts. Then return to the text and read it again, filling out your knowledge of the chapter topics. Finally, try the self-test and exercises in the *Study Guide.* The answers to the questions in these sections appear at the end of the *Study Guide* chapter.

I have tried to make the programmed guide to major concepts more interesting by asking you to recall vocabulary and concepts from the text rather than just repeating information from the previous sentence. I have also concentrated on the most important points and have illustrated these with concrete numerical examples. Each paragraph of the programmed review deals with one or two concepts and requires you to complete one or more statements. You will find the correct answer printed in the margin to the right of each blank. As you work through a paragraph, keep the answers covered with a sheet of paper until you have written your own answers for that paragraph. Then pull the paper down far enough to uncover the correct answers. The purpose of the review is to have you recall and use statistical terminology and concepts; you will benefit from this activity only if you recall the material without looking at the answer and only if you actually write the response in the blank.

At various points in the review you will be asked to perform simple calculations or to complete the calculations outlined in an accompanying table. It is sometimes tempting to skip such activities, but many of my students have found that there is a difference between their ability to understand concepts while reading about them, on the one hand, and to apply them in the solution of numerical problems, on the other. Many students have urged me to encourage you to *regard the numerical activities and exercises as the primary method of obtaining a thorough understanding of the nature and application of statistics*; you should complete them all.

You will also find guided computational examples in the review section. These are tables that outline the computational routine required to calculate a given statistic or to perform a statistical test of significance. Follow these outlines not only for the exercises presented in the *Study Guide* but whenever you need to calculate the statistic in question. If you do so, you will not forget important details or steps and will be less likely to make a simple procedural error.

Self-Test. The self-test questions, although they cannot provide a complete check on your mastery of all the material, do represent a fair selection of basic chapter topics. Thus the self-test functions as a trial examination by which you can evaluate your progress. Since the test covers material from the text and *Study Guide,* you should take it only after you have read the text chapter, done the programmed review, and reread the text to be sure you understand all the important topics in the text in some detail.

Exercises. The exercises enable you to apply the concepts you have studied to new situations and to make creative use of what you have learned. These exercises will be of greatest benefit to you if you do not look at the answer until you have finished working a problem. *Only through doing the exercises can you learn to apply statistical concepts appropriately and accurately to the analysis of data*. To make the exercises relatively painless, I have kept the numbers small and the computations as simple as possible. Many exercises present simplified versions of actual experiments that have had a major impact on thought in the social sciences and thus should be especially interesting to you. Although the material presented in this course is simpler than the statistics performed in some of the actual research projects described, the exercises nevertheless demonstrate why a knowledge of statistics is necessary to read, interpret, or perform research in the behavioral sciences.

Statistical packages. If you are using one of the two computerized statistical packages, MINITAB or SPSS, you should work the entire programmed unit, including any guided computational examples *by hand* first. Then, before doing the exercises, work through the instructions for the computerized statistical package that you or your instructor has selected. The instructions assume you know Windows and how to access the statistical package on your machine, and they typically show you how to do the guided computational example using the computerized package. Then do the exercises using the program when appropriate. Be warned, however, that the computer will perform the calculations, but *it will not help you understand the statistical concepts or interpret the results you obtain*. Also, the purpose of learning to use the program is so that you will be able to use it frequently and efficiently in the future—it may actually take you longer to learn to use it to work the exercises for this course than to do them by hand. Be aware, also, that occasionally a computer program will use a slightly different computational method that may produce a slightly different answer than given in the text or guide. These instances are pointed out in the description of the output from each program.

ROBERT B. McCALL

to the instructor

This *Study Guide* has been prepared to aid students in mastering the basic concepts and applications presented in *Fundamental Statistics for Behavioral Sciences*, Eighth Edition. Each chapter of the *Guide* contains six sections, which are described in the paragraphs that follow.

Concept goals. This section is simply a list of important concepts to be mastered; it ensures that the student is aware of the most crucial topics in each chapter.

Guide to major concepts. This is a semi-programmed summary of the major points made in the corresponding chapter of the text. It is intended to be used as a step-by-step review of only the most important topics after the student has read the text. The presentation is stripped of excess explanation, detail, and secondary considerations. Completing this section of the *Study Guide* requires active involvement from the student, who is asked to recall key terms and concepts from the text or to use principles discussed in the text to solve new problems.

The tone of the guide to major concepts is very concrete and applied; it complements the more theoretical presentation of the text. Immediately after each concept is summarized, it is translated into a numerical example that must be solved. I have encouraged students to explore the application of a statistic by making simple computations on different data sets. In Chapter 3, for example, the variance and standard deviation must be calculated for several small distributions that differ in variability. Then the student is asked to plot the distributions and to label them with the values of s^2 and s; thus the graphical presentation of the concept of variability will be associated with the numerical values of the statistics that index it. Similar exercises illustrate (in Chapter 7) how the correlation coefficient varies as a function of the nature of the scatterplot and (in Chapters 14 and 15) how the mean squares in an analysis of variance are influenced by certain treatment effects.

Whenever possible, major statistical routines described in the programmed unit are organized for the student in guided computational examples. These step-by-step outlines clarify the logical and computational details of important techniques. Students who complete these tables by following the instructions provided will be able to use the same format to solve similar problems in the future.

Self-Test. This covers material presented both in the guide and in the text. Questions may require definitions, explanations, computations, or application of principles to new situations. The test can be used by students to evaluate their progress, since all answers are provided at the end of the chapter.

Exercises. For the most part, exercises require the student to apply concepts and computational routines to new sets of data. They may be used as homework or as the basis of class discussion or laboratory sessions. Many of the exercises are based on actual experiments of major interest in a variety of behavioral sciences.

Answers. Answers to the guided computational examples and all exercises are given, including some of the intermediate quantities so that students may locate their specific errors quickly.

Computerized statistical package instructions. Lastly, two sections give instructions, sample input data, and sample output data, typically for the guided computational example, to students who wish to learn to use the MINITAB or SPSS statistical computer packages. This material is intended to be optional. Teachers must provide instructions for gaining access to one of these packages on the particular machines and systems available to their students. Students are assumed to be familiar with Windows operating systems. The directions given in this *Guide* cover only elementary examples of some of the statistics presented in the text; they do not cover all the options and techniques that each package can perform, and they are not a substitute for the package manual.

I would like to express my gratitude to Richard Sass who prepared the computerized statistical package presentations; Mark Appelbaum of the University of California, San Diego, for his statistical and pedagogical advice; and to Catherine Kelley and Siran Suwan for preparing the manuscript.

Richard Sass thanks MINITAB, Inc., for providing copies of the software as part of their Authors Program.

ROBERT B. McCALL

CHAPTER 1

THE STUDY OF STATISTICS ••••••

CONCEPT GOALS

Be sure that you thoroughly understand the following concepts and how to use them in statistical applications.

- ♦ Properties of scales: magnitude, equal intervals, absolute zero point
- ♦ Types of scales: ratio, interval, ordinal, nominal
- ♦ Variables vs. constants
- ♦ Continuous vs. discrete variables
- ♦ Real limits
- ♦ Rounding numbers
- ♦ Mathematical operations involving the summation sign, $\sum_{i=1}^{N}$
- ♦ The difference between $\sum X$, $\sum X^2$, and $(\sum X)^2$

••••• GUIDE TO MAJOR CONCEPTS

Introduction

The mathematics required to use *Fundamental Statistics for Behavioral Sciences* is quite simple, not more difficult than the level usually required of high school graduates. Indeed, most of the mathematical operations use only elementary algebra. However, if your memory of those operations is a little fuzzy, Appendix I in the textbook and the Appendix at the back of this *Study Guide* will help you review symbols and algebra. If you are not sure whether you already understand this material, try the Self-Test at the end of the *Study Guide* Appendix. If you miss more than two questions, you probably need some review before proceeding.

The study of methods for describing and interpreting quantitative information is called [1]_____ .

There are two types of methods, **descriptive** and **inferential statistics**. Those that organize, summarize, and describe quantitative information are known as [2]_____ , whereas techniques that permit judgments to be made about a larger group of individuals on the basis of data actually collected on a smaller group constitute [3]_____ .

Statistics are often necessary to interpret measurements because almost all data in the behavioral sciences contain [4]_____ . Measurements of the same characteristic in a group of subjects can differ in value for three major reasons: **individual differences**, **measurement error**, and **unreliability**. First, the units (often people) being studied are rarely identical to each other, so one source of variability is [5]_____ . Second, behavioral scientists cannot always measure the attribute or behavior under study as accurately as they would like. This type of variability is called [6]_____ . Third, even if a single person is measured twice under the same circumstances, the measured values may not be identical. This type of variability is called [7]_____ .

Answer Key to Introduction

[1]	statistics	[4]	variability	[7]	unreliability
[2]	descriptive statistics	[5]	individual differences		
[3]	inferential statistics	[6]	measurement error		

Scales of Measurement

An important part of science is **measurement**, which is the orderly assignment of a value to a characteristic. This quantitative description, or [1]_____ , is accomplished with **scales**

of measurement, which are the ordered set of possible numbers that may be obtained by the measurement process. These [2]_____ of measurement may possess properties of **magnitude, equal intervals**, and an **absolute zero point**. If the measurement of some attribute permits one to say whether that attribute in one case is greater than, less than, or equal to that attribute in another case, then the scale has [3]_____ . If each unit of measurement (for example, one second, one rating point, one degree) represents the same amount of the attribute being measured, regardless of where on the scale the unit falls, the scale possesses [4]_____ . Finally, if there is a value that represents none of the attribute being measured, then the scale has an [5]_____ .

If a measurement scale possesses all three of these properties, it is called a **ratio** scale, because the scale makes it possible to use the ratio between two measurements. For example, if a father is 70 inches tall and his son is 35 inches tall, the father is twice as tall as his son; so height in inches (or centimeters) is measured on a [6]_____ scale. If a scale has magnitude and equal intervals but not an absolute zero point, it is called an **interval** scale. Temperature in degrees (Celsius or Fahrenheit) is an example of an [7]_____ scale. Some measurement scales permit only statements of relative magnitude and are called **ordinal**. Rankings of football teams would be an [8]_____ scale. If a scale does not possess any of these three properties, namely it does not possess [9]_____ , [10]_____ , or an [11]_____ , it is called a **nominal** scale. Classification of plant species would be a [12]_____ scale.

Thus, if a scale possesses all three properties, it is a [13]_____ scale; if it has none of them, it is a [14]_____ scale; if it has only magnitude, it is an [15]_____ scale; and if it has only magnitude and equal intervals, it is an [16]_____ scale.

Answer Key to Scales of Measurement

[1]	measurement	[5]	absolute zero point	[9]	magnitude
[2]	scales	[6]	ratio	[10]	equal intervals
[3]	magnitude	[7]	interval	[11]	absolute zero point
[4]	equal intervals	[8]	ordinal	[12]	nominal

[13]	ratio	[15]	ordinal
[14]	nominal	[16]	interval

Variables and Constants

Within any particular context, a **variable** is the general characteristic being measured on a set of people, objects, or events, the members of which may take on different values. If we have a sample of 20 college students and we obtain their Scholastic Assessment Test scores (SAT), then SAT is a [1]_____ that will take on several values within that sample. Even though it has only two values and we usually do not "measure" them, gender may also be a variable if both male and female subjects are in a study. On the other hand, some quantities do not change their value within a given context, and they are called **constants**. The mathematical quantity π always equals 3.1415... and is thus a [2]_____ . Notice that while SAT in the sample mentioned above was a [3]_____ , the average SAT of that sample is a [4]_____ . However, if we obtain several samples of 20 subjects each and calculate the average SAT for each group, then "average SAT" takes on a different value for each sample. In this new context, average SAT is a [5]_____ , but the average taken over all the samples is a [6]_____ for that collection of samples.

Answer Key to Variables and Constants

[1]	variable	[3]	variable	[5]	variable
[2]	constant	[4]	constant	[6]	constant

Continuous and Discrete Variables

A variable may be either **continuous** or **discrete**. A continuous variable is one that theoretically can assume an infinite number of values between any two points on the measurement scale. The length in centimeters of lines drawn by subjects, the longevity in years of American men, and the time in seconds that a subject delays before responding are all examples of [1]_____ variables, because given any two values, one can always name a possible value that will be between them. Actually, there are an infinite number of potential values between any two points for a continuous variable. In contrast, discrete variables are those for which one can assume only a countable number of values between any two points. Since the number of aggressive acts a preschool child commits must be a whole number (1/2 response is impossible), number of aggressive acts is a [2]_____ variable; there is no possible score value between 5 and 6 acts, for example. Actually, this distinction between [3]_____ and [4]_____ variables is a theoretical one, because in practice we round off measures to some convenient level of accuracy (tenths of seconds, whole seconds, etc.), and from a practical standpoint the rounding makes the measures, though not the variables, discrete.

Answer Key to Continuous and Discrete Variables

[1]	continuous	[2]	discrete	[3]	continuous	[4]	discrete

Real Limits

Any single value of a continuous variable actually represents a range of values, roughly composed of the theoretically possible numbers that one would round off to the number in question. For example, if one is measuring time in whole seconds, "23 seconds" represents all the theoretically possible values between 22.5 and 23.5 seconds; similarly, 24 seconds actually stands for values between 23.5 and 24.5 seconds, and so on. The **real limits** of a number, then, are the points falling one-half measurement unit above and one-half measurement unit below that number. If a measurement is in whole seconds, the [1]_____ of 47 seconds are [2]_____ and [3]_____ ; if measurement is in tenths of a second, the real limits of 43.8 seconds are [4]_____ and [5]_____ (the measurement unit is .1 second, one-half of which is .05 second); and if measurement is in hundredths of a second, the real limits of 67.42 seconds are [6]_____ and [7]_____ .

Answer Key to Real Limits

[1]	real limits	[3]	47.5	[5]	43.85	[7]	67.425
[2]	46.5	[4]	43.75	[6]	67.415		

Rounding

If a decimal number is to be rounded to whole units, then the whole-unit portion of the number is increased by 1 (*rounded up*) if the fractional value is .5 or larger; it is left unchanged if the fractional value is less than .5. Rounding to whole numbers, 34.2 becomes [1]__ , 25.5000 becomes [2]__ , and 19.07 becomes [3]__ .

Answer Key to Rounding		
[1] 34	[2] 26	[3] 19

Summation

A great many calculations in statistics require summing specific values. Therefore, many formulas employ a shorthand method for designating the operation of summing. For example, suppose the scores on variable X for five subjects are as follows:

Subject (i)	X_i
1	3
2	6
3	5
4	9
5	2

The symbol X_i stands for the value of variable X for the ith subject; for the data above, [1]$X_3 = $ __ , and [2]$X_4 = $ __ . Frequently, you will need to sum all the X_i scores. For the above example, this operation is symbolized by $\sum_{i=1}^{5} X_i$, in which the Greek letter sigma and its subscripts and superscripts mean "sum the X_i from $i = 1$ to $i = 5$." Written out, $\sum_{i=1}^{5} X_i = X_1 + X_2 + X_3 + X_4 + X_5$. If the number of subjects is N, the operation of summing all N scores for variable X is written $\sum_{i=1}^{N} X_i$, or simply $\sum X$ if it is clear which scores (usually all the available scores) are to be summed. For the data provided above, [3]$\sum_{i=1}^{5} X_i = $ __ , [4]$\sum_{i=3}^{5} X_i = $ __ , [5]$\sum_{i=1}^{2} X_i = $ __ , and [6]$\sum X = $ __ .

Since the summation sign is a frequent element in formulas, it is necessary to understand how to perform simple algebra involving it. Consider the expression $\sum_{i=1}^{N} cX_i$ in which c is a constant and X_i is a variable. This expression tells one to sum over all X from i to N the constant c times the variable. In symbols,

$$\sum_{i=1}^{N} cX_i = cX_1 + cX_2 + \ldots + cX_N$$

But, if the constant c is factored out, one has

$$= c(X_1 + cX_2 + \ldots + X_N)$$
$$\sum_{i=1}^{N} cX_i = c\sum_{i=1}^{N} X_i$$

This idea is simpler than it looks. Suppose for the data above that the constant $c = 2$, and you want to find the sum of all the scores multiplied by $c = 2$. There are two ways to obtain the required total. First, you could multiply each score by $c = 2$ and then add the five products. Stated in symbols, you could determine [7]_____ . To compute the total, add [8] $2(\underline{}) + 2(\underline{}) + 2(\underline{}) + 2(\underline{}) + 2(\underline{}) = \underline{}$. Alternatively, you could add all the scores first and then multiply this sum by $c = 2$. In symbols, obtain [9]_____ by calculating [10] $2(\underline{} + \underline{} + \underline{} + \underline{} + \underline{}) = \underline{}$. Therefore, *the sum of a constant times a variable equals the constant times the sum of the variable*. In symbols, [11]_____ .

Consider the expression $\sum_{i=1}^{N} c$ in which c is a constant. This expression requires adding N c's together. Again, there are two ways to determine this total. If N is 5 and c is 2, you could add five 2s. In symbols, [12]_____ is calculated by [13] $\underline{} + \underline{} + \underline{} + \underline{} + \underline{} = \underline{}$. Alternatively, since multiplication is just a short method of adding the same number over and over again, you could simply multiply five by two. In symbols, the desired total is [14]_____ , which can be calculated by [15] $\underline{}(\underline{}) = \underline{}$. Therefore, the principle is that *the sum of a constant taken N times equals N times the constant*. In symbols, [16]_____ .

Finally, suppose you are asked to find $\sum_{i=1}^{N}(X_i + Y_i)$. This expression requires the sum of two variables over a group of subjects. Again, there are two ways to determine the desired total. You could add the two scores separately for each subject and then add these individual totals. In symbols, you would determine [17]_____ . Using the following table of data,

Subject (i)	X_i	Y_i	$X_i + Y_i$	X_iY_i
1	2	3	[18]____	[19]____
2	7	1	[20]____	[21]____
3	5	6	[22]____	[23]____
	[24]$\sum_{i=1}^{N} X_i =$ __	[25]$\sum_{i=1}^{N} Y_i =$ __	[26]$\sum_{i=1}^{N}(X_i + Y_i)$____	[27]$\sum_{i=1}^{N} X_iY_i =$ ____

you would determine the values for each subject in the $X_i + Y_i$ column and then add those values to obtain the numerical total, [28]__ . Alternatively, you could add the X_i for all subjects (total = [29]__), then add the Y_i for all subjects (total = [30]__), and then add the two sums together to obtain the numerical total [31]__ . In symbols, this latter operation is equivalent to [32]_____ . The rule is that *the summation of a sum of variables is the sum of the summation of each variable.* In symbols, [33]_____ = _____ + _____ .

It will be important for students to recognize the difference between adding and multiplying two variables when a summation across subjects is to be calculated. The difference can be seen by completing the right-hand column of the above table, labeled X_iY_i. While [34]$\sum_{i=1}^{N}(X_i + Y_i) =$ __ , [35]$\sum_{i=1}^{N}(X_iY_i) =$ __ .

Also, it will be necessary for the student to distinguish between $\sum X^2$ and $(\sum X)^2$. The sum of the squared X scores is written symbolically [36]__ , while the squared sum of the X scores is written [37]__ . In terms of the data for the three subjects above, [38]$(\sum X)^2 = (\_\_)^2 =$ __ , while [39]$\sum X^2 =$ __ + __ + __ = __ .

Answer Key to Summation

[1]	5	[8]	3, 6, 5, 9, 2, 50	[15]	$5(2) = 10$
[2]	9	[9]	$c\sum_{i=1}^{N} X_i$	[16]	$\sum_{i=1}^{N} c = Nc$
[3]	25	[10]	$3 + 6 + 5 + 9 + 2 = 50$	[17]	$\sum_{i=1}^{N}(X_i + Y_i)$
[4]	16	[11]	$\sum_{i=1}^{N} cX_i = c\sum_{i=1}^{N} X_i$	[18]	5
[5]	9	[12]	$\sum_{i=1}^{N} c$	[19]	6
[6]	25	[13]	$2 + 2 + 2 + 2 + 2 = 10$	[20]	8
[7]	$\sum_{i=1}^{N} cX_i$	[14]	Nc	[21]	7

[22] 11

[23] 30

[24] 14

[25] 10

[26] 24

[27] 43

[28] 24

[29] 14

[30] 10

[31] 24

[32] $\sum_{i=1}^{N} X_i + \sum_{i=1}^{N} Y_i$

[33] $\sum_{i=1}^{N}(X_i + Y_i)$, $\sum_{i=1}^{N} X_i$, $\sum_{i=1}^{N} Y$

[34] 24

[35] 43

[36] $\sum X^2$

[37] $(\sum X)^2$

[38] $(14)^2 = 196$

[39] $2^2 + 7^2 + 5^2 = 78$

● ● ● ● ●   SELF-TEST

1. Individual differences, measurement error, and unreliability all produce
    a. variability
    b. descriptive statistics
    c. inferential statistics
    d. scales of measurement

2. The failure to obtain the same measured value twice on the same person is known as
    a. individual differences
    b. unreliability
    c. measurement error
    d. variability

3. Indicate the type of measurement scale (ratio, interval, ordinal, or nominal) for each of the following variables.
    _____ a. Age in years of mothers when their first child was born
    _____ b. Type of automobile owned where 1 = American, 2 = Japanese, 3 = Other
    _____ c. Army rank where 1 = Lieutenant, 2 = Captain, 3 = Major, etc., as a measure of authority
    _____ d. Ratings from 1 to 10 which define equal steps pertaining to the livability of U.S. cities as judged by survey respondents

4. Do the following measurements assess discrete or continuous variables?
    _____ a. Number of television sets per household
    _____ b. Average take-home pay of a group of employees
    _____ c. Frequency of bar-pressing by an animal in an operant chamber

5. Determine the real limits of the following numbers.
    a. 90   b. 13.7   c. 30.550

6. Round the following to whole numbers.
    a. 4.6   c. 24.55
    b. 12.5   d. 9.5

7. Given the following data and $c = 2$, perform the indicated summations.

Subject (i)	X_i	Y_i
1	6	2
2	0	8
3	4	5
4	3	3
5	1	6

a. $\sum_{i=1}^{3} X_i + c$

b. $\sum_{i=1}^{3}(X_i + c)$

c. $\sum c(X + Y)$

d. $\sum cX + \sum Y$

e. $(\sum XY) + c$

f. $\sum(XY + c)$

•••••

EXERCISES

1. Determine the real limits for the following numbers. (Assume that the unit of measurement is the smallest place listed.)
    a. 9.0
    b. 9.000
    c. 77.001
    d. .002

2. Round the following to whole numbers.
    a. 11.5
    b. 22.5
    c. 80.503
    d. 23.4599
    e. 36.4999

3. Given the data in the table and $c = 2$, determine the following values.

Subject (i)	X_i	Y_i
1	2	3
2	4	6
3	7	8
4	1	5
5	3	2

a. $\sum_{i=1}^{4} X_i$

b. $\sum_{i=1}^{5} Y_i$

c. $\sum(X + Y)$

d. $\sum cY$

e. $\sum c(X + Y)$

f. $\sum(cX + Y)$

g. $\sum XY + c$

h. $\sum_{i=1}^{3}(Y_i + c)$

•••••

ANSWERS

Self-Test. (1) a. **(2b). (3a)** ratio; **(3b)** nominal; **(3c)** ordinal; **(3d)** interval. **(4a)** discrete; **(4b)** continuous; **(4c)** discrete. **(5a)** 89.5 and 90.5; **(5b)** 13.65 and 13.75; **(5c)** 30.5495 and 30.5505. **(6a)** 5; **(6b)** 13; **(6c)** 25; **(6d)** 10. **(7a)** 12; **(7b)** 16; **(7c)** 76; **(7d)** 52; **(7e)** 49; **(7f)** 57.

Exercises. (1a) 8.95 and 9.05; **(1b)** 8.9995 and 9.0005; **(1c)** 77.0005 and 77.0015; **(1d)** .0015 and .0025. **(2a)** 12; **(2b)** 23; **(2c)** 81; **(2d)** 23; **(2e)** 36. **(3a)** 14; **(3b)** 24; **(3c)** 41; **(3d)** 48; **(3e)** 82; **(3f)** 58; **(3g)** 99; **(3h)** 23.

••••• STATISTICAL PACKAGES •••••

Many chapters in this *Guide* contain a special optional section that provides instructions on how to use the two computer statistical packages, MINITAB and SPSS, to make the computations required in some of the guided computational examples and exercises. These two packages are readily available through most academic bookstores or computing centers and are commonly used in social and behavioral sciences teaching and research settings.

Students should decide with their instructors whether they should use a computer package in conjunction with this course, and if so, they should pick *one* of the packages and use it *throughout* the course (see Foreword to this *Guide*). Further, the instructions in this *Guide* do not cover all details on the use of Windows 95, 98, or later versions for the personal computer, nor do they cover all the features and output each package can deliver. Students should consult the package manuals for additional information. Moreover, the statistical symbols used in the packages will sometimes be different from those used in the text.

The instructions in this *Guide* assume that the statistical package has been properly installed on the hard drive and that you know how to access it. In the instructions that follow, where commands are given in *italics*, it means they appear on the pull-down menus. Instructions in dialog boxes are given in regular type, while information that must be entered from the keyboard appears in **boldface**.

To start a particular program using Windows 95, Windows 98, or Windows NT, select the pro-gram from the *Start>Programs* taskbar. Windows is a registered trademark of Microsoft Corporation.

••••• MINITAB

Introduction

MINITAB is a versatile statistical package with an impressive array of features, which include high-resolution graphics with editing capability. MINITAB is available in both Windows and Macintosh formats, and it also comes in a reasonably priced student version.

The procedures we describe here are based on MINITAB Release 13.0 Statistical Software for Windows 95, Windows 98, and Windows NT. For use on a personal computer with Windows 95, MINITAB requires 16 MB RAM, 24 MB recommended, 486 class or higher processor, 40 MB hard disk space for a normal installation, and either a VGA or an SVGA monitor. MINITAB is a registered trademark of MINITAB, Inc. of State College, Pennsylvania.

Starting MINITAB

From the taskbar in Windows 95, Windows 98, Windows NT4.0, or Windows 2000, select:

Start>Programs>MINITAB 13 for Windows>MINITAB

Everything that happens during a MINITAB session is considered to be part of a MINITAB *Project*. All information pertaining to the current session, including data, graphs and other program output are part of the current Project.

Input information, including data and variables, are entered on and make up the MINITAB *Worksheet*. The Worksheet is itself a part of the current Project.

Entering data

Upon starting the MINITAB session, two windows appear on the screen. The uppermost is the Session window, onto which all textual output will appear. At the bottom half of the screen is the Worksheet window, entitled Worksheet 1, onto which data may be entered in standard spreadsheet format, with rows as observations or subjects, and columns as variables. To enter data, first maximize the Worksheet window.

You may enter all the data values down the first column, and then go on to the next column, or you may enter the data values row by row, filling in each variable as you work down the spreadsheet. When you have finished entering all the data you may review the values and correct as necessary by clicking on the cell to be altered and typing in the corrected value.

Inserting a new column or row

To insert a new variable (i.e., a new column), into the middle of the finished spreadsheet, click anywhere on the column immediately to the right of where the new column is to be added. Go to the pull-down menus at the top of the screen and select:

Editor>Insert Columns

A new blank column will appear on the spreadsheet.

Similarly, to insert a new row into middle of the spreadsheet, point to the case below the row to be added, and carry out the following menu command:

Editor>Insert Rows

The new cells may now be filled in with the data to be inserted. An asterisk character ("*") appearing in the empty cells signifies missing data.

Labeling the columns

In MINITAB, the columns are already designated with default variable names C1, C2, and so on. To label Column 1 with a meaningful variable name, click on the blank space below the column designator C1, type the new variable name in the space, and press *Enter*. Although variable names may contain 31 characters, on some of the output tables only the first eight characters of the variable name will appear.

Saving the data

Spreadsheet data that you have entered in the MINITAB Worksheet window may be saved for use at a later time in the form of a Worksheet file. The following command will create a MINITAB Worksheet file with the extension *mtw*:

> *File>Save Current Worksheet As*
>   (Type in a name for the data file.)
>   Save

If you wish to export data from a MINITAB Worksheet for use in another application, other file types may be created using the file options available under the above command.

Alternatively, all the information about the current MINITAB session may be saved using the *Save Project* command, which will save not only worksheet data but all text and graphics output in a single Project file with the extension *mpj*:

> *File>Save Project As*
>   (Type in a name for the data file.)
>   Save

Note that using the *Save* button on the MINITAB toolbar will employ the *Save Project* command.

We recommend using the *Save Worksheet* command, which saves only the MINITAB Worksheet data, over the *Save Project* command, since program outputs can be easily recreated using the original data. However, the user must be consistent opening and saving either Worksheet or Project files, as data can be lost if the user fails to save worksheet data before exiting MINITAB.

Recalling a previously-saved file

To recall data saved earlier in a MINITAB Worksheet file, use the following command:

> *File>Open Worksheet*
>   (Select the saved Worksheet file.)
>   Open
>   OK

If an earlier session was saved using the *Save Project* command, the data must be retrieved using the *Open Project* command.

Note that using the *Open* and *Save* buttons on the MINITAB toolbar will employ the *Open Project* and *Save Project* commands, respectively.

Running statistical procedures

The *Stat* menu of MINITAB is used to run most of the statistical analyses included in this *Guide*. Boxplots, scatterplots, and other analyses with graphical output are run using the *Graph* menu. Instructions for running these operations are given in the remaining chapters of this *Guide*. Text output from these operations will appear in the Session window, and graphics output will appear in separate Graph windows.

Printing the output

To print the results of any MINITAB commands that appear in the Session window, use the commands:

> *Window>Session*
>   *File>Print Session Window*
>   Print Range: All
>   OK

This command will print all the output from the session. To print only a portion of the output in the Session window, highlight the output and choose "Selection" in the Print Range subcommand above.

Alternatively, you can copy output from the Session window and paste it into a word processing application for editing and printing. First highlight and then copy the desired output from the Session window using the command:

> *Edit>Copy*

Then paste it into a word processor running under Windows. Rather than switching back and forth between the word processing application, it is possible to paste the output directly from the Session window into MINITAB's *Report Pad,* a feature available with Release 13:

> *Window>Project Manager>Report Pad*

From Report Pad, the combined output can then be transferred to the word processor at one time.

Returning to the worksheet window

After carrying out an analysis that produces output, the Session window will be active, and perhaps fill the screen. To return to the Worksheet window to change or add to the data, click anywhere in the Worksheet window, if it is visible. If not visible, pull down the *Window* menu and select the MINITAB Worksheet listed at the bottom of the menu:

> *Window>Worksheet 1 (or Worksheet file name)*

Going on to a new problem

If you wish to begin working on a different exercise, you should clear the spreadsheet. The best way to clear all previous data and output and bring up a new tableau is to use the command:

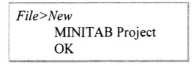

> *File>New*
> MINITAB Project
> OK

You will be prompted to save changes to the current Project. As long as the Worksheet has previously been saved as a file, and no changes to it have been made since, there is no need to save the current Project.

If the Worksheet data have not been saved or if changes have been made to the Worksheet data, choose "Save Separate Pieces," and answer "Yes" to "Save Worksheet 1."

Getting help

Help with using MINITAB is available through Help files accessed through the *Help* menu at the top of the screen. Help files include information on MINITAB calculations and methods, with examples and a glossary of terms. Additional information is available from *Help* buttons that appear in command boxes for selected analyses.

Ending the session

To end the session and exit the MINITAB program:

> *File>Exit*

If you are prompted to save changes to the current Project, select "No." As long as the Worksheet has previously been saved as a file, and no changes to it have been made since, there is no need to save the current Project. To save the Worksheet data, choose "Save Separate Pieces," and answer "Yes" to "Save Worksheet 1."

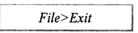

SPSS

Introduction

SPSS is an extensive statistical program typically used by many researchers in the social and behavioral sciences. The procedures we describe here are based on SPSS 10.0 for Windows, Base System.

For use on a personal computer, SPSS requires at least Windows 95 or higher, a Pentium or Pentium-class processor running at 90MHz or faster, 16MB of RAM (64MB recommended), 80MB hard disk space, CD-ROM drive, and SVGA monitor. SPSS is a registered trademark of SPSS, Inc.

Starting SPSS

From the taskbar in Windows 95, Windows 98, Windows 2000 or Windows NT4.0, select:

> *Start>Programs>SPSS for Windows>SPSS 10.0 for Windows*

Entering data

Upon starting the SPSS program, a dialog box will appear. Select "type in data" and click OK. The SPSS Data Editor will fill the screen. This screen is called the SPSS Data View. At this point you may enter the data in the spreadsheet format, with rows as cases or subjects, and columns as variables.

You may enter all the values down the first column, and then go on to the next column, or you may enter the data values row by row, filling in each variable as you go down the spreadsheet. When you have finished entering all the data you may review the values and correct as necessary by clicking on the cell to be altered and typing in the corrected value.

Inserting a new column or row

To insert a new variable (i.e., an additional column), into the middle of the finished spreadsheet, click anywhere on the column immediately to the right of where the new column is to be added. Then go to the pull-down menus at the top of the screen and select:

Data>Insert Variable

A new blank column will appear on the spreadsheet.

Similarly, to insert a new row into the middle of the spreadsheet, point to the case below the row to be added, and carry out the menu command:

Data>Insert Case

Alternatively, you can select "Insert Variable" and "Insert Case" from the SPSS toolbar at the top of the screen. The additional cells may now be filled in with data. A period (".") appearing in the added cells signifies missing data.

Labeling the columns

To label the columns with variable names, click on the tab at the bottom left of the Data View screen marked "Variable View." Enter the variable names for each variable in the Variable View screen and press OK. The SPSS program limits variable names to eight characters, but allows longer names in the "Label" field of the Variable View screen. Any variable labels that are entered in the Label field will appear on the output tables in place of the eight-character variable names.

When finished entering variable names and labels, click on the tab marked "Data View" to return to the original spreadsheet display.

Saving the data

The data entered into the spreadsheet may be saved for use at a later time in the form of an SPSS Save file:

File>Save As
    (Type in a name for the data file.)
    Save

The SPSS *Save* command will create a data file with the extension *sav*. File types for use in different applications may be created using the file options available under the *Save* command.

Recalling a previously-saved file

To recall data saved as an SPSS Save file at an earlier time, use the following command:

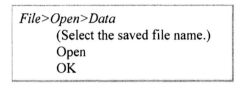

File>Open>Data
    (Select the saved file name.)
    Open
    OK

Note that file options in the *Open* command allow file types to be opened that have been created in different applications.

Running statistical procedures

To carry out operations on the data, the *Analyze* or *Graphs* menu will probably be the most useful. For example, both the *Frequencies* and the *Crosstabs* procedures appear under the *Analyze>Descriptive Statistics* menu. Boxplots and scatterplots are generated using the *Graphs* menu. Instructions for these and other statistical operations are given in the remaining chapters of this *Guide*. The results of these operations will appear in the output window known as the SPSS Viewer. Output appears as graphics on the right side of the Viewer window.

Printing the output

To get a printed copy of the output that appears in the SPSS Viewer window:

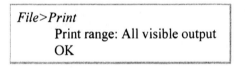

File>Print
    Print range: All visible output
    OK

This command will print all the graphic output that appears on the right side of the Viewer window. To print only a portion of the output showing, highlight the parts desired and choose "Selection" in the Print Range subcommand above. To clear old output, see the section *Going to a new problem*, below.

Returning to the data editor

After carrying out a statistical operation, the SPSS Viewer window will fill the screen. To return to the SPSS Data Editor and perhaps change or add to the data:

Window>SPSS Data Editor

Going to a new problem

If you have been using SPSS for a previous exercise in this *Guide*, you must close or clear both the data window and the output window. Here is a quick way to bring up a new tableau:

File>New>Data

If changes to the spreadsheet data were not saved as a file, a prompt to do so will appear.
    Likewise, to clear old output so that only new results will be printed:

Window>SPSS Viewer
File>Close

It is unnecessary to save the contents of the output viewer; select "No" if prompted.

Getting help

Help with SPSS operations and menus is available through the Index of SPSS commands and keywords, accessed through the menu command:

Help>Topics>Index

Additional information is available from the many published books and manuals describing the SPSS program.

Ending the session

To end the session and exit the SPSS program:

File>Exit

A prompt will appear if there are any files that have not been saved. You are advised not to save the SPSS Viewer files, because these are easily generated from the saved data files.

● ● ● ● ●

CHAPTER **2**

FREQUENCY DISTRIBUTIONS
AND GRAPHING

CONCEPT GOALS

Be sure that you thoroughly understand the following concepts and how to use them in statistical
applications.

- Frequency distributions, relative frequency distributions, cumulative frequency
  distributions, cumulative relative frequency distributions
- Class intervals, number of intervals, size of intervals, lowest interval, mid-point of
  intervals, real and stated limits of intervals
- Histograms and polygons for various kinds of frequency distributions
- Axes, abscissa, ordinate

GUIDE TO MAJOR CONCEPTS

Frequency Distributions

One of the purposes of statistics is to organize, summarize, and describe collections of
measurements (i.e., data). **Frequency distributions** help to accomplish this purpose.

There are many types of frequency distributions. The simplest is a tally of how many times in
a sample of measurements each score value occurs. The score values are listed from the largest at
the top of the table to the smallest at the bottom and then tallies are made after each score value

to indicate how many times that value occurs. By examining the resulting table, or

[1]_____ , one can obtain some idea of the range of score values present and

approximately what score value was typical.

Table 2–1 lists scores on a statistics quiz for a class of 20 students. At the right of the data is a place for you to rewrite all 20 numbers in order of decreasing score value. After you have done that, fill in the three left-hand columns below — Score Value, with the highest score at the top; Tally (that is, a slash for each time that score value appears in the data table); and f (frequency of occurrence) — to make a frequency distribution for these data.

Table 2–1 Frequency Distributions for Scores on a Statistics Quiz

	Scores				Scores Arranged in Descending Order		
4	6	9	5				
9	8	5	7				
7	10	7	6				
5	3	6	9				
8	7	7	6				

Score Value	Tally	f	Relative Frequency	Cumulative Frequency	Cumulative Relative Frequency
		$N = 20$	1.00		

You can see by simply glancing at the frequency distribution that the most common score was [2]__ ; the scores ranged between [3]__ and [4]__ ; nearly half the subjects scored either [5]__ or [6]__ ; and good marks were scores of [7]__ and [8]__ , while poor marks were scores of [9]__ and [10]__ .

Additional information can be obtained from other types of frequency distributions, such as **relative frequency**, **cumulative frequency**, or **cumulative relative frequency** distributions. For example, we often want to know what *proportion* of the total number of cases has been assigned each score value, which information is provided by a [11]_____ distribution. It is called *relative* because the frequencies for each score value are given relative to the total number of measurements, that is, relative to N (relative frequency = frequency of occurrence/N). Fill in the Relative Frequency column of Table 2–1. You can now see that a score of 7 was earned by [12]__ % of the students and that scores of either 6 or 7 were obtained by [13]__ % of the students.

It is also useful to know how many or what proportion of scores *were at a given value or below*. If you scored 8 on the quiz, you might be interested in knowing how many students or what proportion of the class had scores of 8 or lower. Distributions that address these questions are known as [14]_____ distributions. In a cumulative frequency distribution, the entry for each score value represents *the number of cases scoring that value or lower*. A cumulative relative frequency distribution is constructed in the same way, but *the entries are proportions rather than frequencies*. The maximum proportion is 1.00, and proportions become percentages when multiplied by 100. Fill in the Cumulative Frequency and Cumulative Relative Frequency columns of Table 2–1 to produce a [15]_____ distribution and a [16]_____ distribution. Notice that the entry for the score of 5, for example, includes people who scored 5 as well as those who scored less than 5. Thus, 5 or lower was scored by [17]__ % of the students, scores below 5 were recorded for [18]__ %, scores of 5 or above for [19]__ %, and scores higher than 5 for [20]__ %. You can also see that no one scored below [21]__ , that scores of 6 or lower were recorded for [22]__ % of the students, and that if you scored an 8, the percentage of students that scored *higher* than you was [23]__ . See the answer section at the end of this chapter for the completed Table 2–1.

Answer Key to Frequency Distributions							
[1]	frequency	[7]	9	[13]	45	[17]	25
	distribution	[8]	10	[14]	cumulative	[18]	10
[2]	7	[9]	3	[15]	cumulative	[19]	90
[3]	3	[10]	4		frequency	[20]	75
[4]	10	[11]	relative	[16]	cumulative	[21]	3
[5]	6		frequency		relative	[22]	45
[6]	7	[12]	25		frequency	[23]	20%

Class Intervals

The distribution above is quite simple in that it includes only a few score values. In larger distributions, **class intervals** containing several score values are sometimes used instead of a list of individual score values. For example, consider the exam scores of 50 statistics students presented in Table 2–2. As before, the first step is to list all the scores in decreasing order. Do this in the bottom section of Table 2–2 according to the scheme provided. Place the highest scores in each column at the top, and write duplicates next to each other in the same box separated by commas. Scores in the 90s have been entered to illustrate the process. Finish the table now.

Check off scores at the top when you write them at the bottom, and count the scores in the bottom to check that you have 50 when you are finished.

The next task is to determine *how many sets* of score values, called [1]_____ , one should have. Unfortunately, there is no simple rule to answer this question. One needs as many as will summarize and accurately portray the data. To get started, Table 2–3 gives the *maximum* number of intervals for a distribution of a particular size N. For example, the distribution of statistics exam scores in Table 2–2 has [2] $N =$ __ , and Table 2–3 suggests a maximum number of class intervals of [3]__ .

Table 2–2 Statistics Test Scores for Fifty Students

Scores

79	51	67	50	78
62	89	83	73	80
88	48	60	71	79
89	63	55	93✓	71
41	81	46	50	61
59	50	90✓	75	61
75	98✓	53	79	80
70	73	42	72	74
67	73	79	67	85
91✓	67	77	74	77

Ordering of Scores

	90–99	80–89	70–79	60–69	50–59	40–49
–9						
–8	98					
–7						
–6						
–5						
–4						
–3	93					
–2						
–1	91					
–0	90					

Table 2–3 Maximum Number of Class Intervals for Distribution of Size N

N	Number of Intervals	N	Number of Intervals
10	6	80	18
15	8	90	19
20	9	100	20
25	10	125	21
30	11	150	22
40	13	200	23
50	14	350	25
60	15	500	27
70	17	1000	30

The next question is *how big should the intervals be?* The major requirement is that the set of intervals must include all the score values. Subtracting the smallest score from the largest will tell you the range of score values that the set of intervals must cover. For the data in Table 2–2, the largest minus the smallest score is [4] __ − __ = __ . If this range is divided by the maximum number of class intervals to be used, one has an estimate of the minimum size the intervals can be and still include all the scores. Since the maximum number of intervals for $N = 50$ was 14, we divide the range of [5]__ by the maximum number of intervals of [6]__ to obtain the *minimum* size of interval, which is [7]_____ in this case. Since this is the minimum size, we can round this value up to a more convenient size. Usually, we round up to a "round" value, such as 2, 5, or 10 (or some multiple of 10 times these values, like .2, .5, 1.0 or 20, 50, 100). The next "round" values up from 4.07 are [8]__ and [9]__ . The smaller size interval will use a greater number of intervals and give a more detailed picture of the scores; the larger size interval will use a fewer number of intervals and give a more general picture of the distribution. In this case, either choice would be appropriate, and we choose here for illustration the simpler size of 10.

Finally, we need to *determine the lowest interval*. The custom is to start the lowest interval with a value that is equal to or smaller than the smallest observed measurement but also evenly divisible by the size of the interval. Since the smallest score in our data is [10]__ and the interval size is [11]__ , we choose a number equal to or smaller than [12]__ that is also evenly divisible by [13]__ . This number is [14]__ .

The first interval starts with [15]__ , but what does it end with? We have decided that the size of the interval will be 10, and therefore the interval must contain 10 possible score values. Beginning with 40, the 10 score values would begin with [16]__ and end with [17]__ . These are called **stated limits**. Since the first interval will include the scores [18]__ through [19]__and the second interval will include the scores [20]__ through [21]__ , 40–49 and 50–59 are called the [22]_____ of these class intervals.

It is important at this point to recall the concept of **real limits**. If the measurement is in whole numbers, then the real limits of 40 are [23]__ and [24]__ , and the [25]_____ of 49 are [26]__ and [27]__ . Since 40 and 49 are the stated boundaries of the class interval, it follows that the real limits of that interval are [28]__ and [29]__ . The **midpoint** of this interval is the number halfway between these real limits, which is [30]__ .

Now, in Table 2–4, fill in the class intervals for the data in Table 2–2 beginning with the highest at the top, and then complete the remainder of the table.

Table 2–4 Frequency Distributions for the Fifty Statistics Test Scores in Table 2–2

Class Interval	Real Limits	Midpoint	f	Relative Frequency	Cumulative Frequency	Cumulative Relative Frequency

A summary of the steps just described to be used in constructing distributions with grouped data is presented in Table 2–5. For additional practice, consider the hypothetical data presented in Table 2–6. A fundamental concept in the study of achievement is *locus of control*, the extent to which persons believe they personally produce, influence, or control their lives and what happens to them. People who strongly believe that they control the events of their lives are said to be *internally controlled*, while persons who think "things just happen to them" or occur because of luck are said to be *externally controlled*. As might be expected, internally controlled people are more motivated to achieve — to try to attain standards or obtain benefits for themselves — because they believe they largely control these events. Conversely, externally controlled individuals are less motivated, because they believe their efforts are largely irrelevant to what happens to them. A test of locus of control is available, and the scores of 50 individuals are presented in Table 2–6, with higher scores associated with internal control. In the spaces provided, arrange the scores in descending order of magnitude, determine an appropriate set of class intervals, and in Table 2–7 construct the four distributions requested.

Table 2–5 Steps in Constructing Frequency Distributions with Grouped Data

1. Obtain an estimate of the **maximum number of class intervals** from Table 2–3.

2. Calculate the **range** of score values by subtracting the smallest score value from the largest score value in the distribution.

3. Obtain an estimate of the **smallest size of class interval** by dividing the range (obtained in Step 2) by the maximum number of class intervals (obtained in Step 1).

4. **Round up** the estimate of the smallest interval size (obtained in Step 3) to the next "round number" (i.e., round up to .1, .2, .5, 1, 2, 5, 10, 20, 50, 100, etc.).

5. Determine the **lowest class interval** so that its lowest *stated* limit is evenly divisible by the size of the interval (obtained in Step 4).

6. Place the lowest interval at the bottom of the frequency distribution.

7. After constructing the distribution, determine whether the distribution accurately describes the data, and adjust the size and number of intervals if appropriate.

Table 2–6 Locus of Control Scores for Fifty Individuals

Scores

28	16	21	13	25	16	27	17	25	20
21	22	29	23	20	21	19	21	20	22
26	14	27	15	26	29	24	11	28	18
19	25	17	27	26	16	19	26	16	21
26	20	23	20	21	22	25	13	23	22

Ordering of Scores

Table 2–7 Frequency Distributions for the Locus of Control Scores in Table 2–6

Class Interval	Real Limits	Midpoint	f	Relative Frequency	Cumulative Frequency	Cumulative Relative Frequency

(Answers will depend upon the specific class intervals used. Find a classmate who used the same intervals that you did and compare answers.)

Answer Key to Class Intervals

[1]	class intervals	[9]	10	[17]	49	[25]	real limits
[2]	50	[10]	41	[18]	40	[26]	48.5
[3]	14	[11]	10	[19]	49	[27]	49.5
[4]	$98 - 41 = 57$	[12]	41	[20]	50	[28]	39.5
[5]	57	[13]	10	[21]	59	[29]	49.5
[6]	14	[14]	40	[22]	stated limits	[30]	44.5
[7]	4.07	[15]	40	[23]	39.5		
[8]	5	[16]	40	[24]	40.5		

Graphing

At least two kinds of graphs may be drawn for any of the frequency distributions described above, a **histogram** and a **polygon**. One is composed of vertical bars and is called a frequency [1]_____ . The other shows frequency points connected by straight lines and is known as a frequency [2]_____ . The steps in constructing these graphs are described below and summarized in Table 2–8.

We will use the frequency distribution for statistics test scores that you obtained in Table 2–4 to construct a frequency histogram in Figure 2–1. You are given only the **axes**; the **abscissa** and the **ordinate**. The horizontal line, or [3]_____ , should be marked off in [4]_____ . Starting from the left with the midpoint of the lowest interval that you derived in Table 2–4, number the tick marks on this axis and label the axis. The leftmost value marked off on the horizontal [5]_____ , or [6]_____ , will be [7]_____ , and the rightmost value will be [8]_____ . The axis will be labeled as [9]_____ . The vertical axis is called the [10]_____ , and it is marked off in [11]_____ . Beginning with 0 at the bottom, number the tick marks and label this axis.

Table 2–8 Steps in Constructing Histograms and Polygons

Frequency Histogram

1. Draw two axes, with the ordinate approximately three-fourths as long as the abscissa. Mark off the abscissa with values corresponding to the midpoints of the class intervals, and mark off the ordinate in frequencies. Label the axes appropriately.

2. Construct a bar of the histogram over each score value or class interval so that the width of the bar covers the score value or class interval from its lower to its upper real limits (not from midpoint to midpoint) and the height corresponds to the frequency of scores in the interval. There should be no space between bars (except if the abscissa is a nominal scale.)

Frequency Polygon

1. Mark off and label axes as for a frequency histogram, but add one interval below the lowest and one above the highest class interval; assign them 0 frequencies.

2. Place points corresponding to the frequencies of each interval (including the two 0-frequency intervals) directly over the midpoints of each class interval. Connect all adjacent points (including the 0s) with straight lines.

Relative Frequency Histogram or Polygon

1. Plot these in the same way as above, but label the ordinate (and locate the heights of the bars or points) to correspond to relative frequency, not frequency.

Cumulative Frequency Histogram or Polygon

1. Follow the steps for constructing a frequency histogram or polygon, except:
   a. Mark off and label the ordinate for cumulative frequency rather than for frequency.
   b. In drawing a cumulative frequency polygon, place the points over the upper real limit of each class interval, including the lowest interval of 0 accumulated frequencies (note that there is no upper 0-frequency interval).

Cumulative Relative Frequency Histogram or Polygon

1. Plot these in the same way as above, except label the ordinate (and locate the heights of the bars or points) to correspond to cumulative relative frequency.

The histogram is constructed by erecting a bar between the real limits of each class interval, rising to a height equal to the frequency of that interval and having a width equal to the width of the class interval. The leftmost bar of this frequency [12]_____ would thus rest on the abscissa between the real limits of the lowest class interval, which are [13]__ and [14]__ . It would rise to a height of [15]__ frequency units. The next bar would span the abscissa from [16]__ to [17]__ and be [18]__ frequency units tall. Complete this frequency histogram, and then construct one in Figure 2–2 for the locus of control scores that you described with a frequency distribution in Table 2–7.

For **a frequency polygon**, the axes should be labeled in the same way as those for the frequency histogram, except that the abscissa should include one additional interval on the left and one on the right. Mark off and label the axes in Figure 2–3. Locate points over the midpoint of each class interval at a height equal to the number of frequencies in that interval. Do this now. The last point should have been placed over the score value of [19]__ at a height of [20]__ frequency units. Connect adjacent points with straight lines. To make this a polygon (i.e., a closed linear form), the first and last points must be connected to the abscissa at locations corresponding to the [21]_____ of the empty intervals you added just below and just above the intervals containing the lowest and highest scores in the distribution. In this case these zero frequencies would be placed over the score values of [22]__ and [23]__ . Complete the frequency [24]_____ , and construct one in Figure 2–4 for the locus of control scores in Table 2–7.

To graph a **relative frequency histogram** or **polygon**, simply follow the rules above, except that the vertical axis, or [25]_____ , is marked off in units of relative frequency (proportions). Plot the relative frequency data in Table 2–4 both as a histogram and as a polygon on a single graph in Figure 2–5, using the guidelines provided in Table 2–8.

To plot a **cumulative relative frequency polygon** in Figure 2–6 for the data in Table 2–4, mark off and label the abscissa as before, and mark off and label the ordinate with [26]_____ . In contrast to a relative frequency polygon, the points in a cumulative relative frequency polygon must be located over the *upper real limits of the class intervals*, not over the midpoints of the intervals. This is done because each point indicates the proportion of scores *within and below* that interval. Thus, the point for the first interval would be placed over the value [27]__ . Also, a cumulative

relative frequency polygon should be connected at the left with the [28]_____ .
Complete the plot of this cumulative relative frequency polygon in Figure 2–6.

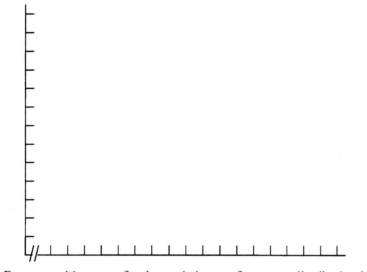

Figure 2–1. Frequency histogram for the statistics test frequency distribution in Table 2–4.

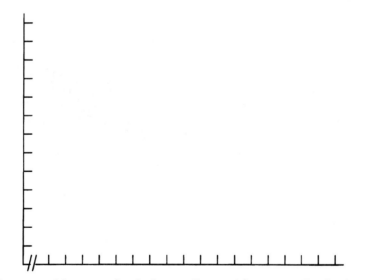

Figure 2–2. Frequency histogram for the locus of control frequency distribution in Table 2–7.

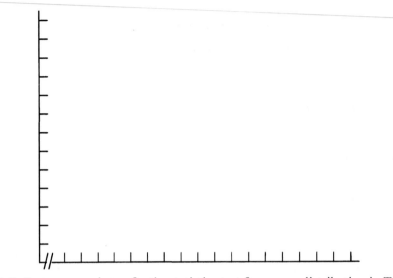

Figure 2–3. Frequency polygon for the statistics test frequency distribution in Table 2–4.

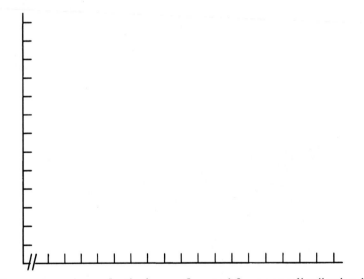

Figure 2–4. Frequency polygon for the locus of control frequency distribution in Table 2–7.

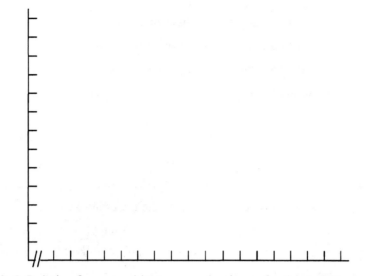

Figure 2–5. Relative frequency histogram and polygon for the statistics test relative frequency distribution in Table 2–4.

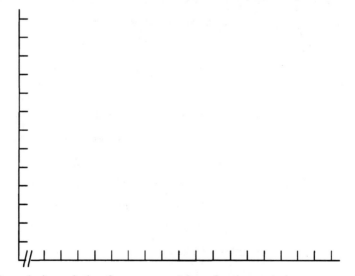

Figure 2–6. Cumulative relative frequency polygon for the statistics test cumulative relative frequency distribution in Table 2–4.

To review: For a frequency histogram, the horizontal axis, known as the

[29]_____ , is marked off in the units of the measurement scale with points located at

the [30]_____ of the class intervals. The vertical axis, known as the

[31]_____ , is marked off in [32]_____ . The axes should

be appropriately [33]_____ . Each bar of the histogram should rise to a height

equivalent to the [34]_____ of scores in that interval, and the sides of the bar should

be located at the [35]_____ of the class interval. A frequency polygon has

the same axes as the histogram, but the points representing frequency are placed over the

[36]_____ of the intervals. The line connecting the points in the polygon meets the

abscissa on both left and right, at the [37]_____ of the next lowest and next

highest intervals. For a relative frequency histogram or polygon, the axes are the same as for

the frequency histogram and polygon, but the ordinate is marked off in units of

[38]_____ . Cumulative graphs require that the ordinate be marked off in

[39]_____ units. For a polygon showing cumulative frequency, the points are

placed over the [40]_____ of each interval. The left end of the line connecting

the points meets the [41]_____ at the midpoint of the next lowest interval

(containing no scores). These guidelines are summarized in Table 2–8 for your convenience in

working the exercises.

Sometimes other types of graphs are used in special situations, such as when the data

represent discrete categories, that is, are represented by a nominal scale. For example, a **bar

graph** may be used to represent a frequency distribution for [42]_____ (or

[43]_____ scale) data. A bar graph is the same as a histogram except that the bars,

which may be oriented vertically or horizontally, do not touch each other. This is because the

separated bars of a [44]_____ represent discrete, unconnected [45]_____ .

Also, the axis of a bar graph representing the categories is marked off with those categories,

spaced in equal steps, not a measurement scale.

A **pie chart** is often used to represent a relative frequency distribution for categorical

(nominal) data. A circle is drawn and wedges are marked off for each category in proportion to the relative frequency of that [46]_____ . The result looks like an unevenly cut pie, which is where the name of [47]_____ comes from.

To construct these two special graphs, consider the data in Table 2–9, which represent the number and proportion of children workers in a county that have various types of educational background. While these backgrounds could be placed on a ratio scale of years of education or an ordinal scale of level of education, they are often thought of as different [48]_____ of education. To graph the frequency data, create a [49]_____ in Figure 2–7 by marking off and labeling the discrete categories along the horizontal axis, called the [50]_____, and frequencies along the vertical axis or [51]_____. Then draw bars centered over each category tick mark that extend upward to a height corresponding to that category's [52]_____. In contrast to a histogram, the bars of a bar graph do [53]_____ touch each other.

**Table 2–9 Frequencies and Relative Frequencies
of Educational Backgrounds of Child Care Workers**

Education	Frequency	Relative Frequency	X360°	Degrees in Pie Chart
Graduate Training	8	.09	X360	
College Degree	15	.17	X360	
Some College	2	.36	X360	
Child Development Associates Certificate	22	.24	X360	
High School	13	.14	X360	
	N = 90	1.00		360

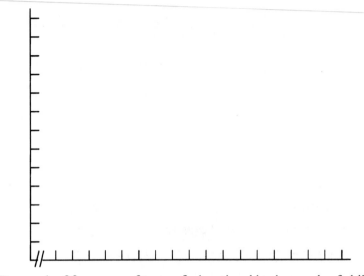

Figure 2–7. Bar graph of frequency of types of educational backgrounds of child care workers.

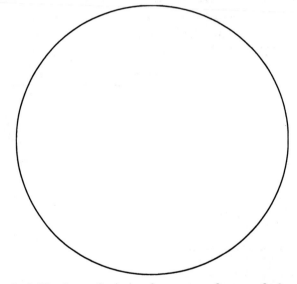

Figure 2–8. Pie chart of relative frequency of types of educational
backgrounds of child care workers.

Construct a pie chart by first determining the number of degrees in the circle that represent each category's [54]_____. To do so, complete the right-hand column of Table 2–9 by multiplying on each row the relative frequency times 360 degrees to obtain the number of degrees of the [55]_____ that should represent the relative frequency of that category . For example, in the case of Graduate Training, multiply the relative frequency of [56]__ by 360°, which equals [57]__ , which is the size of the wedge in the pie chart that is proportional to the 9% of child care workers who had graduate training. Be sure the total number of degrees in this column is 360, although the actual total may be a degree of so off because or founding. Then, with a protractor, mark off a wedge for each category in Figure 2–8 corresponding to the number of degrees for that category, and label each wedge.

Answer Key to Graphing

[1]	histogram	[16]	49.5	[30]	midpoints	[45]	categories
[2]	polygon	[17]	59.5	[31]	ordinate	[46]	category
[3]	abscissa	[18]	7	[32]	frequencies	[47]	pie chart
[4]	score values	[19]	94.5	[33]	labeled	[48]	categories
[5]	axis	[20]	4	[34]	frequency	[49]	bar graph
[6]	abscissa	[21]	midpoints	[35]	real limits	[50]	abscissa
[7]	44.5	[22]	34.5	[36]	midpoints	[51]	ordinate
[8]	94.5	[23]	104.5	[37]	midpoints	[52]	frequency
[9]	Statistics Test	[24]	polygon	[38]	relative	[53]	not
	Score	[25]	ordinate		frequency	[54]	relative
[10]	ordinate	[26]	Cumulative	[39]	cumulative		frequency
[11]	frequencies		Relative	[40]	upper real limit	[55]	pie chart
[12]	histogram		Frequency	[41]	abscissa	[56]	.09
[13]	39.5	[27]	49.5	[42]	categorical	[57]	32°
[14]	49.5	[28]	abscissa	[43]	nominal		
[15]	4	[29]	abscissa	[44]	bar graph		

● ● ● ● ●

SELF-TEST

1. What is the purpose of making a frequency distribution?

2. Define:
   a. frequency distribution
   b. relative frequency distribution
   c. cumulative relative frequency distribution
   d. class interval

3. Describe how to determine the following:
   a. the number of class intervals
   b. the size of the class intervals
   c. the lowest interval

4. If 90 and 95 are the stated limits for a class interval,
   a. what are the real limits of this interval?
   b. what is the size of the interval?
   c. what is the midpoint of the interval?

5. True or false?
   ____ a. The vertical axis is the ordinate.
   ____ b. In a frequency polygon, the points are placed over the lower real limits of each interval.
   ____ c. In a frequency polygon, the first and last points always show frequencies of 0.
   ____ d. In a frequency histogram, the bars span from midpoint to midpoint of adjacent class intervals.
   ____ e. In a cumulative frequency histogram, the bars span from the lower to the upper real limits of each interval.
   ____ f. In a cumulative relative frequency polygon, the points are always over the midpoints of the intervals.
   ____ g. In cumulative polygons, the height of the first point is always 0.
   ____ h. The bars in a bar graph touch each other.
   ____ i. Cumulative relative frequencies for categorical data can be presented in a pie chart.

6.* When should a histogram and when should a polygon be used to display data?

7.* Characterize in words and with graphs:
   a. central tendency
   b. variability
   c. skewness
   d. kurtosis

8.* If the skewness increases or a distribution becomes more platykurtic, what will happen to the variability of the distribution?

Questions preceded by an asterisk can be answered on the basis of the discussion in the text, but the discussion in this Study Guide does not answer them.

● ● ● ● ●   EXERCISES

1. Below are the high temperatures in Fort Lauderdale for the first 25 days of April. Without grouping the data into class intervals, make a frequency distribution, relative frequency distribution, cumulative frequency distribution, and cumulative relative frequency distribution. Then, separately for each of these four distributions, draw a histogram and a polygon.

Temperatures

80	78	75	75	74
75	73	71	73	74
70	79	76	76	77
73	71	77	77	76
77	74	75	76	76

Score Value	f	Relative Frequency	Cumulative Frequency	Cumulative Relative Frequency

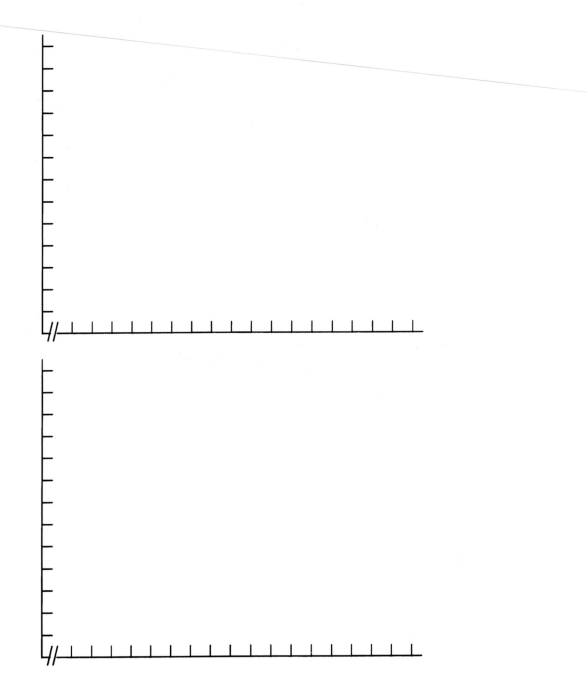

2. Below are 70 scores on a final exam in a class on Gender Roles. Follow the same directions for Exercise 1, but employ the procedures for grouped data. How would you assign the letter grades A, B, C, D, and F to these scores?

3. In exercise #2, if 95+ = A, 85–94 = B, 75–84 = C, 70–74 = D, and 69– = F, determine for these categorical grades their frequencies, relative frequencies, and degrees, and then draw a bar graph and pie chart for these data.

Scores

90	91	85	82	71	75	75
76	85	76	77	70	70	85
70	70	72	79	68	74	75
75	75	73	91	85	82	72
72	85	79	81	92	65	68
80	80	80	65	78	90	94
90	68	87	75	77	95	72
94	90	85	70	93	90	82
70	85	95	65	68	92	80
77	75	92	90	92	85	75

Class Interval	Real Limits	Midpoint	f	Relative Frequency	Cumulative Frequency	Cumulative Relative Frequency

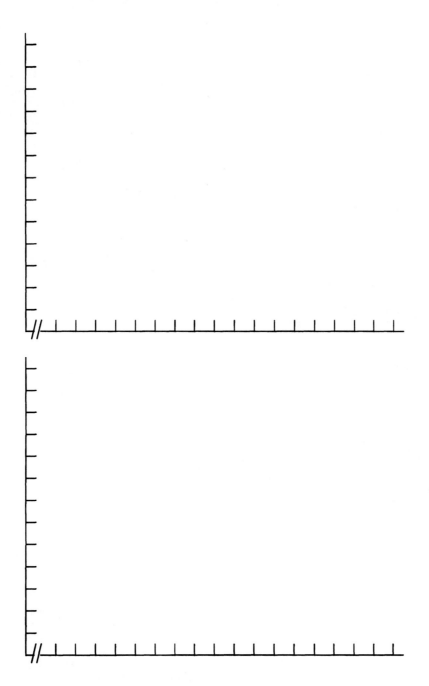

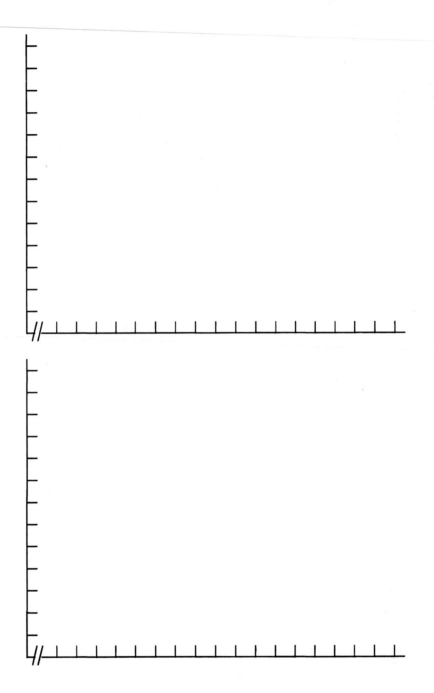

Grade	Frequency	Relative Frequency	X360°	Degrees in Pie Chart
A (95+)			X360	
B (85–94)			X360	
C (75–84)			X360	
D (70–74)			X360	
F (69–)			X360	
	N =	1.0		360

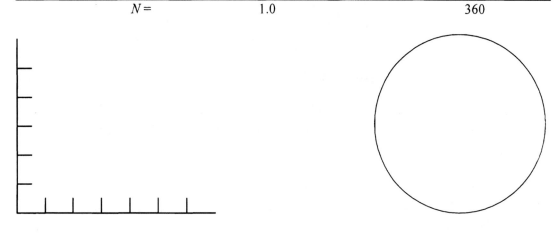

• • • • •   ANSWERS

Table 2–1

Score Value	Tally	f	Relative Frequency	Cumulative Frequency	Cumulative Relative Frequency
10	/	1	.05	20	1.00
9	/ / /	3	.15	19	.95
8	/ /	2	.10	16	.80
7	++++	5	.25	14	.70
6	/ / / /	4	.20	9	.45
5	/ / /	3	.15	5	.25
4	/	1	.05	2	.10
3	/	1	.05	1	.05

Table 2–4

Class Interval	Real Limits	Midpoint	f	Relative Frequency	Cumulative Frequency	Cumulative Relative Frequency
90–99	89.5–99.5	94.5	4	.08	50	1.00
80–89	79.5–89.5	84.5	8	.16	46	.92
70–79	69.5–79.5	74.5	18	.36	38	.76
60–69	59.5–69.5	64.5	9	.18	20	.40
50–59	49.5–59.5	54.5	7	.14	11	.22
40–49	39.5–49.5	44.5	4	.08	4	.08

Table 2–9. The degrees from top to bottom are 32, 61, 130, 86, and 50 (which total 359, not 360, because of rounding).

Self Test. (1) To summarize and describe the data. **(2)** See text pages 29–32. **(3)** See text pages 34–37. **(4a)** 89.5 and 95.5; **(4b)** 6;

(4c) 92.5. **(5a)** T; **(5b)** F; **(5c)** T; **(5d)** F; **(5e)** T; **(5f)** F; **(5g)** T; **(5h)** F; **(5i)** F. **(6)** See text page 45. **(7)** See text pages 46–49. **(8)** Variability increases.

Exercises. (1–3) See the following tables.

(1)

Temperature	f	Relative Frequency	Cumulative Frequency	Cumulative Relative Frequency
80	1	.04	25	1.00
79	1	.04	24	.96
78	1	.04	23	.92
77	4	.16	22	.88
76	5	.20	18	.72
75	4	.16	13	.52
74	3	.12	9	.36
73	3	.12	6	.24
72	0	.00	3	.12
71	2	.08	3	.12
70	1	.04	1	.04
	$N = 25$	1.00		

(2)

Class Interval	Real Limits	Midpoint	f	Relative Frequency	Cumulative Frequency	Cumulative Relative Frequency
95–99	94.5–99.5	97	2	.03	70	1.00
90–94	89.5–94.5	92	15	.21	68	.97
85–89	84.5–89.5	87	9	.13	53	.76
80–84	79.5–84.5	82	8	.11	44	.63
75–79	74.5–79.5	77	16	.23 ·	36	.51
70–74	69.5–74.5	72	13	.19	20	.29
65–69	64.5–69.5	67	7	.10	7	.10

(3)

Grade	Frequency	Relative Frequency	X360°	Degrees in Pie Chart
A	2	.03	X360	11
B	24	.34	X360	122
C	24	.34	X360	122
D	13	.19	X360	68
F	7	.10	X360	36

• • • • • STATISTICAL PACKAGES • • • • •

• • • • •   MINITAB

(To accompany Exercise 1 of Chapter 2)

MINITAB will construct simple frequency (labeled *Count*), cumulative frequency (*CumCnt*), relative frequency (*Percent*), and cumulative relative frequency (*CumPct*) distributions as well as draw dotplots and histograms.

Start the MINITAB program.

For Exercise 1, temperature data for the first 25 days of April were:

80 78 75 75 74 75 73 71 73 74 70 79 76 76 77 73 71 77 77 76 77 74 75 76 76

To enter the above data on the spreadsheet, click on the Data window. Enter the score values down the first column of the spreadsheet, starting with row 1. Strike the down arrow key (↓) or the *Enter* key to register each value. Continue until all values have been entered.

At the top of the first column, click on the blank space below the column designator *C1*. Type the variable name *Scores* in this space. The spreadsheet should appear as follows:

          Scores
          80
          78
          75
          ⋮
          etc.

Check the data you have entered in the spreadsheet and modify as necessary. You may save the data you have entered as follows:

> *File>Save Worksheet As*
>   (Enter folder and file name for the MINITAB Worksheet file.)
>   OK

To generate a frequency distribution of the scores, use the pull-down menus to run the *Tally* command. Click on *Stat*, then *Tables*, and then *Tally*. A dialog box will appear with a variable list. Double-click on the variable *Scores* and it will be transferred across to the variables box.

> *Stat>Tables>Tally*
>   Variables: Scores   [double-click to transfer]
>   Display: Counts, Percents, Cumulative counts, Cumulative percents
>   OK

Running the statistical procedure causes the Worksheet window, which contains the spreadsheet data, to be replaced by the Session window, on which the program output appears. Program output for the frequency distribution is displayed on the following page.

To generate a histogram, use the *Display Descriptive Statistics* command. In addition to the histogram, this command yields a table, which includes the variable mean, standard deviation, and quartiles:

> *Stat>Basic Statistics>Display Descriptive Statistics*
>   Variables: Scores   [double-click to transfer]
>   Graphs:Histogram of data: Yes
>   OK
>   OK

An alternative to the histogram is the dotplot, in which a dot is displayed for each score in the distribution:

> *Graph>Character Graphs>Dotplot*
>   Variables: Scores   [double-click to transfer]
>   OK

The histogram output will appear in a separate graphics window. The statistical table and dotplot outputs are both written to the Session window. To print the output from the Session window:

> *File>Print Session Window*
>   Print Range: All
>   OK

To print the graphics image generated by the *Histogram* command:

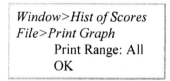

> *Window>Hist of Scores*
> *File>Print Graph*
>   Print Range: All
>   OK

Program output is illustrated below. As an alternative to the MINITAB *Print* command, the user can highlight the desired section of the Session window and copy and paste it directly into MINITAB's *Report Pad,* or into a word processor (see Chapter 1). Graphics output can be copied and pasted in similar fashion.

To exit MINITAB:

> *File>Exit*

There is no need to save changes for the current Project if the Worksheet file has already been saved.

MINITAB Program Output

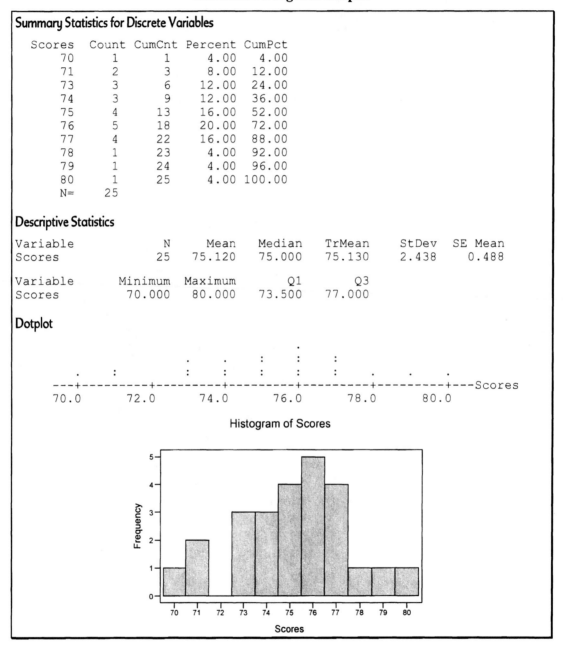

Summary Statistics for Discrete Variables

Scores	Count	CumCnt	Percent	CumPct
70	1	1	4.00	4.00
71	2	3	8.00	12.00
73	3	6	12.00	24.00
74	3	9	12.00	36.00
75	4	13	16.00	52.00
76	5	18	20.00	72.00
77	4	22	16.00	88.00
78	1	23	4.00	92.00
79	1	24	4.00	96.00
80	1	25	4.00	100.00
N=	25			

Descriptive Statistics

Variable	N	Mean	Median	TrMean	StDev	SE Mean
Scores	25	75.120	75.000	75.130	2.438	0.488

Variable	Minimum	Maximum	Q1	Q3
Scores	70.000	80.000	73.500	77.000

Dotplot

```
                                        .
                     .      .      :      :      :
         .     :           :      :      :      :      :      .      .      .
      ---+---------+---------+---------+---------+---------+---------+---Scores
       70.0      72.0      74.0      76.0      78.0      80.0
```

Histogram of Scores

Notice that the program output on the previous page is different in some ways from that presented in the text and this *Guide*. First, scores are listed from the smallest at the top to the largest at the bottom in the frequency distribution. Second, a score value with no frequency (72 in the above example) is simply omitted from the frequency distribution, rather than listed with a frequency count of zero.

●●●●● **SPSS**

(To accompany Exercise 1 of Chapter 2)

SPSS will execute a frequency distribution, a relative frequency distribution ("Percent"), and a cumulative relative frequency distribution ("Cumulative Percent") as well as draw the histogram-like bar chart.

For Exercise 1, temperature "scores" for the first 25 days of April were:

80 78 75 75 74 75 73 71 73 74 70 79 76 76 77 73 71 77 77 76 77 74 75 76 76

Start the SPSS program and select "Type in data," then "OK." The SPSS Data Editor, which consists of a spreadsheet grid, will fill the screen. This screen is known as the SPSS Data View. Enter the data values down the first column of the spreadsheet until all 25 values have been entered. To enter the variable name, click on the tab labeled "Variable View" at the bottom left of the screen. Type in a new variable name *Scores* in place of the default name *var0001*. Next, click the "Data View" tab at the bottom left of the screen to return to the spreadsheet grid.

The spreadsheet should appear as follows:

Scores
80
78
75
⋮
etc.

Check the data that you have entered, modify it if necessary, then save the scores as follows:

File>Save As
    (Enter folder and file name for SPSS Save file.)
    Save

Generate a frequency distribution of the scores and the associated bar chart:

> *Analyze>Descriptive Statistics>Frequencies*
> Variable(s): Scores
>   (Click on the arrow to transfer *Scores* to the "Variables" box.)
> Charts: Chart Type: Bar chart(s)
>   Chart Values: Frequencies
>   Continue
> OK

Program output for this example is illustrated on the following page. Notice that the output is different in some ways from that presented in the text and this *Guide*.

First, scores are listed from the smallest at the top to the largest at the bottom in the frequency distribution and graph.

Second, note that the chart type "Bar chart" will produce a bar for each distinct value of Scores, and only for intervals with one or more counts. The interval around 72, for instance, is not presented on the bar chart because the count is zero for this score. Score values with no frequencies are simply omitted from these two presentations, rather than listed with 0 frequencies.

Print the frequency tables and the bar chart:

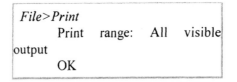

> *File>Print*
>   Print   range: All   visible
> output
>   OK

As an alternative to printing, the user can copy and paste the output tables and graph directly into a word processing application.

Exit SPSS:

> *File>Exit SPSS*
>   Save contents of object viewer: No
>   Save contents of data editor: No

There is no need to save the contents of the Viewer or Data Editor, since they are easily regenerated using the saved data file.

SPSS Program Output

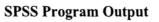

Frequencies

SCORES

		Frequency	Percent	Valid Percent	Cumulative Percent
Valid	70.00	1	4.0	4.0	4.0
	71.00	2	8.0	8.0	12.0
	73.00	3	12.0	12.0	24.0
	74.00	3	12.0	12.0	36.0
	75.00	4	16.0	16.0	52.0
	76.00	5	20.0	20.0	72.0
	77.00	4	16.0	16.0	88.0
	78.00	1	4.0	4.0	92.0
	79.00	1	4.0	4.0	96.0
	80.00	1	4.0	4.0	100.0
	Total	25	100.0	100.0	

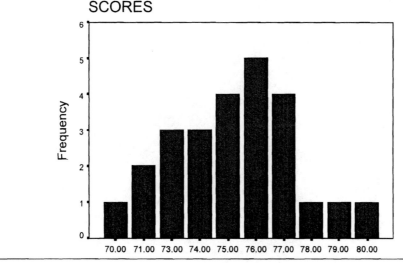

SCORES

● ● ● ● ●

CHAPTER 3

CHARACTERISTICS OF DISTRIBUTIONS ● ● ● ● ●

CONCEPT GOALS

Be sure that you thoroughly understand the following concepts and how to use them in statistical applications.

- ◆ Mean; $\Sigma(X_i - \overline{X}) = 0$ and $\Sigma(X_i - \overline{X})^2$ is a minimum
- ◆ Median
- ◆ Mode; bimodal distribution
- ◆ Advantages of mean, median, and mode
- ◆ Range
- ◆ Variance and standard deviation
- ◆ Population parameters and sample statistics

● ● ● ● ● GUIDE TO MAJOR CONCEPTS

Introduction

Central tendency and **variability** are major concepts in statistics. There are several numerical ways to express the concept of the typical score in a distribution, more formally known as the

[1]_____ of a distribution. Other numerical indices express the extent to which scores in a distribution differ from one another and from their central tendency, that is, they reflect the amount of [2]_____ in a distribution.

Answer Key to Introduction

[1]   central tendency   [2]   variability

Central Tendency

There are at least three types of typical scores, or indicators or measures of [1]_____ , which are the **mean**, **median**, and **mode**. The most common is the arithmetic average, or [2]_____ , which is defined as the sum of the scores divided by the number of scores in the distribution. The mean is symbolized by [3]__ , and its formula can be expressed symbolically as [4]_____ . If a distribution consists of the scores (2, 3, 6, 9, 5), the mean is given by

$$[5]\,\overline{X} = \underline{\hspace{3cm}} = \underline{\hspace{3cm}} = \underline{\hspace{1cm}} .$$

The mean has two characteristics that make it the most commonly used measure of central tendency. The first is that in a distribution the sum of the deviations of the scores about their mean always equals [6]__ . If X_i is any particular score in the sample and $\overline{X}$ is the mean of all the X_i, this relationship can be symbolically written [7]_____ . Two distributions are given in Table 3–1 with space for you to calculate the mean as well as the sum of the deviations of scores about their mean, $\Sigma(X_i - \overline{X})$. Perform these calculations for the X and the Y distributions. Now select any value k that is not equal to the mean of the Y distribution and calculate the deviations of the Y_i scores about the value k instead of about the mean. What do you notice about the sum of the deviations when they are taken about the mean rather than about some other value? The sum about the mean is [8]__ .

Now calculate the columns of Table 3–1 that require the *squared* deviations of scores about their mean and about k. For the X_i, notice that while the sum of deviations about the mean of a distribution is always [9]__ , when the deviations are squared their sum is [10]__ , that is, not 0. These two principles can be written in symbols as

[11] _____ = __

[12] _____ ≠ __

Table 3–1 Mean and Deviations

| Distribution X | | | | Distribution Y | | | | | | |
| Deviations about $\overline{X}$ | | | | Deviations about $\overline{Y}$ | | | | Deviations about k | | |
X_i	$\overline{X}$	$(X_i - \overline{X})$	$(X_i - \overline{X})^2$	Y_i	$\overline{Y}$	$(Y_i - \overline{Y})$	$(Y_i - \overline{Y})^2$	k	$(Y_i - k)$	$(Y_i - k)^2$
2				1						
7				2						
2				8						
9				9						
5				10						
$\Sigma X_i =$		$\Sigma(X_i - \overline{X}) =$	$\Sigma(X_i - \overline{X})^2 =$	$\Sigma Y_i =$		$\Sigma(Y_i - \overline{Y}) =$	$\Sigma(Y_i - \overline{Y})^2 =$		$\Sigma(Y_i - k) =$	$\Sigma(Y_i - k)^2 =$
$N =$ _____				$N =$ _____						
$\overline{X} =$ _____				$\overline{Y} =$ _____						

The second point to observe about the mean is that the sum of *squared* deviations about the mean, while not usually [13]__ is [14]_____ than the sum of squared deviations about any other value, such as the k you selected. The sum of squared deviations about the mean for distribution Y is [15]__ , but the sum of squared deviations about k is [16]_____ , illustrating the fact that the sum of the [17]_____ deviations about the mean is [18]_____ than the sum of squared deviations about any other value.

It is in this sense, sometimes called the **least squares sense**, that the mean is closer to the scores (in terms of squared deviations) than is any other measure of central tendency (any other k.)

To review, the mean is defined by the formula [19]_____ , and it possesses two characteristics that make it a good measure of central tendency. These may be stated symbolically as follows: [20]_____ = __ and [21]_____ is a minimum.

Although the mean is the most common and the best (in the least squares sense) index of central tendency, it is not the only index, nor is it always the most appropriate one to use. For example, the point that divides the distribution into two parts such that an equal number of cases lie above and below that point is the [22]_____ , symbolized by [23]__ . The calculation of the median varies, depending on whether there is an odd or an even number of total cases (i.e., N) in the distribution.

1. **If there is an odd number of cases in the distribution (i.e., N is odd)**, the median is the score value corresponding to the middle case, which will be the $(N+1)/2$ case from the bottom of the distribution. For example, if the distribution is

$$(5, 7, 8, 9, 11)$$

there is an odd number of cases, namely [24] $N =$ __ , so the middle case will be [25] $(N+1)/2 =$ _____ = __ or the third case from the bottom. The score value of the third case is [26]__ , so the [27]_____ is 8. Note that this score value divides the the distribution into two equal parts, since two cases fall below and two cases fall above the score value of 8.

If the distribution is

$$(19, 21, 27, 32, 32, 41, 55)$$

again there is an [28]__ number of cases (i.e., $N = 7$), the middle case is the [29]_____ = _____ = __ case, and the value of the median is [30]__ . This shows that the median is the value of the middle case even when more than one case has that score value.

2. **If there is an even number of cases in the distribution**, the median is half way between (i.e., is the average of) the score values of the two middle cases, which will be cases $N/2$ and $(N/2)+1$ from the bottom of the distribution. Suppose the distribution is

$$(4, 6, 8, 10, 12, 15)$$

Here there is an even number of cases ([31] $N =$ ___) and the two middle cases are the [32] $N/2 =$ _____ case and the [33] $(N/2)+1 =$ _____ case. The median is the average of the score values of these two middle cases, or [34] _____ $=$ ___ . Notice that the point 9, while not actually in the distribution, would separate the distribution into [35] _____ parts consisting of three cases below and three cases above this point.

Now consider the distribution

$$(12, 14, 16, 19, 19, 22, 27, 30)$$

Here, $N = 8$ is [36] _____ , and the middle cases are the [37] _____ $=$ _____ $=$ ___ and [38] _____ $=$ _____ $=$ ___ . The median is the average of their score values, which is simply [39] ___ . This shows that the median is still the average of the values of the middle cases even when those cases have the same score value.

Table 3–2 summarizes these steps in determining the median at the left and then provides three additional examples. Determine the medians for these three distributions now.

The third index of central tendency is the easiest one to compute. It is the most frequently occurring score, called the [40] _____ and symbolized by [41] ___ . In the distribution (2, 4, 6, 6, 6, 5, 5, 10), the most frequent score is [42] ___ , which is called the [43] _____ .

Table 3–2 Computational Examples for Determining the Median (M_d)

	Distribution A	Distribution B	Distribution C
0. Raw distribution:	(4, 10, 2, 15, 1, 3, 11, 9, 4, 3, 10, 14, 11)	(4, 2, 6, 8, 2, 6, 5, 3, 1, 2, 1, 8, 0, 7)	(2.1, 1.9, 2.8, 2.4, 1.6, 2.5, 2.1, 2.4, 1.9, 2.1, 2.0)
1. Order all the cases by score value	(_____)	(_____)	(_____)
2. Determine N:	$N =$ ____	$N =$ ____	$N =$ ____
3. Determine location of M_d:	M_d is at/between cases(s)	M_d is at/between cases(s)	M_d is at/between cases(s)
a. If N is odd, M_d is the value of case $(N+1)/2$	_____	_____	_____
b. If N even, M_d is the average of cases $N/2$ and $(N/2)+1$	_____	_____	_____
4. Determine the value of M_d:	$M_d =$ _____	$M_d =$ _____	$M_d =$ _____

We have examined three indices of central tendency: One is the score value closest in the least squares sense to the scores in the distribution (the [44]_____); one divides the distributions into two equally-sized parts (the [45]_____); and one is the most frequent score (the [46]_____). The values of these three indices are not usually the same for a particular distribution. For example, consider the four distributions in Table 3–3. Calculate the mean, median, and mode for each, and then locate and mark each index of central tendency with its symbol on the scale of measurement corresponding to each distribution in the bottom half of the table.

Table 3–3 Comparison of the Mean, Median, and Mode

	W	X	Y	Z
	2	2	3	3
	3	3	3	5
	5	5	5	5
	6	6	7	<u>7</u>
	<u>9</u>	<u>24</u>	<u>7</u>	
Mean				
Median				
Mode				

Look first at distributions *W* and *X*. Since there is no duplication of scores in either distribution, there is no useful [47]_____ . Observe that the two distributions are identical except for the last score in each, 9 in *W* and 24 in *X*. The difference between these two cases is reflected in a change in the [48]_____ , but it has no effect on the value of the [49]_____ . The formula for the mean, [50]_____ , indicates that value the value of *each* score is entered and has an effect on this statistic. Thus, the measure of central tendency that acts most like a fulcrum or balance point for the distribution of score values along the measurement scales at the bottom of Table 3–3 is the [51]_____ . In contrast, the point that balances cases, not score values, by dividing the cases into two sets having an equal number of cases is the [52]_____ . Only the score value of the *central* cases, regardless of how far the other score values are from them, influences the [53]_____ .Therefore, in distributions that include one or two extreme score values which you regard as atypical, you might prefer the [54]_____ over the [55]_____ as a descriptive index of [56]_____ . Another way of saying the same thing is to observe that distribution X can be described as having positive **skewness**; when distributions are asymmetrical or seriously [57]_____ , one may prefer the [58]_____ over the [59]_____ , because the skewness will have less influence on the [60]_____ than on the [61]_____ .

In determining the mode of distribution Y, you will have noticed that this distribution is [62]_____ . When scores tend to bunch in two places, the mean and median do not reflect this fact but the [63]_____ does.

Distribution Z is a simple example of a symmetrical distribution with one mode. In this case the mean, median, and mode are [64]_____ .

Answer Key to Central Tendency

[1]	central tendency	[14]	smaller	[26]	8
[2]	mean	[15]	70	[27]	median
[3]	$\overline{X}$	[16]	(depends upon your k,	[28]	odd
[4]	$\sum X_i / N$		but > 70)	[29]	$(N+1)/2 = (7+1)/2$
[5]	$\sum X_i / N = 25/5 = 5$	[17]	squared		$= 4$th
[6]	0	[18]	smaller	[30]	32
[7]	$\sum(X_i - \overline{X}) = 0$	[19]	$\overline{X} = \sum X_i / N$	[31]	6
[8]	0	[20]	$\sum(X_i - \overline{X}) = 0$	[32]	$6/2 = 3$rd
[9]	0	[21]	$\sum(X_i - \overline{X})^2$	[33]	$(6/2)+1 = 4$th
[10]	38	[22]	median	[34]	$(8+10)/2 = 9$
[11]	$\sum(X_i - \overline{X}) = 0$	[23]	M_d	[35]	two equal
[12]	$\sum(X_i - \overline{X})^2 \neq 0$	[24]	5	[36]	even
[13]	0	[25]	$(5+1)/2 = 3$	[37]	$N/2 = 8/2 = 4$th

[38]	$(N/2)+1 = 8/2+1$	[47]	mode	[57]	skewed
	$= $ 5th	[48]	mean	[58]	median
[39]	19	[49]	median	[59]	mean
[40]	mode	[50]	$\sum X_i / N$	[60]	median
[41]	M_o	[51]	mean	[61]	mean
[42]	6	[52]	value	[62]	bimodal
[43]	mode	[53]	median	[63]	mode
[44]	mean	[54]	median	[64]	equal
[45]	median	[55]	mean		
[46]	mode	[56]	central tendency		

Variability

Distributions do not differ only with respect to central tendency; they also differ with respect to **variability**. For example, the two distributions (3, 4, 5) and (1, 4, 7) have the same mean and median, but they differ in the extent to which the scores deviate from one another and from their central tendency, a characteristic called [1]_____ .

One measure of variability is simply the difference between the largest and smallest score, a statistic known as the [2]_____ . Thus, for the two distributions given above, the ranges are [3]__ and [4]__ . Although the range provides some idea of the [5]_____ of the scores, it ignores cases less extreme in value than the smallest and largest values. The imprecision of the range as a measure of variability is illustrated by the fact that for (1, 4, 7, 11, 14) and (1, 7, 7, 7, 14) the two ranges are (equal/unequal) [6]_____ , but the first distribution has (more/less) [7]_____ variability than the second because the score values in it deviate more from each other and from their central tendency.

The most common numerical index of variability is the [8]_____ symbolized by [9]__ and defined by the formula [10]_____ .The square root of the variance, symbolized by [11]__ and called the [12]_____ , is also used as an index of variability. The formula for the variance states that the variance equals the sum of [13]_____ of the scores about their [14]_____ divided by the quantity [15]_____ . Thus the variance is roughly akin to the average squared deviation between scores and their mean.

To understand that the variance indeed reflects the degree to which scores deviate from one another, consider Table 3–4. For each of the three distributions, first calculate the mean, the deviations about the mean $(X_i - \overline{X})$, and the squared deviations about the mean $(X_i - \overline{X})^2$; then calculate each variance. Now, to see that the variance is proportional to the sum of the squared deviations between each score and every other score, the second part of the table helps you calculate these values. The pairs of scores within each distribution are already listed for you; square the differences between the numbers in each pair, and add them up to give you the sum of squared differences between each score and every other score, symbolized in the table by $\sum d^2$. It happens that the variance equals that sum divided by twice the number of such pairs of scores, which we have symbolized by $2n_d$ and which is 6 for these particular distributions. If you have not made an error, s^2 and $\sum d^2 / 2n_d$ will be (equal/unequal) [16]_____ . Write the value of s^2 for each distribution in the space provided at the right of the measurement scales drawn at the bottom of the table, and then determine $\sqrt{s^2} = s$ and write it in the available space. Notice that as the scores in the distribution become more spread out (that is, as they deviate more from one another), the variance (increases/decreases) [17]_____ . This illustrates how s^2 (and its cousin, s) reflect the [18]_____ in a distribution.

Table 3–5 presents a guided computational example for the concepts presented above. Complete it now and use it as a model for future computations.

Answer Key to Variability

[1]	variability	[7]	more	[13]	squared deviations
[2]	range	[8]	variance	[14]	mean
[3]	2	[9]	s^2	[15]	$N-1$
[4]	6	[10]	$\sum(X_i - \overline{X})^2/(N-1)$	[16]	equal
[5]	variability	[11]	s	[17]	increases
[6]	equal	[12]	standard deviation	[18]	variability

Table 3–4 Variability and the Variance

Distribution X				Distribution Y				Distribution W			
X_i	$\overline{X}$	$(X_i - \overline{X})$	$(X_i - \overline{X})^2$	Y_i	$\overline{Y}$	$(Y_i - \overline{Y})$	$(Y_i - \overline{Y})^2$	W_i	$\overline{W}$	$(W_i - \overline{W})$	$(W_i - \overline{W})^2$
5				3				1			
6				6				6			
7				9				11			
$\sum X_i =$		$\sum(X_i - \overline{X})^2 =$		$\sum Y_i =$		$\sum(Y_i - \overline{Y})^2 =$		$\sum W_i =$		$\sum(W_i - \overline{W})^2 =$	
$N =$		$N - 1 =$		$N =$		$N - 1 =$		$N =$		$N - 1 =$	
$\overline{X} =$		$s_x^2 =$		$\overline{Y} =$		$s_y^2 =$		$\overline{W} =$		$s_w^2 =$	

Average Squared Difference between Each Pair of Scores

$(7 - 6)^2 =$	$(9 - 6)^2 =$	$(11 - 6)^2 =$
$(7 - 5)^2 =$	$(9 - 3)^2 =$	$(11 - 1)^2 =$
$(6 - 5)^2 =$	$(6 - 3)^2 =$	$(6 - 1)^2 =$
$\sum d_x^2 =$	$\sum d_y^2 =$	$\sum d_w^2 =$
$2n_d = 6$	$2n_d = 6$	$2n_d = 6$
$\sum d_x^2 / 6 \overset{?}{=} s_x^2$	$\sum d_y^2 / 6 \overset{?}{=} s_y^2$	$\sum d_w^2 / 6 \overset{?}{=} s_w^2$

$$s^2 \qquad s$$

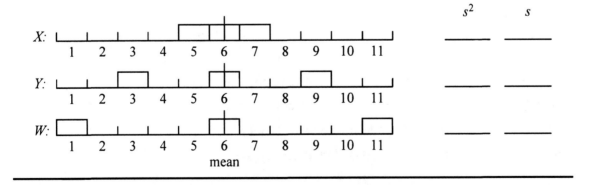

Table 3–5 Guided Computational Examples

X_i	X_i^2	**Central Tendency**
5		1. $\overline{X} = (\sum X_i) / N =$
7		2. $M_d =$ value of middle score $=$
4		$M_d =$
5		3. $M_0 =$ value of most frequent score
9		$M_0 =$
6	—	

$\sum X_i =$ $\qquad$ $\sum X_i^2 =$

$(\sum X_i)^2 =$

$N =$

Variability

1. Range = largest minus smallest score value =

2. $s^2 = [\sum (X_i - \overline{X})^2] / (N - 1) = [N \sum X_i^2 - (\sum X_i)^2] / [N(N - 1)]$ $\qquad$ $=$

    $s = \sqrt{s^2} =$

Statistics and Parameters

Frequently, research is conducted on a small group of subjects, called a [1]_____ , but the results are generalized to a much larger group, called the [2]_____ . A subset of a larger [3]_____ is a [4]_____ . Quantities calculated on a sample are called [5]_____ and symbolized with Arabic letters, such as $\overline{X}$ for the mean and s^2 for the variance of a sample. Quantitative characteristics of populations are called [6]_____ and symbolized with Greek letters such as μ (read "mew") for the mean and σ^2 (read "sigma squared") for the variance of a population. Often sample [7]_____ are used to estimate the values of population [8]_____ .

[1]	sample	[3]	population	[5]	statistics	[7]	statistics
[2]	population	[4]	sample	[6]	parameters	[8]	parameters

● ● ● ● ●   SELF-TEST

1. In what sense is the mean closest to the scores of a distribution?

2. What advantages does the median have over the mean as an index of central tendency?

3. Which index of central tendency assumes an equal-interval scale?

4. For each of the following distributions, indicate which measure of central tendency might be preferred and explain why.
    a. age of students in an urban university
    b. marital status (e.g., single, married, not married but living together as a couple, divorced) of students in a particular college
    c. height of all male students in a particular college

5. Which of the indices of central tendency is not influenced by a single extreme score?

6. Why is the range an imprecise measure of variability?

7.* Why is the standard deviation often preferred to the variance as a descriptive measure of variability?

8. If all the scores in a distribution are negative, will the variance be positive or negative? Explain.

9. What will be the variance if all the scores in a distribution are the same? What will be the standard deviation?

10.* Define *population* and *sample*.

11.* Why does one divide by $N-1$ rather than by N when calculating the variance?

Questions preceded by an asterisk can be answered on the basis of the discussion in the text, but the discussion in this Study Guide does not answer them.

● ● ● ● ●　　　　　　　　　　　　　　　　　　　EXERCISES

1. Calculate the mean, median, mode, range, variance, and standard deviation according to the format of Table 3–5 for each of the following distributions.

X	Y	Z
3	4	3
4	1	1
6	4	9
7	5	2
8	6	7
5	7	5
9	8	5
		5
		9
		4

2. Determine the median following the steps in Table 3–2 for the following distributions.
   a. (4, 2, 24, 1, 3)
   b. (2, 5, 8, 1, 3, 6)
   c. (2, 5, 8, 5, 5, 7)

d. (3, 5, 5, 6, 8)
e. (23, 25, 25, 25, 27, 37)
f. (2.4, 2.1, 7.0, 6.2, 4.6, 3.7, 4.6)

3. Draw distributions such that the following are true.
   a. The median is greater than the mean.
   b. The mode is greater than the mean and the mean is less than the median.
   c. The mean, median, and mode are identical.

4. Calculate the variance with the computational formula given in Table 3–5 for each of the following distributions, and discuss the differences in the s^2 obtained relative to the difference in the variability of scores between the four distributions.
   a. (7, 6, 5, 7, 8, 3)
   b. (−3, −4, −5, −3, −2, −7)
   c. (17, 16, 15, 17, 18, 13)
   d. (70, 60, 50, 70, 80, 30)

● ● ● ● ●　　　　　　　　　　　　　　　　　　　ANSWERS

Table 3–1. $\sum X_i = 25$, $\overline{X} = 5$, $\sum(X_i - \overline{X}) = 0$, $\sum(X_i - \overline{X})^2 = 38$; $\sum Y_i = 30$, $\overline{Y} = 6$, $\sum(Y_i - \overline{Y}) = 0$, $\sum(Y_i - \overline{Y})^2 = 70$; $\sum(Y_i - k)^2 > \sum(Y_i - \overline{Y})^2$.

Table 3–2. Distribution A: (1, 2, 3, 3, 4, 4, 9, 10, 10, 11, 11, 14, 15), $N = 13$, M_d at case 7,

$M_d = 9$. Distribution B: (0, 1, 1, 2, 2, 2, 3, 4, 5, 6, 6, 7, 8, 8), $N = 14$, M_d between cases 7 and 8, $M_d = (3 + 4) / 2 = 3.5$. Distribution C: (1.6, 1.9, 1.9, 2.0, 2.0, 2.1, 2.1, 2.1, 2.4, 2.4, 2.5, 2.8), $N = 12$, M_d between cases 6 and 7, $M_d = (2.1 + 2.1) / 2 = 2.1$.

Table 3–3. Means = 5, 8, 5, 5; medians = 5, 5, 5, 5; modes = none, none, 3 and 7, 5.

Table 3–4. $s_x^2 = 1$, $s_x = 1$, $s_y^2 = 9$, $s_y = 3$, $s_w^2 = 25$, $s_w = 5$.

Table 3–5. $\sum X_i = 36$, $(\sum X_i)^2 = 1296$, $N = 6$, $\sum X_i^2 = 232$, $\overline{X} = 6.0$, $M_d = 5.5$, $M_o = 5$, range $= 5$, $s^2 = 3.2$, $s = 1.79$.

Self-Test. (1) The least squares sense: $\sum(X_i - \overline{X})^2$ is smaller than for any value other than $\overline{X}$. **(2)** The median is unaffected by extreme scores and therefore provides a more representative measure of central tendency when the distribution is substantially skewed. **(3)** The mean assumes an equal interval scale. **(4a)** The median is preferred because the distribution will be skewed to the right; **(4b)** The mode is preferred since the scale is nominal. (The proportion of cases in each category should also be reported.); **(4c)** The mean is preferred because height is usually unimodal and not skewed. (In a large distribution all three indices could be appropriate.) **(5)** The median and probably the mode. **(6)** It ignores the variability of scores between the smallest and largest values. **(7)** Since the standard deviation is expressed in original score units rather than squared units, it is easier to interpret. **(8)** Positive, because $\sum(X_i - \overline{X})^2$ and $N - 1$ will always be positive. **(9)** 0, 0. **(10)** A population is a collection of subjects, events, or scores that have some common characteristics of interest, and a sample is a subgroup of a population. **(11)** To make the statistic s^2 an unbiased estimator of σ^2.

Exercises. (1) For distribution X: $\overline{X} = 6.00$, $M_d = 6$, $M_o =$ no useful mode, range $= 6$, $s^2 = 4.67$, $s = 2.16$; for distribution Y: $\overline{Y} = 5.00$, $M_d = 5.00$, $M_o = 4.00$, range $= 7.00$, $s^2 = 5.33$, $s = 2.31$; for distribution Z: $\overline{Z} = 5.00$, $M_d = 5$, $M_o = 5.00$, range $= 8$, $s^2 = 7.33$, $s = 2.71$. **(2a)** 3; **(2b)** 4; **(2c)** 5; **(2d)** 5; **(2e)** 25; **(2f)** 4.6. **(3)** See page 62 of text. **(4a)** $s^2 = 3.20$; **(4b)** $s^2 = 3.20$: this distribution is the same as in *a* except that a constant of -10 has been added to each score, so the variance remains the same; **(4c)** $s^2 = 3.20$: a constant of 10 has been added to each score in *a*, so the variance remains the same; **(4d)** $s^2 = 320$: a constant of 10 has been multiplied with each score in *a*, so the variance is $10^2 = 100$ times that in *a*; see pages 111–113 of the text for a discussion of these relationships.

• • • • • STATISTICAL PACKAGES • • • • •

• • • • •   MINITAB

(To accompany the guided Computational Example in Table 3–6.)

For a set of scores, MINITAB will determine the mean, median, standard deviation (StDev), minimum, maximum, first quartile (Q1), and third quartile (Q3).

This analysis will examine the number of looks at mother by a child as given in Table 3–6. The *Looks* data consist of 70 observations, strung out in order as follows:

```
47  35  35  34  34  32  31  31  30  29  28  28  28  28  27  27  27  25  24  24
24  23  22  22  22  22  21  21  21  20  20  19  19  18  18  18  17  16  16  16
16  15  15  15  14  14  13  12  12  12  12  11  11  11  10  10   9   9   8   8
 7   6   6   6   6   5   4   4   4   0
```

Start the MINITAB program. To enter data on the spreadsheet, click on the Data window. Enter the number of looks recorded for each child in the first column of the spreadsheet. Label the first column with the variable name *Looks*. To enter the new variable name, point and click on the column heading. The data entered should now appear on the spreadsheet as follows, in rows 1–70:

```
Looks
47
35
35
 :
etc.
```

Save the *Looks* data that you entered:

> *File>Save Worksheet As*
> (Enter folder and file name for the MINITAB Worksheet file.)
> OK

To generate the usual frequency table and the mean and standard deviation of the distribution, use the *Tally* command followed by the *Display Descriptive Statistics* command:

Stat>Tables>Tally
        Variables: Looks   [double-click to transfer]
        Display: Counts, Percents, Cumulative counts, Cumulative percents
        OK

Stat>Basic Statistics> Display Descriptive Statistics
        Variables: Looks   [double-click to transfer]
        OK

The above commands will yield a frequency table, mean, standard deviation, and other descriptive statistics, which will appear in the Session window. A copy of the descriptive statistics and the frequency table for this example appears below and on the following page.

To print the results from the Session window:

Window>Session
File>Print Window
        Print Range: All
        OK

Exit MINITAB:

File>Exit

There is no need to save changes for the current Project if the Worksheet file has already been saved.

MINITAB Program Output

Descriptive Statistics

Variable	N	Mean	Median	TrMean	StDev	SE Mean
Looks	70	18.34	18.00	18.08	9.56	1.14

Variable	Minimum	Maximum	Q1	Q3
Looks	0.00	47.00	11.00	25.50

Summary Statistics for Discrete Variables

Looks	Count	CumCnt	Percent	CumPct
0	1	1	1.43	1.43
4	3	4	4.29	5.71
5	1	5	1.43	7.14
6	4	9	5.71	12.86
7	1	10	1.43	14.29
8	2	12	2.86	17.14
9	2	14	2.86	20.00
10	2	16	2.86	22.86
11	3	19	4.29	27.14
12	4	23	5.71	32.86
13	1	24	1.43	34.29
14	2	26	2.86	37.14
15	3	29	4.29	41.43
16	4	33	5.71	47.14
17	1	34	1.43	48.57
18	3	37	4.29	52.86
19	2	39	2.86	55.71
20	2	41	2.86	58.57
21	3	44	4.29	62.86
22	4	48	5.71	68.57
23	1	49	1.43	70.00
24	3	52	4.29	74.29
25	1	53	1.43	75.71
27	3	56	4.29	80.00
28	4	60	5.71	85.71
29	1	61	1.43	87.14
30	1	62	1.43	88.57
31	2	64	2.86	91.43
32	1	65	1.43	92.86
34	2	67	2.86	95.71
35	2	69	2.86	98.57
47	1	70	1.43	100.00
N=	70			

● ● ● ● ●   **SPSS**

(To accompany the guided computational example in Table 3–6.)

For a set of numbers, SPSS will determine the mean, median, mode, standard deviation, variance, range, and sum of scores.

Start the SPSS program and select "Type in data," then "OK." The Data Editor window should fill the screen.

This analysis will examine the number of looks at mother by a child given in Table 3–6. The *Looks* data consist of 70 observations, strung out in order as follows:

```
47  35  35  34  34  32  31  31  30  29  28  28  28  28  27  27  27  25  24  24
24  23  22  22  22  22  21  21  21  20  20  19  19  18  18  18  17  16  16  16
16  15  15  15  14  14  13  12  12  12  12  11  11  11  10  10   9   9   8   8
 7   6   6   6   6   5   4   4   4   0
```

Enter the observations recorded for the 70 children in the first column of the spreadsheet. To enter the new variable name, click on the tab labeled "Variable View" at the bottom left of the screen. Label the first column with the variable name *Looks*. Go back to the Data View. The data entered should now appear on the spreadsheet as follows, in rows 1–70:

Looks
47
35
35
⋮
etc.

Calculate a frequency table along with the traditional measures of central tendency and variability:

> *Analyze>Descriptive Statistics>Frequencies*
>   Variable(s): Looks
>   Display Frequency Tables: Yes
>   Statistics: Central Tendency: Mean, Median, Mode, Sum
>   Dispersion: Std. Deviation, Variance, Range
>   Continue
>   OK

Print the output generated by the above procedure:

> *File>Print*
>   Print range: All visible output
>   OK

Program output for the summary statistics appears below, and the frequency table output appears on the following page.

Save the *Looks* data that you entered:

> *Window>SPSS Data Editor*
> *File>Save As*
>   (Enter folder and file name for SPSS Save file.)
>   Save

Exit SPSS:

> *File>Exit*

There is no need to save the contents of the Viewer or Data Editor, since they are easily regenerated using the saved data file.

SPSS Program Output

Frequencies

Statistics

LOOKS

N	Valid	70
	Missing	0
Mean		18.3429
Median		18.0000
Mode		6.00[a]
Std. Deviation		9.5612
Variance		91.4170
Range		47.00
Sum		1284.00

a. Multiple modes exist. The smallest value is shown.

LOOKS

		Frequency	Percent	Valid Percent	Cumulative Percent
Valid	.00	1	1.4	1.4	1.4
	4.00	3	4.3	4.3	5.7
	5.00	1	1.4	1.4	7.1
	6.00	4	5.7	5.7	12.9
	7.00	1	1.4	1.4	14.3
	8.00	2	2.9	2.9	17.1
	9.00	2	2.9	2.9	20.0
	10.00	2	2.9	2.9	22.9
	11.00	3	4.3	4.3	27.1
	12.00	4	5.7	5.7	32.9
	13.00	1	1.4	1.4	34.3
	14.00	2	2.9	2.9	37.1
	15.00	3	4.3	4.3	41.4
	16.00	4	5.7	5.7	47.1
	17.00	1	1.4	1.4	48.6
	18.00	3	4.3	4.3	52.9
	19.00	2	2.9	2.9	55.7
	20.00	2	2.9	2.9	58.6
	21.00	3	4.3	4.3	62.9
	22.00	4	5.7	5.7	68.6
	23.00	1	1.4	1.4	70.0
	24.00	3	4.3	4.3	74.3
	25.00	1	1.4	1.4	75.7
	27.00	3	4.3	4.3	80.0
	28.00	4	5.7	5.7	85.7
	29.00	1	1.4	1.4	87.1
	30.00	1	1.4	1.4	88.6
	31.00	2	2.9	2.9	91.4
	32.00	1	1.4	1.4	92.9
	34.00	2	2.9	2.9	95.7
	35.00	2	2.9	2.9	98.6
	47.00	1	1.4	1.4	100.0
	Total	70	100.0	100.0	

● ● ● ● ●

CHAPTER 4

ELEMENTS OF EXPLORATORY DATA ANALYSIS ●●●●●

CONCEPT GOALS

Be sure that you thoroughly understand the following concepts and how to use them in statistical applications.

- ◆ Stem-and-leaf displays, depths, line widths
- ◆ Resistant indicators: Median, fourth-spread, outliers, extreme scores, five-number summary, boxplot

●●●●● GUIDE TO MAJOR CONCEPTS

Introduction

The distributions, graphs, and indicators of central tendency and variability presented in the previous chapters are the traditional means of describing a set of data. Newer approaches, called **exploratory data analysis**, represent alternative techniques for describing data. An approach and a set of tools that are used, often in an unplanned and exploratory manner, to describe and understand the meaning of a set of data represent [1]_____ .

Answer Key to Introduction

[1]   exploratory data analysis

Stem-and-Leaf Displays

The **stem-and-leaf display** is an alternative to the frequency distribution for describing grouped data. An approach that performs all of the summarization functions of the traditional [1]_____ plus has the advantage of combining both the frequency distribution and histogram in one display while preserving more of the information in the original data is the [2]_____ .

For the purpose of constructing a [3]_____ , the numbers in the distribution, which will now be called a **batch**, must be broken down into a part that consists of the smallest digit, called the [4]_____ , and the remaining larger digits, called the [5]_____ . For example, the number 57 would have a stem of [6]__ and a leaf of [7]__ , and the number 23.4 would have 23 as its [8]_____ and .4 as its [9]_____ .

Similar to a frequency distribution, a [10]_____ is an ordered set of all the numbers in the [11]_____ in which the class intervals are defined by the [12]_____ and the size of the class interval is defined by the number of [13]_____ within a stem.

The steps in constructing a stem-and-leaf display, a technique of the general approach to descriptive statistics known as [14]_____ , generally follow those given in Table 2–5 for frequency distributions, but with a few modifications. To be able to compare a stem-and-leaf display with the traditional [15]_____ , the 50 statistics test scores used to construct a frequency distribution in Chapter 2 are reproduced here in Table 4–1. The first step in creating a stem-and-leaf display is to order the data by score value, beginning with the smallest number at the bottom. You did this in Table 2–2, and either refer back to that Table or order the scores again in Table 4–1.

Second, determine generally the stem-and-leaves for the data. The data in Table 4–1 range from the lowest score value of [16]__ to the highest score value of [17]__ , so the tens digit will be the [18]_____ and the ones digit will be the [19]_____.

Third, following the procedures described above for frequency distributions, determine the approximate number of class intervals, which will be called **lines** in the context of a [20]_____ . Recall from constructing the frequency distribution for these data that Table 2–3 in Chapter 2 suggested that the maximum number of intervals for [21] $N =$ __ was [22]__ . Further, the range of score values for these data was equal to [23]_____ . So, as before, the minimum size of an interval is [24] $57 / 14 =$ __ . Then, following the steps in Table 2–5 for constructing a frequency distribution, this minimum size of interval should be rounded *up* to the next "round" value, that is either 2, 5, or 10 (or some multiple of 10 times these "round" values, such as .2, .5, 1.0 or 20, 50, 100). So the interval size, which in the case of a stem-and-leaf display is called the **line width**, for this example will be either [25]__ or [26]__ . Recall, for simplicity, we chose an interval size of 10.

Table 4–1 Statistics Test Scores for Fifty Students

Scores

79	51	67	50	78
62	89	83	73	80
88	48	60	71	79
89	63	55	93✓	71
41	81	46	50	61
59	50	90✓	75	61
75	98✓	53	79	80
70	73	42	72	74
67	73	79	67	85
91✓	67	77	74	77

Ordering of Scores

	90–99	80–89	70–79	60–69	50–59	40–49
–9						
–8	98					
–7						
–6						
–5						
–4						
–3	93					
–2						
–1	91					
–0	90					

Fourth, identify the lowest score, which is [27]__ , and determine the lowest line that would include that score. The score of 41 has a stem of [28]__ , and since 10 is the [29]_____ , the stem of 4 will have [30]__ leaves beginning with 0. In Table 4–2, place at the bottom the first [31]__ of this display, having a stem of [32]__ . Now add all the remaining possible stems until you reach at the top of the display a stem that includes the largest score, [33]__ , which stem is [34]__ .

Table 4–2 A Stem-and-Leaf Display for the Statistics Test Scores in Table 4–1

Statistics Test Scores

Depths ($N = $ __)		(Unit = Point)
	Stem	Leaves

Fifth, go to the ordered data in Table 4–1 (or Table 2–2) and place the leaves of each score on the line corresponding to its stem, beginning with the smallest leaf at the left and increasing in value to the right along the line. These leaves are separated only by a space (i.e., no commas). If no scores exist for a possible stem, keep the stem in the display but enter no leaves.

Sixth, at the left of Table 4–2 you will find a column labeled **depths**. The cumulative frequency of each line is roughly that line's [35]_____ . Calculate the depth of each line, beginning at the bottom of Table 4–2, until you reach the line containing the middle score (between the 25th and 26th score for $N = 50$). That line gets a depth equal to the frequency, not cumulative frequency, of that line alone. This value is [36]__ , and it is enclosed in parentheses to indicate that it is not a cumulative value. Then start at the top of the display, and accumulate frequencies for each stem, or [37]_____ , downward until you again reach the line containing the middle score. Note that if a line has a depth that exactly equals half the number of cases in the [38]_____ (25 in this case), there will be two adjacent lines with that depth and no central line with only its frequency.

Seventh, label the display. Specifically, give it a title (as already printed for Table 4–2), place the N under the heading Depths, and write the unit of measurement over the stem and leaf headings. The unit in this case is [39]__ point. The completed Table 4–2 represents a [40]_____ .

Compare this [41]_____ with the traditional [42]_____ which you completed in Table 2–4 in Chapter 2. The stem-and-leaf display looks somewhat like the frequency distribution would look if tallies rather than simply the number of frequencies were recorded in the frequency distribution. One advantage of a stem-and-leaf display is that it combines the appearance of a frequency histogram with the frequency distribution, preserving more of the original information because the actual leaves are given. Therefore, proponents of this approach to descriptive statistics, called [43]_____ , argue that the techniques provide a more informative description of the data.

The above example used a size of class interval or [44]_____ of 10, so the stems were 10's and the leaves for each stem were the digits 0–9. But we could have used a line width of 5 or, if N were larger, even 2. In this event, a single stem must be divided into two (or five) to produce line widths of 5 (or 2). For example, if the line width were 5, the stem of 4 would be represented twice, once for the five leaves 0–4 and once for the five leaves 5–9. To symbolize this, the stem 4* represents the stem of 4 having leaves 0–4, and the stem 4• represents the stem of 4 having leaves 5–9. In such a display, a score of 53 would be listed next to the stem of [45]__ , and the score of 77 would be listed next to the stem of [46]__ . If 2 rather than 5 is the [47]_____ , then there will be five lines for each stem. In this case, a stem plus

* designates leaves 0 and 1

t designates leaves 2 (two) and 3 (three)

f designates leaves 4 (four) and 5 (five)

s designates leaves 6 (six) and 7 (seven)

• designates leaves 8 and 9.

In this event, a score of 35 will have a stem of [48]__ , 48 a stem of [49]__ , 61 a stem of [50]__ , 96 a stem of [51]__ , and 73 a stem of [52]__ .

For example, Table 4–3 presents the final exam scores given in Exercise 2 in Chapter 2. First determine the lowest and highest score, which are [53]__ and [54]__ , respectively, which gives a range of score values for these data equal to [55]__. The N for this [56]_____ of scores is [57]__ , and referring back in Chapter 2 to Table 2–3 we see that the maximum number of class intervals for this N is [58]__ . Therefore, the minimum size of an interval for these data is [59]_____ , and the interval size, called the [60]_____ , for this example will be either [61]__ or [62]__ . In Table 4–4, complete the stem-and-leaf display using a line width of 5, and in Table 4–5 create a stem-and-leaf display using a line width of 2.

Table 4–3 Final Exam Scores

90	91	85	82	71	75	75
76	85	76	77	70	70	85
70	70	72	79	68	74	75
75	75	73	91	85	82	72
72	85	79	81	92	65	68
80	80	80	65	78	90	94
90	68	87	75	77	95	72
94	90	85	70	93	90	82
70	85	95	65	68	92	80
77	75	92	90	92	85	75

Table 4–4 Stem-and-Leaf Display for Final Exam Scores Using a Line Width of 5

Depths ($N = 70$)	Final Exam Scores (Unit = 1 Point)	
	Stem	Leaves

Table 4–5 Stem-and-Leaf Display for Final Exam Scores Using a Line Width of 2

Depths ($N = 70$)	Final Exam Scores (Unit = 1 Point) Stem	Leaves

Answer Key to Stem-and-Leaf Displays

[1]	frequency distribution	[9]	leaf	[17]	98	[27]	41
[2]	stem-and-leaf display	[10]	stem-and-leaf display	[18]	stem	[28]	4
[3]	stem-and-leaf display	[11]	batch	[19]	leaves	[29]	line width
[4]	leaf	[12]	stems	[20]	stem-and-leaf display	[30]	10
[5]	stem	[13]	leaves	[21]	50	[31]	line
[6]	5	[14]	exploratory data analysis	[22]	14	[32]	4
[7]	7	[15]	frequency distribution	[23]	$98 - 41 = 57$	[33]	98
[8]	stem	[16]	41	[24]	4.07	[34]	9
				[25]	5	[35]	depth
				[26]	10	[36]	181
						[37]	line

[38]	batch	[43]	exploratory	[50]	6*	[58]	17
[39]	1		data analysis	[51]	9s	[59]	30 / 17 = 1.76
[40]	stem-and-leaf	[44]	line width	[52]	7t	[60]	line width
	display	[45]	5*	[53]	65	[61]	2
[41]	stem-and-leaf	[46]	7•	[54]	95	[62]	5
	display	[47]	line width	[55]	30		
[42]	frequency	[48]	3f	[56]	batch		
	distribution	[49]	4•	[57]	70		

Resistant Indicators

The indices of central tendency and variability presented in Chapter 3 are the most traditional and common characteristics used to describe distributions, but they have limitations. One limitation is that the value of many of these indicators depends on the value of every score in the distribution. Ordinarily, this feature is valuable, but if one or two scores are unusually high or low, the mean, range, variance, and standard deviation also will be unusually high or low. It would be helpful to have **resistant indicators**, ones that change relatively little in value if a small portion of the data is replaced with new numbers that may be very different than the original ones. Presumably, [1]_____ "resist" influence by individual scores, especially atypical and very deviant scores, and therefore reflect only the main body of the data.

One [2]_____ of central tendency is the median. Recall from the previous chapter that the value of every score in the distribution, including very deviant scores, influences the value of the [3]_____ , but deviant scores do not influence the value of the [4]_____ . In the following two distributions

A: (2, 4, 6)

B: (2, 4, 100)

the mean of A is [5]__ , while the mean of B is [6]__ ; but the median of both A and B is [7]__ . So the deviant score of 100 influences the value of the [8]_____ but not the [9]_____ ; consequently, the median is a more [10]_____ of central tendency.

The traditional indicators of variability, namely the [11]_____ , [12]_____ , and [13]_____ , are also influenced by the value of every score and especially the value of any very deviant scores. In the above two small distributions, for example, the range of A is [14]_____ and the range of B is [15]_____ . Obviously, the range is influenced a great deal by the one deviant score of 100, and the variance and standard deviation will also be influenced by this extreme score. Therefore, it would be helpful to have an indicator of variability that was more [16]_____ to the values of unusual and deviant scores.

One such indicator is called the **fourth-spread**, and its definition is based upon the concept of **depth** in **stem-and-leaf displays**. Table 4–6 presents a stem-and-leaf display for the number of looks at mother that $N = 70$ ten-month infants made during a 20-minute free play session in a study of attachment. At the left of the table are the depths. Recall that the depth of line 1* is [17]__ , which means that 26 of the 70 cases have scores of [18]__ or [19]_____ . Similarly, for the line 3*, the [20]_____ is 9, which means that [21]__ of the [22]__ scores in the batch are [23]__ or [24]_____ . Recall also that the depth of (13) for line 1• means that this line contains [25]__ cases, and that it contains the middle score value, or [26]_____ . The median score value has a depth of $(N + 1) / 2$. *If N is an odd number*, this depth will be a whole number, and the median is the value of the case having that depth. That is, if the depth of the median is 11, the median is the value of the [27]__ score from the bottom (or top). *If N is an even number*, the depth of the median will be fractional. For example, the batch in Table 4–6 has an $N = 70$, so the depth of the median is [28]$(N + 1) / 2 =$ _____ = __ . The median is the average of the values of the [29]__ and [30]__ scores, or [31]_____ .

Just as there is a depth of the median, there are also **depths of the fourths**. Whereas the median is the middle score value that divides the batch in half, the fourths (plus the median) divide the [32]_____ approximately into [33]_____ . The depths of the fourths is given by depths of the fourths $= [(\text{depth of median}) + 1] / 2$ in which a fractional depth of the median is first rounded down to the next lowest integer. In the present example, the depth of the median was [34]__ , which must be rounded down to [35]__ before determining the depth of the [36]_____ , which is [37]_____ . Therefore, in this batch, the **fourths** are the values of the [38]__ score from the top, called the **upper fourth**, F_U, and from the bottom, called the **lower fourth**, F_L. The value of the 18th case from the bottom is in the line with a stem of [39]__ . Since 14 cases exist below this line, one needs four more cases from line 1*. Counting cases (i.e., leaves) from left to right (i.e., in increasing value) along line 1*, the fourth case has a leaf of [40]__ representing a score value of [41]__ , so the value of the [42]_____ , symbolized by [43]__ , is [44]__ . Now, to obtain the 18th case from the top, we note that the depth of line 2• is 18, which means that this line contains the 18th case and it is the last case on this line. But remember that you are counting *down* over *decreasing* score values, so you must count down from right to left within a line. Thus, the 18th case has a leaf of [45]_____ representing a score value of [46]__ , so the value of the [47]_____ , or [48]__ , is [49]__ . If the depth of a fourth is fractional (e.g., 9.5), the fourth is the average of the scores bordering the fraction (e.g., in this case the average of the values of the [50]__ and [51]__ cases.)

Now the resistant indicator of variability is the **fourth-spread**, which is the difference in score values between the upper and lower fourths:

$$\text{fourth - spread} = \text{upper fourth} - \text{lower fourth}$$
$$\text{fourth - spread} = F_U - F_L$$

In the present example, the [52]_____ equals [53]_____ .

The fourth-spread approximately defines the middle half of the batch. Thus, roughly half the infants in this example looked at their mothers between [54]__ and [55]__ times. Because it is the middle half of the cases and it is based upon the median not the mean, the [56]_____ is not influenced by unusual deviant scores and is therefore a [57]_____ of variability.

The fourths help define **outliers**, cases whose values are substantially deviant from the group and would have little likelihood of being obtained again if a new sample were taken. Outliers are cases that fall 1.5 times the fourth-spread above or below the fourths, that is,

$$\text{below } F_L - 1.5 \text{ (fourth-spread) or}$$
$$\text{above } F_U + 1.5 \text{ (fourth-spread)}$$

Table 4–6 Guided Computational Example of Resistant Indicators

Number of Looks at Mother

Depths ($N = 70$)	(Unit = 1 Look) Stem	Leaves
1	4●	7
1	4*	
2	3●	5 5
9	3*	0 1 1 2 4 4
18	2●	5 7 7 7 8 8 8 8 9
31	2*	0 0 1 1 1 2 2 2 2 3 4 4 4
(13)	1●	5 5 5 6 6 6 6 7 8 8 8 9 9
26	1*	0 0 1 1 1 2 2 2 2 3 4 4
14	0●	5 6 6 6 6 7 8 8 9 9
4	0*	0 4 4 4

Median

The **median** is the value of the score having a depth of $(N + 1)/2$. The median has a depth of $(N + 1)/2 = \underline{\hspace{2cm}} = \underline{\hspace{0.5cm}}$.
If the depth of the median is a whole number, the value of the median is the value of the case having this depth. If the depth of the median is fractional, the value of the median is the average of the values of the cases bordering this fractional depth.

$$M_d = \underline{\hspace{0.5cm}}$$

Fourth-Spread

Depth of the fourths = (depth of the median) + 1/2 in which any fractional depth of the median is first rounded down to the next whole number. Depths of the fourths = $[(\underline{\hspace{0.3cm}}) + 1]/2 = \underline{\hspace{2cm}} = \underline{\hspace{0.5cm}}$.

The **lower fourth**, F_L, is the score value of the case with a depth of a fourth counted up from the bottom of the batch. F_L is the value of the __ case from the bottom which is $F_L = \underline{\hspace{0.5cm}}$.

The **upper fourth**, F_U, is the score value of the case with a depth of a fourth counted down from the top of the batch. F_U is the value of the __ case from the top which is $F_U = \underline{\hspace{0.5cm}}$.

The **fourth-spread** is the difference in values between the upper and lower fourths:

$$\text{fourth - spread} = \text{upper fourth} - \text{lower fourth}$$
$$= F_U - F_L$$
$$\text{fourth - spread} = \underline{\hspace{3cm}} = \underline{\hspace{0.5cm}}$$

Outliers and Extreme Scores

Outliers are cases whose values fall either

$$\text{below } F_L - 1.5 \text{ (fourth - spread)} = \underline{\hspace{3cm}} = \underline{\hspace{0.5cm}} \text{ or}$$
$$\text{above } F_U + 1.5 \text{ (fourth - spread)} = \underline{\hspace{3cm}} = \underline{\hspace{0.5cm}}$$

So the score value of __ is an outlier.

Extreme scores are the lowest (***LEx***) and highest (***UEx***) scores in the batch excluding outliers. The extreme scores are *LEx* __ and *UEx* __ .

Recall that the fourth-spread for this example was [58]___ , [59] $F_L = $ ___ , and $F_U = $ [60]___ . So the cutoffs for [61]_____ are: [62] $F_L - 1.5$ (fourth-spread) = _____ and [63] $F_U + 1.5$ (fourth-spread) = _____ .Since there can be no negative number of looks at mother, the lower fourth is taken to be, not −10, but [64]___ . Note that these cutoffs of [65]___ and [66]___ define one score as an [67]_____ , namely the score value of [68]___ .

Extreme scores are the lowest and highest scores in the batch excluding outliers. Eliminating the outlier score of 47, the next highest score was [69]___ and the lowest score was [70]___ , which are the [71]_____ of the batch. They are represented by **LEx** for the lower extreme score and **UEx** for the upper extreme score. Thus, [72] $LEx = $ ___ and [73] $UEx = $ ___ .

The lower portion of Table 4–6 provides a guided computational example of these resistant indicators. Complete it now.

These indicators can be presented in a special table or graphically. A table containing the major resistant indicators of central tendency and variability is called a **five-number summary**. Table 4–7 presents the general format for the five-number summary for the information obtained in Table 4–6. Study the notation under the display and then fill in the values from Table 4–6 in their proper places in the [74]_____ at the top of Table 4–7.

A graphical display of the same information is called a **boxplot**, and a guide for constructing a boxplot is given at the bottom of Table 4–7. Follow those instructions and label the sample [75]_____ at the bottom of the table.

Notice the nice picture the boxplot provides of the nature of the scores in the batch. The box, which spans the [76]_____ , represents the central [77]_____ of the batch. It is the main body of data exclusive of the upper and lower quarters of the batch that could possibly contain deviant scores. The resistant indicator of central tendency, the [78]_____ , resides within the box. The ends of the lines are defined by the [79]_____ and [80]_____ scores. This is basically the range of the batch ignoring [81]_____ , which are presented with Xs for completeness. Asymmetry in the plot, conveyed by a longer line to one versus the other side of the box, would imply skewness. In this case, the batch appears symmetrical except for the [82]_____ .

Table 4–7 Guided Example of Presentations of Resistant Indicators

Five Number Summary

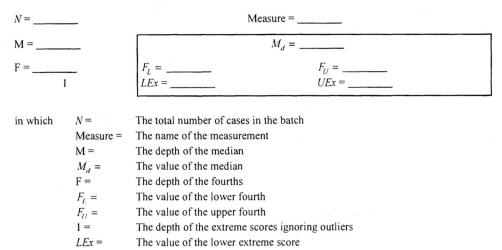

$N =$ _____   Measure = _____

$M =$ _____

$M_d =$ _____

$F =$ _____

$F_L =$ _____ $F_U =$ _____

1                      $LEx =$ _____ $UEx =$ _____

in which		
$N =$	The total number of cases in the batch
Measure =	The name of the measurement
$M =$	The depth of the median
$M_d =$	The value of the median
$F =$	The depth of the fourths
$F_L =$	The value of the lower fourth
$F_U =$	The value of the upper fourth
1 =	The depth of the extreme scores ignoring outliers
$LEx =$	The value of the lower extreme score
$UEx =$	The value of the upper extreme score

Boxplot

1. Mark off abscissa in units of the measurement scale and label. Draw an ordinate without scale and label the batch(es) to the left of the ordinate.
2. Draw a rectangular box for each batch that stretches on the measurement scale between the lower fourth (F_L) and upper fourth (F_U).
3. Within the box, draw a vertical line at the median (M_d).
4. Draw horizontal lines in each direction from the box, extending to the lower extreme score (LEx) and to the upper extreme score (UEx).
5. Locate each outlier, if any, with an X and label that case, if appropriate (e.g., with initials).
6.

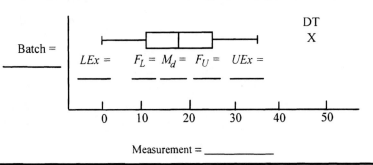

Batch = _____

DT
X

$LEx =$ $F_L =$ $M_d =$ $F_U =$ $UEx =$

_____   ___ ___ ___   _____

0   10   20   30   40   50

Measurement = _____

Answer Key to Resistant Indicators

[1]	resistant indicators	[29]	35th	[57]	resistant indicator
[2]	resistant indicator	[30]	36th	[58]	14
[3]	mean	[31]	$(18 + 18) / 2 = 18$	[59]	11
[4]	median	[32]	batch	[60]	25
[5]	4	[33]	fourths	[61]	outliers
[6]	35.3	[34]	35.5	[62]	$11 - 1.5(14) = -10$
[7]	4	[35]	35	[63]	$25 + 1.5(14) = 46$
[8]	mean	[36]	fourths	[64]	0
[9]	median	[37]	$(35 + 1) / 2 = 18$	[65]	0
[10]	resistant indicator	[38]	18th	[66]	46
[11]	range	[39]	1*	[67]	outlier
[12]	variance	[40]	1	[68]	47
[13]	standard deviation	[41]	11	[69]	35
[14]	$6 - 2 = 4$	[42]	lower fourth	[70]	0
[15]	$100 - 2 = 98$	[43]	F_L	[71]	extreme scores
[16]	resistant	[44]	11	[72]	0
[17]	26	[45]	5	[73]	35
[18]	14	[46]	25	[74]	five-number summary
[19]	lower	[47]	fourth	[75]	boxplot
[20]	depth	[48]	F_U	[76]	fourths
[21]	9	[49]	25	[77]	half
[22]	70	[50]	9th	[78]	median
[23]	30	[51]	10th	[79]	lower
[24]	higher	[52]	fourth-spread	[80]	upper extreme
[25]	13	[53]	$25 - 11 = 14$	[81]	outliers
[26]	median	[54]	11	[82]	outlier
[27]	11th	[55]	25		
[28]	$(70 + 1) / 2 = 35.5$	[56]	fourth-spread		

● ● ● ● ●   SELF-TEST

1. A stem-and-leaf display is an alternative to
    a. a frequency distribution
    b. a relative frequency distribution
    c. a histogram
    d. both a frequency distribution and histogram

2. What are the similarities and differences between cumulative frequency and depths?

3. If the line width is 10, the number 54 has a stem of
    a. 10   c. 4
    b. 50   d. 5

4. If the line width is 2, the number 54 has a stem of
    a. 5t   c. 5s
    b. 5f   d. 4

5. Which pair of concepts below are most similar to one another?
    a. depth and relative frequency
    b. fourth-spread and line width
    c. frequency distribution and batch
    d. outlier and extreme score

6. Line width is the same as
    a. interval size   c. real limits
    b. fourth-spread   d. batch

7. A stem of 8 plus the following symbol has leaves of which values?
    a. 8s has leaves __ and __ .
    b. 8t has leaves __ and __ .
    c. 8• has leaves __ and __ .
    d. 8f has leaves __ and __ .
    e. 8* has leaves __ and __ .

8.* What are the advantages of using stem-and-leaf displays, five-number summaries, and boxplots over more traditional descriptive methods?

9. What are the five numbers in a five-number summary?

10. What are the six possible values that can be plotted in a boxplot?

11. What value represents a resistant indicator for the variability in a batch?
    a. Outliers
    b. Depths of the fourths
    c. Fourth-spread
    d. Median

12. The resistant indicator of central tendency is the
    a. depth   c. fourth-spread
    b. mean   d. median

Questions preceded by an asterisk can be answered on the basis of the discussion in the text, but the discussion in this Study Guide does not answer them.

● ● ● ● ●   EXERCISES

1. Two basketball teams will meet for the league championship. They have played essentially the same teams during the season and they have identical won-loss records. Sports writers are arguing that Allegheny is a better team than Laurel Highlands because they have scored a higher average number of points per game. Below are the points scored by each team respectively during the season. Create stem-and-leaf displays and five-number summaries separately for each team, and then construct a single boxplot comparing the two teams (see text for how to draw two plots on one graph). Interpret this information in view of the sports writers' claim.

Allegheny: 70, 68, 86, 99, 74, 65, 80, 83, 78, 64, 79, 81, 97, 73, 72, 88, 79, 82, 82, 99, 68, 75, 66, 73, 75, 87, 77, 84, 74, 78

Laurel Highlands: 51, 67, 88, 80, 83, 76, 72, 79, 83, 85, 70, 74, 83, 87, 59, 72, 74, 83, 86, 75, 65, 77, 73, 82, 87, 86, 76, 84, 72, 77

● ● ● ● ●   ANSWERS

Table 4–2

| | Statistics Test Scores | |
| Depths ($N = 50$) | (Unit = 1 Point) | |
	Stem	Leaves
4	9	3 8
12	8	0 0 1 3 5 8 9 9
(18)	7	0 1 1 2 3 3 3 4 4 5 5 7 7 8 9 9 9 9
20	6	0 1 1 2 3 7 7 7 7
11	5	0 0 0 1 3 5 9
4	4	1 2 6 8

Table 4–4

Depths ($N = 70$)	Final Exam Scores (Unit = 1 Point)	
	Stem	Leaves
2	9•	5 5
17	9*	0 0 0 0 0 0 1 1 2 2 2 2 3 4 4
26	8•	5 5 5 5 5 5 5 7
34	8*	0 0 0 0 1 2 2 2
(16)	7•	5 5 5 5 5 5 5 5 6 6 7 7 7 8 9 9
20	7*	0 0 0 0 0 0 1 2 2 2 2 3 4
7	6•	5 5 5 8 8 8 8

Table 4–5

Depths ($N = 70$)	Final Exam Scores (Unit = 1 Point)	
	Stem	Leaves
4	9f	4 4 5 5
9	9t	2 2 2 2 3
17	9*	0 0 0 0 0 0 1 1
17	8•	
18	8s	7
26	8f	5 5 5 5 5 5 5 5
29	8t	2 2 2
34	8*	0 0 0 0 1
(3)	7•	8 9 9
33	7s	6 6 7 7 7
28	7f	4 5 5 5 5 5 5 5 5
19	7t	2 2 2 2 3
14	7*	0 0 0 0 0 0 1
7	6•	8 8 8 8
3	6s	
3	6f	5 5 5

Table 4–6. Depth of the median $= (70 + 1) / 2 = 35.5$, $M_d = 8$; Depth of the fourths $= (35 + 1) / 2 = 18$; F_L is the 18th case from the bottom, $F_L = 11$; F_U is the 18th case from the top, $F_U = 25$; fourth-spread $= 25 - 11 = 14$; outliers exist below $11 - 1.5(14) = -10 = 0$ and above $25 + 1.5(14) = 46$, score value 47 is an outlier; $LEx = 0$, $UEx = 35$.

Table 4–7. $N = 70$, Measure = Looks at Mother, $M = 35.5$, $M_d = 18$, $F = 18$, $F_L = 11$, $F_U = 25$, $LEx = 0$, $UEx = 35$.

Self-Test. (1) d. **(2)** They both represent cumulative frequencies. In a cumulative frequency distribution, frequencies are cumulated only in one direction, up from the bottom or lowest interval all the way to the top or highest interval. In a stem-and-leaf display, depth is a cumulation of frequencies in both directions. One starts at the bottom and accumulates frequencies upward until reaching the line with the middle score; then one starts at the top and accumulates downward until reaching the line containing the middle score. The line containing the middle score receives, in parentheses, a depth equal to its frequency, not cumulative frequency. **(3)** d. **(4)** b. **(5)** c. **(6)** a. **(7a)** 6, 7; **(7b)** 2, 3; **(7c)** 8, 9; **(7d)** 4, 5; **(7e)** 0, 1. **(8)** Resistant indicators are less subject to the influence of unusual deviant scores. The stem-and-leaf display provides all the information in the frequency distribution, cumulative frequency distribution, and histogram in one display and preserves more of the detail of the data. The five-number summary and boxplot provide tabular and graphical representation to resistant indicators that convey central tendency, variability, outliers, and skewness. **(9)** The median, M_d; the value of the lower fourth, F_L; the value of the upper fourth, F_U; the value of the lower extreme score, LEx; the value of the upper extreme score, UEx. **(10)** LEx, F_L, M_d, F_U, UEx, and the value of any outliers. **(11)** c. **(12)** d.

Exercises. (1) See the following.

Allegheny Points per Game			Laurel Highlands Points per Game		
Depths ($N = 30$)	(Unit 1 = Points) Stem	Leaves	Depths ($N = 30$)	(Unit 1 = Point) Stem	Leaves
3	9•	7 9 9	6	8•	5 6 6 7 7 8
3	9*		13	8*	0 2 3 3 3 3 4
6	8•	6 7 8	(6)	7•	5 6 6 7 7 9
12	8*	0 1 2 2 3 4	11	7*	0 2 2 2 3 4 4
(7)	7•	5 5 7 8 8 9 9	4	6•	5 7
11	7*	0 2 3 3 4 4	2	6*	
5	6•	5 6 8 8	2	5•	9
1	6*	4	1	5*	1

Allegheny

$N = 30$ Points per Game

$M = 15.5$ $\quad M_d = 78$

$F = 8$ $\quad F_L = 73 \qquad F_U = 83$

1 $\quad LEx = 64 \qquad UEx = 97$

Outliers are beyond 58–98; 99, 99 are outliers

Laurel Highlands

$N = 30$ Points per Game

$M = 15.5$ $\quad M_d = 77$

$F = 8$ $\quad F_L = 72 \qquad F_U = 83$

1 $\quad LEx = 59 \qquad UEx = 88$

Outliers are beyond 55.5–99.5; 51 is an outlier

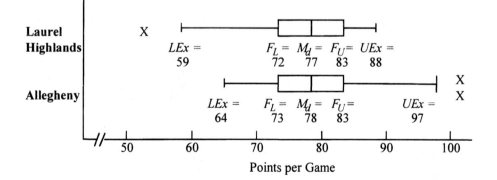

Generally, the teams are nearly the same except Allegheny can occasionally have very high-scoring games and Laurel Highlands can occasionally have very low-scoring games.

● ● ● ● ● STATISTICAL PACKAGES ● ● ● ● ●

● ● ● ● ●   MINITAB

(To accompany the guided Computational Example in Table 4–6.)

For a set of scores, MINITAB will generate descriptive statistics for exploratory data analysis, construct a stem-and-leaf display and draw a boxplot.

This analysis will examine the number of looks at mother by a child given in Table 4–6 (and earlier in Table 3–6). The *Looks* data consist of 70 observations, strung out in order as follows:

```
47  35  35  34  34  32  31  31  30  29  28  28  28  28  27  27  27  25  24  24
24  23  22  22  22  22  21  21  21  20  20  19  19  18  18  18  17  16  16  16
16  15  15  15  14  14  13  12  12  12  12  11  11  11  10  10   9   9   8   8
 7   6   6   6   6   5   4   4   4   0
```

Start the MINITAB program. You will have to enter the observations recorded for the 70 children in the first column of the spreadsheet, unless you have previously entered the data for these observations in Chapter 3. In that case, retrieve the MINITAB Worksheet file as follows:

> *File>Open Worksheet*
>   (Select the saved Worksheet file.)
>   Open
>   OK

The data entered should now appear on the spreadsheet as follows, in rows 1–70:

Looks
47
35
35
⋮
etc.

Two kinds of descriptive analyses can be carried out on the variable. The first is to calculate the usual frequency table and the mean and standard deviation of the distribution as we did in Chapters 2 and 3.

A second strategy, which is used in this chapter, is exploratory data analysis. A stem-and-leaf display for describing grouped data will be generated in place of the frequency table, and a graphics display of a boxplot will illustrate variability.

To generate the descriptive statistics, the stem-and-leaf display, and its associated boxplot:

> *Graph>Stem-and-leaf*
> 　　　　Variables: Looks　　　　　　[double-click to transfer]
> 　　　　OK

> *Stat>Basic Statistics>Display Descriptive Statistics*
> 　　　　Variables: Looks　　　　　　[double-click to transfer]
> 　　　　Graphs: Boxplot of data: Yes
> 　　　　　　　　OK
> 　　　　OK

The above commands will yield tabular output in the Session window, and a graphics image of the boxplot. This output is shown below and on the next page.

Notice that the above output is different in some ways from that presented in the text and this *Guide*. First, scores are listed from the smallest at the top to the largest at the bottom in the stem-and-leaf display. Second, score values with no frequencies are simply omitted from the frequency distribution, rather than listed with 0 frequencies. Third, each of the 11 stems is listed in the stem-and-leaf display (fewer stems could have been used), so each instance of each leaf is indicated with a 0. Finally, notice that the line in the boxplot represents the range of scores, not the *LEx* to the *UEx*, so no outliers are plotted.

To print the results from the Session window:

> *Window>Session*
> *File>Print Session Window*
> 　　　　Print Range: All
> 　　　　OK

To print the boxplot:

> *Window>Boxplot of Looks*
> *File>Print Graph*
> 　　　　Print Range: All
> 　　　　OK

Exit MINITAB:

File>Exit

MINITAB Program Output

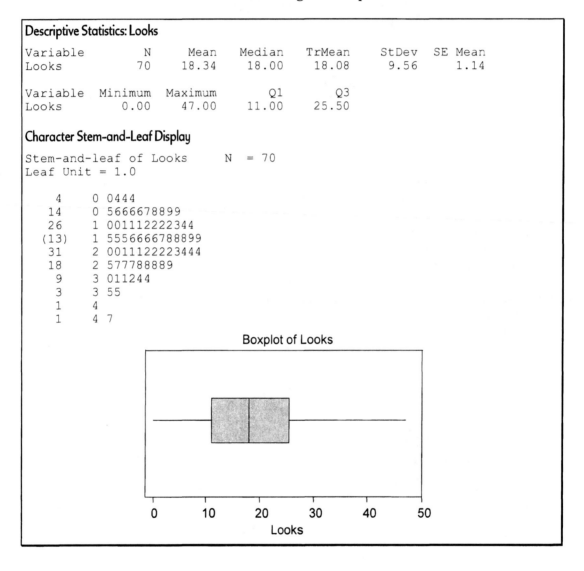

Descriptive Statistics: Looks

Variable	N	Mean	Median	TrMean	StDev	SE Mean
Looks	70	18.34	18.00	18.08	9.56	1.14

Variable	Minimum	Maximum	Q1	Q3
Looks	0.00	47.00	11.00	25.50

Character Stem-and-Leaf Display

```
Stem-and-leaf of Looks     N  = 70
Leaf Unit = 1.0

    4     0 0444
   14     0 5666678899
   26     1 001112222344
  (13)    1 5556666788899
   31     2 0011122223444
   18     2 577788889
    9     3 011244
    3     3 55
    1     4
    1     4 7
```

Boxplot of Looks

● ● ● ● ●   SPSS

(To accompany the guided computational example in Table 4–6.)

For a set of numbers, SPSS will generate descriptive statistics for exploratory data analysis and produce a stem-and-leaf plot and a boxplot.

Start the SPSS program. The Data Editor window will fill the screen.

This analysis will examine the number of looks at mother by a child given in Table 4–6 (and earlier in Table 3.6). The *Looks* data consist of 70 observations, strung out in order as follows:

```
47  35  35  34  34  32  31  31  30  29  28  28  28  28  27  27  27  25  24  24
24  23  22  22  22  22  21  21  21  20  20  19  19  18  18  18  17  16  16  16
16  15  15  15  14  14  13  12  12  12  12  11  11  11  10  10  9   9   8   8
7   6   6   6   6   5   4   4   4   0
```

You will have to enter the observations recorded for the 70 children in the first column of the spreadsheet, unless you have previously entered the data for these observations in Chapter 3. In that case, retrieve the SPSS Save file as follows:

> *File>Open>Data*
>   (Select the saved file name.)
>   Open
>   OK

Two kinds of descriptive analyses can be carried out on these data. The first strategy is to calculate a frequency table along with the traditional measures of central tendency and variability, as we did in Chapters 2 and 3.

A second strategy, which is used in this chapter, is to employ exploratory data analysis. A stem-and-leaf display for describing grouped data will be generated in place of the frequency table of Chapter 2, and a graphics display of a boxplot will illustrate variability in place of the standard deviation of Chapter 3.

To generate the descriptive statistics, the stem-and-leaf display, and its associated boxplot:

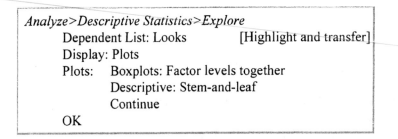

Analyze>Descriptive Statistics>Explore
        Dependent List: Looks   [Highlight and transfer]
        Display: Plots
        Plots: Boxplots: Factor levels together
                  Descriptive: Stem-and-leaf
                  Continue
     OK

The SPSS output for the stem-and-leaf table and the boxplot is shown on the next two pages. Notice that substantially more information is provided than has been presented thus far in the text. Further, the boxplot is displayed vertically, rather than horizontally.

Print the stem-and-leaf display and the boxplot output:

File>Print
        Print range: All visible output
        OK

Exit SPSS:

File>Exit

SPSS Program Output

Explore

Case Processing Summary

	Cases					
	Valid		Missing		Total	
	N	Percent	N	Percent	N	Percent
LOOKS	70	100.0%	0	.0%	70	100.0%

Descriptives

			Statistic	Std. Error
LOOKS	Mean		18.3429	1.1428
	95% Confidence Interval for Mean	Lower Bound	16.0631	
		Upper Bound	20.6227	
	5% Trimmed Mean		18.0952	
	Median		18.0000	
	Variance		91.417	
	Std. Deviation		9.5612	
	Minimum		.00	
	Maximum		47.00	
	Range		47.00	
	Interquartile Range		14.5000	
	Skewness		.384	.287
	Kurtosis		-.164	.566

LOOKS

```
   LOOKS Stem-and-Leaf Plot

    Frequency     Stem &   Leaf

        4.00       0 .   0444
       10.00       0 .   5666678899
       12.00       1 .   001112222344
       13.00       1 .   5556666788899
       13.00       2 .   0011122223444
        9.00       2 .   577788889
        6.00       3 .   011244
        2.00       3 .   55
        1.00  Extremes     (>=47)

   Stem width:      10.00
   Each leaf:        1 case(s)
```

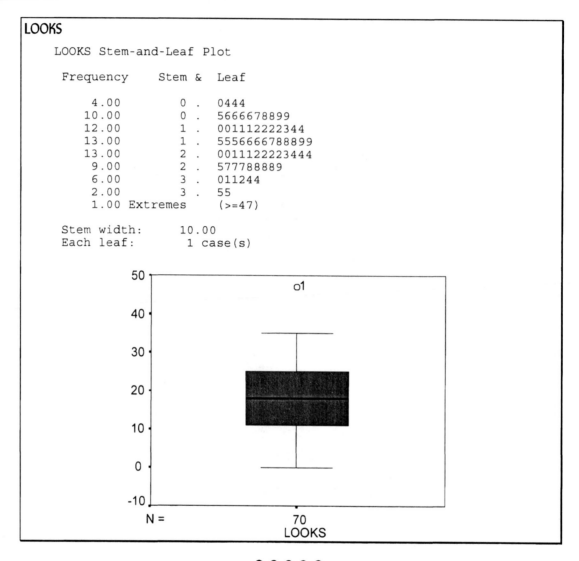

•••••

CHAPTER 5

INDICATORS OF RELATIVE STANDING •••••

CONCEPT GOALS

Be sure that you thoroughly understand the following concepts and how to use them in statistical applications.

- ◆ Percentile points and ranks
- ◆ Standard scores, z
- ◆ Mean, variance, and standard deviation of standard scores
- ◆ Normal distribution
- ◆ Standard normal distribution

••••• GUIDE TO MAJOR CONCEPTS

Percentiles

Simply knowing that you scored 88 on a statistics exam does not always tell you much about how well you did. For example, you would feel somewhat better if you knew that 88 was above the mean, but even if you knew that 88 was 10 points above the mean, you might still wonder how many other students scored that well. Thus, we need techniques that indicate the place of individual scores in a distribution. These techniques are called indicators of [1]_____ .

The most common indicators of relative standing are the **percentile point** and **percentile rank**. The score value below which the proportion P of the cases in the distribution lie is the Pth [2]_____ . The proportion P of the cases is known as the [3]_____ of that score value. For example, if .75 of the cases in a distribution scored lower than 88, then 88 is the [4]_____ and .75 is its [5]_____ . Percentile points are score values, but percentile ranks are proportions, designated by a capital P with a subscript corresponding to the desired proportion. Therefore, the 75th percentile rank is symbolized by [6]__ . Since proportion times 100 equals percent, P_{75}, called the 75th [7]_____ , refers to the score value, or [8]_____ , for which [9]__ % of cases lie (above/below) [10]_____ its value. As such, percentile rank is identical to the [11]_____ of its corresponding score value.

In the last chapter, we calculated the median for a group of scores. Since the median is that point in the distribution below which .50 of the cases fall, the median is identical to the percentile rank [12]_____ . In addition, we might want to know how to determine percentile points corresponding to percentile ranks other than P_{50}. The percentile point corresponding to the Pth percentile rank is given by

$$Percentile\ point\ \ X = L + \left[\frac{P(N) - n_b}{n_w}\right]i$$

in which

$P =$ the percentile rank of the required point (that is, the proportion of cases falling below the desired point; P ranges between 0 and 1.00)

$L =$ the lower real limit of the score value containing the required percentile point

$N =$ the total number of cases in the entire distribution

$n_b =$ the number of cases falling below L

$n_w =$ the number of cases falling within the score value containing the required percentile point

$i =$ the size of the score value measurement unit ($i = 1$ if the data are in whole numbers; $i = .1$ if the data are in tenths; and so on)

This formula looks more forbidding than it really is. Notice that $P(N)$ is simply the number of cases in the distribution which must lie below the desired score value. Suppose that the distribution at hand is the one presented in Table 5–1. Then if we want the 35th percentile point and there are 40 observations in the sample, [13] $P =$ ___ , [14] $N =$ ___ , and [15] $P(N) =$ _____ = ___ . Therefore, we seek the score value such that [16]___ cases fall (above/below) [17]_____ that point. Looking at Table 5–1, the fourteenth lowest score is [18]___ . Since the score value 61 represents the interval from 60.5 to 61.5, this is the interval which must contain the desired percentile point. Therefore, [19] $L =$ ___ , [20] $P(N) =$ ___ , [21] $n_b =$ ___ , [22] $n_w =$ ___ and [23] $i =$ ___ , and [24] $X =$ _____ = _____ = ___ . Therefore, 61.5—the upper real limit of the 14th score—is the score value below which 35% of the distribution falls. In symbols, [25] ___ = ___ .

Similarly, if we want to compute the 45th percentile point for the data in Table 5–1, first calculate [26] $P(N) =$ _____ = ___ to determine that the desired point lies in the interval [27]_____ . Then [28] $L =$ ___ , [29] $P(N) =$ ___ , [30] $n_b =$ ___ , [31] $n_w =$ ___ , [32] $i =$ ___ , and [33] $X =$ _____ = _____ = ___ . So, [34] ___ = ___ .

Sometimes we know the score and want to find its percentile rank. The formula above can be transposed to give $P = [n_w(X - L) + in_b] / Ni$ in which

$P =$ the desired percentile rank (that is, the proportion of cases lying below X; P ranges between 0 and 1.00)

$X =$ the score value for which the percentile rank is desired

$L =$ the lower real limit of X

$n_w =$ the number of cases having the score value X

$n_b =$ the number of cases having a score value lower than X

$N =$ the total number of cases in the entire distribution

$i =$ the size of the score value measurement unit ($i = 1$ if the data are in whole numbers; $i = .1$ if the data are in tenths; and so on)

Table 5–1 Distribution of Scores on a Statistics Examination for a Class of Forty Students

Student	Score	Student	Score	Student	Score	Student	Score
0	97	30	80	20	72	10	56
39	93	29	79	19	72	9	55
38	92	28	78	18	72	8	55
37	91	27	78	17	71	7	55
36	88	26	78	16	70	6	55
35	85	25	78	15	65	5	51
34	85	24	76	14	61	4	49
33	84	23	75	13	60	3	49
32	83	22	75	12	59	2	48
31	82	21	74	11	58	1	46

Looking at Table 5–1, [35] $X =$ ___ , [36] $L =$ ___ , [37] $n_w =$ ___ , [38] $n_b =$ ___ , [39] $N =$ ___ ,

[40] $i =$ ___ , and [41] $P =$ _____ = _____ = ___ .

In symbols, [42] ___ = ___ .

Suppose that the percentile rank for the score 55 is desired. Then, [43] $X =$ ___ , [44] $L =$ ___ ,

[45] $n_w =$ ___ , [46] $n_b =$ ___ , [47] $N =$ ___ , [48] $i =$ ___ , and

[49] $P =$ _____ = _____ = ___ . In symbols, [50] ___ = ___ .

Answer Key to Percentiles

[1]	relative standing	[8]	percentile point	[14]	40
[2]	percentile point	[9]	75	[15]	$.35(40) = 14$
[3]	percentile rank	[10]	below	[16]	14
[4]	percentile point	[11]	cumulative	[17]	below
[5]	percentile rank		relative frequency	[18]	61
[6]	$P_{.75}$	[12]	P_{50}	[19]	60.5
[7]	percentile rank	[13]	.35	[20]	14

[21]   13

[22]   1

[23]   1

[24] $L + [(P(N) - n_b) / n_w]i,$

      $60.5 + [(14 - 13) / 1]1$

      $= 61.5$

[25] $P_{.35} = 61.5$

[26] $.45(40) = 18$

[27]   71.5 to 72.5

[28]   71.5

[29]   18

[30]   17

[31]   3

[32]   1

[33] $L + [(P(N) - n_b) / n_w]i,$

      $71.5 + [(18 - 17) / 3]1$

      $= 71.8$

[34] $P_{.45} = 72$

[35]   74

[36]   73.5

[37]   1

[38]   20

[39]   40

[40]   1

[41] $[n_w(X - L) + in_b] / N_i$

      $= [1(74 - 73.5) + 1(20)]$

÷40(1) = .5125

[42] $P_{.51} = 74$

[43]   55

[44]   54.5

[45]   4

[46]   5

[47]   40

[48]   1

[49] $[(n_w(X - L) + in_b) / N_i]$

      $= [4(55 - 54.5) + 1(15)]$

      $÷40(1) = .175$

[50] $P_{.175} = 55$

Standard Scores

In statistics we often convert scores on one scale (e.g., the X scale) into scores on another scale, called z, by the formula $z_i = (X_i - \overline{X}) / s_x$. Such a z_i is called a **standard score**. This transformation to a [1]_____ is common in the social and behavioral sciences. The distribution of X's with a mean $\overline{X}$ and a standard deviation s_x becomes a distribution of z's which has mean 0 and standard deviation 1.00. To illustrate this, consider the distribution of X's presented in Table 5–2, which has a mean $\overline{X} = 5$ and a standard deviation $s_x = 2$. Transform the X's into z's with the above formula, and fill in the columns of the table. Then calculate the mean and standard deviation of the z's. You should find that the mean of the z's is [2]$\overline{z} =$ ___ and that the standard deviation of the z's is [3]$s_z =$ ___ .

Now look at the bottom of the table. The X's have been located on the X scale of measurement with boxes. Position the z scores in their proper place on the z scale in the same way. Notice that the *relative position* of the scores in the distribution of z's (is/is not) [4]___ the same as for the X 's. Standardizing does not change the form of the distribution, only its [5]_____ of measurement.

Table 5–2 Converting X_i to z_i

X_i	$\overline{X}$	$z_i = (X_i - \overline{X}) / s_x$	$(z_i - \overline{z})$	$(z_i - \overline{z})^2$
2	5			
4	5			
5	5			
5	5			
6	5			
8	5			

$\sum X_i = 30$ $\qquad\qquad \sum z_i = \underline{\quad}$ $\qquad\qquad \sum(z_i - \overline{z})^2 = \underline{\quad}$

$N = 6$ $\qquad\qquad\qquad N = \underline{\quad}$ $\qquad\qquad\qquad N - 1 = \underline{\quad}$

$\overline{X} = 5$

$s_x = 2$ $\qquad\qquad \overline{z} = \dfrac{\sum z_i}{N} = \underline{\quad}$ $\qquad\qquad s_z^2 = \dfrac{\sum(z_i - \overline{z})^2}{N - 1} = \underline{\quad}$

$\qquad\qquad\qquad\qquad\qquad\qquad\qquad\qquad s_z = \sqrt{s_z^2} = \underline{\quad}$

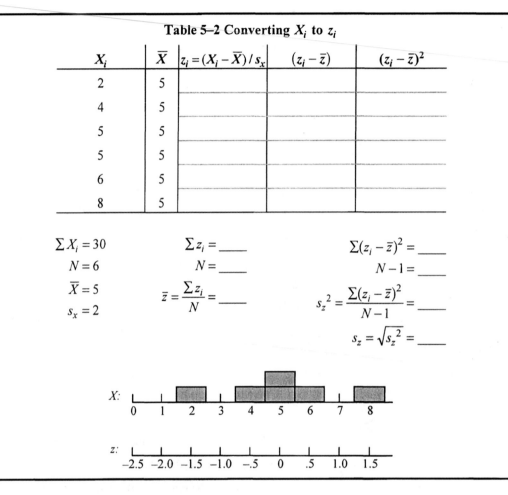

The fact that the standard deviation of the z's is always equal to [6]__ implies that the unit of measurement of the z scale is equal to its [7]_____ . Therefore, $z = 1.50$ indicates that such a score falls 1.5 [8]_____ to the right of the mean. Also, in an X distribution with mean 50 and standard deviation 10, a score of 70 is [9]__ standard deviations above the mean. Thus, its corresponding z score is [10]__ .

In summary, the transformation of any X distribution to z units employs the formula

[11]$z_i = $ _____ .

Although the mean and standard deviation of the original distribution were respectively $\overline{X}$ and s_x, the mean of the z's will always be [12]__ and the standard deviation will always be [13]__ , regardless of the values of $\overline{X}$ and s_x. Thus, z scores are expressed in [14]_____ units. It is in this sense that z scores are said to be [15]_____ , because any X distribution can be transformed into a z distribution with $\overline{z}$ = [16]__ and [17]s_z = __ .

Answer Key to Standard Scores

[1]	standard score	[7]	standard deviation	[13]	1
[2]	0	[8]	standard deviations	[14]	standard deviation
[3]	1.00	[9]	2	[15]	standard scores
[4]	is	[10]	2.00	[16]	0
[5]	scale	[11]	$(X_i - \overline{X}) / s_x$	[17]	1.00
[6]	1.00	[12]	0		

Standard Normal Distribution

Converting to z scores has distinct advantages if the original X distribution is a special type, one having a frequency distribution that looks something like Figure 5–1, which statisticians call a [1]_____ distribution. A normal distribution is defined theoretically by a specific mathematical equation, and there are normal distributions having different means and standard deviations. However, if the original X distribution is normal in form and then the scores are converted to z scores, such a distribution of z scores is called the **standard** [2]_____ **distribution**.

Although any distribution can be transformed into a z distribution, not any distribution can be transformed into a standard *normal* distribution; this is possible only if the original X distribution is a [3]_____ distribution. Normality of the X distribution is required because transforming to z scores does not change the form of the distribution (look back at your work in Table 5–2.)

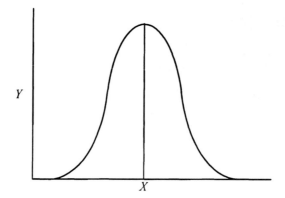

Figure 5–1. A normal distribution.

An important feature of the standard normal distribution is that all the percentile ranks are known for each possible value of z. In fact, the percentiles of the [4]_____ distribution are presented in Table A in Appendix 2 of the text. Open your text to Table A. The column labeled z lists z values from 0.00 to 4.00; the other two columns list the proportion of the area under the normal curve that lies between certain z values. We can interpret proportion of area as proportion of cases, so simply remember the l verbaequation: proportion of [5]_____ = proportion of [6]_____ . For each z in Table A, the proportion of cases found between the mean of the z distribution ($\bar{z} = 0$) and the listed value of z is given in the second column; the proportion of cases having higher z scores than the listed z value is presented in the third column. To find the percentage of cases, note that the percentage = 100 times the proportion. For example, for a z value of 1.25, the second column of the table states that .3944, or 39.44%, of the cases in a standard normal distribution would have z values between [7]$z =$ ___ and [8]$z =$ ___ . The third column indicates that [9]_____ , or [10]_____ %, would have z scores (lower/higher) [11]_____ than 1.25.

You can use Table A to obtain percentile ranks and other information for any z value in a normal distribution if you remember a few facts about the standard normal distribution. First, the standard normal is a symmetrical distribution with one mode. Therefore, the mean, median, and mode all have the same value, namely [12]$z =$ ___ . Second, z values to the left of 0 are [13]_____ , while those to the right of $z = 0$ are [14]_____ . Third, since the distribution is symmetrical about 0, the proportion of cases between $z = 0$ and $z = +.75$ is equal to the proportion of cases between $z = 0$ and [15]$z = $ ___ .

Given this information, a number of problems can be solved with Table A. First, the proportion of cases falling to the right of $z = +.61$, for example, is approximately [16]___ , and the proportion falling to the left of $z = -.61$ is [17]___ .

The proportion of cases falling to the *left* of $z = +.61$ is the sum of the proportion between $z = 0$ and $z = .61$ which is [18]___ plus the proportion to the left of $z = 0$ which is [19]___ for a total of [20]___ .

The proportion of cases falling between $z = -1.00$ and $z = +1.00$ can also be determined from Table A. Problems of this sort can be solved more easily if you sketch the given information on a standard normal distribution. In the first blank graph of Figure 5–2, draw vertical lines through the distribution at $z = -1.00$ and $z = +1.00$, and shade in the area between them. You can now see that the proportion of area between $z = -1.00$ and $+1.00$ is the amount between $z = 0$ and $z = +1.00$ plus the amount between $z = 0$ and $z = -1.00$. Because the normal curve is [21]_____ about $z = 0$, the required proportion is [22]____ + ____ = ____ . Using Table A and the graphs provided, determine the proportion of area between $z = -1.96$ and $z = +1.96$: [23]____ + ____ = ____ ; between $z = 1.73$ and $z = 1.02$: [24]____ + ____ = ____ ; and between $z = -1.56$ and $z = -.21$: [25]____ + ____ = ____ .

Now suppose that an X distribution is normal, with $\overline{X} = 70$ and $s_x = 5$. What proportion of the cases scored higher than $X = 77$? To solve this problem, $X = 77$ first must be translated into a z score as follows: [26]$z = (X_i - \overline{X}) / s_x = $ _____ = ___ . Then, by looking in Table A, determine the proportion of cases that lies to the (right/left) [27]_____ of [28]$z = $ ___ , which is [29]___ .

What proportion of cases fall between $X = 95$ and $X = 88$ in a normal distribution with $\overline{X} = 85$ and $s_x = 5$? First, look at Figure 5–3, which presents this normal distribution. Locate the points 88 and 95 on the X scale, draw vertical lines at these points, and shade in the area between them. This is the area requested. Now, transform these X values into their z equivalents:

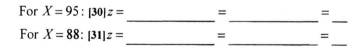

For $X = 95$: [30]$z = $ _____ = _____ = ___
For $X = 88$: [31]$z = $ _____ = _____ = ___

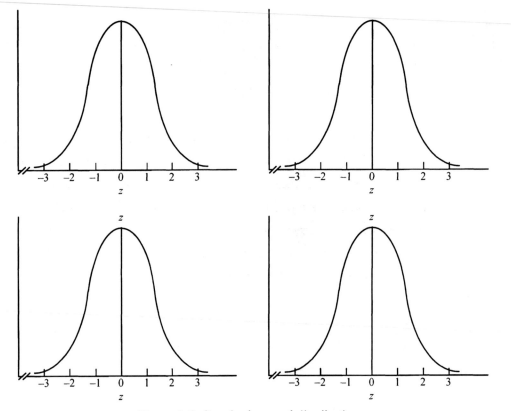

Figure 5–2. Standard normal distributions.

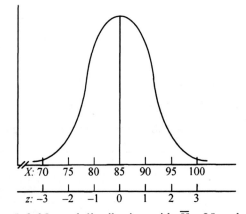

Figure 5–3. Normal distribution with $\overline{X} = 85$ and $s_x = 5$.

Mark these points on the z scale in Figure 5–3. The required area can be determined by obtaining the proportion of area between $z = 0$ and $z = 2.00$, which is [32]___ , and subtracting the area between $z = 0$ and $z = .60$, which is [33]___ . Thus, the required area is [34] ____ – ____ = ____ .

Suppose that you are asked a slightly different question: In a normal distribution with $\overline{X} = 40$ and $s_x = 10$, what score value has a percentile rank of .67? Look at Figure 5–4, which displays the standard normal distribution. First, determine what point along the z scale is at the 67th percentile. This is the z value for which [35]___ % of the total area lies to its (left/right) [36]___ . Since the proportion of area to the left of $z = 0$ is [37]___ , the required point must be such that [38].67–.50 = ___ of the area falls between $z = 0$ and this point. These values are already sketched in on Figure 5–4. Go to Table A and look down the *second* column, which gives the proportion of area between $z = 0$ and the z of that row of the table, until you find the value [39]___ . The corresponding z value is [40]$z =$ ___ . Mark this on the z scale in Figure 4–4. Translating this z into an X_i score in a distribution with $\overline{X} = 40$ and $s_x = 10$ can be accomplished with the usual formula and a little algebra:

$$z = \frac{X_i - \overline{X}}{s_x}$$

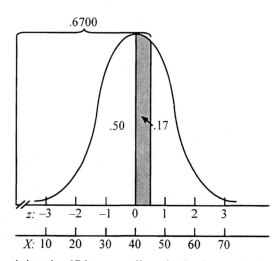

Figure 5–4. Determining the 67th percentile point in the standard normal distribution.

Substitute the known values of $z_i = .44$, $\overline{X} = 40$, and $s_x = 10$, and solve for X_i:

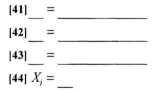

[41] __ = _____

[42] __ = _____

[43] __ = _____

[44] X_i = __

Therefore, the score value with a percentile rank of 67 is [45]__ .

Steps in solving these kinds of problems are summarized in Table 5–3.

Table 5–3 Steps in Determining Proportions of Cases in Normal Distribution

1. Draw a picture of a normal distribution.

2. Put the X scale under the abscissa if X values are given in the problem; put the z scale under the abscissa if z values are given in the problem.

3. Put the other scale (z or X) as an extra abscissa under the previous scale in the manner of Figures 5–3 and 5–4.

4. Locate on the appropriate scale any X or z values given in the problem.

5. Shade in the area under the curve requested by or given in the problem.

6. Convert relevant X scores to z scores or the reverse.

7. Determine relevant areas or z values from Table A, Appendix 2 of the text.

8. Use the above information to determine the specific answer to the question (e.g., add or subtract appropriate areas.)

Answer Key to Standard Normal Distribution

[1]	normal	[5]	area	[9]	.1056
[2]	normal	[6]	cases	[10]	10.56
[3]	normal	[7]	0	[11]	higher
[4]	standard normal	[8]	1.25	[12]	0

[13]	negative	[25]	$.4406 - .0832 = .3574$	[35]	67
[14]	positive	[26]	$(77 - 70) / 5 = 1.40$	[36]	left
[15]	$-.75$	[27]	right	[37]	.5000
[16]	.27	[28]	1.40	[38]	.17
[17]	.27	[29]	.0808	[39]	.1700
[18]	.2291	[30]	$(X_i - \overline{X}) / s_x$	[40]	.44
[19]	.5000		$= (95 - 85) / 5 = 2.00$	[41]	$.44 = (X_i - 40) / 10$
[20]	.7291	[31]	$(X_i - \overline{X}) / s_x$	[42]	$.44 = X_i / 10 - 4$
[21]	symmetrical		$= (88 - 85) / 5 = .60$	[43]	$4.44 = X_i / 10$
[22]	$.3413 + .3413 = .6826$	[32]	.4772	[44]	44.4
[23]	$.4750 + .4750 = .9500$	[33]	.2257	[45]	44.4
[24]	$.4582 - .3461 = .1121$	[34]	$.4772 - .2257 = .2515$		

● ● ● ● ●   SELF-TEST

1. In any distribution, if a score of 50 is at the 75th percentile, 75 is the percentile _____ corresponding to the percentile _____ of 50.

2. Your score is at the 72nd percentile rank in a sample of 75 people. How many people scored above you?

3. If you earn a score of 97 on a mathematics exam and a score of 23 on an English exam, is it possible for your percentile rank to be higher in English than in mathematics? Explain.

4. Suppose that your score of 23 on the English exam gives you a percentile rank of 85. One week after returning your exams, your instructor announces that an arithmetic error has been discovered and that he is increasing all exam scores by 30 points. What will be your new percentile rank?

5. What is the relationship between cumulative relative frequency and percentile rank?

6.* In the equation $Y = kX + c$ in which X is transformed to Y:
    a. Which term(s) are constants?
    b. Which term(s) change the location of the origin?
    c. Which term(s) change the size of the unit of measurement?
    d. Which term(s) change the variance of the distribution?

7.* If we have an X distribution such that $\overline{X} = 20$ and $s_x = 4$, and if X is then transformed into Y by the equation $Y = 3X + 1$, what will $\overline{Y}$, s_y^2, and s_y equal?

8.* Write the transformation equation and answer the same questions as in question 7 with the X's transformed into the z distribution.

9.* Why is it advantageous for a personnel selection officer to convert into standardized form the scores of applicants on three different selection tests, rather than just averaging the particular scores before deciding which applicant to hire?

10. In the standard normal distribution, the mean is __ , the variance is __ , the standard deviation is __ , and the total area under the curve is __ .

11. Suppose there are two tests that are equally valid in predicting whether a trainee will successfully complete a particular program. Candidate A scores 22 on the first test and 102 on the second test, for a total of 124. Candidate B scores 20 on the first test and 104 on the second test, also for a total of 124. Given that the first test has a mean of 20 and standard deviation of 2, and that the second test has a mean of 100 and a standard deviation of 20, which candidate appears more likely to be successful in the training program?

12. If John scored 23 on a geology test and this was equivalent to a z score of .60, what was the standard deviation of the scores in John's class if the mean was 20?

13.* If the mean of a normal distribution of history exam grades is 80 and the standard deviation is 5, all (or essentially all, that is, 99.74%) the scores will probably fall between what two values?

14.* Suppose that you have a sample of 25 scores on a test of scholastic performance and you want to use the standard normal distribution to determine percentiles for each student. What two assumptions must you make to do this? Explain why.

15.* If scores on a test of mathematical ability are transformed by the equation $Y = 3[(X_i - \overline{X}) / s_x] + 5$, what will be the mean and standard deviation of the Y distribution?

Questions preceded by an asterisk can be answered on the basis of the discussion in the text, but the discussion in this Study Guide does not answer them.

● ● ● ● ●   EXERCISES

Exercises 1–3 refer to the following data.

Subject	X	Subject	X	Subject	X	Subject	X
40	95	30	88	20	83	10	73
39	94	29	87	19	83	9	72
38	94	28	86	18	82	8	71
37	92	27	86	17	80	7	71
36	91	26	86	16	80	6	68
35	89	25	85	15	79	5	63
34	88	24	85	14	78	4	57
33	88	23	84	13	75	3	53
32	88	22	84	12	75	2	53
31	88	21	84	11	73	1	51

1. Determine the percentile points corresponding to the following ranks.
   a. $P_{.10}$ c. $P_{.60}$ e. $P_{.75}$
   b. $P_{.225}$ d. $P_{.80}$ f. $P_{.25}$
   g.* The interquartile range

2. Determine percentile ranks for the following score values.
   a. 72   c. 84   e. 88
   b. 80   d. 86   f. 95

3. In what sense is it correct and in what sense is it incorrect to say that someone who scored at P_{75} did three times as well as someone who scored at P_{25} on the same test?

4.* Given an X distribution having $\overline{X} = 100$ and $s_x = 10$, determine the mean, variance, and standard deviation after the following transformations.

Transfor-mation	Mean	Variance	Standard Deviation
none	100	100	10
$Y = X + 10$			
$Y = 2X$			
$Y = 3X + 4$			
$Y = 4(X + 1)$			

5. Determine the z score for X_i under the following conditions.

$\overline{X}$	s_x	X_i	z
35	5	45	
25	3	23.5	
50.3	3.3	49.2	
−15	6.5	−7.7	

6. Determine the proportion of cases in the standard normal distribution that fall between the mean and a z score of
   a. −1.00   c. .55   e. −3.17
   b. 1.96   d. 1.33   f. 0

7. Determine the proportion of cases in the standard normal distribution which have z scores higher than:

   a. -1.00 c. .75

   b. 1.96   d. 0

8. Determine the percentile rank of the following z scores in the standard normal distribution.

   a. 1.96   c. 0   e. .04

   b. $-.35$ d. 2.33   f. .35

9. Determine the proportion of cases in the standard normal distribution falling between the following z values.

   a. -1.96 and $+1.96$

   b. -1.645 and $+1.645$

   c. -1.00 and $+1.00$

   d. $-.50$ and $+1.50$

   e. -1.33 and $-.33$

   f. .45 and 1.20

10. In a normal population with mean 20 and standard deviation 5, what proportion of cases score:

    a. more than 15? 18? 20? 21? 30?

    b. between 15 and 25? 10 and 30? 17.2 and 21.5? 21.5 and 22?

11. In the distribution in question 10, what score did a person have if $z = .43$? If $z = -.54$? If that person was at $P_{.50}$? At P_{33}?

12. Assume that scores on one part of the Scholastic Assessment Test are normally distributed with mean 500 and standard deviation 100.

    a. If Snoot U. takes students only from the top 20%, what score should you have before you consider applying?

    b. If Smithville College will consider anyone with a score of 600 or better, what percentage fewer applicants can Smithville expect than Snoot U.?

    c. What score does it take to be in the top 4%?

● ● ● ● ●   ANSWERS

Self-Test. (1) Rank, point. **(2)** 21. **(3)** Yes, because percentile ranks are relative positions, and all the scores on your mathematics test could be higher than all the scores on the English exam. **(4)** You remain at the 85th percentile. **(5)** Cumulative relative frequency and percentile rank are essentially the same thing. **(6a)** k and c; **(6b)** c; **(6c)** k; **(6d)** k. **(7)** 61; 144; 12. **(8)** $z = (X_i - \overline{X})/s_x$; 0; 1; 1. **(9)** The results of three different tests can be compared more accurately if they are converted to distributions, such as the z, which will have the same mean and standard deviation. **(10)** 0; 1; 1; 1.00. **(11)** Candidate A. **(12)** 5. **(13)** 65 and 95. **(14)** You must assume that the population distribution of scores on the test is normal in form and that the sample is large enough for $\overline{X}$ and s_x to be reasonably accurate estimators of the mean and standard deviation of that population distribution. **(15)** Mean = 5; standard deviation = 3.

Exercises. (1a) 57.5; **(1b)** 72.5; **(1c)** 85.0; **(1d)** 88.1; **(1e)** 87.70; **(1f)** 73.0; **(1g)** 73.0 to 87.70. **(2a)** $P_{.2125}$; **(2b)** $P_{.40}$; **(2c)** $P_{.5375}$; **(2d)** $P_{.6625}$; **(2e)** $P_{.7875}$; **(2f)** $P_{.9875}$. **(3)** Three times as many people scored below P_{75} as below P_{25}, but the numerical value of the percentile point corresponding to P_{75} would probably not be three times that of P_{25}. **(4)** Means = 110, 200, 304, 404; variances = 100, 400, 900, 1600; standard deviations = 10, 20, 30, 40. **(5)** 2.00; −.50; −.33; 1.12. **(6a)** .3413; **(6b)** .4750; **(6c)** .2088; **(6d)** .4082; **(6e)** .4992; **(6f)** 0. **(7a)** .8413; **(7b)** .0250; **(7c)** .2266; **(7d)** .5000. **(8a)** $P_{.9750}$; **(8b)** $P_{.3632}$; **(8c)** $P_{.5000}$; **(8d)** $P_{.9901}$; **(8e)** $P_{.5160}$; **(8f)** $P_{.6368}$. **(9a)** .9500; **(9b)** .9000; **(9c)** .6826; **(9d)** .6247; **(9e)** .2789; **(9f)** .2113. **(10a)** .8413; .6554; .5000; .4207; .0228. **(10b)** .6826; .9544; .3302; .0375. **(11)** 22.15; 17.3; 20.0; 17.8. **(12a)** 584 to 585; **(12b)** 4.13%; **(12c)** 675.

● ● ● ● ● STATISTICAL PACKAGES ● ● ● ● ●

● ● ● ● ●　　　　　　　　　　　MINITAB

(To accompany Table 5–1.)

MINITAB will produce percentiles and calculate standard scores for all values in a distribution. The data in Table 5–1 represent a distribution of scores for a class of 40 students:

97 93 92 91 88 85 85 84 83 82 80 79 78 78 78 78 76 75 75 74 72 72 72 71 70 65 61 60 59 58 56 55 55 55 55 51 49 49 48 46

Start the MINITAB program. To enter data on the spreadsheet, click on the Data window. Enter the 40 score values in the first column. Label the top of the column with the variable name *Scores*. To enter the variable name, click on the space at the top of the column and type in the name. The data you entered should appear on the spreadsheet as follows, in rows 1–40:

Scores
97
93
92
⋮
etc.

Save the *Scores* data that you entered:

> *File>Save Worksheet As*
> (Enter folder and file name for the MINITAB Worksheet file.)
> OK

To carry out this exercise, calculate the mean and standard deviation of the distribution of *Scores*. To calculate the mean and standard deviation:

> *Stat>Basic Statistics>Display Descriptive Statistics*
> Variables: Scores   [double-click to transfer]
> OK

Next the distribution of *z* scores will be calculated from *Scores* using the *Standardize* command, which be placed in a new variable named *Zscores*. Finally, frequency tables for both *Scores* and *Zscores* will be generated using the *Tally* command. To calculate the *z* scores and place them in a new variable:

> *Calc>Standardize*
> Input column(s): Scores   [double-click each to transfer]
> Store results in: **Zscores**   [type in]
> Subtract mean and divide by standard deviation: Yes
> OK

To generate the frequency tables:

> *Stat>Tables>Tally*
> Variables: Scores Zscores   [double-click to transfer]
> Display: Counts, Percents, Cumulative counts, Cumulative percents
> OK

The output from the above command displays the frequency (Count), cumulative frequency (CumCnt), relative frequency (Percent), and cumulative relative frequency (CumPct) distributions. It is the latter distribution (CumPct) that gives the percentile rank for each score value in the distribution. However, the program does not interpolate within a score value when duplicate cases exist. Also, percentile points (score values corresponding to specific percentiles) can be determined from the output table only for the specific percentile ranks (CumPct) actually reported there.

To print the output from the Session window:

> *File>Print Session Window*
> Print Range: All
> OK

Exit MINITAB:

> *File>Exit*

On exiting, MINITAB will ask if you want to save changes to the current Project. The z-scores have been calculated and placed on the Worksheet as a new variable. To save the updated Worksheet, choose "Save Separate Pieces," and answer "Yes" to "Save Worksheet."

MINITAB Program Output

Descriptive Statistics

Variable	N	Mean	Median	TrMean	StDev	SE Mean
Scores	40	70.75	73.00	70.72	14.20	2.25

Variable	Minimum	Maximum	Q1	Q3
Scores	46.00	97.00	56.50	81.50

Summary Statistics for Discrete Variables

Scores	Count	CumCnt	Percent	CumPct	Zscores	Count	CumCnt	Percent	CumPct
46	1	1	2.50	2.50	-1.74279	1	1	2.50	2.50
48	1	2	2.50	5.00	-1.60196	1	2	2.50	5.00
49	2	4	5.00	10.00	-1.53154	2	4	5.00	10.00
51	1	5	2.50	12.50	-1.39071	1	5	2.50	12.50
55	4	9	10.00	22.50	-1.10905	4	9	10.00	22.50
56	1	10	2.50	25.00	-1.03863	1	10	2.50	25.00
58	1	11	2.50	27.50	-0.89780	1	11	2.50	27.50
59	1	12	2.50	30.00	-0.82738	1	12	2.50	30.00
60	1	13	2.50	32.50	-0.75697	1	13	2.50	32.50
61	1	14	2.50	35.00	-0.68655	1	14	2.50	35.00
65	1	15	2.50	37.50	-0.40489	1	15	2.50	37.50
70	1	16	2.50	40.00	-0.05281	1	16	2.50	40.00
71	1	17	2.50	42.50	0.01760	1	17	2.50	42.50
72	3	20	7.50	50.00	0.08802	3	20	7.50	50.00
74	1	21	2.50	52.50	0.22885	1	21	2.50	52.50
75	2	23	5.00	57.50	0.29927	2	23	5.00	57.50
76	1	24	2.50	60.00	0.36968	1	24	2.50	60.00
78	4	28	10.00	70.00	0.51051	4	28	10.00	70.00
79	1	29	2.50	72.50	0.58093	1	29	2.50	72.50
80	1	30	2.50	75.00	0.65134	1	30	2.50	75.00
82	1	31	2.50	77.50	0.79218	1	31	2.50	77.50
83	1	32	2.50	80.00	0.86259	1	32	2.50	80.00
84	1	33	2.50	82.50	0.93301	1	33	2.50	82.50
85	2	35	5.00	87.50	1.00342	2	35	5.00	87.50
88	1	36	2.50	90.00	1.21467	1	36	2.50	90.00
91	1	37	2.50	92.50	1.42592	1	37	2.50	92.50
92	1	38	2.50	95.00	1.49633	1	38	2.50	95.00
93	1	39	2.50	97.50	1.56675	1	39	2.50	97.50
97	1	40	2.50	100.00	1.84841	1	40	2.50	100.00
N=	40				N=	40			

● ● ● ● ●   **SPSS**

(To accompany Table 5–1.)

SPSS will calculate frequency tables for raw scores and for z scores. Percentile ranks may be approximated using the Cumulative Percent column of the frequency table. The program does not interpolate when duplication of scores exists near a desired percentile, so answers may differ slightly from the sample answers in the *Guide*. The program will also calculate percentile points for specific percentiles on request.

The data in Table 5–1 are:

97 93 92 91 88 85 85 84 83 82 80 79 78 78 78 78 76 75 75 74 72 72 72 71 70 65 61 60 59 58 56 55 55 55 55 51 49 49 48 46

Start the SPSS program. The Data Editor window will fill the screen. Enter the 40 data values in the first column of the spreadsheet. To enter the new variable name, click on the tab labeled "Variable View" at the bottom left of the screen. Label the first column with the variable name *Scores*. Go back to the Data View. The data you entered should appear on the spreadsheet as follows, in rows 1–40:

Scores
97
93
92
⋮
etc.

The *Descriptives* procedure can be used to calculate standard scores:

> *Analyze>Descriptive Statistics>Descriptives*
> Variable(s): Scores   [highlight and transfer]
> Save standardized values as variables: Yes
> OK

The standard scores are calculated and placed in column 2 of the spreadsheet, in a new variable called *Zscores*. To see the spreadsheet again:

> *Window>SPSS Data Editor*

The last step is to generate frequency tables for the two variables:

Zscore(SCORES)

		Frequency	Percent	Valid Percent	Cumulative Percent
Valid	1.84841	1	2.5	2.5	2.5
	1.56675	1	2.5	2.5	5.0
	1.49633	1	2.5	2.5	7.5
	1.42592	1	2.5	2.5	10.0
	1.21467	1	2.5	2.5	12.5
	1.00342	2	5.0	5.0	17.5
	.93301	1	2.5	2.5	20.0
	.86259	1	2.5	2.5	22.5
	.79218	1	2.5	2.5	25.0
	.65134	1	2.5	2.5	27.5
	.58093	1	2.5	2.5	30.0
	.51051	4	10.0	10.0	40.0
	.36968	1	2.5	2.5	42.5
	.29927	2	5.0	5.0	47.5
	.22885	1	2.5	2.5	50.0
	.08802	3	7.5	7.5	57.5
	.01760	1	2.5	2.5	60.0
	-.05281	1	2.5	2.5	62.5
	-.40489	1	2.5	2.5	65.0
	-.68655	1	2.5	2.5	67.5
	-.75697	1	2.5	2.5	70.0
	-.82738	1	2.5	2.5	72.5
	-.89780	1	2.5	2.5	75.0
	-1.03863	1	2.5	2.5	77.5
	-1.10905	4	10.0	10.0	87.5
	-1.39071	1	2.5	2.5	90.0
	-1.53154	2	5.0	5.0	95.0
	-1.60196	1	2.5	2.5	97.5
	-1.74279	1	2.5	2.5	100.0
	Total	40	100.0	100.0	

● ● ● ● ●

CHAPTER 6

REGINALD REGRESSION •••••

CONCEPT GOALS

Be sure that you thoroughly understand the following concepts and how to use them in statistical applications.

- ◆ Regression constants, slope, intercept
- ◆ Scatterplot
- ◆ Regression line
- ◆ Least squares criterion
- ◆ Standard error of estimate

 GUIDE TO MAJOR CONCEPTS

Straight Lines

Regression procedures are designed to predict the value of one variable from knowledge of another variable. Specifically, [1]_____ permits us to determine the equation that best describes a straight-line, or [2]_____ , relationship, even if the two variables in question are not perfectly related (that is, even if all the points do not fall exactly on the straight line).

Suppose we make two measurements on each of three people. Call the two variables X and Y. The simplest linear relationship between these variables occurs when Y always equals X, which can be expressed by the equation [3]_____ . In that case, no matter what the specific values of X and Y, Y will always equal X. Below is a table for three subjects. Given the X values already presented in the table, determine the Y values according to this equation, plot these values on the graph provided (Figure 6–1), draw the line passing though these points, and label the line with its equation.

$$Y = X$$

Subject	Y	X
a	[4]__	0
b	[5]__	1
c	[6]__	3

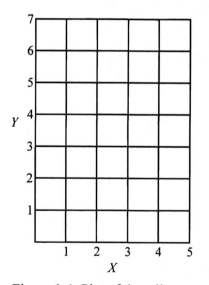

Figure 6–1. Plot of three lines.

Now consider a second relationship. Suppose Y is always twice the value of X. This verbal rule can be expressed by the equation [7]_____ . Using the same X values as above, fill in the appropriate Y values in the table below using this new equation.

$$Y = 2X$$

Subject	Y	X
a	[8]__	0
b	[9]__	1
c	[10]__	3

Plot the new line on the same graph as the first (Figure 6–1), and label it with its equation.

These two lines differ in **slope**, which we will symbolize by b and which is the vertical distance divided by the horizontal distance between any two points on the line. Consider the line $Y = X$ and the two points, (1, 1) and (3, 3), which are on the line. To travel on the graph between these two points, you must go up [11]_ units and then to the right [12]_ units. Since the definition of b, the [13]_____ , is the [14]_____ distance between any two points on the line divided by the [15]_____ distance between them, we have in this case that

[16]$b =$ _____ = __ .

Now consider the line $Y = 2X$ and the points (1, 2) and (3, 6) which lie on this line. To travel between these points on the line in Figure 6–1, you must go vertically [17]_ units and then horizontally [18]_ units. The slope for this line is [19]$b =$ _____ = __ .

You will obtain the same value for the slope if you travel between the two points in the opposite direction, from (3, 6) to (1, 2). To do so, you must understand that positive values are at the top and to the right in a graph, so when you travel upward or to the right you are going in a [20]_____ direction. However, when you travel downward or to the left, you are going in a [21]_____ direction. Therefore, when you go from (3, 6) to (1, 2) you must travel vertically (downward) [22]_ units and laterally (left) [23]_ units. Thus, the slope is

[24]$b =$ _____ = __ .

So we see that the slope of a line can be determined by using the formula $b = (y_2 - y_1) / (x_2 - x_1)$ in which b is the slope and (x_1, y_1) and (x_2, y_2) are any two points on the line. Using the formula [25] $b =$ _____ the slope for the line $Y = 2X$ given two other points (2, 4) and (4, 8) is [26] $b =$ _____ = _____ = ___ . Using the points in the reverse order, (4, 8) and (2, 4), the slope is [27] $b =$ _____ = _____ = _____ = ___ .

Notice that the slope of the line $Y = 2X$ is 2, which is twice the slope of the line $Y = X$. Examine their equations:

$$Y = X$$
$$Y = 2X$$

The only difference between them is the 2 in the second equation. The number in front of the X is called its coefficient. When the equation of a line is in the form $Y = bX + a$, the slope of the line is always b, the coefficient of X. The value of b in the equation $Y = 2X$ is [28]___ , and in $Y = X$ it is [29]___ .

Now consider a third possible relationship between Y and X. Suppose Y is always equal to twice the value of X plus 1. This verbal rule can be written mathematically as the equation [30]_____ . Below is a table containing the same X values as in the previous examples. Fill in the appropriate Y values using the above equation, plot these points on the same graph (Figure 6–1), draw the line connecting these points, and label it with its equation.

$$Y = 2X + 1$$

Subject	Y	X
a	[31]___	0
b	[32]___	1
c	[33]___	3

Look at the graph of this line and compare it with the graph of $Y = 2X$. Note that the line you just drew is always 1 unit higher than $Y = 2X$. It is customary to assess this difference along the vertical or Y-axis, where $X = 0$. The point where a line intersects the Y axis is called its **y-intercept**.

By substituting $X = 0$ into the equation of the line, you can determine the value of the
[34]_____ .

Equation	Substituting $X = 0$	Value of Equation at y-Intercept
$Y = 2X$	[35] $Y =$ ___	[36] $Y =$ ___
$Y = 2X + 1$	[37] $Y =$ ___	[38] $Y =$ ___

Thus, the difference between the equations at $X = 0$ (i.e., at their [39]_____) is [40]___
unit. However, we could have seen this fact by simply looking at the equations of the two lines;
the value of Y obtained from using a particular value of X in the second equation will always be 1
more than the value of Y obtained for the same value of X in the first equation.

$$Y = 2X$$
$$Y = 2X + 1$$

When the equation of a line is in the form $Y = bX + a$, the y-intercept of the line is always a. For
the two equations above, the y-intercepts, symbolized by [41]___ , are respectively [42]___ and [43]___ .

A straight line represents the relationship between two variables X and Y, and the general
equation for any straight line is given by [44]_____ , in which a is the
[45]_____ and b is the [46]_____ of the line.

Figure 6–2 presents graphs of three lines, A, B, and C. Determine their equations:
A [47]_____ , B [48]_____ , C [49]_____ .

On the graph provided in Figure 6–3, draw lines describing the following relationships and
label them with their equations:

1. A baby-sitter earns $5 an hour but must pay the agency $3 for each night of work. Determine
   the equation and draw the line representing the amount earned (Y) as a function of the hours
   worked (X). [50]_____ .

2.   Suppose that you rent a set of six wine goblets for a special dinner party. In addition to a rental fee, a deposit of $10 on the set of glasses is required. Each glass costs $2 if broken. Plot the relationship between the amount of money (Y) you will receive back from your deposit and the number (X) of glasses that are broken. [51]_____ .

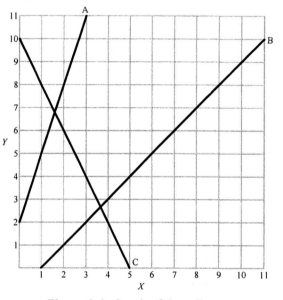

Figure 6–2. Graph of three lines.

Knowing the equation of a line helps not only to describe the relationship between two variables but to predict a specific Y value from knowledge of a specific X value. Determine the following values both by using the equations you determined immediately above and by drawing in Figure 6–3, at the appropriate X value, a vertical line that is perpendicular to the X-axis and that intersects the line of the relationship at the required Y value.

1.   Using the relationship in number 1 above, how much will the baby-sitter earn in 4 hours? [52]_____ .

2.   In number 2 above, how much will you get back from your $10 deposit if you or your guests break two glasses? [53]_____ .

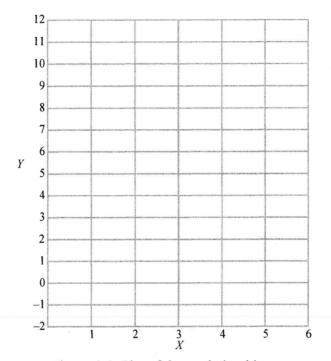

Figure 6–3. Plot of three relationships.

Answer Key to Straight Lines

[1]	regression	[13]	slope	[25]	$(y_2 - y_1) / (x_2 - x_1)$
[2]	linear	[14]	vertical	[26]	$(8 - 4) / (4 - 2) = 4 / 2$
[3]	$Y = X$	[15]	horizontal		$= 2$
[4]	0	[16]	$2 / 2 = 1$	[27]	$(y_2 - y_1) / (x_2 - x_1)$
[5]	1	[17]	4		$= (4 - 8) / (2 - 4)$
[6]	3	[18]	2		$= -4 / -2 = 2$
[7]	$Y = 2X$	[19]	$4 / 2 = 2$	[28]	2
[8]	0	[20]	positive	[29]	1
[9]	2	[21]	negative	[30]	$Y = 2X + 1$
[10]	6	[22]	–4	[31]	1
[11]	2	[23]	–2	[32]	3
[12]	2	[24]	$-4 / -2 = 2$	[33]	7

[34]	y-intercept	[41]	a	[48]	$Y = X - 1$
[35]	2(0)	[42]	0	[49]	$Y = -2X + 10$
[36]	0	[43]	1	[50]	$Y = 5X - 3$
[37]	2(0) + 1	[44]	$Y = bX + a$	[51]	$Y = 10 - 2X$
[38]	1	[45]	y-intercept	[52]	$Y = 5(4) - 3 = \$17$
[39]	y-intercepts	[46]	slope	[53]	$Y = 10 - 2(2) = \$6$
[40]	1	[47]	$Y = 3X + 2$		

Regression

In the graphs you have drawn in this chapter, all the points fall precisely on the line. The relationship between X and Y was errorless or [1]_____ . When two variables from the behavioral sciences are examined for the nature of their relationship, the observed data points (e.g., actual grades and SAT scores) rarely fall precisely along a straight line. A pictorial display of each pair of points in a relationship is called a **scatterplot**. The verbal SAT scores and grade averages for 20 students are listed in Table 6–1. Plot these 20 points on the graph provided (Figure 6–4) to form a [2]_____ .

Table 6–1 Verbal SAT Scores and Grades for a Sample of 20 College Students

Verbal SAT	Freshman Grades	Verbal SAT	Freshman Grades
510	1.3	659	2.1
558	0.8	670	1.8
569	1.1	679	2.9
581	1.3	687	1.8
603	1.5	693	1.8
612	0.9	700	3.6
618	3.0	710	2.2
633	1.1	724	2.3
643	1.1	739	3.8
651	1.5	767	1.7

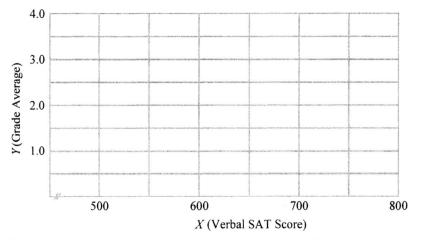

Figure 6–4. Scatterplot of grade average as a function of Verbal SAT score.

Notice that the points show a generally increasing pattern but certainly do not fall precisely along a single straight line. One possible explanation of this is that, while there may indeed be a theoretically perfect linear relationship between scholastic assessment and college performance, there are many factors that produce variability in our measurements of these characteristics and thus cloud such a relationship. But if we had to fit a straight line to these points, what would be the best line we could draw? Statisticians define the best line as the one for which the sum of the squared vertical distances between the points and the line is as small as possible. This is called the criterion of [3]_____ .

To see how the **least squares criterion** works, it will be helpful to have a small sample of numbers such as those presented in Table 6–2. The line of relationship, called the [4]_____ , for this small set of data is $\hat{Y} = .9X = 1.5$, in which the symbol $\hat{Y}$ (read "Y predicted") is used because we can only estimate or predict Y imperfectly. Fill in the values that are missing from the first three columns of Table 6–2 by calculating $\hat{Y}$ for each X value (using the regression equation given above), calculating $(Y_i - \hat{Y})$, and then squaring this difference. The sum of the column $(Y_i - \hat{Y})$ should be zero (but rounding off numbers makes it .4 in this case). However, the sum of the column $(Y_i - \hat{Y})^2$ will not usually be zero. In this case it equals approximately [5]__ .

Table 6–2 Illustration of the Least Squares Criterion

		The Regression Line, $\hat{Y}=.9X+1.5$			An Alternative Line, $\hat{Y}=X+2$		
X_i	Y_i	$\hat{Y}$	$(Y_i-\hat{Y})$	$(Y_i-\hat{Y})^2$	$\hat{Y}$	$(Y_i-\hat{Y})$	$(Y_i-\hat{Y})^2$
1	3						
4	3						
2	4						
7	9						
5	6						
			$\Sigma(Y_i-\hat{Y})=$	$\Sigma(Y_i-\hat{Y})^2=$		$\Sigma(Y_i-\hat{Y})=$	$\Sigma(Y_i-\hat{Y})^2=$

Plot the regression line for these data in Figure 6–5. Next, place a point on the graph for each of the five points. Then draw a vertical dotted line between each Y_i point and the regression line, checking to see that the distance corresponds to the values for $Y_i-\hat{Y}$ that you calculated in Table 6–2. These vertical distances represent the error in the regression line, and the sum of their squared values should be as small as possible, according to the [6]_____ .

Now, plot the line $\hat{Y}=X+2$ on the same graph (Figure 6–5), and draw with wavy lines the deviations between each point and this line. The new line looks as if it might be a reasonable summary of the imperfect linear relationship for these data. However, if the regression equation given initially is really the best line in the sense of least squares, then the sum of the squared differences, $(Y_i-\hat{Y})^2$, between each point and the best regression line should be (larger/smaller) [7]_____ than the corresponding sum computed for the alternative line, $Y=X+2$. In short, over all five points, the dotted lines should be shorter than the wavy lines you have drawn in Figure 6–5. Calculate in Table 6–2 the values of $\hat{Y}_i$, $(Y_i-\hat{Y})$, and $\Sigma(Y_i-\hat{Y})^2$ for this alternative line. Is $\Sigma(Y_i-\hat{Y})^2$ greater than 6.7? [8]_____ . Then the new line is not is good because the error is greater over the set of five points even if this alternate line fit three of the five points exactly. It is in this sense that the best fit line is defined as the one for which the sum of squared deviations, symbolized [9]_____ , is a [10]_____ .

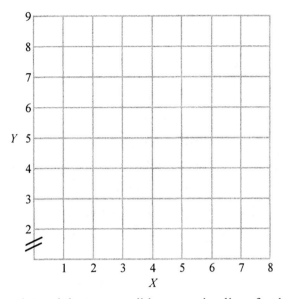

Figure 6–5. The scatterplot and the two possible regression lines for the data in Table 6–2.

Answer Key to Regression							
[1]	perfect	[4]	regression line	[6]	least squares	[8]	Yes (it is 10)
[2]	scatterplot	[5]	6.7		criterion	[9]	$\Sigma(Y_i - \hat{Y})^2$
[3]	least squares			[7]	smaller	[10]	minimum

Standard Error of Estimate

We have seen that a regression line can be constructed even if the relationship between two variables is not perfect. The **standard error of estimate** is a measure of the **error** in predicting Y from a knowledge of X. In the discussion of the least squares criterion, it was said that the regression line is selected so that the sum of the squared deviations of the points from the line is a minimum. These squared deviations are also called the squared [1]_____ of the points about the line, because the sum of squared deviations of points about the line is a measure of how *inaccurately* the regression line represents the relationship between two variables. A statistic that is roughly the average squared error per point in using the regression line is the

[2]_____ , symbolized by $s_{y \cdot x}$ and defined by

$$s_{y \cdot x} = \sqrt{\frac{\Sigma(Y_i - \hat{Y})^2}{N-2}}.$$

To understand how this quantity works as a measure of [3]_____ , consider the two sets of data given in Table 6–3. First plot the points given in Table 6–3 on the graphs provided in Figure 6–6, which already have regression lines drawn. (Note: these are not precisely the true regression lines, but they will simplify computation.) Then, draw with dotted lines the vertical distance between each point and the line. This should give you a visual display of the relative error in using the regression line as an index of the linear relationship in the two sets of data. Now, in Table 6–3 calculate $(Y_i - \hat{Y})$, $(Y_i - \hat{Y})^2$, $\Sigma(Y_i - \hat{Y})^2$, and $s_{y \cdot x}$ for each data set. For set A, [4]$s_{y \cdot x} = $ ___ ; for set B, [5]$s_{y \cdot x} = $ ___ .

Table 6–3 Comparison of Standard Errors of Measurement

Set A					Set B				
X_i	Y_i	$\hat{Y}$	$(Y_i - \hat{Y})$	$(Y_i - \hat{Y})^2$	X_i	Y_i	$\hat{Y}$	$(Y_i - \hat{Y})$	$(Y_i - \hat{Y})^2$
2	1	2			2	3	2		
4	5	4			4	2	4		
6	7	6			6	4	6		
8	7	8			8	10	8		
10	11	10			10	9	10		

$N = $ $\Sigma(Y_i - \hat{Y})^2 = $ $N = $ $\Sigma(Y_i - \hat{Y})^2 = $

$s_{y \cdot x} = \sqrt{\dfrac{\Sigma(Y_i - \hat{Y})^2}{N-2}} = \sqrt{} = \sqrt{}$ $s_{y \cdot x} = \sqrt{\dfrac{\Sigma(Y_i - \hat{Y})^2}{N-2}} = \sqrt{} = \sqrt{}$

$s_{y \cdot x} = $ _____ $s_{y \cdot x} = $ _____

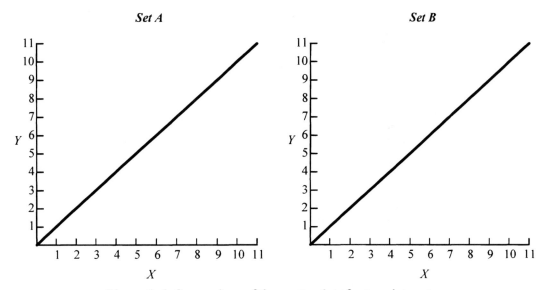

Figure 6–6. Comparison of the scatterplots for two data sets.

Notice that the standard error of estimate is smaller for set *A* than for set *B*, indicating that the line approximates the location of the actual data points better for set [6]__ than set [7]__ . You should also be able to see from your scatterplot that the points cluster about the line more closely for set [8]__ than set [9]__ .

To summarize the computational routines necessary to calculate values for the concepts presented in this chapter, consider the following situation. A teacher gives two quizzes to a class. The scores of the 11 students are given in Table 6–4. Using the computational outline provided, determine the regression equation to predict scores on the second test from scores on the first, and calculate the standard error of estimate for this relationship. Use this Guided Computational format to solve future problems.

Answer Key to Standard Error of Estimate

[1]	errors	[3]	error	[6]	*A*	[9]	*B*
[2]	standard error	[4]	1.29	[7]	*B*		
	of estimate	[5]	2.16	[8]	*A*		

Table 6–4 Guided Computational Example

Student	Test 1 X	Test 2 Y	X^2	Y^2	XY
a	3	1			
b	6	6			
c	4	5			
d	3	4			
e	8	8			
f	9	10			
g	2	3			
h	1	0			
i	4	5			
j	5	6			
k	2	8			

$N =$ $\sum X =$ $\sum Y =$ $\sum X^2 =$ $\sum Y^2 =$ $\sum XY =$

$(\sum X)^2 =$ $(\sum Y)^2 =$

Intermediate Quantities

$(\text{I}_{XY}) = N(\sum XY) - (\sum X)(\sum Y)$ $(\text{II}_X) = N\sum X^2 - (\sum X)^2$ $(\text{III}_Y) = N\sum Y^2 - (\sum Y)^2$

$=$ $=$ $=$

$(\text{I}_{XY}) =$ $(\text{II}_X) =$ $(\text{III}_Y) =$

Statistical Computations

$\overline{X} = \sum X / N =$ $\overline{Y} = \sum Y / N =$

$s_x^2 = (\text{II}_X) / N(N-1) =$ $s_y^2 = (\text{III}_Y) / N(N-1) =$

$s_x = \sqrt{s_x^2} =$ $s_y = \sqrt{s_y^2} =$

$b = (\text{I}_{XY}) / (\text{II}_X) =$ $=$

$a = \overline{Y} - b\overline{X} =$ $=$

$\hat{Y} = bX + a =$ For $X = 6$, $\hat{Y} =$

$s_{y \cdot x} = \sqrt{\left[\dfrac{1}{N(N-2)} \right] \left[(\text{III}_Y) - \dfrac{(\text{I}_{XY})^2}{(\text{II}_X)} \right]} =$

• • • • •   SELF-TEST

1. The equation for a regression line is
    $\hat{Y} = bX + a$ in which
    a. __ is the predicted variable
    b. __ is the predicting variable
    c. __ is the y-intercept
    d. __ is the slope

2. Find the slope and y-intercept of each of
    the following lines.
    a. $Y = X$ c. $2Y = 4X - 8$
    b. $Y = .5X + 2$ d. $X + 2Y = 6$

3. State what is known under the following
    circumstances:
    a.* The regression line always passes
        through the point (__ , __).
    b. If $a = 0$, the regression line passes
        through the point with the
        coordinates (__ , __).
    c. If $b = 1$, what angle does the regres-
        sion line have relative to the X-axis?
    d.* If $\overline{Y} = 4$, $\overline{X} = 4$, and $a = 6$, is b posi-
        tive or negative?
    e. Describe the relationship if $s_{y \cdot x} = 0$.
    f. If $(4, 2)$ and $(2, 4)$ are points on the
        line, is b positive or negative?
    g. If a is negative and b is positive, the
        regression line crosses the X-axis to
        the (left/right) of the origin.

4. Define the following in words:
    a. Y_i b. $\overline{Y}$ c. $\hat{Y}$

5. The least squares criterion selects the
    regression line such that what quantity is
    a minimum?

6.* Applying the regression equation is
    inappropriate when the relationship
    between X and Y is not _____
    or when the value of X is outside the
    _____ of values upon which the
    regression equation was based.

7.* In a regression equation:
    a. What units is a expressed in?
    b. What units is b expressed in?

8. $s_{y \cdot x}$
    a.* is expressed in which units, X or Y?
    b.* can never be (greater/smaller) than
        s_y.
    c. is based upon which deviations?
    d. differs from the standard deviation of
        the Y scores (i.e., s_y) in which
        respects?

9. Indicate whether each of the following
    sets of facts could or could not possibly
    occur simultaneously. If the set is
    impossible, explain why.
    a. $a = 12$, $b = 2$, $s_y = 1.5$, $s_{y \cdot x} = .5$
    b. $a = -5$, $b = -1$, $s_{y \cdot x} = -2$
    c. $s_y = 5$, $s_{y \cdot x} = 5$, $b = 2$
    d. $Y = 20$ at $X = 12$, $s_{y \cdot x} = 2$, and
        $(12, 28)$ is a typical score

*Questions preceded by an asterisk can be answered on the basis of the discussion in the text,
but the discussion in this Study Guide does not answer them.*

EXERCISES

1. A personnel manager for an industrial firm gave job application tests for manual dexterity and visual spatial-relations perception to each of the last fifteen people hired for assembly positions. In addition, these employees have been rated on a scale from 1 to 10 (10 is the best score) for their success on the job after six months. These data are presented in Table 6–5. Calculate the means, variances, standard deviations, regression constants, and standard error of estimate: first, for predicting job success from manual dexterity and, second, for predicting job success from spatial-relations skill. Use the format of Table 6–4 as a computational guide.

2. June Ryan applies for a position as an assembler with the above company. She scores 38 on the dexterity test and 9 on the spatial test. Calculate the predicted job success rating from these two measurements. Which test is the more accurate predictor of job success and why?

Table 6–5 Data for Exercises

Manual Dexterity	Spatial Skill	Job Success
24	6	2
41	10	9
35	7	6
28	4	4
35	11	5
48	4	10
40	8	4
28	7	5
38	9	9
36	6	4
29	10	1
33	9	5
25	8	5
25	8	6
37	6	9

• • • • •

ANSWERS

Table 6–4. $N = 11$, $\sum X = 47$, $\sum Y = 56$, $\sum X^2 = 265$, $\sum Y^2 = 376$, $\sum XY = 297$, $(\sum X)^2 = 2209$, $(\sum Y)^2 = 3136$, $(\mathbf{I_{XY}}) = 635$, $(\mathbf{II_X}) = 706$, $(\mathbf{III_Y}) = 1000$, $\overline{X} = 4.27$, $\overline{Y} = 5.09$, $s_x^2 = 6.42$, $s_y^2 = 9.09$, $s_x = 2.53$, $s_y = 3.02$, $b = .90$, $a = 1.25$, $\hat{Y} = .90X + 1.25$, $\hat{Y}_{X=6} = 6.65$, $s_{y \cdot x} = 2.08$.

Self-Test. (1a) $\hat{Y}$; **(1b)** X; **(1c)** a; **(1d)** b. **(2a)** 1; 0; **(2b)** .5, 2; **(2c)** 2; –4; **(2d)** –.5; 3. **(3a)** $(\overline{X}, \overline{Y})$; **(3b)** $(0, 0)$; **(3c)** 45° angle; **(3d)** negative; **(3e)** all points fall on the regression line; **(3f)** negative; **(3g)** right. **(4a)** Y_i = the actual Y score for the ith subject; **(4b)** $\overline{Y}$ = mean of the observed Y scores; **(4c)** $\hat{Y}$ = predicted Y score at a given X, (i.e., the regression line). **(5)** $\sum(Y_i - \hat{Y})^2$. **(6)** linear; range. **(7a)** Y units; **(7b)** b is unitless. **(8a)** Y units; **(8b)** greater; **(8c)** $\sum(Y_i - \hat{Y})^2$; **(8d)** deviations are taken about the regression line, not the mean, and the divisor is $N - 2$, not $N - 1$. **(9a)** Possible; **(9b)** impossible because $s_{y \cdot x}$ cannot be less than 0; **(9c)** impossible, because b must be 0 if $s_{y \cdot x} = s_y$; **(9d)** (12, 28) is not likely a

"typical" score since it would be 4 standard errors above the regression line.

Exercises. (1) Predicting job success from manual dexterity: $N = 15$, $\sum X = 502$, $\sum Y = 84$, $\sum X^2 = 17468$, $\sum Y^2 = 568$, $\sum XY = 2982$, $(\sum X)^2 = 252004$, $(\sum Y)^2 = 7056$; $(\mathbf{I_{XY}}) = 2562$, $(\mathbf{II_X}) = 10016$, $(\mathbf{III_Y}) = 1464$; $\overline{X} = 33.47$, $\overline{Y} = 5.6$, $s_x^2 = 47.70$, $s_y^2 = 6.97$, $s_x = 6.91$, $s_y = 2.64$, $b = .26$, $a = -2.96$ is exact, -3.10 if rounded numbers are used; $s_{y \cdot x} = 2.04$, $\hat{Y} = .26X - 2.96$. Predicting job success from spatial test: $N = 15$, $\sum X = 113$, $\sum Y = 84$, $\sum X^2 = 913$, $\sum Y^2 = 568$, $\sum XY = 624$, $(\sum X)^2 = 12769$, $(\sum Y)^2 = 7056$; $(\mathbf{I_{XY}}) = -132$, $(\mathbf{II_X}) = 926$, $(\mathbf{III_Y}) = 1464$; $\overline{X} = 7.53$, $\overline{Y} = 5.6$, $s_x^2 = 4.41$, $s_y^2 = 6.97$, $s_x = 2.10$, $s_y = 2.64$, $b = -.14$, $a = 6.67$ is exact, 6.65 if rounded numbers are used; $s_{y \cdot x} = 2.72$, $\hat{Y} = -.14X + 6.67$. **(2)** 6.92; 5.41; The manual dexterity test is the more accurate test, because its standard error is smaller.

●●●●● STATISTICAL PACKAGES ●●●●●

●●●●●   MINITAB

(To accompany the guided computational example in Table 6–4.)

MINITAB will calculate the regression of a dependent variable onto a predictor variable as in the example shown in Table 6–4. The program will calculate the regression constants (called "coef") for the slope and y-intercept of the least squares regression line, and determine the standard error of estimate (called "S"). It will also plot the least squares regression line. The dependent variable is Y; the predictor variable X. In this example, the Y variable is *Test2*; it is predicted by the X variable, *Test1*.

Start the MINITAB program. In the Data window enter the scores for the predictor variable *Test1* in the first column, and the corresponding scores for the dependent variable *Test2* in the second column. Label the variable names by typing them in at the top of the columns. The data you entered should consist of eleven pairs of scores, which appear on the spreadsheet as follows:

Test1	Test2
3	1
6	6
4	5
3	4
8	8
9	10
2	3
1	0
4	5
5	6
2	8

Save the data that you have entered in a MINITAB Worksheet file:

File>Save Worksheet As
        (Enter folder and file name for the Worksheet file.)
        OK

Carry out the linear regression analysis and plot the least-squares estimate:

Stat>Regression>Fitted Line Plot
      Response (Y): Test2   [double-click to transfer]
      Predictor (X): Test1   [double-click to transfer]
      Type of Regression Model: Linear
      OK

Make sure the two variable names are entered in the correct order.

To print the graph of the plot, and to print the regression table from the Session window:

Window>Fitted Line Plot
File>Print Window
      Print Range: All
      OK

Window>Session
File>Print Session Window
      Print Range: All
      OK

To exit MINITAB:

File>Exit

There is no need to save changes for the current Project if the Worksheet file has already been saved.

Program output for this example appears on the next page. The graph shows the least squares regression line. In the regression table, the regression equation, in this example, $Y = 1.25 + 0.899 * X$, appears first. The regression constants appear under the heading "Coef" along with other information that is not needed at this point. Specifically, the y-intercept is 1.248, which is the "coefficient" of the "constant" term, and the slope is 0.8994, which is the "coefficient" of X. The standard error of estimate ($s_{y \cdot x}$) is 2.081, which is labeled "S."

MINITAB Program Output

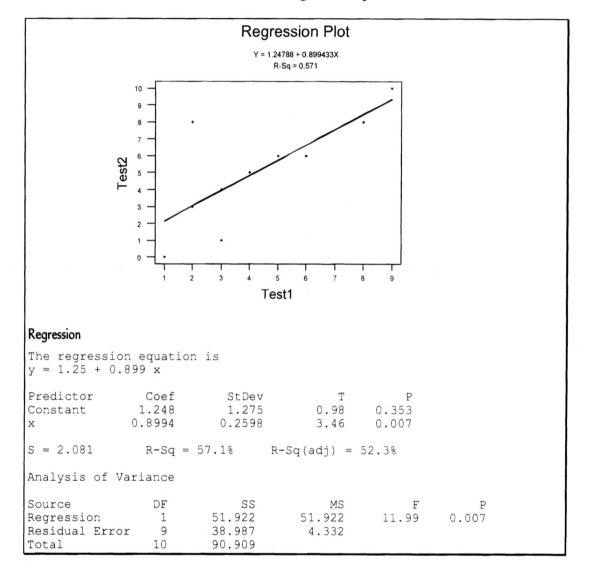

Regression

```
The regression equation is
y = 1.25 + 0.899 x

Predictor        Coef        StDev           T          P
Constant        1.248        1.275        0.98      0.353
x              0.8994       0.2598        3.46      0.007

S = 2.081       R-Sq = 57.1%      R-Sq(adj) = 52.3%

Analysis of Variance

Source           DF          SS          MS          F          P
Regression        1      51.922      51.922      11.99      0.007
Residual Error    9      38.987       4.332
Total            10      90.909
```

● ● ● ● ●   **SPSS**

(To accompany the guided computational example in Table 6–4.)

SPSS will calculate the regression of a dependent variable onto a predictor variable as in the example shown in Table 6–4. The program will calculate the regression constants (called "B") for the slope and y-intercept of the least squares regression line, and determine the standard error of estimate. The dependent variable is called Y; the predictor or independent variable, X. In this example, the Y variable is *Test 2*; it is predicted by the X variable, *Test1*.

Start the SPSS program. The Data Editor window will fill the screen. To enter the variable names, click on the tab labeled "Variable View" at the bottom left of the screen. Label the first two columns with the variable names *Test1* and *Test2*. Go back to the Data View.

Enter the eleven pairs of scores, the predictor variable score *Test1* going in the first column, and the dependent variable score *Test2* going in the second column. The data you entered should consist of eleven pairs of scores, which should appear on the spreadsheet as follows:

Test1	Test2
3	1
6	6
4	5
3	4
8	8
9	10
2	3
1	0
4	5
5	6
2	8

Carry out the simple linear regression analysis:

> *Analyze>Regression>Linear*
> > Dependent: Test2   [highlight and transfer]
> > Independent: Test1   [highlight and transfer]
> > Method: Enter
> > OK

Make sure that the two variables are entered into the program in the correct order.

The output at this point contains much more information than is needed. Refer to the output, which is illustrated on the following pages. On the output, you will see three tables labeled Model Summary, ANOVA, and Coefficients, respectively.

The regression constants appear in the Coefficients table under the heading "B." Specifically, the y-intercept is 1.248, which is the coefficient of the "Constant" term, and the slope is 0.899, which is the coefficient of *Test1*. The standard error of estimate ($s_{y \cdot x}$) is 2.0813, which is listed in the rightmost column of the Model Summary table.

Print the regression output:

> *File>Print*
> > Print range: All visible output
> > OK

Save the data that you entered:

> *Window>SPSS Data Editor*
> *File>Save As*
> > (Enter folder and file name for SPSS Save file.)
> > Save

Exit SPSS:

> *File>Exit*

There is no need to save the contents of the Viewer files.

SPSS Program Output

Regression

Variables Entered/Removed[b]

Model	Variables Entered	Variables Removed	Method
1	TEST1[a]	.	Enter

a. All requested variables entered.

b. Dependent Variable: TEST2

Model Summary

Model	R	R Square	Adjusted R Square	Std. Error of the Estimate
1	.756[a]	.571	.523	2.0813

a. Predictors: (Constant), TEST1

ANOVA[b]

Model		Sum of Squares	df	Mean Square	F	Sig.
1	Regression	51.922	1	51.922	11.986	.007[a]
	Residual	38.987	9	4.332		
	Total	90.909	10			

a. Predictors: (Constant), TEST1

b. Dependent Variable: TEST2

Coefficients[a]

Model		Unstandardized Coefficients		Standardized Coefficients	t	Sig.
		B	Std. Error	Beta		
1	(Constant)	1.248	1.275		.979	.353
	TEST1	.899	.260	.756	3.462	.007

a. Dependent Variable: TEST2

● ● ● ● ●

CHAPTER 7

CORRELATION • • • • • •

CONCEPT GOALS

Be sure that you thoroughly understand the following concepts and how to use them in statistical applications.

- ◆ Correlation
- ◆ $\Sigma(Y_i - \overline{Y})^2$, $\Sigma(Y_i - \hat{Y})^2$, $\Sigma(\hat{Y} - \overline{Y})^2$
- ◆ The relation between r, s_y, and $s_{y\cdot x}$
- ◆ Effects on r of a restricted range of scores, of the use of extreme groups or combined groups, and of an extreme score

• • • • • GUIDE TO MAJOR CONCEPTS

Correlation Coefficient

The square of the **correlation coefficient** is an index that reflects the proportion of variability in the Y variable that is associated with Y's linear relationship with variable X. This statistic was developed by Karl Pearson and is sometimes called the Pearson product-moment [1]_____ .

Consider Table 7–1. At the top is a scatterplot of five points that describe an approximately linear relationship between variables X and Y. The value of the points (i.e., Y_i), the mean of the

Y's (i.e., $\overline{Y}$), and the value of the regression line $\hat{Y}_i$ at each X value are provided. The first column left vacant in the table at the bottom of Table 7–1 is for the simple deviations between each Y_i *value and the mean of the Y's*. This difference is symbolized by [2]_____ .
These deviations, when squared, summed, and divided by $N-1$, yield the [3]_____ of the Y_i, an expression of the total variability in the Y_i scores. Now, calculate $(Y_i - \overline{Y})$ for each score, and mark each deviation on the scatterplot with a straight vertical line drawn between the point (Y_i) and the mean $(\overline{Y})$.

Now consider only the point (9, 10) at the top right of the graph and in the first row of the table. The total distance between that point and the mean of the $Y's$ is symbolized by [4]_____ . Numerically, it equals [5]_____ = __ . As you can see in the scatterplot, this total distance is composed of two parts, the distance from the mean to the regression line, symbolized by [6]_____ , and the distance from the regression line to the point, written [7]_____ .

Fill in these symbol expressions in the appropriate parentheses at the right of the graph. Then determine the numerical value of these two distances for the point (9, 10) and write them in the first row of the table. Notice that $(Y_i - \overline{Y}) = (\hat{Y}_i - \overline{Y}) + (Y_i - \hat{Y}_i)$, which is numerically verified, since [8] __ = __ + __ . On the graph, mark the distance between the mean and the regression line $(\hat{Y}_i - \overline{Y})$ with a wavy line and the distance between the regression line and the point $(Y_i - \hat{Y}_i)$ with a dotted line. Place these lines next to the continuous straight line you drew indicating the total distance, $(Y_i - \overline{Y})$.

Now proceed *in the table* to the second point (7, 6). Determine algebraically the total deviation $(Y_i - \overline{Y})$ and then its two components $(\hat{Y}_i - \overline{Y})$ and $(Y_i - \hat{Y}_i)$, but watch the direction of the subtraction and the sign of your answer. Again, you should obtain the numerical equation [9] __ = __ + __ . Draw these distances on the graph; notice that after you have drawn the wavy line for $(\hat{Y}_i - \overline{Y})$ you must "come back," or go down, from the line to the point $(Y_i - \hat{Y}_i)$, which is the same as adding the negative distance $-.5$. Fill in the columns of the table that call for the deviations of the remaining points, and draw the distances on the graph. Total the columns.

Table 7–1 Numerical Illustration of the Correlation Coefficient

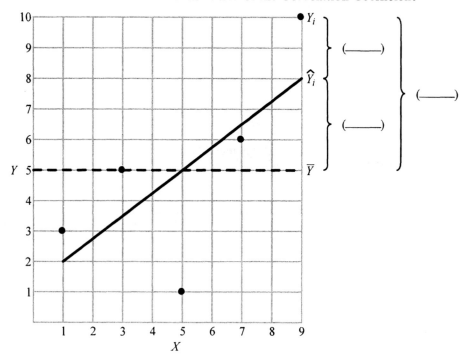

				Deviations			Squared Deviations		
				Total	Relationship	Error	Total	Relationship	Error
X_i	Y_i	$\overline{Y}$	$\hat{Y}_i$	$(Y_i - \overline{Y})$	$(\hat{Y}_i - \overline{Y})$	$(Y_i - \hat{Y}_i)$	$(Y_i - \overline{Y})^2$	$(\hat{Y}_i - \overline{Y})^2$	$(Y_i - \hat{Y}_i)^2$
9	10	5	8.0						
7	6	5	6.5						
5	1	5	5.0						
3	5	5	3.5						
1	3	5	2.0						
25	25			____ = ____ + __			____ = ____ + __		

Table 7–1 Numerical Illustration of the Correlation Coefficient (Continued)

Variance

$$\text{Variance of } Y = s_y{}^2$$

$$= \frac{\text{sum of total squared deviations of points about their mean}}{N-1}$$

$$= \underline{\hspace{1.5cm}} = \underline{\hspace{1.5cm}} = \underline{\hspace{1.5cm}}$$

Correlation

$$\text{Correlation squared} = r^2 = \frac{\text{sum of squared deviations associated with } Y\text{'s relationship to } X}{\text{sum of total squared deviations of points about their mean}}$$

$$= \underline{\hspace{1.5cm}} = \underline{\hspace{1.5cm}} = \underline{\hspace{1.5cm}}$$

$$\text{Correlation coefficient} = r = \sqrt{\frac{\text{sum of squared deviations associated with } Y\text{'s relationship to } X}{\text{sum of total squared deviations of points about their mean}}}$$

$$= \sqrt{\underline{\hspace{1.5cm}}} = \sqrt{\underline{\hspace{1.5cm}}} = \underline{\hspace{1.5cm}}$$

Standard Error of Estimate

$$\text{Standard error of estimate} = s_{y \cdot x} = \sqrt{\frac{\text{sum of squared deviations of points associated with error}}{N-2}}$$

$$= \sqrt{\underline{\hspace{1.5cm}}} = \sqrt{\underline{\hspace{1.5cm}}} = \underline{\hspace{1.5cm}}$$

The above process has illustrated that the total deviation between [10]_____ and their [11]_____ can be broken into two parts, the distance between the [12]_____ and the [13]_____ plus the distance between the [14]_____ and the [15]_____ . This relationship can be expressed symbolically as [16]_____ = _____ + _____ .

It is important to interpret these three parts conceptually. The differences between points and their mean $(Y_i - \overline{Y})$ represent the **total** deviation, as used in the common measure of variability, the [17]_____ . The distances between the regression line and the points $(Y_i - \hat{Y}_i)$ reflect the **error** in Y remaining after prediction of Y is made from the regression line. These distances contribute to the statistic called the [18]_____.The distance between the mean and the regression line $(\hat{Y}_i - \overline{Y})$ represents the segment of the total deviation that is associated with Y's **relationship** to X. Thus, the total deviation between points and their mean can be divided into a part associated with Y's [19]_____ to X and a part that remains as [20]_____ in predicting Y from that relationship (i.e., from the regression line). A simple verbal equation expresses this relationship: [21] _____ = _____ + _____ .

However, as we have seen from our study of the variance, variability is usually expressed in *squared* deviations. One reason for this is that deviations that are not squared add up to zero over all the points. Did yours? Fill in the remaining three columns of Table 7–1, which require you to square the deviations that you have already filled in. Add the squared deviations in each column. Note that for squared deviations the equation "total = relationship + error" no longer holds for individual points; for the point (9, 10) for example, [22]__ ≠ __ + __ . However, for the *sums* of the columns (which are no longer zero), the equation "total = relationship + error" does hold: [23]__ = __ + __ .

At the bottom of the table you will find verbal expressions of the formulas for the variance, correlation, and standard error of estimate. Under each verbal statement, write the algebraic representation of the sum of the appropriate squared deviations and then the numerical value of the statistic for these data.

To check yourself: The total variability in Y_i can be expressed by the statistic called the [24]_____, which equals the sum of squared deviations for total, [25]$\sum(Y_i - \overline{Y})^2 = $ __ , divided by [26]$N - 1 = $ __ . So [27]$s_y^2 = $ __ / __ = __ .

The degree of relationship between X and Y can be expressed by the statistic called the [28]_____ . To obtain its value, determine the proportion of the total variability that is associated with Y's relationship to X by dividing the sum of squared deviations associated with the relationship, [29]$\sum(\hat{Y}_i - \overline{Y})^2 = $ __ by the total squared deviations, [30]$\sum(Y_i - \overline{Y})^2 = $ __ , which proportion equals [31]__ / __ = __ . The square root of this value is the [32]_____ which equals [33]__ .

The error in this relationship can be expressed by the statistic called the

[34]_____ , symbolized by [35]__ . It equals the square root of the sum of squared deviations for error, [36] $\sum(Y_i - \hat{Y})^2 =$ __ , divided by [37] $N - 2 =$ __ , which ratio equals [38]__ , and its square root, $s_{y \cdot x} = $ [39]__ .

In statistics, the formula that defines a concept is commonly not the most convenient formula to use for computation. The computational formula for the correlation coefficient is

$$r = \frac{N(\sum XY) - (\sum X)(\sum Y)}{\sqrt{[N\sum X^2 - (\sum X)^2][N\sum Y^2 - (\sum Y)^2]}}$$

A guided computational example is presented in Table 7–2. Notice that you first calculate X^2, Y^2, and XY. After summing these quantities, determine the three intermediate quantities shown, which are the same intermediate quantities used in the previous chapter (Table 6–4), and they can be used to obtain most of the statistics presented in Chapters 2–7. These quantities are to be substituted into the formula for r. Complete the calculation of the example.

Answer Key to Correlation Coefficient

[1]	correlation coefficient	[12]	mean	[21]	total = relationship + error	[30]	46
[2]	$(Y_i - \overline{Y})$	[13]	regression line			[31]	22.5 / 46 = .49
[3]	variance	[14]	regression line			[32]	correlation coefficient
[4]	$(Y_i - \overline{Y})$	[15]	point	[22]	$25 \neq 9 + 4$		
[5]	$10 - 5 = 5$	[16]	$(Y_i - \overline{Y}) = (\hat{Y}_i - \overline{Y}) + (Y_i - \hat{Y}_i)$	[23]	$46 = 22.5 + 23.5$	[33]	.70
[6]	$(\hat{Y}_i - \overline{Y})$			[24]	variance	[34]	standard error of estimate
[7]	$(Y_i - \hat{Y}_i)$			[25]	46		
[8]	$5 = 3 + 2$	[17]	variance	[26]	4	[35]	$s_{y \cdot x}$
[9]	$1 = 1.5 + (-.5)$	[18]	standard error of estimate	[27]	$46 / 4 = 11.5$	[36]	23.5
[10]	points			[28]	correlation coefficient	[37]	3
[11]	mean	[19]	relationship			[38]	7.83
		[20]	error	[29]	22.5	[39]	2.80

Table 7–2 Guided Computational Example

Case	X	Y	X^2	Y^2	XY
a	7	4			
b	5	6			
c	6	4			
d	4	7			
e	2	5			

$N =$ $\sum X =$ $\sum Y =$ $\sum X^2 =$ $\sum Y^2 =$ $\sum XY =$

$(\sum X)^2 =$ $(\sum Y)^2 =$

Intermediate Quantities

$(\mathbf{I_{XY}}) = N(\sum XY) - (\sum X)(\sum Y) =$

$(\mathbf{II_X}) = N\sum X^2 - (\sum X)^2 =$

$(\mathbf{III_Y}) = N\sum Y^2 - (\sum Y)^2 =$

$$r = \frac{N(\sum XY) - (\sum X)(\sum Y)}{\sqrt{[N\sum X^2 - (\sum X)^2][N\sum Y^2 - (\sum Y)^2]}} = \frac{(\mathbf{I_{XY}})}{\sqrt{(\mathbf{II_X})(\mathbf{III_Y})}} = \qquad =$$

Factors Affecting *r*

Since the correlation coefficient is an abstract, unitless index of the degree of relationship between two variables, it will be helpful to observe how its value changes under different conditions. Table 7–3 presents four examples. The scores in the X and Y distributions are the same in each of the four cases, but the X-Y pairings are different from case to case. Consequently, much of the computational labor has been eliminated, and only the numerator of r needs to be calculated (the denominator is always 200). Compute the value of r in each case, and plot the points on the graphs provided.

Case A illustrates a special and unlikely occurrence, a [1]_____ relationship. In this case, all the points fall on the line, so Y_i and $\hat{Y}_i$ always have the same values. Therefore, $\Sigma(Y_i - \overline{Y})^2$ and $\Sigma(\hat{Y}_i - \overline{Y})^2$ are (equal/unequal) [2]_____ , which means that the correlation coefficient, defined as $r = \sqrt{[\Sigma(\hat{Y} - \overline{Y})^2] / [\Sigma(Y_i - \overline{Y})^2]}$ will equal [3]__ .

Table 7–3 Some Examples of Correlation

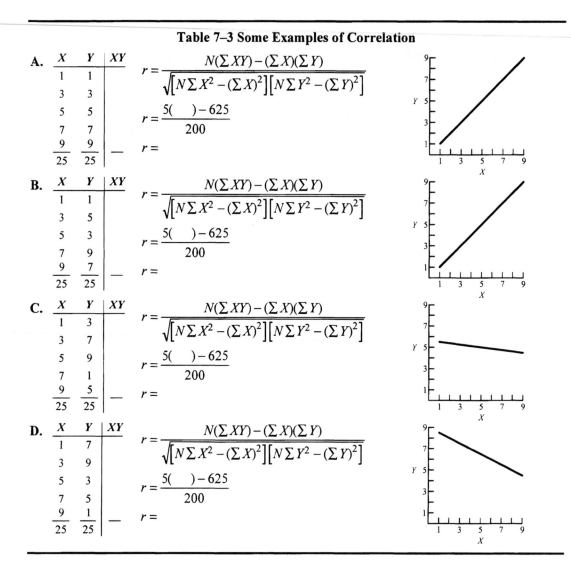

A comparison of cases A and B illustrates the fact that the closer the points cluster about the line, the higher is the value of r (assuming that s_y is the same, which it is in these examples.) Draw the vertical lines connecting each point in B to the regression line to see this more closely. When squared, these deviations contribute to the statistic [4]__ . Therefore, under the special circumstances of this comparison, as the standard error of estimate becomes larger the correlation becomes [5]_____ . Instead of $r = 1.00$ as in A, the [6]$r = $ __ in B.

Case C illustrates a situation in which there is almost no relationship between X and Y. Here, the regression line does not improve prediction very much, so the correlation is [7]__ . If the regression line did not aid prediction *at all*, the correlation coefficient would equal [8]__ .

Case D illustrates a [9]_____ relationship; high Y values tend to be associated with (high/low) [10]_____ X values. The [11]$r = $ __ . It should be observed that correlations of $-.80$ and $+.80$ represent (the same/a different) [12]_____ degree of relationship; only the direction of the relationship is different.

It is important to interpret the correlation coefficient in relation to the sample of participants that contributed data for its calculation. Table 7–4 presents some circumstances that can drastically alter the value of r. The age (X) and language proficiency score (Y) for 14 children are presented, and the subjects are divided into six subgroups, (a, b, c, d, e, and f) for the purpose of illustrating several facts. The N and the intermediate quantities (I_{XY}), (II_X), and (III_Y) are given for the following four sets of subjects: (1) over all subgroups; (2) just over subgroups b, c, and d; (3) just over subgroups b, c, d, and f; and (4) just over subgroups a, b, d, e, and f. For each of these four sets of groups, draw the scatterplot and compute r now.

Case I, involving all 14 subjects, will serve as a reference group for the other situations. Since the correlation over the entire age range is [13]__ , you would conclude that there is a fairly high relationship between age and language performance. However, this relationship is limited to the ages studied. If the ages were 42 to 50 instead of 2 to 10, there might not be any relationship. Similarly, suppose that a teacher in a special school reads that the correlation between age and language ability is .72. As a result, the teacher decides to group the children, whose ages range from 4 to 8, into three age groups to make each class more homogeneous in language ability. However, consider just the data for four-, six-, and eight-year-olds (where we *restrict* the range to subgroups b, c, and d). Here in Section II of Table 7–4 you found the correlation to be only [14]__ , quite a reduction from the value of [15]__ for the entire group. Thus the correlation coefficient is influenced by the range of values sampled; restricting the range of the variables often makes the correlation coefficient smaller.

Table 7–4 Interpreting the Correlation Coefficient in Special Circumstances

Group	Age X	Language Score Y
a	2	1
	2	2
b	4	2
	4	3
	4	5
c	6	2
	6	4
	6	6
	6	7
d	8	3
	8	5
	8	6
e	10	6
f	10	9

Summary	N	(I_{XY})	(II_X)	(III_Y)
All groups	14	784	1232	969
b, c, and d	10	80	240	281
b, c, d and f	11	276	424	530
a, b, d, e, and f	10	560	880	536

I. All Groups $(a - f)$

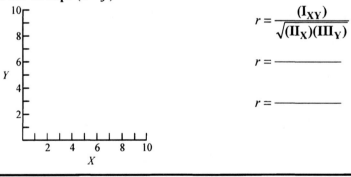

$$r = \frac{(I_{XY})}{\sqrt{(II_X)(III_Y)}}$$

$$r = \underline{\hspace{2cm}}$$

$$r = \underline{\hspace{2cm}}$$

Table 7–4 Interpreting the Correlation Coefficient in Special Circumstances (Continued)

II. Restricted Range (*b*, *c*, and *d*)

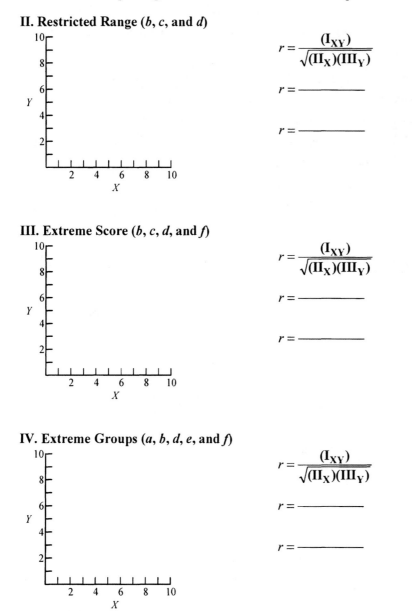

$$r = \frac{(I_{XY})}{\sqrt{(II_X)(III_Y)}}$$

$$r = \text{\underline{\hspace{2cm}}}$$

$$r = \text{\underline{\hspace{2cm}}}$$

III. Extreme Score (*b*, *c*, *d*, and *f*)

$$r = \frac{(I_{XY})}{\sqrt{(II_X)(III_Y)}}$$

$$r = \text{\underline{\hspace{2cm}}}$$

$$r = \text{\underline{\hspace{2cm}}}$$

IV. Extreme Groups (*a*, *b*, *d*, *e*, and *f*)

$$r = \frac{(I_{XY})}{\sqrt{(II_X)(III_Y)}}$$

$$r = \text{\underline{\hspace{2cm}}}$$

$$r = \text{\underline{\hspace{2cm}}}$$

Suppose that one mother begged the same teacher to let her 10-year-old child stay one more year in the special school. Suppose that this child is case *f*. What effect can one child have on a correlation? When you calculated *r* for the extreme-score example (subgroups *b*, *c*, *d*, and *f*) in Section III of Table 7–4, you found [16]*r* = ___ , compared to [17]__ without that subject. Obviously, one subject with [18]_____ scores can change a correlation quite substantially.

Suppose that the original researcher who investigated the relationship between age and language has access only to 2- and 4-year-olds in a nursery school and 8- and 10-year-olds from two classes in a public school. The correlations you found in Section IV of Table 7–4 for such a situation (where we concentrate on the *extreme groups a, b, d, e, and f*) is [19]__ , compared to *r* for the total group of [20]__ , indicating that special sampling involving extreme groups can also influence *r*. It is clear that the value of the correlation coefficient is highly dependent upon the distribution and range of values included.

Answer Key to Factors Affecting r

[1]	perfect	[5]	smaller	[9]	negative	[13]	.72	[17]	.31
[2]	equal	[6]	.80	[10]	low	[14]	.31	[18]	extreme
[3]	1.00	[7]	−.10	[11]	−.80	[15]	.72	[19]	.82
[4]	$s_{y \cdot x}$	[8]	0	[12]	the same	[16]	.58	[20]	.72

● ● ● ● ●   ## SELF-TEST

1. Which of the following measures reflects the variability in *Y* associated with differences in *X*? Which reflects the total variation in *Y*? Which reflects the variation in *Y* not associated with differences in *X*?

    a. $\Sigma(Y_i - \overline{Y})^2$ c. $\Sigma(\hat{Y} - \overline{Y})^2$
    b. $\Sigma(Y_i - \hat{Y})^2$

2.* The correlation coefficient varies in size as a function of the relative sizes of s_y^2 and $s_{y \cdot x}^2$. Explain this relationship.

3. The value of *r* ranges between __ and __ .

4. When no linear relationship exists between *X* and *Y*, *r* = __ .

5. If *r* = .60, what proportion of the variability in *Y* is associated with the variability in *X*? What proportion is not associated with *X*?

6.* If *r* = .70 between age of grade-school children and broad jump distance in feet, what do you know about this relationship if jumping distance is measure in meters instead of feet?

7.* Under what circumstances is r equal to the slope, b, of the regression line of Y on X?

8.* What is the relationship, if any, between the correlation of X and Y and the correlation of Y and X?

9. Why might the correlation between scores on a test designed to predict success in college and subsequent college grades be lower for students at a very expensive private school than for students at State U?

10. The Smith Reading Diagnostic Test is reported to be a valid measure of reading skill because it correlated .75 with another measure of reading proficiency in a sample of 1000 children drawn from grades 1 to 6. Mrs. Jones, a reading specialist in the New York public schools, wants to use this test to select third-grade children who are having reading problems so that they can be given special training. What do you know about the validity of the Smith test for this purpose, that is, about the correlation between the Smith test and reading proficiency for third graders?

11. Suppose that within a sample of 100 male subjects an $r = .50$ is obtained between two variables. Indicate what is

likely to happen to the size of r (will it increase, decrease, remain essentially unchanged, or change substantially in a direction that cannot be predicted?) in the following situations.

a. N is increased to 150.
b. The range of X values is restricted by eliminating some abnormally low scores.
c. Two groups of subjects, one at each extreme of the X scale, are used as subjects.
d. A single subject with extremely high positive X and Y scores is added to the sample.
e. 10 subjects, all of whom scored $\overline{X}$ and $\overline{Y}$, are added.
f. 50 female subjects, whose within-group r is also .50 but who have a different mean and variance than the males, are combined in the same sample.

12. Suppose that the number of hours a child spends watching television programs regarded as violent correlates .70 with the tendency of these children toward aggressive social behavior. Comment on the possibility of concluding that viewing violent programs causes aggressive social behaviors.

13.* What is r under the following conditions?
a. $s_y = s_{y \cdot x} \neq 0$
b. $s_y < s_{y \cdot x}$
c. $s_{y \cdot x} = 0$ and $s_y \neq 0$

*Questions preceded by an asterisk can be answered on the basis of the discussion in the text, but the discussion in this Study Guide does not answer them.

● ● ● ● ●   EXERCISES

1. It has often been suggested that artistic ability is incompatible with analytical reasoning. Below are data from a hypothetical study in which researchers examined the relationship between these two abilities by giving tests designed to measure analytical reasoning and artistic skills to each child in a sample of boys and girls. Calculate the correlation between these measures within each sex group according to the scheme of the guided computational example in Table 7–2.

Males		Females	
Analytical Reasoning Ability	Artistic Ability	Analytical Reasoning Ability	Artistic Ability
5	6	6	5
7	8	8	7
3	1	4	0
1	4	2	3
8	3	9	2
2	2	3	1
6	7	7	6

2. Using the data in exercise 1, calculate the correlation for the two sexes combined into one sample. Explain any differences.

3. Suppose that the scores for analytical reasoning and artistic ability were transformed into standard scores separately within each sex and variable. Would the correlations in problems 1 and 2 change? Explain.

● ● ● ● ●   ANSWERS

Table 7–2. $N = 5$, $\sum X = 24$, $\sum Y = 26$, $\sum X^2 = 130$, $\sum Y^2 = 142$, $\sum XY = 120$, $(\sum X)^2 = 576$, $(\sum Y)^2 = 676$; $(\mathbf{I_{XY}}) = -24$, $(\mathbf{II_X}) = 74$, $(\mathbf{III_Y}) = 34$.

Table 7–3. $r = 1.00$, $.80$, $-.10$, $-.80$.

Self-Test. (1a) $\sum(Y_i - \overline{Y})^2$ reflects the total variability in the Y scores; **(1b)** $\sum(Y_i - \hat{Y})^2$ reflects the variability in Y remaining after predicting with the regression line (i.e., the error); **(1c)** $\sum(\hat{Y} - \overline{Y})^2$ reflects the variability in Y attributable to X. **(2)** $r^2 = 1 - (s_{y \cdot x}^2)/s_y^2$, so as $s_{y \cdot x}^2$ becomes small or s_y^2 becomes large, r will increase. **(3)** -1.00 and $+1.00$. **(4)** 0. **(5)** $.36$; $.64$. **(6)** $r = .70$. **(7)** If $s_x^2 = s_y^2$ as when X and Y are both standardized. **(8)** The two r's are the same value. **(9)** Since the expensive private school is presumable highly selective, its student range would be more narrow than State's. **(10)** Very little. Since reading is related to age, it is possible that the $r = .75$ for grades 1–6 is due to age and that the correlation within the third grade is quite different because of a restricted range of scores. **(11a)** Essentially no change; **(11b)** decrease; **(11c)** increase; **(11d)** increase; **(11e)** essentially no change; **(11f)** change but the direction depends on the particular values. **(12)** Not proved by this information, because correlation does not necessarily imply causality. **(13a)** .00; **(13b)** impossible; **(13c)** ±1.00.

Exercises. (1) For males: $(I_{XY}) = 149$, $(II_X) = 292$, $(III_Y) = 292$; $r = .51$; for females:

$(I_{XY}) = 149$, $(II_X) = 292$, $(III_Y) = 292$; $r = .51$. **(2)** For sexes combined: $(I_{XY}) = 547$, $(II_X) = 1217$, $(III_Y) = 1217$, $r = .45$; although the correlation within males is the same as within females, the correlation for the combined sample is smaller because of differences in the means for the two groups. **(3)** The r for each sex would not be affected, because when all scores are standardized the changes in the units and origins do not influence r. However, the r for the combined group would change, because some scores (i.e., males) would be transformed differently than other scores (i.e., females.)

••••• STATISTICAL PACKAGES •••••

•••••   MINITAB

(To accompany the guided computational example in Table 7–2.)

MINITAB will calculate the correlation between two variables and will produce a scatterplot. The variables consist of pairs of values in the same manner as for the simple regression analysis.

Start the MINITAB program. In the Data window enter the five pairs of data from Table 7–2 for the two variables X and Y into the first two columns of the spreadsheet. Label the two columns with the variable names X and Y. To enter the variable names, type them in at the top of the columns. The data you entered should appear on the spreadsheet as follows:

X	Y
7	4
5	6
6	4
4	7
2	5

Save the data that you entered:

> *File>Save Worksheet As*
>   (Enter folder and file name for the Worksheet file.)
>   OK

Calculate the Pearson correlation between *X* and *Y*:

> *Stat>Basic Statistics>Correlation*
>   Variables: X Y   [double-click each to transfer]
>   Display p-values: Yes
>   OK

Graph the scatterplot for the joint distribution:

> *Graph>Plot*
>   Graph variables:
>   Graph 1,Y: Y   [double-click to transfer]
>   Graph 1,X: X   [double-click to transfer]
>   OK

Print the output from the Session window and the graph of the scatterplot:

> *Window>Session*
> *File>Print Session Window*
>   Print Range: All
>   OK

> *Window>Plot 'Y' * 'X'*
> *File>Print Graph*
>   Print Range: All
>   OK

Exit MINITAB:

> *File>Exit*

There is no need to save changes for the current Project if the Worksheet file has already been saved.

MINITAB Program Output

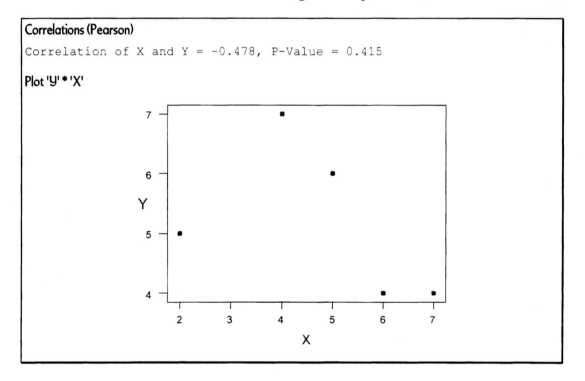

Correlations (Pearson)

Correlation of X and Y = -0.478, P-Value = 0.415

Plot 'Y' * 'X'

The output shows the correlation between X and Y to be $-.478$. The significance level p associated with the correlation (see Chapter 10) is 0.415.

● ● ● ● ●   **SPSS**

(To accompany the guided computational example in Table 7–2.)

SPSS will the graph the scatterplot and calculate the correlation between two variables. The variables are paired in essentially in the same manner as for the simple regression analysis.

Start the SPSS program. The Data Editor window will fill the screen. Enter the five pairs of data for the two variables X and Y into the first two columns of the SPSS Data Editor spreadsheet. To enter the variable names, click on the tab labeled "Variable View" at the bottom left of the screen. Label the first two columns with the variable names X and Y. Go back to the Data View.

The five pairs of scores you entered should appear on the spreadsheet as follows:

X	Y
7	4
5	6
6	4
4	7
2	5

Generate the scatterplot for the joint distribution:

> *Graphs>Scatter*
>   Simple:
>   Define
>   Y Axis: Y   [highlight and transfer]
>   X Axis: X   [highlight and transfer]
>   OK

Calculate the correlation coefficient between X and Y and its significance:

> *Analyze>Correlate>Bivariate*
>   Variables: X and Y   [highlight and transfer]
>   Correlation coefficients: Pearson
>   Test of significance: Two-tailed
>   OK

The output table, which is illustrated on the following page, shows the correlation between X and Y to be $-.478$. The significance associated with the correlation (see Chapter 10) is $p = .415$. To print the graph and the table:

> *File>Print*
>   Print range: All visible output.
>   OK

To save the data that you entered:

> *Window>SPSS Data Editor*
> *File>Save As*
>   (Enter folder and file name for SPSS Save file.)
>   Save

Exit SPSS:

> *File>Exit*

SPSS Program Output

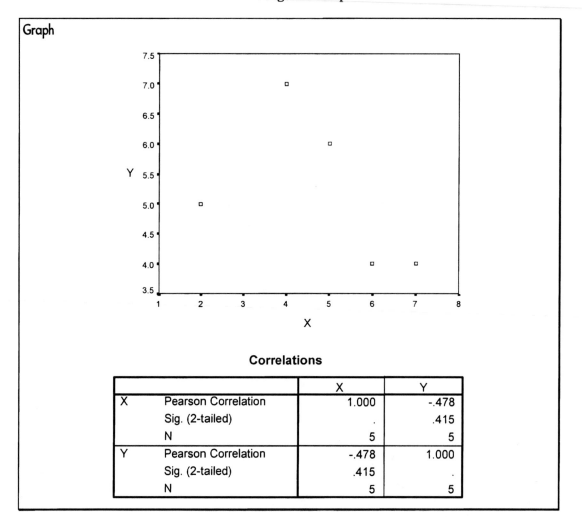

Graph

Correlations

		X	Y
X	Pearson Correlation	1.000	-.478
	Sig. (2-tailed)	.	.415
	N	5	5
Y	Pearson Correlation	-.478	1.000
	Sig. (2-tailed)	.415	.
	N	5	5

●●●●●

CHAPTER 8

SAMPLING, SAMPLING DISTRIBUTIONS, AND PROBABILITY •••••

CONCEPT GOALS

Be sure that you thoroughly understand the following concepts and how to use them in statistical applications.

- ♦ Population, parameter
- ♦ Sample, statistic
- ♦ Random and independent sampling
- ♦ Empirical and theoretical sampling distributions
- ♦ Standard error and its relationship to the standard deviation

••••• GUIDE TO MAJOR CONCEPTS

Samples and Populations

When performing a research project, scientists usually observe only a **sample** of subjects or events selected from a larger **population**. After making the measurements, certain **statistics**, such as the mean and the variance, are often calculated on the sample and used to estimate their corresponding **parameters** in the population. Quantities and indices determined on a small [1]_____ of subjects are known as [2]_____ . The sample is only a subset of a larger [3]_____ whose characteristics are called [4]_____ . Research in the behavioral sciences often consists of calculating certain [5]_____ on a

[6]_____ of subjects for the purpose of estimating and inferring the values of corresponding [7]_____ in the [8]_____ .

Obviously, if statistics are to be good estimators of parameters, they must be based on a good sample of observations. Most frequently, a scientist attempts to obtain a **simple random sample**, one in which each subject or observation in the population has an **equal likelihood** of being selected and is picked **independently** of any other observation. Thus, in a [9]_____ sample, observations of subjects are selected [10]_____ from one another and in such a way that each element of the population has an [11]_____ of being chosen.

Answer Key to Samples and Populations						
[1]	sample	[4]	parameters	[7]	parameters	[10]	independently
[2]	statistics	[5]	statistics	[8]	population	[11]	equal
[3]	population	[6]	sample	[9]	simple random		likelihood

Sampling Distributions

In addition to the population distribution and sample distribution of raw scores, one of the most important ideas in inferential statistics is that of a **sampling distribution**. A distribution of a statistic (the mean, for example) calculated on separate independent samples of size N from a given population is called a [1]_____ . Notice that it is not composed of unmodified direct observations; it is a distribution of a [2]_____ determined on numerous samples of such observations. While the sample and population distributions are composed of raw scores, a [3]_____ is the distribution of a [4]_____ determined on each of several independent [5]_____ of raw scores taken from the [6]_____ of raw scores.

As a concrete example of a sampling distribution, we will now create an **empirical sampling distribution**. That is, we will actually calculate the mean for each of several samples selected from a single population of values and form a distribution of those means. Since this distribution of means will actually be observed, it is called an [7]_____ distribution. In contrast, most sampling distributions used by statisticians are **theoretical**. Such distributions, based upon mathematical concepts as opposed to actual observations, are called [8]_____ .

At the bottom of Table 8–1 are some numbers in boxes. Cut or carefully tear these out and separate them (or make your own set on another piece of paper). Suppose that these are raw scores for the whole population; they are listed in the left column of the table. The population distribution has a mean of 5 and a standard deviation of 2.16. Notice that Greek letters μ (mu) and σ (sigma) are used to designate these quantities, because they are population [9]_____ , not sample [10]_____ . A graphic display of this frequency distribution is also presented in the table. Now put your 12 population values into a hat or some other opaque container, mix, and draw out a sample of four numbers at random by picking a number, replacing it in the container, picking a second number, *replacing* it, etc. Write the four numbers in the space under "Observed Sample Distributions of Raw Scores"; calculate the mean, $\overline{X}$, for this sample and write it in the third column of Table 8–1. That has already been done for sample a, so repeat the process until you have a total of 10 samples. When you are finished, add up the 10 sample $\overline{X}$'s and obtain their average value ($\overline{X}_{\overline{x}}$). The formulas in Table 8–1 for the mean and standard deviation, formerly written in terms of the raw scores, X_i, are now expressed in terms of $\overline{X}_j$, because the means, $\overline{X}_j$, are the scores in an empirical sampling distribution of the mean.

Now, look down the column labeled "Sampling Distribution of the Mean." The figures under "$\overline{X}$" are the means of the 10 samples you collected. Since the sample mean is a statistic, this column represents a distribution of a statistic and is thus an empirical [11]_____ . Specifically, it is the [12]_____ of the [13]_____. In the lower right corner of the Table 8–1, place squares on the frequency distribution graph for each of the 10 means, locating them over their value on the abscissa; you can see that a new distribution (a distribution of means) has been created.

Now consider the task of estimating the mean of the population distribution of raw scores (supposing that it is too difficult to calculate directly). The population value is symbolized by μ_x and, in this case, we know that it equals [14]__ . We can estimate the mean of the population of raw scores by selecting a single sample of raw scores and calculating the sample [15]_____ , symbolized by [16]__ . For the first sample, this value is [17]__ . For the second sample, it is [18]_____ . But we can also estimate the mean of the population of raw scores, symbolized by [19]__ , with the average of the ten sample means which you have just calculated and which equals [20]_____ .

Table 8–1 Creating an Empirical Sampling Distribution of the Mean

Population Distribution of Raw Scores	Observed Sample Distributions of Raw Scores ($N_x = 4$)	Sampling Distribution of the Mean $\overline{X}$	$\overline{X}^2$
1	**a.** (6, 1, 5, 6)	**a.** 4.5	
2	**b.** (, , ,)	**b.**	
4	**c.** (, , ,)	**c.**	
4	**d.** (, , ,)	**d.**	
4	**e.** (, , ,)	**e.**	
5	**f.** (, , ,)	**f.**	
5	**g.** (, , ,)	**g.**	
6	**h.** (, , ,)	**h.**	
6	**i.** (, , ,)	**i.**	
6	**j.** (, , ,)	**j.**	
8			
$\underline{9}$			
60		$\sum \overline{X} =$	$\sum \overline{X}^2 =$

$$\mu_x = 5$$
$$\sigma_x = 2.16$$

$$\left(\sum \overline{X} \right)^2 =$$

$$\overline{X}_{\bar{x}} = \frac{\sum \overline{X}_i}{N_{\bar{x}}} = \frac{\sum \overline{X}}{10} =$$

$$\sigma_{\bar{x}} = \frac{\sigma_x}{\sqrt{N_x}} = \frac{2.16}{\sqrt{4}} = 1.08 \quad s_{\bar{x}} = \sqrt{\frac{N \sum \overline{X}_j^2 - \left(\sum \overline{X}_j \right)^2}{N^2 (N-1)}} = \sqrt{\frac{10 \sum \overline{X}_j^2 - \left(\sum \overline{X}_j \right)^2}{90}} =$$

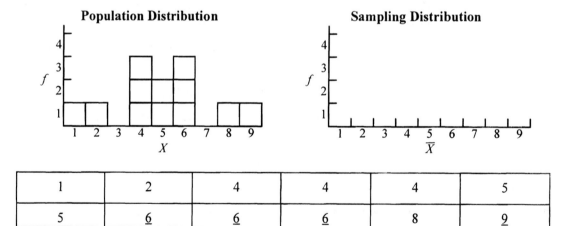

1	2	4	4	4	5
5	$\underline{6}$	$\underline{6}$	$\underline{6}$	8	$\underline{9}$

Here the concept of a **theoretical sampling distribution** is important. A theoretical sampling distribution is a distribution of a statistic over an uncountable number of samples. The theoretical sampling distribution of the mean is the distribution of the mean of an uncountable number of samples of a given size. The **mean** of the theoretical sampling distribution of the mean is symbolized by μ_x in which the μ indicates that the quantity is a [21]_____ of a [22]_____ , and the subscript $\bar{x}$ denotes that it is the mean of a distribution of means (namely, of the [23]_____ of the [24]_____). Since these two theoretical means are equal, a fact that can be expressed in symbols as [25]_____ ,there is no need to retain their subscripts, so it will be understood that μ without subscripts refers both to the mean of the [26]_____ of [27]_____ and to the mean of the theoretical [28]_____ of the [29]_____ . The empirical average of the ten sample means is represented by $\overline{X}_{\bar{x}}$, the mean of the means, and both $\overline{X}$ and $\overline{X}_{\bar{x}}$ are estimators of [30]__ .

Answer Key to Sampling Distributions

[1]	sampling distribution	[11]	sampling distribution	[22]	population distribution
[2]	statistic	[12]	sampling distribution	[23]	sampling distribution
[3]	sampling distribution	[13]	mean	[24]	mean
[4]	statistic	[14]	5	[25]	$\mu_x = \mu_{\bar{x}}$
[5]	samples	[15]	mean	[26]	population
[6]	population	[16]	$\overline{X}$	[27]	raw scores
[7]	empirical sampling	[17]	4.5	[28]	sampling distribution
[8]	theoretical sampling	[18]	$\left(\text{your } \overline{X}_b\right)$	[29]	mean
	distributions	[19]	μ_x	[30]	μ
[9]	parameters	[20]	$\left(\text{your } \overline{X}_{\bar{x}}\right)$		
[10]	statistics	[21]	mean		

Standard Error of the Mean

The sampling distribution of the mean has an average value; it also has a standard deviation. The standard deviation of the theoretical sampling distribution of the mean is symbolized by $\sigma_{\bar{x}}$, in which σ indicates a [1]_____ of a population distribution and the subscript $\bar{x}$ refers to the [2]_____ of the [3]_____ . Statisticians call this quantity, symbolized by [4]__ , the **standard error of the mean**. Immediately below where you calculated the average of the 10 sample means, compute their standard deviation, $s_{\bar{x}}$, which will constitute an empirical estimate of the [5]_____ of the [6]_____ .

There is a specific relationship between the *theoretical* standard error of the mean ($\sigma_{\bar{x}}$) and the theoretical standard deviation of the population of raw scores (σ_x):

$$\sigma_{\bar{x}} = \frac{\sigma_x}{\sqrt{N}}$$

This equation states that the theoretical standard error of the mean ($\sigma_{\bar{x}}$) for samples of size N equals the standard deviation of the population of raw scores divided by $\sqrt{N}$. If the standard deviation of the population of raw scores is 20, the standard error of the mean for samples of size 16 equals [7]_____ . Thus, relative to the standard deviation of raw scores, the standard error of the mean will always be (larger/smaller) [8]_____ .

If the standard deviation of a single sample of scores (s_x) is an estimate of its corresponding population parameter, [9]__ , then s_x from a sample could be substituted for σ_x in this formula to give an estimate of the standard error of the mean:

$$\sigma_{\bar{x}} = \frac{\sigma_x}{\sqrt{N}}$$

$$[10]\, s_{\bar{x}} = \frac{\overline{\quad\quad}}{\sqrt{N}}$$

Therefore, an estimate of $\sigma_{\bar{x}}$, written [11]__ , can be calculated on the basis of only one sample of cases, by dividing the [12]_____ of a single sample by the square root of [13]__ . For example, the standard deviation for the first sample of four cases in Table 8–1 equals 2.38. For this sample [14]$s_x = $ ___ and [15]$N = $ ___ so we estimate $\sigma_{\bar{x}}$ with

$$[16]\, s_{\bar{x}} = \underline{\quad\quad\quad\quad} = \underline{\quad\quad\quad\quad} = \underline{\quad} .$$

The standard error of a statistic is an index of **sampling error**. That is, the mean from one sample will probably not precisely equal the mean from another sample, as demonstrated by your calculations in Table 8–1. This variation from sample to sample in the value of a statistic is called [17]_____ . Since a standard deviation of a score represents its variability or the extent to which the scores deviate from one another, the standard deviation of the mean, called the [18]_____ , is an index of variability in the value of the mean from sample to sample, or[19]_____ . To summarize: A distribution of a statistic is called a [20]_____ . If that statistic is the mean, its distribution is called the [21]_____ of the [22]_____ . The mean of the theoretical sampling distribution of the mean equals the mean of the population of raw scores; this statement can be symbolized by [23]_____ . Therefore, both these quantities are represented simply by [24]__ . The standard deviation of the theoretical sampling distribution of the mean is symbolized by [25]__ and is called the [26]_____ of the [27]_____ . Its relationship to the standard deviation of the population of raw scores can be expressed by [28]_____ . Since the standard deviation of a single sample of scores, [29]__ , estimates [30]__ , the standard error of the mean may be estimated from a single sample of N raw scores by the formula [31]_____ .

Answer Key to Standard Error of the Mean

[1]	standard deviation	[12]	standard deviation	[21]	sampling distribution
[2]	sampling distribution	[13]	N	[22]	mean
[3]	mean	[14]	2.38	[23]	$\mu_{\bar{x}} = \mu_x$
[4]	$\sigma_{\bar{x}}$	[15]	4	[24]	μ
[5]	standard error	[16]	$s_x / \sqrt{N} = 2.38 / \sqrt{4}$	[25]	$\sigma_{\bar{x}}$
[6]	mean		$= 1.19$	[26]	standard error
[7]	$20 / \sqrt{16} = 5$	[17]	sampling error	[27]	mean
[8]	smaller	[18]	standard error of the	[28]	$\sigma_{\bar{x}} = \sigma_x / \sqrt{N}$
[9]	σ_x		mean	[29]	s_x
[10]	s_x	[19]	sampling error	[30]	σ_x
[11]	$s_{\bar{x}}$	[20]	sampling distribution	[31]	$s_{\bar{x}} = s_x / \sqrt{N}$

Interpretation of Sampling Distributions

But what information does the standard error of the mean, $s_{\bar{x}}$, convey? It is an expression of the accuracy of estimating the population mean μ with a sample mean $\overline{X}$. Since the standard error of the mean is the [1]_____ of the sampling distribution of the mean, $s_{\bar{x}}$ estimates the extent to which means of samples of size N vary one from another. The more similar the value of a statistic from sample to sample, the (larger/smaller) [2]_____ its standard error. Therefore, the sample mean is most accurate as an estimator of the population mean when its [3]_____ is as (large/small) [4]_____ as possible.

The sampling distribution of the mean and its standard error possess two very important properties. The first is that regardless of the form of the population distribution of raw scores, as the sample size gets larger the sampling distribution of the mean becomes more normal in form. For example, instead of drawing samples of size $N = 4$ in Table 8–1, suppose that each of the 10 samples was of size $N = 6$ or $N = 8$; then the larger sample size would make the sampling distribution of the mean more [5]_____ in form, even if the population distribution of raw scores was highly skewed left or right. This fact is important because it means that when the sample size is large the percentiles of the normal distribution can be applied to the [6]_____ of the [7]_____ . (If the population distribution is normal, then so is the sampling distribution of the mean for *any* sample size.)

The second property is that the standard error of the mean becomes smaller as the size of the samples used to obtain the sampling distribution increases. If the 10 samples each had been of size $N = 6$ or 8 or 20, the size of $s_{\bar{x}}$ would have decreased as N (increased/decreased) [8]_____ . Since the standard error reflects the extent to which the sample mean varies from one sample to another, this observation implies that means computed on small samples will tend to vary (more/less) [9]_____ than means computed on larger samples. Therefore, X is a more accurate estimator of μ when it is determined on a (large/small) [10]_____ sample.

Answer Key to Interpretation of Sampling Distributions							
[1]	standard deviation	[3]	standard error	[6]	sampling distribution	[8]	increased
		[4]	small			[9]	more
[2]	smaller	[5]	normal	[7]	mean	[10]	large

Applications

How can we use this information to make decisions about the results of our experiments? As an example, suppose that a psychologist and a physician know that a population of college students asked to remember 15 nouns can recall an average of 7 with a standard deviation of 2. Thus, the population parameters of this normal distribution are [1]_____ and [2]_____ . Now the scientists would like to know whether a certain drug has any influence on such memory performance. They first randomly select a student from the population, administer the drug, and record the number of correctly recalled nouns for this drugged student. If the student's score falls at a very low percentile relative to the nondrugged population, then perhaps the drug has retarded memory performance. If the student scores at a high percentile, perhaps the drug has improved memory performance. Following scientific convention, the researcher decides that $P_{.025}$ and $P_{.975}$ will be cutoff limits; a score by the drugged individual equivalent to a percentile for non-drugged individuals between these boundaries will be regarded as usual nondrugged performance, while a percentile more extreme than these values will suggest that the drug has actually had an effect.

Suppose the drugged student's actual score is 11. Since the population distribution is normal in form, this score can be translated into the standard normal deviate defined by:

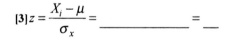

$$[3]\, z = \frac{X_i - \mu}{\sigma_x} = \underline{\hspace{3cm}} = \underline{\hspace{1cm}}$$

Looking in Table A, Appendix 2 of your text, you can see that [4] $z =$ ___ corresponds to a percentile rank of [5] ___ , which is a very good performance. So the drug probably helps memory.

This result encourages the scientists to observe a group of 20 students performing the same task while under the influence of the drug. Suppose the group mean performance is 8.4. How can the scientists determine a percentile rank for this mean, since it is based on a group rather than on a single score? The theoretical sampling distribution of the mean is normally distributed; its mean is symbolized by [6]__ , and its standard deviation, symbolized by $\sigma_{\bar{x}}$, can be determined by the formula [7]_____ . Thus, the observed mean of 8.4 can be translated into a standard normal deviate with respect to the sampling distribution of the mean in essentially the same manner as above:

$$[8]\, z = \frac{\bar{X} - \mu}{\sigma_{\bar{x}}} = \frac{\bar{X} - \mu}{\sigma_x / \sqrt{N}} = \underline{\hspace{3cm}} = \underline{\hspace{1cm}}$$

Looking in Table A, we see that a score of [9]$z = $ ___ corresponds to a percentile rank of [10]__ , which is high enough for the scientists to conclude that the drug probably facilitates memory performance.

Suppose that an educator knows that in a given school system the mean reading score at the end of first grade is 72 with a standard deviation of 10, and 16 children who are instructed with a new reading program have a mean score of 78. If the new program is actually no better than the old one, at what percentile would this special sample fall in the sampling distribution for samples of size $N = 16$?

$$[11]\, \mu = \underline{\hspace{1cm}} , \quad [12]\, \sigma_x = \underline{\hspace{1cm}}$$
$$[13]\, N = \underline{\hspace{1cm}} , \quad [14]\, \sigma_{\bar{x}} = \underline{\hspace{3cm}}$$
$$[15]\, z = (\bar{X} - \mu) / \sigma_{\bar{x}} = \underline{\hspace{3cm}} = \underline{\hspace{1cm}}$$

which has a percentile rank of [16]__ . Since this is beyond $P_{.975}$, it is likely that the new reading program is better than the old one.

Table 8–2 presents guided computational examples as a summary of the points made in this chapter.

Table 8–2 Guided Computational Examples

1. Given a population distribution with mean $\mu = 30$ and $\sigma_x = 6$, the mean $\mu_{\bar{x}}$ and standard deviation (standard error) $\sigma_{\bar{x}}$ of the theoretical sampling distribution of the mean for samples of size $N = 36$ are

$$\mu_{\bar{x}} = \mu_x = \mu = \underline{\quad}$$
$$\sigma_{\bar{x}} = \sigma_x / \sqrt{N} = \underline{\quad} = \underline{\quad}$$

2. If only a single sample of size $N = 36$ is available with mean $\bar{X} = 32$ and standard deviation $s_x = 8$, the parameters μ and $\sigma_{\bar{x}}$ may be estimated respectively by

$$\bar{X}_{\bar{x}} = \bar{X} = \underline{\quad}$$
$$s_{\bar{x}} = s_x / \sqrt{N} = \underline{\quad} = \underline{\quad}$$

3. The percentile rank of a *single score* $X_i = 43$ taken from the normal population in number 1 above can be determined from Table A of Appendix II with

$$z = (X_i - \mu_x) / \sigma_x = \underline{\quad} = \underline{\quad}$$
$$\text{percentile rank} = \underline{\quad}$$

So the probability of a randomly selected score being 43 or higher is $1.00 - .985 = .015$.

4. The percentile rank of a *mean* $\bar{X} = 27.25$ based on a sample of size $N = 16$ drawn from the population in number 1 above can be determined from Table A with

$$z = (\bar{X} - \mu) / \sigma_{\bar{x}} = (\bar{X} - \mu) / (\sigma_x / \sqrt{N}) = \underline{\quad} = \underline{\quad}$$
$$\text{percentile rank} = \underline{\quad}$$

So the probability of a sample of size $N = 16$ having a mean of 27.25 or more is $1.00 - .0336 = .9664$. This assumes that the population distribution of raw scores is normal in form or that N is large enough so that the sampling distribution of the mean is normal.

Answer Key to Applications

[1] $\mu = 7$

[2] $\sigma_x = 2$

[3] $(11 - 7)/2 = 2.00$

[4] 2.00

[5] .9772

[6] μ

[7] $\sigma_{\bar{x}} = \sigma_x / \sqrt{N}$

[8] $(8.4 - 7)/(2/\sqrt{20})$
    $= 3.13$

[9] 3.13

[10] .9991

[11] 72

[12] 10

[13] 16

[14] $10/\sqrt{16} = 2.50$

[15] $(78 - 72)/2.50 = 2.40$

[16] .9918

●●●●● SELF-TEST

1. A quantity computed on a sample is a _____ , whereas that quantity determined on an entire population is called a _____ .

2. What is a simple random sample?

3. Explain the differences between the population distribution of raw scores, an observed sample distribution of raw scores, and a sampling distribution.

4. The standard deviation of a sampling distribution of means is called the

   _____ .

5. Imagine a theoretical distribution of variances determined on all possible samples of size N drawn from a given population of scores. What would such a distribution be called, and what would be the special name given to the standard deviation of such a distribution?

6. What is the relationship between the mean of the theoretical sampling distribution of the mean and the mean of the population of raw scores? What is the relationship between the standard deviation of the theoretical sampling distribution of the mean and the standard deviation of the population of raw scores?

7. The variability of the theoretical sampling distribution of the mean will (always, often) be (smaller than, equal to, larger than) the variability of the population of raw scores.

8. Explain how it is possible to estimate the parameters of a sampling distribution of the mean by observing only one sample.

9. Under what conditions can one assume that the sampling distribution of the mean is normal in form?

10.* Under what conditions are the mean and variance of a theoretical sampling distribution independent of each other?

11.* What is an idealized experiment?

12.* What is the relationship between probability and theoretical relative frequency?

13. If a population of scores is normally distributed with $\mu = 50$ and $\sigma_x = 8$, determine the following probabilities.

a. Sampling a score of 54 or lower, 54 or higher.

b. Sampling a score of 24 or lower, 24 or higher.

c. Obtaining a mean of 52 or higher with a sample of 16 observations, with a sample of 64 observations.

d. Obtaining a mean of 46 or lower with a sample of size 36, with a sample of size 4.

e. Obtaining a mean between 46 and 49 for a sample of size 16.

Questions preceded by an asterisk can be answered on the basis of the discussion in the text, but the discussion in this Study Guide does not answer them.

EXERCISES

1. Are the following procedures likely to produce a simple random sample of the stated population? Explain why or why not?
   a. There are six sections of Introductory Psychology being taught this semester. The classes are labeled one through six and a die toss is used to select which section is the sample of all introductory psychology students. The sample size is 30.
   b. Selecting the person listed in the upper right-hand corner of every fifth page of the telephone book as a sample of the telephone owners with listed numbers in the city.
   c. Selecting every third senior that answers an advertisement in the school paper as a sample of seniors.

   d. From a file of 150 questions, each one written on a card, selecting the first 20 questions after the cards were thoroughly shuffled as a sample of all the questions in the file.

2. Determine $\sigma_{\bar{x}}$ under the following conditions:
   a. $\sigma_x = 5$, $N = 16$
   b. $\sigma_x = 20$, $N = 36$
   c. $\sigma_x = 8$, $N = 64$
   d. $\sigma_x = 25$, $N = 100$

3. Suppose that a psychologist has developed a test to measure test anxiety in college students. The mean of a large population of students who have taken the test is 85 with $\sigma_x = 10$. The psychologist devises a test anxiety reduction technique

that he teaches to a random selection of students. Tentatively assuming that knowing the technique has no effect on anxiety scores, what is the probability of a student who has received training scoring as low or lower than the following?

a. 80   c. 77
b. 92   d. 70

4. Again assuming that the training in exercise 3 has no effect, what is the probability of obtaining a sample mean as low or lower than the following means, given the indicated sample sizes.

a. $\overline{X} = 80$, $N = 9$
b. $\overline{X} = 80$, $N = 16$
c. $\overline{X} = 92$, $N = 25$
d. $\overline{X} = 83$, $N = 100$

5. IQ is approximately normally distributed in the population with $\mu = 100$ and $\sigma_x = 16$. Suppose an educator obtains a truly random sample of three-year-old children and provides them with an intensive home education program administered by parents. After two years of the program, the researcher gives the children an IQ test. If the program has had no real effect on IQ, what is the probability of the group scoring as high as the following or higher?

a. $\overline{X} = 108$, $N = 25$
b. $\overline{X} = 104$, $N = 16$
c. $\overline{X} = 104$, $N = 100$

● ● ● ● ●   ANSWERS

Table 8–2. (1) $\mu = 30$; $\sigma_{\overline{x}} = 1.00$. **(2)** $\overline{X} = 32$; $s_{\overline{x}} = 1.33$. **(3)** $z = 2.17$; 98.5th percentile. **(4)** $z = -1.83$; 3.36th percentile.

Self-Test. (1) Statistic; parameter. **(2)** Each observation in the population has an equal likelihood of being included in the sample, and the observations are selected independently of one another. **(3)** A population distribution of raw scores is a distribution of raw scores in a specified population; an observed sample distribution of raw scores is a distribution of raw scores from a sample from that population;

a sampling distribution is a distribution of a statistic based upon repeated samples of size N from that population. **(4)** Standard error of the mean. **(5)** Sampling distribution of the variance, standard error of the variance. **(6)** $\mu_{\overline{x}} = \mu_x = \mu$, $\sigma_{\overline{x}} = \sigma_x / \sqrt{N}$. **(7)** Always; smaller (except of course when $N = 1$). **(8)** $\overline{X}$ estimates μ and $s_{\overline{x}} = s_x / \sqrt{N}$ (based upon one sample of size N) estimates $\sigma_{\overline{x}}$. **(9)** If the population of raw scores is normal or if the size of the sample is sufficiently large. **(10)** If the population distribution of raw scores is normal (or symmetrical) and the observations are independently and randomly sampled. **(11)** An idealized experiment is a hypothetical experiment composed of an unlimited number of identical repetitions of an event in which all natural factors contributing to the outcome of such events have an appropriate chance of influencing the result. **(12)** Theoretical relative frequency can be interpreted as probability. **(13a)** .6915, .3085; **(13b)** .0006, .9994; **(13c)** .1587, .0228; **(13d)** .0013, .1587; **(13e)** .2857.

Exercises. (la) No, students were not independently selected, once one student was selected (the section), the entire sample was selected; **(1b)** yes; **(1c)** no, only seniors who responded to the advertisement were eligible for the sample; **(1d)** yes. **(2a)** 1.25; **(2b)** 3.33; **(2c)** 1.00; **(2d)** 2.50. **(3a)** .3085; **(3b)** .7580; **(3c)** .2119; **(3d)** .0668. **(4a)** .0668; **(4b)** .0228; **(4c)** .9998; **(4d)** .0228. **(5a)** .0062; **(5b)** .1587; **(5c)** .0062.

● ● ● ● ●

CHAPTER 9

INTRODUCTION TO HYPOTHESIS TESTING: TERMINOLOGY AND THEORY

• • • • •

CONCEPT GOALS

Be sure that you thoroughly understand the following concepts and how to use them in statistical applications.

- ◆ Assumptions for statistical tests:
  - ■ Random and independent sampling
  - ■ Normality of sampling distribution
- ◆ Null and alternative hypotheses
- ◆ Significance level
- ◆ Critical values and decision rules
- ◆ Theoretical relative frequency distributions z and t
- ◆ Sampling error
- ◆ Type I and Type II decision errors
- ◆ Directional and nondirectional tests
- ◆ Degrees of freedom

• • • • •   GUIDE TO MAJOR CONCEPTS

Statistical Inference

Suppose a psychologist and a physician, knowing that a population of normal subjects recalls an average of 7 of 15 nouns ($\sigma_x = 2$) after an 80-minute delay, wondered whether administering a certain drug would influence memory performance in a group of 20 subjects. The researchers decided that if the mean of the drugged group fell between $P_{.025}$ and $P_{.975}$ in the non-drugged population, then the performance of the drugged group would be sufficiently typical of non-drugged people that it would not be interpreted as evidence that the drug had had an effect. However, if the performance of the drugged group was more extreme than these percentile ranks, then the researchers would conclude that the drug probably did have an effect. The mean for the group of drugged people was 8.4, and the standard normal deviate for this mean was

$$z = \frac{\overline{X} - \mu}{\sigma_x / \sqrt{N}} = \frac{8.4 - 7}{2 / \sqrt{20}} = 3.13$$

which has a percentile rank of .9991. Since this would be a very unusual and extreme level of performance for non-drugged individuals, the scientists concluded that the drug probably did influence performance. We now consider this example in greater detail.

Assumptions and Hypotheses

The statistical procedure used by scientists requires certain **assumptions** about the data. Statements about the population that are held to be true throughout the statistical analysis constitute its[1]_____ . The first assumption is that the subjects composing the drugged group were **randomly** and **independently** sampled from the same population as the non-drugged subjects. For the statistical procedures to give accurate probabilities, one must make the

[2]_____ that the subjects in the drugged group were [3]_____ and
[4]_____ sampled from the same [5]_____ as the non-drugged subjects.

The second assumption is that the theoretical sampling distribution of the means of non-drugged subjects is **normal** in form. This assumption is necessary because the percentiles of the standard normal distribution are not accurate unless the population distribution of the statistic being evaluated $(\overline{X})$ is [6]_____ in form. Thus, the assumptions of this statistical technique are that the subjects are [7]_____ and [8]_____ sampled from a common population and that the sampling distribution of the mean is [9]_____ in form.

Next, the logic of the process requires that the scientists state some **hypotheses** about what might be true of this situation. Whereas *assumptions* are held to be true throughout the statistical process and are not tested, statements that represent a set of two or more contradictory and often exhaustive possibilities, only one of which can actually be the case, are known as [10]_____ . For example, one could hypothesize that the observed mean of 8.4 might be reasonably typical of a sample of non-drugged individuals (i.e., the drug has no demonstrable effect). Conversely, the observed performance might be very atypical of the performance of non-drugged people (i.e., the drug has an effect). Both of these [11]_____ cannot be true, so one is tentatively held to be true, and this hypothesis is designated the **null hypothesis, H_0**. In this case, the scientists temporarily suppose that the observed mean is typical of non-drugged performance, that is, that the drug has no effect; this supposition is formally stated as the [12]_____ . An **alternative hypothesis, H_1**, states that the drug does have an effect. The null hypothesis is symbolized by [13]__ , while its alternative is designated [14]__ . In this case,

H_0: The observed mean is computed on a sample drawn from a population with $\mu = 7$ (i.e., the drug has no effect).

H_1: The observed mean is computed on a sample drawn from a population with $\mu \neq 7$ (i.e., the drug has some effect).

In summary, two [15]_____ , which are usually mutually exclusive and exhaustive, are stated. The one that is tentatively held to be true is called the [16]_____ , symbolized by [17]__ . The other is designated the [18]_____ hypothesis, represented by [19]__ . In the present case, the two hypotheses are:

[20] H_0: _____

_____

[21] H_1: _____

_____

Answer Key to Assumptions and Hypotheses

[1]	assumptions	[10]	hypotheses	[19]	H_1
[2]	assumption	[11]	hypotheses	[20]	The observed mean is computed on a sample drawn from a population with $\mu = 7$.
[3]	randomly	[12]	null hypothesis		
[4]	independently	[13]	H_0		
[5]	population	[14]	H_1		
[6]	normal	[15]	hypotheses	[21]	The observed mean is computed on a sample drawn from a population with $\mu \neq 7$.
[7]	randomly	[16]	null hypothesis		
[8]	independently	[17]	H_0		
[9]	normal	[18]	alternative		

Significance Level

The question of whether a sample mean of 8.4 is typical or not typical of the non-drugged population is decided by the **significance level** (or **critical level**), symbolized by the Greek letter α (alpha). The probability value that forms the boundary between rejecting and not rejecting the null hypothesis is the [1]_____ , or [2]__ . That is, if it is probable that the sample mean of 8.4 comes from a population having $\mu = 7$ and $\sigma_x = 2$, then the null hypothesis will not be rejected. Behavioral scientists usually choose a significance level of .05 or one chance in 20 that such a result should occur if the null hypothesis is true, although other values are possible as well. Thus, if the probability is greater than .05 that H_0 is true, do not reject H_0; otherwise, reject H_0. In this case, we say that the [3]_____ is [4]__ ; in symbols, [5]_____ .

Answer Key to Significance Level

[1]	significance level	[3]	significance level	[5]	$\alpha = .05$
[2]	α	[4]	.05		

Decision Rules

Such a probability value needs to be translated into terms that permit a decision with respect to the null hypothesis. Such statements are called **decision rules**, since they specify how high or low the sample mean must be for H_0 to be rejected. Statements that designate the statistical conditions necessary for rejecting the null hypothesis are called [1]_____ . Decision rules are determined by obtaining the points in a theoretical relative frequency distribution (e.g., the standard normal) corresponding to the percentile ranks dictated by α. If the significance level is .05 and the performance of drugged individuals could be better or worse than that of non-drugged individuals, one needs the percentile points corresponding to $P_{.025}$ and $P_{.975}$ of the standard normal distribution. These critical values define a range which in the long run will contain 95% of the means of samples from a population with $\mu = 7$ and $\sigma_x = 2$. The task is to determine what values of z define the middle [2]__ % of the [3]_____ distribution. Thus, look at Table A in the Appendix of your text, not with a specific z value in mind, but with a given proportion of area (i.e., probability) in mind. To find $P_{.975}$, scan the column giving proportions of area between the mean and a specific z. We want to find the value [4]___ . Alternatively, look down the column giving the proportions beyond a given value of z, searching for the value [5]___ . The corresponding z in either case is [6]___ . So the z value corresponding to $P_{.025}$ is [7]___ , and that corresponding to $P_{.975}$ is [8]___ . After translating the observed mean $\overline{X} = 8.4$ into a standard normal deviate—a value which is called "z observed" or z_{obs}—we can state the statistical conditions necessary for a decision on H_0, statements called [9]_____ . If [10]___ falls between [11]___ and [12]___ , we shall not reject H_0; if it falls outside these values, the decision will be to [13]_____ . We can state these rules using the symbols z_{obs}, ± 1.96, $<$, $\leq$, and $\geq$, as follows:

If [14]_____ , do not reject H_0.

If [15]_____ or [16]_____ , reject H_0.

Answer Key to Decision Rules

[1]	decision rules	[7]	−1.96	[13]	reject H_0
[2]	95	[8]	1.96	[14]	$-1.96 < z_{obs} < 1.96$
[3]	standard normal	[9]	decision rules	[15]	$z_{obs} \leq -1.96$
[4]	.4750	[10]	z_{obs}	[16]	$z_{obs} \geq 1.96$
[5]	.0250	[11]	−1.96		
[6]	1.96	[12]	1.96		

Computation and Decision

Given that the experiment has produced a group mean of 8.4, the remaining task is one of **computation** and **decision**. First, the observed mean must be translated into a [1]_____ by the formula

$$z_{obs} = \frac{\overline{X} - \mu}{\sigma_x / \sqrt{N}}$$

In this particular example, [2]$\overline{X} =$ ___ , [3]$\mu =$ ___ , [4]$\sigma_x =$ ___ , and [5]$N =$ ___ , so we get the result [6]$z_{obs} =$ _____ $=$ ___ . Then z_{obs} must be compared with the decision rules: Does z_{obs} fall within the limits of the first rule or the second? In this case, [7]$z_{obs} =$ ___ corresponds to the (first/second) [8]_____ rule, so H_0 is [9]_____ .

What does it mean to *reject* H_0? It means deciding that the drug very probably did have an effect on this type of memory performance, because the statistical evidence is that a mean of 8.4 for a sample of 20 individuals is very unlikely to occur by **sampling error** alone. Sampling error must be considered because even if a group of 20 people was tested *without* receiving the drug, its mean likely would not precisely equal the population mean, $\mu = 7$, nor would its group mean likely equal the observed mean of a second or third group of 20 non-drugged individuals. Samples of individuals do not all have the same mean, and such variation in the mean from sample to sample is attributed to [10]_____ . In the previous chapter we noted that a measure of the amount of sampling error is given by the [11]_____ of the mean. In the present case, the standard error equals [12]$\sigma_{\overline{x}} = \sigma_x / \sqrt{N} =$ _____ $=$ ___ . Consequently, the rationale of the statistical test is to construct the sampling distribution of the mean for samples of size $N = 20$ and ask how likely it is that the observed mean could deviate that much from the population mean simply as a function of [13]_____ . Since $\overline{X} = 8.4$ corresponds to a value of $z_{obs} = 3.13$ in the [14]_____ of the mean, a value that has a percentile rank of .9991, the observed mean is very unlikely to deviate from the population mean by [15]_____ alone. Thus, the null hypothesis is probably wrong, and the researchers decide to [16]_____ , concluding that the drug probably did have an effect.

To summarize this basic process of statistical inference: first we must make the

[17]_____ that the subjects have been [18]_____ and [19]_____

sampled and that the sampling distribution of the mean is [20]_____ in form. We then

propose two contradictory [21]_____ :

[22] __ : _____

_____

[23] __ : _____

_____

We tentatively adopt the [24]_____ , symbolized by [25]__ . Then we arbitrarily select a

probability value, the [26]_____ , or [27]__ ; the customary value of a is [28]__ . This

probability value marks the difference between a decision to [29]_____ H_0 and to

[30]_____ H_0. After stating this probability in terms of standard normal deviates, we

can formalize the [31]_____ as follows:

If [32]_____ , do not reject H_0.

If [33]_____ or [34]_____ , reject H_0.

After conducting the experiment, we translate the observed group mean into a [35]_____

by the formula [36]$z_{obs} =$ _____ . If z_{obs} comes under the second

decision rule, we decide to [37]_____ , because the observed mean is so different from

the population mean of non-drugged individuals that such a discrepancy would not be likely on

the basis of [38]_____ alone.

Answer Key to Computation and Decision

[1]	standard normal deviate	[6]	$(8.4 - 7)/(2/\sqrt{20}) = 3.13$	[11]	standard error
[2]	8.4	[7]	3.13	[12]	$2/\sqrt{20} = .447$
[3]	7	[8]	second	[13]	sampling error
[4]	2	[9]	rejected	[14]	sampling distribution
[5]	20	[10]	sampling error	[15]	sampling error

[16]	reject H_0	[23]	H_1, The observed mean is computed on a sample drawn from a population with $\mu \neq 7$.	[30]	not reject
[17]	assumptions			[31]	decision rules
[18]	randomly			[32]	$-1.96 < z_{obs} < 1.96$
[19]	independently			[33]	$z_{obs} \leq -1.96$
[20]	normal	[24]	null hypothesis	[34]	$z_{obs} \geq 1.96$
[21]	hypotheses	[25]	H_0	[35]	standard normal deviate
[22]	H_0, The observed mean is computed on a sample drawn from a population with $\mu = 7$.	[26]	significance level	[36]	$(\overline{X} - \mu)/(\sigma_x / \sqrt{N})$
		[27]	α	[37]	reject H_0
		[28]	.05	[38]	sampling error
		[29]	reject		

Decision Errors

Statistical inference helps researchers make a decision in the face of partial evidence, but it does not guarantee that the decision is correct. **Decision errors** occur when the statistical process leads to a wrong decision either to reject or not to reject H_0. There are two kinds of [1]_____ . A **Type I** error occurs when the statistical process leads to rejection of H_0 when H_0 is actually correct. In the example of the drugged individuals the statistical process led to the decision to reject H_0, but that decision might be incorrect: the drug may actually have had no effect. If this had been true, we would have made a [2]_____ of the kind called [3]_____ . Given the logic of the statistical procedure, one should expect to make such mistakes occasionally. Even if the drug had no effect, a small percentage of groups would still have mean values more extreme than the limits set in the decision rules, as a result of sampling error alone. That percentage would equal a. If $\alpha = .05$, then when the null hypothesis is actually true, the statistical procedures will lead us to make a mistake and incorrectly reject H_0 in [4]__ % of the decisions. In short, given $\alpha = .05$, the probability of a [5]_____ error is [6]__ .

The second kind of mistake that can occur is called a **Type II** error. When the null hypothesis is actually wrong but the statistical process declares that H_0 should not be rejected, statisticians say that a [7]_____ error has occurred.

To review: there are two kinds of possible incorrect statistical results, called
[8]_____ . If the null hypothesis is actually true but the statistical process decided to
reject it, a [9]_____ error has been committed. Conversely, if the null hypothesis is
actually false but the statistical procedure decides not to reject it, a [10]_____ error has
occurred.

Answer Key to Decision Errors

[1]	decision errors	[4]	5	[7]	Type II	[10]	Type II
[2]	decision error	[5]	Type I	[8]	decision errors		
[3]	Type I	[6]	.05	[9]	Type I		

Directional Tests

In the example of drugged and non-drugged individuals, the researchers could not reasonably
predict in advance whether the drug might have a facilitating or retarding effect on memory.
Consequently, the alternative hypothesis had to be phrased as

H_1:   The observed mean is computed on a sample drawn from a population with $\mu \neq 7$.

This means that H_0 would be rejected if the observed mean were *either* very high or very low
relative to the population mean. This is called a **nondirectional** alternative and leads to a **two-
tailed** statistical test, because the direction of the possible result is not specified and extreme
values in either tail of the sampling distribution will result in rejecting H_0. Thus, if one cannot
firmly predict whether the observed mean will be greater or smaller than the population mean, a
[1]_____ alternative and a [2]_____ test are required.

However, suppose that on the basis of a popular theory or other experiments, the researcher
could confidently predict that the drug would *not* retard memory but might help it. In this case,
the alternative hypothesis would be

H_1:   The observed mean is computed on a sample drawn from a population with $\mu > 7$.

This is a **directional** alternative, and it prompts a **one-tailed** test of H_0. In this event, an observed mean must be greater than P_{95} to reject H_0. P_{95} is selected instead of P_{975} because $\alpha = .05$ means that H_0 is to be rejected when the value of z_{obs} is in a range too extreme to be attained by more than 5% of the cases by sampling error alone. Since the drug is not likely to produce extremely low scores, drug-induced deviations are likely to be only positive. The entire critical region thus is placed in one tail of the distribution to keep the probability of a type I error at a, since the researchers know before the experiment that it is almost impossible to obtain an extreme value in the other tail. Therefore, P_{95} is the critical value for a [3]_____ alternative (a [4]_____ test) at [5]$\alpha = $ ___ .

Answer Key to Directional Tests

[1]	nondirectional	[3]	directional	[5]	.05
[2]	two-tailed	[4]	one-tailed		

The *t* Distribution

In the example given in this and the previous chapter, the population standard deviation, σ_x, and the population standard error of the mean, σ_x were known values. This rarely happens in actual research practice. We have already seen that the sample $s_{\bar{x}}$ is an estimator of the population $\sigma_{\bar{x}}$. Thus, substituting $s_{\bar{x}}$ for $\sigma_{\bar{x}}$, the formula translating an observed mean into a standard score becomes [1]_____ .

However, when $\sigma_{\bar{x}}$ is estimated by $s_{\bar{x}}$, the standard normal distribution is not the appropriate theoretical sampling distribution to use. A new distribution, the *t distribution*, is used to determine the probability that an observed mean could be obtained by sampling error alone. When the standard error of the mean is estimated with [2]___ , the appropriate distribution and formula are [3] ___ = _____ .

It happens that there is a different *t* distribution for every size of sample, or more accurately, for every number of **degrees of freedom** in the calculation of the statistic being examined. In this case, the number of degrees of freedom, *df*, is $N - 1$. The critical values of *t* for directional and nondirectional tests for several different degrees of freedom are presented in Table B in Appendix 2 in your text. Look at that table now. Suppose a sample of 20 people was being considered; the particular t distribution to be used depends on the number of [4]_____ , and in this case, [5] $df =$ _____ = __ . Not knowing in advance whether the drug would help or hinder memory, the scientists proposed a [6]_____ alternative with $\alpha = .05$. The value in the table corresponding to these circumstances is [7]__ . Since the t distribution, like the z, is symmetrical about its mean of 0, the two critical values are [8]__ and [9]__ . The decision rules are

If [10]_____ , do not reject H_0.

If [11]_____ or [12]_____ , reject H_0.

Suppose this same experiment had yielded a sample mean of 9.1 and a sample standard deviation of 3, based upon $N = 25$. Since the standard error of the mean $s_{\bar{x}}$ equals the sample standard deviation divided by the square root of N (i.e., $s_{\bar{x}} = s_x / N$) and the population mean is still $\mu = 7$, then [13] $t_{obs} =$ _____ = _____ = __ . The decision would be to [14]_____ .

Similarly, suppose 16 people had been observed and a directional test conducted because other research indicated the drug should help (not hinder) memory. Also assume for this example that $\alpha = .01$. Therefore the critical value of t at $\alpha = .01$ would be [15]_____ , and the decision rules would be

If [16]_____ , do not reject H_0.

If [17]_____ , reject H_0.

Finally, given a normal population with $\mu = 80$, what is the probability that a sample of 25 should have a mean as extreme as 71 (nondirectional) by sampling error alone if $s_x = 20$? Use $\alpha = .05$. Complete all the details of this problem in Table 9–1.

Table 9–1 Guided Computational Example

Hypotheses

H_0: _____

_____

H_1: _____

_____

(directional/non-directional)

Assumptions and Conditions

1. _____

2. _____

Significance Level

$\alpha =$ __

Decision Rules

If _____ , do not reject H_0.

If _____ , reject H_0.

Computation

$t = (\overline{X} - \mu)/(s_x/\sqrt{N}) =$ _____ $=$ _____

$df = N - 1 =$ __

Decision

_____ (Reject/Do not reject) H_0.

---

[7]	2.093	[11]	$t_{obs} \leq -2.093$	[14]	reject H_0
[8]	−2.093	[12]	$t_{obs} > 2.093$	[15]	2.602
[9]	2.093	[13]	$(\overline{X} - \mu)/(s_x/\sqrt{N}) =$	[16]	$t_{obs} < 2.602$
[10]	$-2.093 < t_{obs} < 2.093$		$(9.1 - 7)/(3/\sqrt{25}) = 3.50$	[17]	$t_{obs} \geq 2.602$

● ● ● ● ●   # SELF-TEST

1.* What is wrong with the following statements?
   a. "The statistical test found the statistical assumptions to be invalid."
   b. "The statistical test rejected both hypotheses."
   c. "The statistical test proved that the null hypothesis could not possibly be correct."

2. Why is it necessary to assume that the sampling distribution of the mean is normal?

3. Although direct knowledge of the shape of the sampling distribution of the mean is rare, its normality may be assumed under what two conditions?

4. Why is it necessary to hold tentatively that the null hypothesis is true?

5. What relationship does the significance level have to the probability of a Type I error?

6.* Why do we never *accept* H_0?

7. What role does the sampling distribution play in the logic of hypothesis testing?

8. What is a critical value?

9. Define Type I and Type II errors.

10.* Define the *power* of a test.

11. When a directional alternative is appropriate, why is the entire critical region placed in one tail?

12. Under what circumstances is it necessary to use the *t* rather than *z* distribution?

13.* Define and give an example of degrees of freedom.

14. What is the critical value for a one-tailed *t* test of a score from a single group if $\alpha = .05$, $N = 17$, and $s_x = 3$?

*Questions preceded by an asterisk can be answered on the basis of the discussion in the text, but the discussion in this Study Guide does not answer them.

• • • • •   EXERCISES

1. If the population average income for owners of Mamma Mia Pizza Shops is \$40,000 with $\sigma_x = \$5500$, what is the probability that a sample of 121 owners who have had a special course on pizza store management should average \$40,800 a year if the course really has no influence on income levels? Follow the general outline given in Table 9–1 in setting up and solving this problem. Use $\alpha = .05$, non-directional.

2.* The population distribution of annual incomes in exercise 1 is not likely to be normal in form. How did you handle this problem?

3. The population mean brain-weight at 90 days of age for a particular strain of inbred mice is 3.36 grams. A group of 25 of these mice is reared in a special environment designed to stimulate diverse kinds of learning. The 90-day mean brain-weight of these mice is 3.40 with $s_x = .05$. Following the outline in Table 9–1, test the hypothesis that the special environment has no effect on brain-weight. Use $\alpha = .05$.

4. Suppose it is known from a national survey that 18-year-olds rate their relationship with their parents to be 2.75 on a scale ranging from 1 (very poor) to 5 (very good). However, a sample of 16 adolescents who had recently been arrested for delinquent acts had an average rating of 1.97 with a standard deviation of 1.20. Previous research also discovered a similar difference. Test the hypothesis that there is no evidence that delinquents feel that their relationship with their parents is less good than the population of nondelinquents. Again follow the outline in Table 8–1 and use $\alpha = .05$.

• • • • •   ANSWERS

Table 9–1. Hypotheses: H_0: The observed mean is computed on a sample drawn from a population with $\mu = 80$. H_1: The observed mean is computed on a sample drawn from a population with $\mu \neq 80$ (nondirectional.) *Assumptions*: The subjects are randomly and independently sampled; the sampling distribution of the mean is normal. *Significance level*: $\alpha = .05$. *Decision rules*: Non-directional test with $df = N - 1 = 24$. If $-2.064 < t_{obs} < 2.064$, do not reject H_0. If $t_{obs} \leq -2.064$ or

$t_{obs} \geq 2.064$, reject H_0. *Computation*:
$t_{obs} = -2.25$; $df = 24$. *Decision*: Reject H_0.

Self-Test. (1a) The statistical procedures test the hypotheses, not the assumptions; **(1b)** Since the null and alternative hypotheses are mutually exclusive, they both cannot be false; **(1c)** The logic of the statistical test permits the rejection of the null hypothesis because a sample value was improbable, but even if a value is extremely unlikely, it is never shown to be impossible. **(2)** Normality of the sampling distribution of the mean is required to use the percentiles of the standard normal or t theoretical relative frequency distributions. **(3)** Normality is assumed if X is normally distributed in the population or if N is large, because the sampling distribution of the mean approaches normality as N becomes large. **(4)** Statistical logic requires that H_0 be held true and the statistical results examined to determine if the findings are consistent with H_0. **(5)** The significance level (a) is the probability of a Type I error. **(6)** The statistical procedures tentatively assume H_0 to be true until there is evidence sufficient to contradict that hypothesis. Therefore, the evidence can only contradict H_0, because H_0 has already been *assumed* (not *proved*) true. **(7)** The

sampling distribution and its standard error represent the extent to which statistics would be expected to vary from sample to sample on the basis of sampling error alone. **(8)** The critical value(s) define the boundary between rejecting and not rejecting H_0. **(9)** A Type I error occurs when H_0 is actually true but the statistical decision is to reject it. A Type II error occurs when H_0 is actually false but the statistical decision is not to reject it. **(10)** The power of a test is the probability of correctly rejecting H_0. **(11)** The entire critical region is placed in one tail to keep the probability of a Type I error at a, because such an error is almost impossible to make in the other tail under these circumstances. **(12)** When $\sigma_{\bar{x}}$ is estimated with $s_{\bar{x}}$. **(13)** The number of degrees of freedom is the number of quantities that are free to vary when calculating a statistic. The df for $\overline{X}$ is N; for s_x it is $N-1$. **(14)** 1.746.

Exercises. (1) *Hypotheses*: H_0: The observed mean is computed on a sample from a population with $\mu = 40,000$. H_1: The observed mean is computed on a sample drawn from a population with $\mu \neq 40,000$. *Assumptions*: The subjects are randomly and independently sampled, and $\overline{X}$ is normally distributed. *Significance level*: .05. *Decision rules*: Given a non-directional test at .05, if $-1.96 < z_{\text{obs}} < 1.96$, do not reject H_0; if $z_{\text{obs}} \leq -1.96$ or $z_{\text{obs}} \geq 1.96$, reject H_0. *Computation*: $z_{\text{obs}} = 1.60$. *Decision*: Do not reject H_0. The evidence is not strong enough to conclude that the course is associated with a higher income level. **(2)** The sample size was large enough to assume that the sampling distribution of $\overline{X}$ was normal even if the population distribution of X was not. **(3)** Given a nondirectional test at .05 with $df = 24$, critical value are ± 2.064; $t_{\text{obs}} = 4.00$.

Reject H_0. **(4)** Given a directional test at .05 with $df = 15$, the critical value of t is 1.753. If $t_{\text{obs}} > -1.753$, do not reject H_0. If $t_{\text{obs}} \leq -1.753$, reject H_0. $t_{\text{obs}} = -2.60$. Reject H_0. (Note: Sometimes when testing directional hypotheses, the sequence of the means in the numerator is arranged to produce a positive difference. In this case, the signs and inequalities would be reversed accordingly in the critical values, decision rules, and a.)

CHAPTER 10

ELEMENTARY TECHNIQUES OF HYPOTHESIS TESTING • • • • •

CONCEPT GOALS

Be sure that you thoroughly understand the following concepts and how to use them in statistical applications.

- ◆ *t* test of the difference between two independent group means
- ◆ *t* test of the difference between two correlated group means
- ◆ Test of the significance of *r*
- ◆ Test of the difference between two correlation coefficients

• • • • • GUIDE TO MAJOR CONCEPTS

Introduction

This chapter presents several techniques of statistical inference commonly used in social science. Although the formulas differ from one technique to another, it is important to realize that the basic logic of the process is the same in each case. First, we assume for the entire analysis that the data and population have certain characteristics. These are the [1]_____ of the analysis. Then we pose a set of mutually exclusive and usually exhaustive [2]_____ about the parameters of the population and tentatively hold one of the hypotheses to be true. This is the [3]_____ . A probability level called the [4]_____ is selected and used to

205

specify a set of [5]_____ . Then we evaluate the observed data relative to an appropriate

[6]_____ distribution, usually a known theoretical [7]_____ distribution, such

as the [8]_____ or the [9]_____ distribution. This observed z, t, or other

statistic is compared to the [10]_____ to make the decision whether to

[11]_____ the [12]_____. This comparison reveals the probability that the

observed results would occur under the null hypothesis by [13]_____ alone.

Answer Key to Introduction

[1]	assumptions	[6]	sampling	[11]	reject
[2]	hypotheses	[7]	relative frequency	[12]	null hypothesis
[3]	null hypotheses	[8]	standard normal	[13]	sampling error
[4]	significance level	[9]	t		
[5]	decision rules	[10]	decision rules		

t Tests

Several approaches to be presented rely on the t distribution. Although the specific terms of the formulas that translate the statistics into t values differ, the general logic of the formulas is the same. Recall from the previous chapter that $t = (\overline{X} - \mu) / s_{\overline{x}}$. This expression is quite general: it could be written

$$t = \frac{(\text{a value}) - (\text{population mean of such values})}{(\text{estimate of the standard error of such values})}$$

That is, if the "value" is a sample statistic, then a sample statistic minus the population mean of all such statistics divided by an estimate of the standard error of that statistic is distributed as t. In the previous chapter the sample statistic was the sample mean. The population mean of sample means is symbolized by [1]__ , and an estimate of the standard error of such means is symbolized by [2]__ .

But now suppose that the sample statistic is the difference between two sample means. Then the formula will read: the difference between two sample means minus the difference between those means in their [3]_____ divided by an estimate of the [4]_____ of the difference between means is distributed as [5]___ . If the difference between two sample means is symbolized by $\overline{X}_1 - \overline{X}_2$, the difference between their population means by $\mu_1 - \mu_2$, and the estimated standard error of this difference by $s_{\overline{x}_1 - \overline{x}_2}$, then the formula will read

$$[6]\, t = \left(\right) - \left(\right) / .$$

The null hypothesis states that the two population parameters do not differ from each other, that is, that $\mu_1 = \mu_2$ and thus that $[7]\, \mu_1 - \mu_2 = $ ___ . Therefore, under the null hypothesis the formula reduces to $t = (\overline{X}_1 - \overline{X}_2) / s_{\overline{x}_1 - \overline{x}_2}$ and one needs only to determine the proper expression for $s_{\overline{x}_1 - \overline{x}_2}$.

Answer Key to t Tests

[1]	μ	[4]	standard error	[6]	$(\overline{X}_1 - \overline{X}_2) - (\mu_1 - \mu_2) /$
[2]	$s_{\overline{x}}$	[5]	t		$s_{\overline{x}_1 - \overline{x}_2}$
[3]	populations			[7]	0

Independent Groups

The problem discussed in the last chapter concerning the effect of a drug on memory performance would be better approached by having two separate samples that are treated exactly alike except that one group receives an injection of the drug and the other group receives an injection of a neutral saline solution. We could then directly compare the performance of the drugged group with that of the control group, which received the neutral saline solution. Statistically, that amounts to determining the probability that the two observed sample means differ from each other by [1]_____ alone. We shall consider this approach in detail.

The basic question is whether the drug has an effect. We can translate this into two mutually exclusive and exhaustive statistical hypotheses, the **null hypothesis** and an **alternative hypothesis**. We want to decide whether the means of the populations of nondrugged and of drugged individuals are really identical. The proposition that they are identical, which we will tentatively assume to be true, is called the [2]_____ . It can be stated in symbols as [3]__ : _____ .

On the other hand, these population means might not be equal. This is the [4]_____ , which we can write as [5]__ : _____ .

The assumptions necessary to address these questions are (1) that the individuals in the two groups are **randomly** and **independently** sampled, (2) that the two groups are **independent** of each other, (3) that the population variances for the two groups are **homogeneous**, and (4) that the distribution of $\overline{X}_1 - \overline{X}_2$ is **normal** in form. If the participants are to be typical of the population, they must be [6]_____ and [7]_____ sampled. Moreover, the two groups cannot be matched or related in any way; that is, the groups must be [8]_____ of each other. If the groups are to be compared in the proposed manner, they must have the same variance in the population, a characteristic referred to as [9]_____ of [10]_____ . To use the percentiles of the t distribution, the distribution of $\overline{X}_1 - \overline{X}_2$ must be [11]_____ , which will be the case if the two population distributions of raw scores are [12]_____ or if the sample sizes are [13]_____ .

The next step is to determine the **degrees of freedom**, adopt a **significance level**, and state the **decision rules**. Suppose $N_1 = 15$ and $N_2 = 13$. The number of degrees of freedom for the statistical test to be made is $N_1 + N_2 - 2$. In this case the [14]_____ equal [15]__ + __ − __ = __ . Suppose we select .05 as the [16]_____ . We can now state the [17]_____ . Looking at the t distribution in Table B of Appendix 2 of the text, we see that a nondirectional test at the .05 level with $df = 26$ has critical values of [18]__ and [19]__ . If the observed value of t is between –2.056 and +2.056, the decision rule will be [20]_____ . In this case we would have insufficient evidence that the drug has had an effect. However, if the observed value of t is less than or equal to –2.056 or greater than or equal to +2.056, then we would decide to [21]_____ ; that is, we would conclude that the drug probably has an effect.

A formal guided outline of this example is given in Table 10–1. In the appropriate places in that table, state the hypotheses, assumptions, and decision rules. Then complete the computational procedures outlined in the table.

Table 10–1 Guided Computational Example for a Test of the Difference between Two Independent Means

Hypotheses

H_0: _____

H_1: _____ (nondirectional/directional)

Assumptions and Conditions

1. The subjects are _____ and _____ sampled.

2. The groups are _____ .

3. The population variances are _____ .

4. The population distribution of _____ is _____ in form.

Decision Rules (from Table B of Appendix 2 in the text)

Given a significance level of __ , a _____ test, and $df = N_1 + N_2 - 2 = \underline{\ \ }$:

If _____ , _____ .

If _____ , _____ .

Computation

	Drugged	Non-Drugged
	$N_1 = 15$	$N_2 = 13$
	$\overline{X}_1 = 9.1$	$\overline{X}_2 = 7.0$
	$s_1^2 = 9$	$s_2^2 = 4$

$$t_{obs} = \frac{\overline{X}_1 - \overline{X}_2}{\sqrt{\left[\dfrac{(N_1-1)s_1^2 + (N_2-1)s_2^2}{N_1 + N_2 - 2}\right]\left[\dfrac{1}{N_1} + \dfrac{1}{N_2}\right]}} = \underline{\hspace{3cm}} = \underline{\hspace{1.5cm}}$$

Decision

_____ H_0.

Since [22]t_{obs} = __ , which comes under the [23]_____ decision rule, we
[24]_____ H_0. Thus, the data suggest that the observed difference between the means of
the drugged and non-drugged samples was so large relative to what one would expect by
[25]_____ alone that the samples probably do not come from populations having the
same means. That is, the drug is probably effective.

Answer Key to Independent Groups

[1]	sampling error	[8]	independent	[15]	$15 + 13 - 2 = 26$	[21]	reject H_0
[2]	null hypothesis	[9]	homogeneity	[16]	significance	[22]	2.14
[3]	$H_0: \mu_1 = \mu_2$	[10]	variance		level	[23]	second
[4]	alternative	[11]	normal	[17]	decision rules	[24]	reject
	hypothesis	[12]	normal	[18]	−2.056	[25]	sampling error
[5]	$H_1: \mu_1 \neq \mu_2$	[13]	large	[19]	+2.056		
[6]	randomly	[14]	degrees of	[20]	do not reject		
[7]	independently		freedom		H_0		

Correlated Groups

Consider another situation. An educator tests a sample of 12 nursery-school children to determine
how well they grasp the concept of conservation of volume. This is tested by determining whether
they realize that an amount of clay remains the same regardless of whether it is rolled into the
shape of a long sausage or into a compact ball. The educator then institutes a program designed to
give the children experiences that should improve their understanding of conservation of volume.
After the training sessions, the same test that was initially given to the children is repeated. The
children scored a mean of 6.0 on the first testing, but after the training the mean was 7.5. How
likely is it that the mean score would have risen to 7.5 even without the training program, simply
as a function of sampling error? That is, is the training program effective?

There is an important difference between the previous example and this one. Whereas before
the measurements were made on two groups that were [1]_____ , the pretraining and
posttraining scores in this situation are assessed on the same children. Therefore, the groups of
measurements are **correlated**. Whenever the measurements in the groups of scores are not

independent but [2]_____ , a slightly different statistical procedure for testing the null hypothesis is required.

The hypotheses are determined in the same way as for the previous case. The hypothesis to be tested, namely the [3]_____ , is that the population means for the first and second testings are identical. In symbols, [4]__ : _____ . The statement of the [5]_____ is slightly different in this particular problem. Whereas the previous example had a **nondirectional** alternative, this test has a **directional** alternative. Before, we wondered whether the drug had any effect, positive or negative. Thus the alternative hypothesis was [6]_____ and was written [7]__ : _____ . In the present situation, no one would expect the children to perform less well on the second test than on the first one, so the alternative is said to be [8]_____ . Given that μ_1 is the population mean on the first test and μ_2 the population mean on the second test, the alternative hypothesis can be written [9]__ : _____ .

The assumptions for this test are that the children have been [10]_____ and [11]_____ sampled and that the pairs of scores have been obtained from the same or related individuals. That is, the two sets of measurements are [12]_____ . A third assumption is that the distribution of the differences between pairs of scores is [13]_____ .

If we adopt the .05 level of [14]_____ with $N - 1 = 12 - 1 = 11$ [15]_____ , we determine the critical value by searching in the t table under a [16]_____ test at the [17]__ level with [18]$df = $ __ . Look up in Table B of your text this [19]_____ , which is [20]__ . You can now state two [21]_____ , being careful to remember that this is a [22]_____ test. Therefore, [23]_____ , [24]_____ ; [25]_____ , [26]_____ .

The computational procedure is somewhat different in the case of correlated groups, and it is summarized in Table 10–2. Notice that the posttraining and pretraining test scores are listed in that order, since the second score is expected to be larger and the decision rule for rejecting H_0 was for large positive t's. Then the scores are subtracted, and the remainder is placed in the column D_i. Do this now. Then square these values and place the results in the column D_i^2. Now separately total the D_i and D_i^2 columns, compute $(\sum D_i)^2$, and calculate the value of t_{obs} with the formula provided. The logic of this procedure is that the differences between test scores, D_i, should have a mean that approaches zero in the long run if there is no difference in the populations from which the samples were drawn. The above formula yields a t_{obs} which can be used to obtain the probability that on the average the [27]___ deviate from [28]_____ by [29]_____ alone.

The value of t_{obs} for these data is [30]___ , which is consistent with the decision rule to [31]_____ . The teaching program apparently improved performance of the children. Finish Table 10–2 now, and use it as a guide for solving future problems of this type.

Answer Key to Correlated Groups

[1]	independent	[12]	correlated	[23]	If $t_{obs} < 1.796$		
[2]	correlated	[13]	normal	[24]	do not reject H_0		
[3]	null hypothesis	[14]	significance	[25]	If $t_{obs} \geq 1.796$		
[4]	$H_0: \mu_1 - \mu_2$	[15]	degrees of freedom	[26]	reject H_0		
[5]	alternative hypothesis	[16]	directional	[27]	D_i		
[6]	nondirectional	[17]	.05	[28]	zero		
[7]	$H_1: \mu_1 \neq \mu_2$	[18]	11	[29]	sampling error		
[8]	directional	[19]	critical value	[30]	2.45		
[9]	$H_1: \mu_2 > \mu_1$	[20]	1.796	[31]	reject H_0		
[10]	randomly	[21]	decision rules				
[11]	independently	[22]	directional				

Significance of r

Suppose a researcher takes a random sample of 42 women between 18 and 50 years of age and gives them a questionnaire to assess their attitudes toward women's roles in society. Higher scores are interpreted to indicate a more feminist attitude. The researcher observes a correlation of −.33 between age and a feminist attitude; that is, younger women tend to receive higher scores than older women. The researcher wants to know the probability that such a correlation is a chance result, and that the population correlation is actually $\rho = .00$. That is, the value of −.33 observed for r may be merely a consequence of [1]_____ .

Table 10–2 Guided Computational Example for a Test of the Difference between Two Correlated Means

Hypotheses H_0: _____ H_1: _____ (nondirectional/directional)

Assumptions and Conditions

1. The subjects have been _____ and _____ sampled.

2. The scores of the two groups are _____ .

3. The population distribution of D_i is _____ (i.e., X_1 and X_2 distributions are normal or N is large).

Decision Rules (from Table B of Appendix 2 in the text)

Given a significance level of __ , a _____ test, and $df = N - 1 =$ ___ :

If _____ : _____ .

If _____ : _____ .

Data and Computation

Participant	X_2 Second Test	X_1 First Test	$D_i = (X_{2i} - X_{1i})$	D_i^2
A	6	5		
B	7	6		
C	3	4		
D	6	4		
E	2	2		
F	3	1		
G	4	2		
H	4	5		
I	7	5		
J	4	5		
K	9	7		
L	6	3		

$N =$ ___ $\sum D_i =$ ___ $\sum D_i^2 =$ ___

$(\sum D_i)^2 =$ ___

$$t_{obs} = \frac{\sum D_i}{\sqrt{[N \sum D_i^2 - (\sum D_i)^2]/(N-1)}} = \underline{\hspace{3cm}} = \underline{\hspace{3cm}}$$

Decision   _____ H_0 .

The hypotheses are that the correlation in the population is zero versus that it is not zero. Specifically, the null hypothesis is [2]_____ , while the alternative hypothesis is [3]_____ . One must assume that the participants are [4]_____ and [5]_____ sampled and that the distributions of both X (attitude score) and Y (age) are [6]_____ in form.

The critical values of r for various df are listed in Table C in Appendix 2 of the text. Turn to Table C now, and observe that it is very similar in form to the t table. To use it, first decide whether the alternative hypothesis is [7]_____ or [8]_____ and adopt a [9]_____ . In the present example, the alternative hypothesis is that the population correlation is not .00, so a [10]_____ test is required. Notice in Table C that the $df = N - 2$ are listed down the left side. Assuming a significance level of .05 and remembering that $N = 42$ (and thus $df = N - 2 = 40$), we see that the critical value of r is [11]___ . This means that if the observed r is less than or equal to $-.3044$ or greater than or equal to $.3044$, then H_0 should be rejected. For this illustration, $r = -.33$, so H_0 is [12]_____ . It appears that the younger the woman, the more feminist her attitude. A formal summary of this problem is presented in Table 10–3, which you should complete now.

Answer Key to Significance of r

[1]	sampling error	[5]	independently	[9]	significance level
[2]	$H_0: \rho = 0$	[6]	normal	[10]	nondirectional
[3]	$H_1: \rho \neq 0$	[7]	directional	[11]	.3044
[4]	randomly	[8]	nondirectional	[12]	rejected

The Difference between Two Correlation Coefficients

Suppose a researcher is interested in the relationship between the number of hours per week that children viewed aggressive or violent television programs and the number of physically aggressive acts those children displayed during two weeks of nursery school. The correlation between these two measurements is .46 for a group of 23 boys but only .22 for a sample of 28 girls. Do the sexes really differ in the degree of this relationship? Specifically, what is the probability that the observed difference between .46 and .22 is simply a consequence of [1]_____ and that in the population there is actually no difference between the two correlations?

Table 10–3 Guided Computational Example for a Test of the Significance of a Correlation Coefficient

Hypotheses

H_0: _____

H_1: _____ (nondirectional/directional)

Assumptions and Conditions

1. Subjects are _____ and _____ sampled.

2. The population distributions of both X and Y are _____ in form.

Decision Rules (from Table C of Appendix 2 in the text)

Given a significance level of __ , a _____ test, and $df = N - 2 =$ __ :

If _____ , _____ .

If _____ , _____ .

Computation

$r_{obs} =$ __

Decision

_____ H_0.

The hypotheses are that the population correlations are equal versus that they are not equal. In symbols, the null hypothesis is [2]_____ and the alternative is [3]_____ . It is assumed that the subjects are [4]_____ and [5]_____ sampled, that the two groups are [6]_____ of each other, and that the population distributions of X and Y for both groups are [7]_____ in form. Both N_1 and N_2 must be large—greater than [8]__ —for an accurate result, because this statistical test requires the use of the standard normal distribution. For a nondirectional test at the .05 level, Table A in Appendix 2 of the text shows that the critical values of z are [9]__ , and the decision rules are [10]_____ , [11]_____ ; [12]_____ , [13]_____ .

The computation of z_{obs} proceeds as follows. First, an unusual step is taken—the values of r, .46 and .22 in this case, must be transformed into z_r values by using Table D in Appendix 2 of the text. Correlation coefficients are not usually normally distributed, and this transformation normalizes them so that the standard normal distribution can be used. Turn to this table now. Notice that the table lists values of r from .000 to .995 and their corresponding transformed values, z_r. For $r_1 = .46$, [14] $z_{r_1} = $ ___ , and for $r_2 = .22$, [15] $z_{r_2} = $ ___ . Then use the formula

$$z_{obs} = \frac{z_{r_1} - z_{r_2}}{\sqrt{\dfrac{1}{N_1 - 3} + \dfrac{1}{N_2 - 3}}}$$

in which N_1 and N_2 are the number of pairs of scores entering into r_1 and r_2, respectively. In this example, [16] $N_1 = $ ___ and [17] $N_2 = $ ___ . Thus,

[18] $z_{obs} = $ _____ $= $ _____ $= $ __

This value of z_{obs} does not exceed the z_{crit} of ± 1.96, so H_0 (is/is not) [19] _____ rejected. A formal outline of this problem is presented in Table 10–4, which you should now complete.

Answer Key to The Difference between Two Correlation Coefficients

[1]	sampling error	[9]	± 1.96	[16]	23
[2]	$H_0: \rho_1 = \rho_2$	[10]	If $-1.96 < z_{obs} < 1.96$	[17]	28
[3]	$H_1: \rho_1 \neq \rho_2$	[11]	do not reject H_0	[18]	$[.497 - .224]$
[4]	randomly	[12]	If $z_{obs} \leq -1.96$ or		$\div \sqrt{[(1/20) + (1/25)]} = $
[5]	independently		$z_{obs} \geq 1.96$		$.273 / .300 = .91$
[6]	independent	[13]	reject H_0	[19]	is not
[7]	normal	[14]	.497		
[8]	20	[15]	.224		

Table 10–4 Guided Computational Example for a Test of the Difference between Two Correlation Coefficients

Hypotheses

H_0: _____

H_1: _____ (nondirectional/directional)

Assumptions and Conditions

1. The subjects are _____ and _____ sampled.

2. The two groups are _____ .

3. The population distributions of X and Y for both groups are _____ in form.

4. Both N_1 and N_2 are greater than __ .

Decision Rules

Given a significance level of __ and a _____ test:

If _____ , _____ .

If _____ , _____ .

Computation

	Group 1 (Boys)	Group 2 (Girls)
	$N_1 = 23$	$N_2 = 28$
	$r_1 = .46$	$r_2 = .22$
	$z_{r_1} =$ __	$z_{r_2} =$ __

$$z_{obs} = \frac{z_{r_1} - z_{r_2}}{\sqrt{\dfrac{1}{N_1 - 3} + \dfrac{1}{N_2 - 3}}} = \underline{\hspace{3cm}} = \underline{\hspace{2cm}}$$

Decision

_____ H_0 .

● ● ● ● ●   SELF-TEST

1. The formula for testing a single sample mean $[t = (\overline{X} - \mu) / s_{\overline{x}}]$ can be generalized to handle any sample statistic. Express the generalized formula in words.

2. If the sample statistic is the difference between two means, what is the null hypothesis?

3. Why must a different statistical technique be employed when the same individuals are measured twice than when the two groups of measurements are made on different random samples?

4. Under what conditions will the assumption of a normal distribution of $\overline{X}_1 - \overline{X}_2$ be met?

5. In a test of two correlated means, what is the mean of the sampling distribution, assuming the null hypothesis to be true?

6. Why is it necessary to assume in so many of the techniques described in this chapter that the sample distribution is normal in form?

7.* How is it possible to have a significant correlation between two variables for girls and no significant correlation for boys, but no significant difference between the two correlations? What does such a situation tell us about interpreting statistical significance?

8.* Is it possible for there to be a significant difference between two correlated means but no correlation between the two sets of measures on which means were computed? Explain.

*Questions preceded by an asterisk can be answered on the basis of the discussion in the text, but the discussion in this Study Guide does not answer them.

● ● ● ● ●   EXERCISES

Follow the appropriate guided computational example as an outline for each statistical test requested in these exercises. Assume the .05 level of significance except where another is stated, but you will need to decide whether the alternative hypothesis is directional or nondirectional from the information given in the question.

1. Two samples of 21 men each are brought into a room and told they are to help another person in the next room learn a

simple problem by giving him an electric shock as a punishment for wrong responses. The participant has a dial with 20 levels of shock that he can administer, 20 being the highest level. Another person is with the participant during the observation; he encourages one group of participants to administer higher and higher levels of shock, whereas he does not so encourage members of the other group. The person supposedly receiving the shocks and the "persuader" are really actors, but the people administering the "shocks" do not know this. The point of the study is to determine whether people are influenced by pressure from others when given the opportunity to hurt other individuals without fear of disapproval. The hypothetical results are these: The average shock level administered by the people who were encouraged to use higher levels was $16.2(s_1^2 = 12)$, and that administered by the other group was $13.8(s_2^2 = 13)$. Evaluate the significance of this difference.[1]

2. Psychologists interested in the vulnerability of eye witnesses to the effects of leading questions showed a film of a traffic accident to a group of college students. The students then completed a questionnaire that included the critical question of how fast two automobiles were traveling when they collided. Thirty of the students were asked "About how fast were the cars going when they smashed into each other?" Thirty other students had the same question but with the less violent word "contacted" substituted for "smashed into." The "smashed" group's mean speed estimate was 40.5 with $s_1 = 5.0$. The "contacted" group's mean was 31.0 with $s_2 = 4.5$. Test the significance of the difference between these means.[2]

3. It has been found that leadership, or status, in colonies of male monkeys is related to the level of the male hormone testosterone in the animal's blood: Higher levels correspond to higher status. Such a correlation might indicate that the testosterone level causes the leadership qualities, but the causality could also be in the other direction. As an experiment, 10 male monkeys were reared individually, and their testosterone levels were recorded. Then the 10 males were put together in a large living environment for two months, after which their leadership status and testosterone levels were recorded. The resulting data included testosterone levels before and after the group living experience and the correlations between testosterone levels and leadership. They are shown in the accompanying table. If the level of testosterone causes leadership status, then there should be a strong positive correlation between the two testosterone levels (before and after group living) and

1   Adapted from S. Milgram, "Group Pressure and Action Against a Person," *Journal of Abnormal and Social Psychology*, 69 (1964): 137-43.

2   Adapted from E. F. Loftus and J. C. Palmer, "Reconstruction of Automobile Destruction: An Example of the Interaction between Language and Memory," *Journal of Verbal Learning and Verbal Behavior*, 13 (1974): 585–589.

between each testosterone assessment and the leadership rating. Furthermore, there should be no difference between the average testosterone level before the group living and that after it. On the other hand, if the direction of causality is reversed and leadership status causes the testosterone levels to change, then there should be no correlation between testosterone level before the group living and leadership, but there should be a significant correlation between testosterone level after the group living and leadership. Statistically evaluate:

a. the correlation between testosterone level before group living and leadership

b. the correlation between testosterone level after group living and leadership

c. the mean difference between testosterone level before the group living and the level after it

| Subject | Testosterone Level | | Leadership |
	Before	After	After
a	5	7	6
b	9	8	7
c	5	5	7
d	6	8	6
e	2	6	4
f	2	6	5
g	7	8	7
h	2	6	4
i	3	11	12
j	4	7	8

$r = .83$

$r = -.10$

What do these results indicate about the direction of causality between testosterone levels and social leadership among monkeys?[3]

4. It is frequently important to ask whether certain personality traits remain consistent as individuals grow up. For example, is a child who is aggressive at age 5 also likely to be aggressive at age 18? The Fels Research Institute in Yellow Springs, Ohio, conducted a longitudinal study of children who were seen regularly throughout their childhood in a variety of testing and social contexts, and they were rated for social and intellectual behavior. For 27 males, the correlation between aggressiveness at age 5 and the same variable at age 18 was .39, whereas the correlation for a sample of 32 girls was .21. Assume that a personality theory predicts that aggressiveness should be consistent over age for both sexes.[4]

a. Are each of these values of r significantly different from zero?

b. Is the degree of this relationship different for the two sexes?

---

3 Based on, but not identical to, studies by I. Bernstein and T. Gordon reported in *Newsweek* (International Edition), 27 August 1973, p. 46.

4 Based on, but not identical to, studies by J. Kagan and H. A. Moss, *Birth to Maturity* (New York: John Wiley & Sons, 1962.)

• • • • •   ANSWERS

Table 10–1. H_0: $\mu_1 = \mu_2$, H_1: $\mu_1 \neq \mu_2$; randomly, independently; independent; homogeneous; $\overline{X}_1 - \overline{X}_2$, normal; .05, nondirectional, 26. If $-2.056 < t_{obs} < 2.056$, do not reject H_0. If $t_{obs} \leq -2.056$ or $t_{obs} \geq 2.056$, reject H_0. $t_{obs} = 2.14$. Reject H_0.

Table 10–2. H_0: $\mu_1 = \mu_2$, H_1: $\mu_2 > \mu_1$; randomly, independently; correlated; normal; .05, directional, 11. If $t_{obs} < 1.796$, do not reject H_0. If $t_{obs} \geq 1.796$, reject H_0. $N = 12$, $\sum D_i = 12$, $\sum D_i^2 = 34$, $(\sum D_i)^2 = 144$, $t_{obs} = 2.45$. Reject H_0.

Table 10–3. H_0: $\rho = 0$, H_1: $\rho \neq 0$; randomly, independently; normal; .05, nondirectional, 40. If $-.3044 < r_{obs} < .3044$, do not reject H_0. If $r_{obs} \leq -.3044$ or $r_{obs} \geq .3044$, reject H_0. $r_{obs} = -.33$. Reject H_0.

Table 10–4. H_0: $\rho_1 = \rho_2$, H_1: $\rho_1 \neq \rho_2$; randomly, independently; independent; normal; 20; .05, nondirectional. If $-1.96 < z_{obs} < 1.96$, do not reject H_0. If $z_{obs} \leq -1.96$ or $z_{obs} \geq 1.96$, reject H_0. $z_{r_1} = .497$, $z_{r_2} = .224$, $z_{obs} = .91$. Do not reject H_0.

Self-Test. (1) The formula states that a value (e.g., a statistic) minus its population value divided by an estimate of the standard error of that value is distributed as t. **(2)** $\mu_1 = \mu_2$. **(3)** When the groups of measurements are correlated (as when the same or matched subjects contribute a score to each distribution), the standard error is different than when the two distributions are independent, thus a different procedure is required. **(4)** If the two population distributions are normal or if the sample sizes are large regardless of the form of their population. **(5)** 0. **(6)** This permits the use of the percentiles of the standard normal or t distribution. **(7)** For samples of 27 males and 27 females, a correlation of .33 for the girls would be significant but an $r = .31$ for the boys would not be significant; yet there would be no significant difference between .33 and .31. Saying that there is a correlation for girls and no correlation for boys but no difference between them depends on using a dichotomous relationship/no relationship decision. In fact, the probability of each H_0 is a continuum, and the probabilities should be stated. The problem of "accepting the null" must also be recalled here. The nonsignificant correlation cannot be directly translated into the conclusion that *no* correlation exists for boys. **(8)** Yes, because the correlation between two sets of measures is independent of the means.

Exercises. (1) Follow the format of Table 10–1 for a *t* test of independent groups. Nondirectional test at .05 with $df = 40$, $t_{crit} = 2.021$, $t_{obs} = 2.20$. Reject H_0. **(2)** Follow the format of Table 10–1 for a *t* test of independent groups. Nondirectional test at .05 with $df = 58$, $t_{crit} = 2.00$ (approximately), $t_{obs} = 7.74$ (can vary with rounding procedures). Reject H_0. **(3a)** Follow the format of Table 10–3 for the significance of a correlation. Nondirectional test at .05 with $df = 8$, $r_{crit} = \pm.63$, $r_{obs} = -.10$. Do not reject H_0. **(3b)** Follow the same format and r_{crit} as for (3a) but $r_{obs} = .83$. Reject H_0.

(3c) Follow the format of Table 10–2 for a *t* test of correlated groups. Nondirectional test at .05 with $df = 9$, $t_{crit} = \pm 2.262$, $t_{obs} = 3.36$ (may vary with rounding procedures). Reject H_0. Since there was a correlation between hormone level and social leadership after but not before the group rearing and since testosterone levels rose after group rearing, social activity may alter hormone level rather than the reverse. **(4a)** Follow the format of Table 10–3 for the significance of a correlation. For males: A directional test at .05 with $df = 25$, $r_{crit} = .3233$, $r_{obs} = .39$. Reject H_0. For females: A directional test at .05 with $df = 30$, $r_{crit} = .2960$, $r_{obs} = .21$. Do not reject H_0. **(4b)** Follow the format of Table 10–4. A nondirectional test at .05, $z_{crit} = \pm 1.96$, $z_{r_1} = .412$, $z_{r_2} = .213$, $z_{obs} = .72$. Do not reject H_0.

● ● ● ● ● **STATISTICAL PACKAGES** ● ● ● ● ●

● ● ● ● ●   **MINITAB**

(To accompany the guided computational example in Table 10–2.)

MINITAB will compute a *t* test for two means based upon two independent samples and for a mean difference based on one sample or from two correlated samples. While MINITAB will compute correlation coefficients and their significance (see Chapter 7), it does not test the significance of the difference between two *r*s. These tests can be performed by looking in the tables in your text (see example, Table 10–3) or by making a simple calculation (see example, Table 10–4).

Two Independent Means (Table 10-1)

Table 10–1 of the *Guide* gives an example of a *t* test of two means based upon two independent samples, but the raw data are not presented. So, to create a new example of the effects of a drug on memory, new raw data are presented below.

Drug (1)	Non-Drug (2)
12, 9, 13, 6, 11, 11, 14, 10, 10, 12, 9, 7, 13, 12	7, 4, 8, 9, 5, 7, 10, 6, 6, 8, 9, 7, 7, 6, 9

Two methods of data entry are possible for this example. If you are entering data from the above table, the first method, which is simplest, is to place the two groups of memory measures in two separate columns. In the first column place the memory measure for the group that received drug; the second column contains the measure for the group that did not receive the drug. The number of cases in each group does not have to be equal for the independent sample *t* test.

Start the MINITAB program. To enter data on the spreadsheet, click on the Data window. Enter the values from the two groups into the first two columns of the spreadsheet, respectively. Label the two columns with the variable names *Drug* and *Nondrug*. To enter the variable names, type them in at the top of the columns. The data you have entered should now appear on the spreadsheet as follows:

Drug	Nondrug
12	7
9	4
13	8
6	9
11	5
11	7
14	10
10	6
10	6
12	8
9	9
7	7
13	7
12	6
	9

To save the data that you entered as a MINITAB Worksheet:

File>Save Worksheet As
  (Enter folder and file name for the MINITAB Worksheet file.)
  OK

To carry out the independent sample *t* test:

> *Stat>Basic Statistics>2-Sample t*
>   Samples in different columns: Yes
>   First: Drug   [double-click to transfer]
>   Second: Nondrug
>   Assume equal variances: Yes
>   Options: Alternative: not equal
>   OK
>   OK

The accompanying program output, which reflects the first method of data entry, contains more information than you need at this point. For current purposes, the top of the table gives the N, mean, and standard deviation for the two groups, and the second line from the bottom of the table indicates that the $t = 4.64$, the probability of a t this large or larger with a two-tailed test is equal to .0001, and the number of degrees of freedom is 27. If a one-tailed test is needed, the Alternative subcommand can be changed to "greater than" if the Drug group is expected to have a higher mean than the Nondrug group. If the reverse is true, the alternative should be set to "less than."

The second method of data entry, which MINITAB calls the "stacked" method, is to code a treatment variable (*Trt*) to indicate whether or not the group received the drug, and place the memory score in a single outcome variable (*Meas*). In the first column of the spreadsheet enter the treatment code *Trt* (1=Drugged; 2=Non-Drugged). In the second column enter the value for the memory measure *Meas*. The spreadsheet for using the second method of data entry should appear as follows:

Trt	Meas
1	12
1	9
1	13
⋮	⋮
1	12
2	7
2	4
2	8
⋮	⋮
2	9

The *t* test for stacked data entry can be carried out by selecting the "Samples in one column" subcommand in MINITAB, as shown below:

> *Stat>Basic Statistics>2-Sample t*
>   Samples in one column: Yes
>   Samples: Meas   [double-click to transfer]
>   Subscripts: Trt
>   Assume equal variances: Yes
>   Options: Alternative: not equal
>   OK
>   OK

Except for the variable names, the result obtained using either method is the same.
    To print the output from the Session window:

> *File>Print Session Window*
>   Print Range: All
>   OK

To input data for the next computational example, open a new spreadsheet:

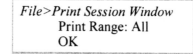

MINITAB Program Output

```
Two Sample T-Test and CI: Drug, Nondrug

Two sample T for Drug vs Nondrug
 N Mean StDev SE Mean
Drug 14 10.64 2.31 0.62
Nondrug 15 7.20 1.66 0.43

Difference = mu Drug - mu Nondrug
Estimate for difference: 3.443
95% CI for mu Drug - mu Nondrug: ( 1.921, 4.965)
T-Test of difference = 0 (vs not =): T-Value = 4.64 P-Value= 0.000 DF= 27
Both use Pooled StDev = 2.00
```

Two Correlated Means (Table 10–2)

When two means are based on a single group of individuals (for example, pre-posttest scores) or on two correlated samples (for example, parent-child pairs), the means are no longer independent and the independent sample *t* test is not valid. MINITAB can be used to perform a *t* test on two correlated means, as long as the data are entered in pairs.

In this example, the two variables are entered as paired test scores, *Test1* and *Test2*. In the Data window, enter the scores from Table 10–2 for *Test1* and *Test2* in the first two columns. Label the columns *Test1* and *Test2*.

The spreadsheet for the correlated sample *t* test should appear as follows:

Test1	Test2
5	6
6	7
4	3
4	6
2	2
1	3
2	4
5	4
5	7
5	4
7	9
3	6

To save the worksheet data:

> *File>Save Worksheet As*
>   (Enter folder and file name for the MINITAB Worksheet file.)
>   OK

To compare the means of the two correlated samples:

> *Stat>Basic Statistics>Paired t*
>   First sample: Test1   [double-click to transfer]
>   Second sample: Test2
>   Options: Test mean: 0
>   Alternative: less than
>   OK
>   OK

Note that the example in Table 10–2 is a directional test, which is specified in the command by setting Alternative to "less than," meaning that *Test2* is expected to be larger than *Test1,* so the difference *Test1 – Test2* will be "less than" zero. This is indicated on the last line of the output as "T-Test of mean difference = 0 (vs < 0)."

To print the output from the Session window, select the new portion, then:

> *File>Print Session Window*
> Print Range: Selection
> OK

Exit MINITAB:

> *File>Exit*

MINITAB Program Output

```
Paired T-Test and CI: Test1, Test2

Paired T for Test1 - Test2

 N Mean StDev SE Mean
Test1 12 4.083 1.782 0.514
Test2 12 5.083 2.065 0.596
Difference 12 -1.000 1.414 0.408

95% CI for mean difference: (-1.899, -0.101)
T-Test of mean difference= 0 (vs<0): T-Value= -2.45 P-Value= 0.016
```

● ● ● ● ●   SPSS

(To accompany the guided computational example in Table 10–2.)

SPSS will compute a *t* test for two means from independent samples and a mean difference from one sample or two correlated samples. The SPSS *Bivariate* command will compute correlation coefficients (see Chapter 7) and test the significance of a Pearson *r*, but it will not test the significance of the difference between two *r*s (see Table 10–4).

Two Independent Means (Table 10-1)

Table 10–1 of the *Guide* gives an example of a *t* test of two means based upon two independent samples, but the raw data are not presented. So, to create a new example of the effects of a drug on memory for words, new raw data are presented below.

Drugged (1)	Non-Drugged (2)
12, 9, 13, 6, 11, 11, 14, 10, 10, 12, 9, 7, 13, 12	7, 4, 8, 9, 5, 7, 10, 6, 6, 8, 9, 7, 7, 6, 9

SPSS requires "stacked" data entry consisting of two variables: a treatment variable with a code for drugged and non-drugged groups (*Trt*), and the measurements of memory (*Meas*).

Start the SPSS program. The Data Editor window should fill the screen. The data are entered by giving the group number (1=Drugged; 2=Non-Drugged) followed by the measurement value, one individual per line. Label the two columns with the variable names *Trt* and *Meas*. To enter the variable names, click on the bottom tab labeled "Variable View" and label the first two variables X and Y. Go back to the Data View. The spreadsheet should appear as follows:

Trt	Meas
1	12
1	9
1	13
⋮	⋮
1	12
2	7
2	4
2	8
⋮	⋮
2	9

Carry out the *t* test analysis to test for a difference of means:

Analyze>Compare Means>Independent-Samples T Test
      Test Variable(s): Meas   [highlight and transfer]
      Grouping Variable: Trt
      Define Groups: Use specified values
          Group 1: 1
          Group 2: 2
          Continue
    OK

The top table on the output shown below gives the codes you entered for the groups (listed as 1.00 and 2.00) plus the N, mean, standard deviation, and standard error of the mean for the two groups. The bottom table has two rows. The row labeled "Equal variances assumed" gives the results of the *t* test for the procedure described in your text (ignore the lower row). Note that the probabilities listed for the *t* test are two-tailed, appearing under the heading "Sig. (2-tailed)." For directional hypotheses, divide the listed p value in half.

To print the output, make sure the SPSS Viewer window is on the screen. Click on the yellow box next to the heading "T-Test" on the *left* side of the SPSS view window. This will highlight the portion of the output to be printed. Since the output from this program is wider than normal, a better result can be obtained if it is printed across the length of the page in landscape orientation. To print the output in landscape orientation:

File>Print
    Properties>Paper
        Orientation: Landscape
        OK
    Print range: Selection
    OK

To save the data that you entered and clear the spreadsheet for new data entry:

File>Save As
    (Enter folder and file name for SPSS Save file.)
    Save
File>New>Data

SPSS Program Output

Group Statistics

	TRT	N	Mean	Std. Deviation	Std. Error Mean
MEAS	1.00	14	10.6429	2.3074	.6167
	2.00	15	7.2000	1.6562	.4276

Independent Samples Test

		Levene's Test for Equality of Variances		t-test for Equality of Means					95% Confidence Interval of the Difference	
		F	Sig.	t	df	Sig. (2-tailed)	Mean Difference	Std. Error Difference	Lower	Upper
MEAS	Equal variances assumed	1.580	.220	4.641	27	.000	3.4429	.7419	1.9206	4.9651
	Equal variances not assumed			4.588	23.469	.000	3.4429	.7504	1.8922	4.9935

Two Correlated Means (Table 10–2)

When the two means are based on a single group of individuals (for example, pre-posttest scores) or on two correlated samples (for example, parent-child pairs), each pair of measures is entered on a separate line on the spreadsheet. In this example, the two variables to be entered are the paired test scores, *Test1* and *Test2*.

In the Data Editor window enter the scores for *Test1* in the first column and the corresponding scores for *Test2* in the second column. Label the columns *Test1* and *Test2* in the "Variable View" screen. The spreadsheet for the correlated sample *t* test should appear as follows:

Test1	Test2
5	6
6	7
4	3
4	6
2	2
1	3
2	4
5	4
5	7
5	4
7	9
3	6

Run the analysis for comparing the means of two correlated samples:

> *Analyze>Compare Means>Paired-Samples T Test*
>   Paired Variables: Test1 — Test2   [highlight both variables and transfer]
>   OK

The output for this example appears on the next page. Values of N, the mean and standard deviation for each group are reported in the top table. The correlation between the two tests, and the significance of the correlation coefficient obtained, is reported in the middle table.

Note that the probability, .032, listed on the bottom output table under "Sig. (2-tailed)" is nondirectional. Since the example in Table 10–2 is directional, the listed probability value must be halved. The mean difference and *t* value are negative because the program subtracts the second variable from the first. Since we hypothesized that the second test score would be higher than the first, this result is consistent with our hypothesis, and it is therefore appropriate to report that the one-tailed probability is .016.

To print the output, make sure the SPSS Viewer window is on the screen. Click on the lower yellow box next to the second heading for "T-Test" on the *left* side of the SPSS view window. This will highlight the new portion to be printed. Since this output is also wider than normal, a better result can be obtained if it is printed in landscape orientation.

To print the output in landscape orientation:

> *File>Print*
> > Print range: Selection
> > OK

To save the data that you entered:

> *Window>SPSS Data Editor*
> *File>Save As*
> > (Enter folder and file name for SPSS Save file.)
> > Save

Exit SPSS:

> *File>Exit*

SPSS Program Output

T-Test

Paired Samples Statistics

		Mean	N	Std. Deviation	Std. Error Mean
Pair 1	TEST1	4.0833	12	1.7816	.5143
	TEST2	5.0833	12	2.0652	.5962

Paired Samples Correlations

		N	Correlation	Sig.
Pair 1	TEST1 & TEST2	12	.739	.006

Paired Samples Test

		Paired Differences							
					95% Confidence Interval of the Difference				
		Mean	Std. Deviation	Std. Error Mean	Lower	Upper	t	df	Sig. (2-tailed)
Pair 1	TEST1 - TEST2	-1.0000	1.4142	.4082	-1.8985	-.1015	-2.449	11	.032

● ● ● ● ●

CHAPTER 11

BEYOND HYPOTHESIS TESTING: EFFECT SIZE AND INTERVAL ESTIMATION ● ● ● ● ●

CONCEPT GOALS

Be sure that you thoroughly understand the following concepts and how to use them in statistical applications.

- ◆ The limitations of hypothesis testing
- ◆ The difference between statistical significance and scientific or practical importance
- ◆ Indices of size of effect for correlations and for the difference between means
- ◆ Confidence intervals for a single mean, a single correlation coefficient, the difference between two independent means, and the difference between two independent correlations

● ● ● ● ● GUIDE TO MAJOR CONCEPTS

Introduction

The procedures of traditional hypothesis testing described in Chapters 8–10 provide a clever logic and strategy for deciding whether a particular statistic or difference between two statistics is likely to reflect values or differences in the population that are different from zero. However, these [1]_____ procedures have several limitations.

First, the decision provided by traditional procedures provides very little information. Specifically, if the result is that the null hypothesis should be rejected, we have learned that

[2]_____ relationship or difference likely exists in the population, but not much else including [3]_____ of a relationship or difference likely exists. Conversely, if the evidence is not sufficient to reject the null hypothesis, we know almost nothing—insufficient evidence exists to confirm that a relationship or difference exists.

Second, the traditional hypothesis testing decision is based on an arbitrary cutoff—typically the [4]__ level of [5]_____ . But this level is [6]_____ ; why should it not be some other value?

Third, the simple reject/do not reject H_0 decision seems artificial. The traditional process gives a reject/do not reject [7]_____ in a situation in which there is actually a continuum of uncertainty.

Fourth, the decision of traditional hypothesis testing depends on [8]__, the number of cases in the sample. The larger the N, the (more/ less) [9]_____ likely the decision will be to reject the null hypothesis.

The latter fact leads to the conclusion that essentially any correlation coefficient will be significant and any difference between means or correlation coefficients will be significant if the [10]__ is large enough. Stated another way, all null hypotheses are [11]_____ . This is because it is unlikely in the population that the actual value of statistic or a difference between two statistics will be exactly zero among the infinite number of possible values, and that all null hypotheses would be rejected if N is sufficiently [12]_____ .

Therefore, the simple reject/do not reject the [13]_____ of traditional hypothesis testing is not very informative, and other procedures can provide more information, especially about a [14]_____ of a statistic or the difference between two statistics. For example, it is possible for a correlation coefficient to be [15]_____ significant but very small in size if [16]__ is large; and it is possible for a correlation coefficient not to be statistically significant but nevertheless to be very [17]_____ in value if N is very [18]_____ .
Therefore, there is a difference between whether a statistic, in this case the correlation coefficient but it could be the difference between two means, is [19]_____ versus the
[20]_____ of that correlation or difference between means. The size of a statistic or difference between two statistics may well reflect the theoretical or practical importance of the

phenomenon under study. For example, a very large sample size may reveal that a program of government services produces statistically significantly greater numbers of families who are able to leave government-supported welfare programs, but the size of the difference in terms of the increased number of families who leave the welfare roles may be very small and the cost per family very high. Therefore, [21]_____ does not necessarily imply theoretical or practical [22]_____ , and indices of the size of the relationship or difference often provides information on the theoretical or practical importance of the observation.

Answer Key to Introduction

[1]	traditional hypothesis testing	[8]	N	[16]	N
[2]	some	[9]	more	[17]	large
[3]	how much	[10]	N	[18]	small
[4]	.05	[11]	false	[19]	statistically significant
[5]	significance	[12]	large	[20]	size
[6]	arbitrary	[13]	null hypothesis	[21]	statistical significance
[7]	decision	[14]	size	[22]	importance
		[15]	statistically		

Indices of Size

In the case of a single correlation, an index of the size of the relationship can be obtained by squaring the sample correlation coefficient. The proportion of variance in one measurement, Y, that is associated with variability in another set of measurements, X, is given by [1]__ . If the correlation between infant vocalization and later IQ is .74 for females, then [2]_____ % of the variability in female adult IQ is associated with individual differences in infant vocalizations. This represents a (small/large) [3]_____ relationship, but it may or may not be [4]_____ , depending upon the size of [5]__ .

It is also possible to obtain an estimate of the proportion of variance associated with the difference between means. The general logic is similar to that underlying the use of the proportion of variance associated with the correlation coefficient as a measure of the

[6]_____ of the relationship. That is, it is possible to estimate the proportion of the total variability in the measure of interest that is associated with the difference in means between the groups. Specifically, scores will differ from one another because participants differ from each other within a group and because scores differ from one another between groups. So an index of the proportion of variance associated with the difference between group means represents the proportion of total variability in scores that is associated with differences between groups and not differences between scores within groups.

This index of the [7]_____ of the difference between means is given by a statistic called omega squared, which is given by the following formula:

$$\text{Estimated } \omega^2 = \frac{t_{\text{obs}}^2 - 1}{t_{\text{obs}}^2 + N_1 + N_2 - 1}$$

in which t_{obs} is the observed t from the t test for independent groups and N_1 and N_2 are the sample sizes of the two groups. In the previous chapter, the difference between two independent means was determined for an example that tested the effect of a drug on memory performance by comparing one group of 15 participants ($N_1 = 15$) who received the drug on a memory test versus another group of 13 participants ($N_2 = 13$) who were given a neutral saline solution that is known not to have any effect on memory. The drug group remembered an average of 9.1 words ($\overline{X}_1 = 9.1$) versus 7.0 for the non-drugged group ($\overline{X}_2 = 7.0$) which produced a $t_{\text{obs}} = 2.14$ ($t_{\text{obs}} = 2.14$). Substituting the appropriate values into the formula for omega squared produces

$$\text{Estimated } \omega^2 = \frac{t_{\text{obs}}^2 - 1}{t_{\text{obs}}^2 + N_1 + N_2 - 1}$$

$$[8]\text{Estimated } \omega^2 = \frac{(\underline{})^2 - 1}{(\underline{})^2 + (\underline{}) + (\underline{}) - 1} = \underline{} = \underline{}$$

Therefore, the drug accounted for [9] _____ % of the variability in memory recall scores.

These procedures are summarized in a guide to computation in Table 11–1.

Table 11–1 Guided Computational Examples for Estimated Reporting of Variance

Proportion of Variance Associated with a Correlational Relationship

The proportion of variance in Y associated with individual differences in X:

Estimated Proportion of Variance $= r^2$

If $r = .74$,

Estimated Proportion of Variance $= r^2 = (\ \_\ )^2 = \ \_\_\ = \ \_\ \%$

Proportion of Variance Associated with a Difference between Two Independent Means

Estimated $\omega^2 = (t_{obs}^2 - 1) / (t_{obs}^2 + N_1 + N_2 - 1)$

If $t_{obs}^2 = 2.14$, $N_1 = 15$, and $N_2 = 13$,

Estimated $\omega^2 = [(\ \_\ )^2 - 1] / [(\ \_\ )^2 + \_\_ + \_\_ - 1] = (\ _____\ ) / (\ _____\ ) = \ \_\_\_\_\_$

Answer Key to Indices of Size					
[1]	r^2	[5]	N	[8]	$(2.14)^2$, $(2.14)^2 + 15 +$
[2]	54.76%	[6]	size		$13 - 1 = .11$
[3]	large	[7]	size	[9]	11%
[4]	statistically significant				

Confidence Intervals for Other Parameters

Traditional hypothesis testing procedures estimate the value of parameters, an approach called **point estimation**. Thus, testing the null hypothesis that $\mu = .00$ or $\mu_1 - \mu_2 = 0$ provides the probability that these parameters are a specific value—that is, it represents [1]_____ . But these procedures only help us decide how likely it is that the population parameter is a specific value; they do not tell us the range of values that is likely to include the population parameter. Procedures that provide this range are called **interval estimation**. Therefore, determining the probability that $\mu = .00$, for example, represents [2]_____ , while determining that the probability is .95 that the interval .12 to .35 contains the population μ is an example of [3]_____ . Clearly, more information, especially about the possible size of the population parameter, is provided by [4]_____ .

The interval likely to contain the population parameter is called a confidence interval, the limits that define this [5]_____ are called confidence limits, and the "confidence" is the probability that the stated interval contains the population parameter. Therefore, when one says that the probability is .95 that the population correlation value is between .12 and .35, then .95 is the [6]_____ , .12 and .35 are the [7]_____ , the interval .12 to .35 is the [8]_____ , and the entire procedure is one example of the general approach of [9]_____ . Interval estimation, in addition to obtaining estimates of the proportion of variance associated with certain variables, constitutes another approach to estimating the [10]_____ of a parameter—a relationship or difference between means, for example.

Confidence intervals for a single mean. Suppose a school system will qualify for extra state financial assistance if the average first grade readiness score of all the children in the school is below 100. To decide whether it is worth testing all children in the school, the school psychologist takes a sample of $N = 25$ children and obtains an average score of $\overline{X} = 94$. Since the sample mean is an estimate of the population [11]_____ , that is $\overline{X}$ estimates μ, then 94 is a [12]_____ of the population mean of that school. But what range of values is likely to include the population mean for the school; that is, what is the [13]_____ of the population mean?

The sampling distribution of the mean is likely to be normal in form, and in a normal distribution 95% of the values will fall between -1.96 and $+1.96$ standard deviations of the mean. In this case, we have the sampling distribution of the mean and the standard error of the sampling distribution of the mean is $\sigma_x / \sqrt{N}$. Suppose we know from the very large standardization sample of the readiness test that the standard deviation of scores is 15. Therefore, the standard error of the mean will be [14] __ / __ = __ / __ = __ . Therefore, 95% of the means of a sampling distribution of means should fall between [15] $-1.96\sigma_{\overline{x}} = -1.96(3) =$ __ and [16] $+1.96\sigma_{\overline{x}} = +1.96(3) =$ __ . Since the sample mean, $\overline{X} = 94$, is an unbiased estimate of the population μ, then the confidence limits for the mean are

$$[17]\ \overline{X} - 1.96\sigma_{\overline{x}} = \underline{\hspace{2cm}} = \underline{\hspace{0.5cm}}$$
$$[18]\ \overline{X} + 1.96\sigma_{\overline{x}} = \underline{\hspace{2cm}} = \underline{\hspace{0.5cm}}$$

Therefore, 88.12 and 99.88 are the [19]_____ for the mean, 88.12 to 99.88 is the [20]_____ for the mean, ± 1.96 was chosen to include 95% of sample means so the degree of confidence in this interval is [21]__ %, and therefore the probability is that 95 out of every such 100 intervals calculated on separate samples would include the population mean for this school. Since the interval does not include the national average of 100, the administrator can conclude that it is likely that the average for his school falls between 88.12 and 99.88 or just below average.

Confidence intervals can be determine for any desired degree of confidence. While the above example represented a [22]__ % confidence interval, other intervals could be determined for 90%, 99%, or any other desired degree of [23]_____ . The degree of confidence is determined by selecting the number of standard errors of the mean in a normal distribution below and above the population mean that includes the specified proportion of cases. In the above example, 1.96 was selected because Table 2 in Appendix 2 of your text shows that in a normal distribution .025 or 2 1/2% of the distribution falls above $z = 1.96$ standard deviation units and [24]__ % falls below [25]_____ standard deviation units, and therefore 95% of the distribution will fall between [26]_____ and [27]_____ standard deviations of the mean. Table A shows that .005 or ½% of the area in a normal distribution falls to the right of $z = 2.575$ and [28]__ = __ % falls to the left of [29]_____ because the standard normal distribution is symmetrical. Therefore, if the school administrator wanted to determine the interval that was 99% likely that such an interval would contain the population mean, the confidence limits would be given by the formula:

$$\overline{X} - 2.575\sigma_{\overline{x}}$$
$$\overline{X} + 2.575\sigma_{\overline{x}}$$

Specifically for the sample obtained with $\overline{X} = 94$ and $\sigma_{\overline{x}} = 15 / \sqrt{25} = 3$, the 99% [30]_____ would be

[31] _____ = _____
[32] _____ = _____

Notice that at this degree of confidence, the interval with greater confidence is smaller/larger [33]_____ and in this case includes the national average of 100.

The above procedures for determine a [34]_____ for a single population mean have assumed that the population standard error of the mean, $\sigma_{\bar{x}}$, is known. If this value is not known, which is most often the case, the procedure for estimating confidence intervals is slightly different. The general formula for determining a confidence interval when $\sigma_{\bar{x}}$ is estimated with

[35]__ = _____ is given by $\bar{X} \pm t_\alpha(s_{\bar{x}})$ in which

$\bar{X}$ = the sample mean

$\alpha = 1 -$ the level of confidence desired

t_α = the critical value of t corresponding to a nondirectional test of significance level α

$s_{\bar{x}}$ = the sample standard of the mean ($s_{\bar{x}} = s_x / \sqrt{N}$).

For example, to determine 95% confidence limits for the example above in which the school administrator took a sample of $N = 25$ students and found a mean readiness score of $\bar{X} = 94$ with a standard deviation of $s_x = 10$, the level of confidence desired is [36]__ so that

[37]α = _____ = __ . Now, instead of using the standard normal distribution, which is appropriate when $\sigma_{\bar{x}}$ is known, we learned in previous chapters that when $s_{\bar{x}}$ is used to estimate the standard error of the mean we must use a different distribution, namely the [38]__ distribution. We can turn to Table B in Appendix 2 to determine the critical value of t corresponding to a

[39]_____ test at significance level [40]__ . But a different critical value exists for each degree of freedom, and in the case of a single sample mean the degrees of freedom are

[41]_____ = _____ = __ . Therefore, [42]t_α = _____ . Since the sample standard deviation was $s_x = 10$, the [43]$s_{\bar{x}}$ = _____ = _____ = __ . Therefore, the [44]_____ for 95% confidence limits are

[45]$\bar{X} \pm t_\alpha(s_{\bar{x}})$ = _____ = _____ = _____ . If a 99% confidence interval is desired, the same approach is used except that t_α will be the critical value of t corresponding to a nondirectional test at significance level [46]__ , which according to Table B in Appendix 2 is

[47]__ . This confidence interval as well as all of the others determined above for a single population mean are presented in Table 11–2 which provides a guided computational routine for these calculations, which should be completed now.

Table 11–2 Guided Computational Examples for Confidence Intervals for a Single Mean

If $\sigma_{\bar{x}} = \sigma_x / \sqrt{N}$ is known: $\overline{X} \pm z_\alpha(\sigma_{\bar{x}})$ or $\overline{X} \pm z_\alpha(\sigma_x / \sqrt{N})$ in which

$\overline{X}$ = the sample mean

$\alpha = 1-$ the level of confidence desired

z_α = the critical value of z corresponding to a nondirectional test at significance level α

$\sigma_{\bar{x}}$ the population standard error of the mean $\sigma_{\bar{x}} = \sigma_x / \sqrt{N}$

95% Limits:

$\overline{X} = 94$

$\alpha = 1-.95 = .05$

$z_\alpha = $ ___

$\sigma_x = 15$

$N = 25$

$\sigma_{\bar{x}} = \sigma_x / \sqrt{N} = $ _____ = __

$\overline{X} \pm z_\alpha(\sigma_{\bar{x}}) = $ _____

= _____

= _____ and _____

99% Limits:

$\overline{X} = 94$

$\alpha = 1-.99 = 0.1$

$z_\alpha = $ ___

$\sigma_x = 15$

$N = 25$

$\sigma_{\bar{x}} = \sigma_x / \sqrt{N} = $ _____ = __

$\overline{X} \pm z_\alpha(\sigma_{\bar{x}}) = $ _____

= _____

= _____ and _____

If $s_{\bar{x}} = s_x / \sqrt{N}$ is known: $\overline{X} \pm t_\alpha(s_{\bar{x}})$ or $\overline{X} \pm t_\alpha(s_x / \sqrt{N})$ in which

$\overline{X}$ = the sample mean

$\alpha = 1-$ the level of confidence desired

t_α = the critical value of t corresponding to a nondirectional test at significance level α

$s_{\bar{x}}$ = the sample standard error of the mean $(s_{\bar{x}} = s_x / \sqrt{N})$

95% Limits:

$\overline{X} = 94$

$\alpha = 1-.95 = .05$

$N = 25$

$df = N - 1 = $ _____ = __

$t_\alpha = $ _____

$s_x = 10$

$s_{\bar{x}} = s_x / \sqrt{N} = $ _____ = __

$\overline{X} \pm t_\alpha(s_{\bar{x}}) = $ _____

= _____

= _____ and _____

99% Limits:

$\overline{X} = 94$

$\alpha = 1-.99 = 0.1$

$N = 25$

$df = N - 1 = $ _____ = __

$t_\alpha = $ _____

$s_x = 10$

$s_{\bar{x}} = s_x / \sqrt{N} = $ _____ = __

$\overline{X} \pm t_\alpha(s_{\bar{x}}) = $ _____

= _____

= _____ and _____

It is important to understand how to interpret a confidence interval. For one thing, the level of confidence applies to the interval, not to the population mean. The population mean is a (fixed/variable) [48]_____ value, whereas the sample mean and the confidence interval are (the same/different) [49]_____ from sample to sample. Therefore, it is *not* correct to say that "the probability is .95 that the population mean falls within the confidence interval," because this implies that the value of μ (varies/is fixed) [50]_____ and might or might not happen to land in the stated interval. Actually, it is the [51]_____ that is variable, and so the correct statement is that "the probability is .95 that such an interval includes the population value." Notice that the probability statement applies to all such intervals, not to a specific interval once it is calculated. The specific interval 88.12 to 99.88 either contains or does not contain the [52]_____ ; it is *not* 95% likely. Therefore, the appropriate conclusion is that "the 95% confidence interval is 88.12 to 99.88" or that "we are 95% confident that the interval 88.12 to 99.88 includes the population mean." Therefore, what varies from sample to sample is the [53]_____ not to the [54]_____ , and the level of confidence applies to the [55]_____ not to the [56]_____ .

Confidence intervals for other statistics. Confidence intervals can be calculated for essentially any statistic. Three values are needed in each case. First, one must calculate the sample [57]_____ that will estimate the population parameter that one is interested in. Second, one needs an estimate of the variability of that statistic that is reflected in its [58]_____ . Third, one needs to determine in an appropriate theoretical sampling distribution the [59]_____ for a [60]_____ test at the desired [61]_____ corresponding to 1- the desired level of [62]_____ . These critical values represent the number of standard errors above and below the sample statistic that define the [63]_____ that define the desired [64]_____ .

Confidence intervals for a single correlation. The Pearson correlation coefficient, *r*, estimates the extent of relationship between two variables, *X* and *Y*, and the traditional significance test assesses the probability of the null hypothesis that the population correlation is [65]__ . But one can also determine a range of values that define an interval in which we have a stated level of [66]_____ that the population correlation falls within its boundaries.

For example, recall that a correlation of $r = .74$ was observed for a sample of $N = 27$ girls between vocalizations during infancy and later IQ. We can construct a 95% confidence interval by transforming the observed $r = .74$ into its z transformed equivalent from Table D in your text which is [67]__ . Since this is a 95% confidence interval, [68]$\alpha = 1 - $__ $= $__ , and the value in the standard normal distribution that represents a [69]_____ test at the .05 level is [70]__ . Therefore, the critical values are represented by

$$[71] z_r \pm z_\alpha \sqrt{\frac{1}{N-3}} = \underline{\hspace{4cm}} = \underline{\hspace{2.5cm}} = \underline{\hspace{0.6cm}} \text{ and } \underline{\hspace{0.6cm}} .$$

However, it must be remembered that these values are z transformed values which must be converted back by Table D in the text to rs. This produces the confidence interval in terms of rs of [72]__ to [73]__ . A guided computational format is provided for this calculation in Table 11–2 which should be completed at this time.

Notice that the obtained confidence interval does not include the value [74]__ , so it is unlikely that the [75]_____ is .00. In addition, we are [76]__ confident that the interval [77]__ to [78]__ contains the population value.

Confidence intervals for the difference between two independent means. In traditional hypothesis testing, we often test the null hypothesis that the difference between two sample means in the population is [79]__. We estimate that population difference on the basis of the sample data with the statistic [80]_____   , and the hypothesis testing procedures help us to decide whether the observed statistic differs from a population value of 0 by [81]_____ alone. But we could also calculate a confidence interval for the population difference between two means based on the sample data, which would provide an [82]_____ of the population difference between those means.

A confidence interval for the difference between two independent means is defined by the confidence limits given by Table 11–3.

**Table 11–3 Guided Computational Example for Constructing
Confidence Intervals for Other Statistics**

Confidence Intervals for a Single Correlation
The confidence interval for a single correlation coefficient is defined by the confidence limits
that are given by $z_r \pm z_\alpha \sqrt{1/(N-3)}$ in which
  r = the observed sample correlation
  z_r = the z transformed value for the observed sample r (Table D of the text)
  $\alpha = 1-$ the desired level of confidence
  z_α = the critical value of z for a nondirectional test at the significance level α (Table A of the text)

The z_r 's obtained above must be transformed back to r's using Table D in the text.

For 95%, $r = .74$ for a sample of $N = 27$
  $z_r = \underline{\quad}$
  $\alpha = 1 - \underline{\quad} = \underline{\quad}$
  $z_\alpha = \underline{\quad}$
  $z_r \pm z_\alpha \sqrt{1/(N-3)} = \underline{\hspace{4cm}} = \underline{\hspace{2cm}} = \underline{\quad}$ and $\underline{\quad}$

So the 95% confidence interval in terms of rs is between $\underline{\quad}$ and $\underline{\quad}$.

Confidence Intervals for the Difference Between Two Independent Means
The confidence interval for the difference between two independent means is defined by the
confidence limits given by $(\overline{X}_1 - \overline{X}_2) \pm t_\alpha(s_{\overline{x}_1 - \overline{x}_2})$ in which
  $\overline{X}_1$ = the sample mean of the first group
  $\overline{X}_2$ = the sample mean of the second group
  $(\overline{X}_1 - \overline{X}_2)$ = the point estimate of the difference between group means
  $\alpha = 1-$ the level of confidence desired
  t_α = the critical t value corresponding to a nondirectional test at significance level α with
      $df = N_1 + N_2 - 2$ (Table B in the text)
  $s_{\overline{x}_1 - \overline{x}_2}$ = the estimated standard error of the difference between means which equals

$$s_{\overline{x}_1 - \overline{x}_2} = \sqrt{\left[\frac{(N_1 - 1)s_1^2 + (N_2 - 1)s_2^2}{N_1 + N_2 - 2}\right] \cdot \left[\frac{1}{N_1} + \frac{1}{N_2}\right]}$$

Table 11–3 Guided Computational Example for Constructing
Confidence Intervals for Other Statistics (Continued)

For 95% confidence limits, given $N_1 = 17$, $\overline{X}_1 = 40$, $s_1^2 = 16$, $N_2 = 15$, $\overline{X}_2 = 35$, $s_2^2 = 18$

$(\overline{X}_1 - \overline{X}_2) = $ _____ $= $ ___

$\alpha = 1 - $ ___ $= $ ___

$df = N_1 + N_2 - 2 = $ _____ $= $ ___

$t_\alpha = $ _____

$s_{\overline{x}_1 - \overline{x}_2} = $ _____ $= $ _____ $= $ ___

$(\overline{X}_1 - \overline{X}_2) \pm t_\alpha(s_{\overline{x}_1 - \overline{x}_2}) = $ _____ $= $ _____ $= $ ___ and ___

Confidence Intervals for the Difference Between Two Independent Correlations

The confidence interval for the difference between two independent correlations is defined by the confidence limits given by $(z_{r_1} - z_{r_2}) \pm z_\alpha(s_{z_{r_1} - z_{r_2}})$ in which

$z_{r_1} = $ the z transformation of r_1, (Table D in the text)

$z_{r_2} = $ the z transformation of r_2 (Table D in the text)

$\alpha = 1 - $ level of confidence desired

$z_\alpha = $ the critical value of z for a nondirectional test a significance level α (Table A in the text)

$s_{z_{r_1} - z_{r_2}} = $ the standard error of the difference between two z-transformed correlations which equals

$$s_{z_{r_1} - z_{r_2}} = \sqrt{\frac{1}{N_1 - 3} + \frac{1}{N_2 - 3}}$$

The z transformed limits must be transformed back to rs by using Table D in the text.

For 95% confidence limits given $N_1 = 27$, $r_1 = .74$, $N_2 = 22$, $r_2 = .09$:

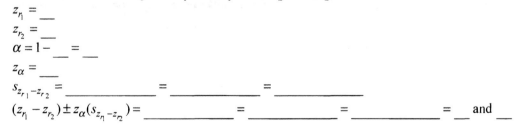

$z_{r_1} = $ ___

$z_{r_2} = $ ___

$\alpha = 1 - $ ___ $= $ ___

$z_\alpha = $ ___

$s_{z_{r_1} - z_{r_2}} = $ _____ $= $ _____ $= $ _____

$(z_{r_1} - z_{r_2}) \pm z_\alpha(s_{z_{r_1} - z_{r_2}}) = $ _____ $= $ _____ $= $ _____ $= $ ___ and ___

So the 95% confidence interval for the difference in rs is ___ and ___ .

Recall the example comparing the number of aggressive actions displayed by a group of 17 young boys whose parents had recently divorced ($\overline{X}_1 = 40$, $s_1^2 = 16$) versus a group of 15 boys whose parents had not divorced ($\overline{X}_2 = 35$, $s_2^2 = 18$). To determine 95% confidence limits for this example, [83]$(\overline{X}_1 - \overline{X}_2) = \underline{\quad} - \underline{\quad} = \underline{\quad}$

[84]$\alpha = 1 - \underline{\quad} = \underline{\quad}$

[85]$df = \underline{\qquad\qquad} = \underline{\quad}$

[86]$t_{.05} = \underline{\qquad\qquad}$

[87]$s_{\overline{x}_1 - \overline{x}_2} = \underline{\qquad\qquad\qquad} \times \underline{\qquad\qquad} = \underline{\qquad\qquad} = \underline{\quad}$

Therefore, the confidence limits are

$$[88](\overline{X}_1 - \overline{X}_2) \pm t_{.05}(s_{\overline{x}_1 - \overline{x}_2}) = \underline{\qquad\qquad} = \underline{\qquad\qquad} = \underline{\quad} \text{ and } \underline{\quad}$$

This means that we are [89]__ % [90]_____ that the interval [91]___ to [92]___ contain the population difference in means of aggressive acts for these two groups. Notice that since this interval does not contain the value [93]__ traditional hypothesis testing would [94]_____ the null hypothesis and conclude that some difference exists in the population; the confidence interval suggests that young boys of divorced parents are 95% likely to display in round numbers between [95]__ and [96]__ more aggressive acts in the observational situation. A guided computational example for this exercise is given in Table 11–3, which you should complete now.

Confidence intervals for the difference between two independent correlations. Just as one can test the null hypothesis that the difference in the population between two independent correlations is 0, one can also create [97]_____ for the difference between two independent correlations.

Such a confidence interval is given by $(z_{r_1} - z_{r_2}) \pm z_\alpha(s_{z_{r_1} - z_{r_2}})$ in which

z_{r_1} = the z transformation of r_1 (Table D in the text)

z_{r_2} = the z transformation of r_2 (Table D in the text)

$\alpha = 1 -$ level of confidence desired

z_α = the critical value of z for a nondirectional test a significance level α (Table A in the text)

$s_{z_{r_1} - z_{r_2}}$ = the standard error of the difference between two z-transformed correlations which equals

$$s_{z_{r_1} - z_{r_2}} = \sqrt{\frac{1}{N_1 - 3} + \frac{1}{N_2 - 3}}$$

The z transformed limits must be transformed back to rs by using Table D in the text.

Recall the example in which the amount of vocalization made during an observation at 12 months of age was used to predict IQ at 26 years of age for a sample of $N_1 = 27$ females for whom the correlation $r_1 = .74$ compared to a sample of $N_2 = 22$ males for whom the correlation was $r_2 = .09$. To construct a 95% confidence interval for the difference in the population of these correlations, we first need to transform the sample rs into their z transformed equivalence using Table D in the text:

$$[98] z_{r_1} = \underline{} \text{ and } [99] z_{r_2} = \underline{} \, .$$

For 95% confidence limits $[100] \alpha = 1 - \underline{} = \underline{}$ and the standard normal $[101] z_{.05} = \underline{}$. The standard error of the difference between two z-transformed correlations is

$$[102] s_{z_{r_1} - z_{r_2}} = \underline{} = \underline{} = \underline{} \, .$$

Therefore, the confidence limits in z-transformed values are

$$[103] (z_{r_1} - z_{r_2}) \pm z_\alpha (s_{z_{r_1} - z_{r_2}}) = \underline{} \pm \underline{} = \underline{} = \underline{} \text{ and } \underline{} \, .$$

But it must be remembered that these are z- transformed values which must be transformed back into rs using Table D in the text, which produces the limits of the difference in rs to be $[104]\underline{}$

and [105]__ . Therefore, we are [106]__ % confident that the population difference between the genders for this predictive relationship is [107]__ to [108]__ . Since this interval does not include [109]__ , the genders are likely different in the extent of this relationship, and the size of that difference is likely to be moderate to very substantial. Table 11–3 presents a guided computational illustration of this procedures, which you should complete now.

Answer Key to Confidence Intervals for Other Parameters

[1]	point estimation	[23]	confidence	[45]	$94 \pm 2.064(2) =$
[2]	point estimation	[24]	2.5		$94 \pm 4.128 = 89.872$ and
[3]	interval estimation	[25]	-1.96		98.128
[4]	interval estimation	[26]	-1.96	[46]	.01
[5]	confidence interval	[27]	$+1.96$	[47]	2.797
[6]	confidence	[28]	$.005 = 1/2\%$	[48]	fixed
[7]	confidence limits	[29]	-2.575	[49]	different
[8]	confidence interval	[30]	confidence limits	[50]	varies
[9]	interval estimation	[31]	$94 - 2.575(3) = 86.275$	[51]	confidence interval
[10]	size	[32]	$94 + 2.575(3) = 101.725$	[52]	population mean
[11]	mean	[33]	larger	[53]	confidence interval
[12]	point estimate	[34]	confidence interval	[54]	population mean
[13]	interval estimation	[35]	$\sigma_{\bar{x}} = s_x / \sqrt{N}$	[55]	confidence interval
[14]	$\sigma_x / \sqrt{N}$, $15/\sqrt{25} = 3$	[36]	.95	[56]	population mean
[15]	-5.88	[37]	$1 - .95 = .05$	[57]	statistic
[16]	$+5.88$	[38]	t	[58]	standard error
[17]	$94 - 5.88 = 88.12$	[39]	nondirectional	[59]	critical values
[18]	$94 + 5.88 = 99.88$	[40]	.05	[60]	nondirectional
[19]	confidence limits	[41]	$N - 1 = 25 - 1 = 24$	[61]	significance level
[20]	confidence interval	[42]	2.064	[62]	confidence
[21]	95%	[43]	$s_x / \sqrt{N} = 10/\sqrt{25} = 2$	[63]	confidence limits
[22]	95%	[44]	critical values	[64]	confidence interval

[65] .00

[66] confidence

[67] .950

[68] $1-.95=.05$

[69] nondirectional

[70] 1.96

[71] $.95 \pm 1.96\sqrt{1/(27-3)} =$
      $.950 \pm .400 = .550$ and
      1.35

[72] .50

[73] .88

[74] .00

[75] population correlation

[76] 95%

[77] .50

[78] .88

[79] 0

[80] $\overline{X}_1 - \overline{X}_2$

[81] sampling error

[82] interval estimation

[83] $40 - 35 = 5$

[84] $1 - .95 = .05$

[85] $17 + 15 - 2 = 30$

[86] 2.042

[87] $[\sqrt{16(16)+14(18)}$
      $\div\sqrt{17+15-2}] \times$
      $\sqrt{(1/17)+(1/15)} =$
      $\sqrt{(16.933)(.1255)} = 1.458$

[88] $5 \pm 2.042(1.458) =$
      $5 \pm 2.977 = .023$ and
      7.977

[89] 95%

[90] confident

[91] 2.023

[92] 7.977

[93] 0

[94] reject

[95] 2

[96] 8

[97] confidence intervals

[98] .95

[99] .090

[100] $1 - .95 = .05$

[101] 1.96

[102] $\sqrt{1/(27-3)+1/(22-3)}$
      $= \sqrt{.0417+.0526} = .307$

[103] $(.950 - .090) \pm$
      $1.96(.3071) = .860 \pm .602$
      $= .258$ and 1.462

[104] .25

[105] .90

[106] 95%

[107] .25

[108] .90

[109] .00

● ● ● ● ●   SELF-TEST

1. Traditional hypothesis testing procedures
    a. estimate the size of a relationship
    b. give the probability of the null
        hypothesis
    c. estimate how much of a relationship
        or difference likely exists in the
        population
    d. none of the above

2. A major limitation of traditional
    hypothesis testing is that
    a. it provides only a dichotomous
        reject/do not reject decision
    b. the decision is based upon acceptance
        of an arbitrary level of significance
    c. the procedure does not provide
        information on the extent of
        relationship or difference
    d. all of the above

3.   Why are all null hypotheses false?

4.   What are two statistical approaches to describing the size of a relationship or difference?

5.   What do estimates of the size of the relationship or difference have to do with its scientific or practical importance as opposed to its statistical significance?

6.*   Which is an index of proportion of variance associated with a difference between two independent means?
   a. r^2
   b. t^2_{obs}
   c. ω^2
   d.   all of the above

7.*   If the correlation coefficient between risk factors and school performance is .60, what is the proportion of variance in school performance that is associated with early risk factors?
   a.   36%
   b.   the $\sqrt{.60} = .77$
   c.   .60
   d.   none of the above

8.*   Why is ω^2 often less generalizable as an estimate of the proportion of variance associated with group mean differences than is r^2 as a measure of the proportion of variance in one measure that is associated with differences in another?

9.   The probability statement or degree of confidence in a confidence interval applies to the
   a.   parameter
   b.   the specific interval calculated
   c.   all such intervals based on separate samples
   d.   none of these

10.   Technically, which of the following statements is correct?
   a.   the probability is .95 that the interval 27 to 39 contains the population mean
   b.   the probability is .95 that the population mean falls within the interval 27 to 39
   c.   in 95 out of every 100 such intervals we would expect the population parameter to fall within their limits
   d.   95 out of every 100 such intervals determined on independent samples would contain the population parameter

11.   The greater the confidence
   a.   the smaller the confidence interval
   b.   the larger the confidence interval
   c.   the interval does not change
   d.   the interval could be larger or smaller

12.   What does the size of the confidence interval tell you about sampling error?

Questions preceded by an asterisk can be answered on the basis of the discussion in the text, but the discussion in this Study Guide does not answer them.

● ● ● ● ●

EXERCISES

1. Suppose a sample of $N = 27$ girls has a mean score of 12 ($s_{\bar{x}_1} = 3$, $s^2_{x_1} = 243$) and a sample of $N = 22$ boys had a mean of 23 ($s_{\bar{x}_2} = 4$, $s^2_{x_2} = 352$) on an assessment of spontaneous vocalizations at 12 months of age (for mean difference $t_{obs} = -1.86$). Later, at 6 years of age the average IQ's of the same group of girls is 102 ($s_{\bar{y}_1} = 3.5$, $s^2_{y_1} = 330.75$), and the average IQ for the group of boys is 96 ($s_{\bar{y}_2} = 4$, $s^2_{y_2} = 352$). The $t_{obs} = 1.23$ for IQ between genders. The correlation between 12-month vocalization score and 6-year IQ was .68 for the girls and .07 for boys.

   a. Determine the proportion of variance associated with the difference between the genders for the mean vocalization scores.

   b. Determine the proportion of variance between the genders for the mean IQ scores.

   c. Determine the proportion of variances in IQ scores associated with 12-month vocalization scores for girls and separately for boys.

   d. Determine 95% and 99% confidence limits for the mean vocalization scores for girl and separately for boys.

   e. Determine the 95% and 99% confidence limits for the correlation between vocalization and IQ for girls and separately for boys.

   f. Determine the 95% and 99% confidence limits for the differences between the genders in mean vocalization scores and separately in mean IQ.

   g. Determine the 90% and 95% confidence limits for the difference in correlations between vocalization and IQ for the two gender.

● ● ● ● ●

ANSWERS

Table 11–1. $r^2 = (.74)^2 = .5476 = 55\%$; est. $\omega^2 = [(2.14)^2 - 1] / [(2.14)^2 + 15 + 13 - 1]$ $= 3.5796 / 31.5796 = .11$

Table 11–2. If σ_x is known—95%: $z_\alpha = 1.96$, $\sigma_{\bar{x}} = 15 / \sqrt{25} = 3$, $94 \pm 1.96(3)$ $= 94 \pm 5.88 = 88.12$ and 99.88. 99%: $z_\alpha = 2.575$,

$\sigma_{\bar{x}} = 15 / \sqrt{25} = 3$, $94 \pm 2.575(3)$ $= 94 \pm 7.725 = 86.275$ and 101.725. If s_x estimates σ_x—95%: $df = 25 - 1 = 24$, $t_\alpha = 2.064$, $s_{\bar{x}} = 10 / \sqrt{25} = 2$, $94 \pm 2.064(2)$ $= 94 \pm 4.128 = 89.872$ and 98.128. 99%: $df = 25 - 1 = 24$, $t_\alpha = 2.797$, $s_{\bar{x}} = 10 / \sqrt{25} = 2$, $94 \pm 2.797(2) = 94 \pm 5.594 = 88.406$ and 99.594.

Table 11–3. Confidence interval for a correlation: $z_r = .950$, $\alpha = 1-.95 = .05$, $z_\alpha = 1.96$; $s_{z_{r_1} - z_{r_2}} = .950 \pm 1.96\sqrt{1/(27-3)} = .950 \pm .400$ $= .550$ and 1.350, $.50$ to $.88$. Confidence interval for the difference between two independent means: $\overline{X}_1 - \overline{X}_2 = 40 - 35 = 5$, $\alpha = 1-.95 = .05$, $df = 17 + 15 - 2 = 30$, $t_{.05} = 2.042$,

$$s_{\overline{x}_1 - \overline{x}_2} = \sqrt{\left[\frac{(17-1)16 + (15-1)18}{17 + 15 - 2}\right]\left[\frac{1}{17} + \frac{1}{15}\right]}$$
$$= \sqrt{\left[\frac{256 + 252}{30}\right][.1255]} = 1.458$$

$5 \pm 2.042(1.458) = 5 \pm 2.977 = 2.023$ and 7.977. Confidence interval for the difference between two independent correlations: $z_{r_1} = .950$, $z_{r_2} = .090$, $\alpha = 1-.95 = .05$, $z_{.05} = 1.96$,

$$s_{z_{r_1} - z_{r_2}} = \sqrt{\frac{1}{27-3} + \frac{1}{22-3}} = \sqrt{.0417 + .0526}$$
$$= .3071,$$
$(.950 - .090) \pm 1.96(.3071)$
$$= .860 \pm .602 = .258 \text{ and } 1.462, .25 \text{ and } .90$$

Self-Test. (1) b. **(2)** d. **(3)** Except if the population value is *exactly* 0, a significance test will reject H_0 if N is large enough. **(4)** Estimates of the proportion of variance associated with the relationship or difference and confidence intervals for the population parameter. **(5)** Estimates of size guard against a relationship or difference being statistically significant (perhaps because of a large N) but which are not large enough effects to justify practical actions or influence theory. **(6)** c. **(7)** a. **(8)** Samples are more likely to be fairly random or representative when correlations are calculated, whereas groups are often defined specifically and are not random or representative conditions so ω^2 can only be generalized to those specific groups. **(9)** c. **(10)** d. **(11)** b. **(12)** The greater the sampling error, the wider the confidence interval, because the standard error of the parameter is used in calculating the interval.

Exercises. (1a) 4.78%; **(1b)** 1.04%; **(1c)** 46.24%, .49%; **(1d)** 95%: 5.832 to 18.168; 99%: 3.663 to 20.337; 95%: 14.68 to 31.32; 99%: 11.676 to 34.24; **(1e)** 95%: .41 to .84; 99%: .30 to .88; 95%: −.36 to .48; 99%: −.48 to .58; **(1f)** 95%: −20.88 to −1.12; 99%: −24.20 to 2.20; 95%: −4.67 to 16.67; 99%: −8.26 to 20.26; **(1g)** 90%: .25 to .86; 95%: .16 to .88. Note: Answers depend on interpolation of t and rounding practices.

●●●●● STATISTICAL PACKAGES ●●●●●

●●●●●   MINITAB

(To accompany the guided computational examples in Chapter 11.)

MINITAB will compute confidence intervals for a single mean and for the difference between two independent means. The program will not compute confidence intervals for a correlation coefficient, nor for the difference between two correlations.

Confidence Interval for a Single Mean

Unlike the computational examples shown in this chapter, MINITAB computes confidence intervals directly from the raw data. Since the raw data are not presented in Table 11–2, we will employ the *Looks* data first presented in Table 3–6, consisting of 70 observations on the number of looks at mother by a child. Since this example involves a single mean and $\sigma_{\bar{x}}$ is not known, the *1-Sample t* command will be used. A 95% confidence interval for the mean number of looks will be determined.

Retrieve the MINITAB Worksheet file for the *Looks* data as follows:

> *File>Open Worksheet*
>   (Select the saved *Looks.mtw* file.)
>   Open
>   OK

Refer to Chapter 3 to re-enter the data if the *Looks* data were not saved at that time. A confidence interval may be computed using the *1-Sample t* command:

> *Stat>Basic Statistics>1-Sample t*
>   Variables: Looks   [double-click to transfer]
>   Test mean: **0**   [arbitrary value]
>   Options: Confidence level: 95%
>   Alternative: not equal
>   OK
>   OK

The two parameters listed under "Options" are the default for this command. Note also that a particular value for "Test mean" is not necessary for calculating a confidence interval. We used zero, but any numeric value will work. If, instead of zero, the sample mean is entered, the calculated t statistic will be zero, with resulting p value of 1.0. The values shown for t and p on the program output may be ignored. For the *Looks* data, the sample mean is 18.34 and the 95% confidence limits are from 16.06 to 20.62.

To print the MINITAB output, select the output in the Session Window, then:

> *File<Print Session Window*
> Print Range: Selection
> OK

MINITAB Program Output

```
One-Sample T: Looks
Test of mu = 0 vs mu not = 0

Variable N Mean StDev SE Mean
Looks 70 18.34 9.56 1.14

Variable 95.0% CI T P
Looks ( 16.06, 20.62) 16.05 0.000
```

Confidence Interval for the Difference between Two Independent Means

Table 11–3 gives an example for computing a confidence interval for the difference between two independent means, but the raw data are not presented. To illustrate the computation using the MINITAB program, we will employ the drug data created for use in the first computer exercise of Chapter 10:

Drug (1)	Non-Drug (2)
12, 9, 13, 6, 11, 11, 14, 10, 10, 12, 9, 7, 13, 12	7, 4, 8, 9, 5, 7, 10, 6, 6, 8, 9, 7, 7, 6, 9

Since the example involves two independent groups and $\sigma_{\bar{x}_1 - \bar{x}_2}$ is not known, the *2-Sample t* command will be used. A 95% confidence interval for the mean difference will be determined.

Retrieve the MINITAB Worksheet file for the drug data as follows:

> *File>Open Worksheet*
> (Select the saved drug data Worksheet file.)
> Open
> OK

A confidence interval may be computed using the *2-Sample t* command:

> *Stat>Basic Statistics>2-Sample t*
> Samples in different columns: Yes
> First: Drug   [double-click to transfer]
> Second: Nondrug
> Assume equal variances: Yes
> Options: Confidence level: 95%
> Test mean:0.0
> Alternative: not equal
> OK
> OK

The three options listed—confidence level of 95%, test mean of zero, and a non-directional alternative hypothesis—are default options. A pooled estimate for the standard error is specified, which assumes equal variances. The shaded lines of the program output appearing below (which is identical to that shown in the example of Chapter 10) reveal that the mean difference is 3.443, for which 95% confidence limits are from 1.921 to 4.965.

Note: to accommodate the "stacked" method of data entry, in which a treatment variable (*Trt*) is coded to indicate whether or not an individual received the drug (1=Drug; 2=Non-Drug), choose "Samples in one column." Refer to Chapter 10 for details.

To print the MINITAB output, select the output in the Session Window, then:

> *File>Print Session Window*
> Print Range: Selection
> OK

Exit MINITAB:

> *File>Exit*

MINITAB Program Output

```
Two Sample T-Test and CI: Drug, Nondrug

Two sample T for Drug vs Nondrug
 N Mean StDev SE Mean
Drug 14 10.64 2.31 0.62
Nondrug 15 7.20 1.66 0.43

Difference = mu Drug - mu Nondrug
Estimate for difference: 3.443
95% CI for mu Drug - mu Nondrug: (1.921, 4.965)
T-Test of difference = 0 (vs not =): T-Value = 4.64 P-Value= 0.000 DF= 27
Both use Pooled StDev = 2.00
```

● ● ● ● ●   SPSS

(To accompany the guided computational examples in Chapter 11.)

SPSS will compute confidence intervals for a single mean and for the difference between two independent means. Confidence intervals for a single correlation coefficient, or for the difference between two correlations are not computed.

Confidence Interval for a Single Mean

Unlike the computational examples shown in this chapter, the SPSS program is designed to compute confidence intervals directly from the raw data. Since raw data are not presented in Table 11–2, we will employ the *Looks* data first presented in Table 3–6, consisting of 70 observations on the number of looks at mother by a child. Since this example involves a single mean, and because $\sigma_{\bar{x}}$ is not known, the *One-Sample T Test* command will be used. A 95% confidence interval for the mean number of looks will be determined.

Retrieve the SPSS Save file for the *Looks* data of Chapter 3. If the data were saved in a file named *Looks.sav*, recall the file as follows:

> *File>Open>Data*
> (Select the *Looks.sav* file.)
> Open
> OK

Refer to Chapter 3 to re-enter the data if the *Looks* data were not saved at that time. A confidence interval may be computed as follows:

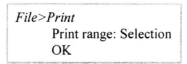

Analyze>Compare Means>One-Sample T Test
       Test Variable(s): Looks   [highlight and transfer]
       Test Value: **0**
       Options: Confidence Interval: 95%
               Continue
    OK

The 95% confidence level listed under "Options" is the default for this command, as is the value of zero for "Test Value." Note also that a particular test value is not necessary for calculating a confidence interval; any numeric value will work. If, instead of zero, the sample mean is entered, the calculated t statistic will be zero, with resulting p value of 1.0. The values shown for t, df and *Sig.* on the program output may be ignored. For the *Looks* data, the sample mean is shown to be 18.3429 with 95% confidence limits from 16.0631 to 20.6227.

To print the output, highlight the portion to be printed, then:

File>Print
       Print range: Selection
       OK

SPSS Program Output

T-Test

One-Sample Test

			Test Value = 0			
					95% Confidence Interval of the Difference	
	t	df	Sig. (2-tailed)	Mean Difference	Lower	Upper
LOOKS	16.051	69	.000	18.3429	16.0631	20.6227

Confidence Interval for the Difference between Two Independent Means

Table 11–3 gives an example for computing a confidence interval for the difference between two independent means, but the raw data are not presented. To illustrate the confidence interval computation using SPSS, we will employ the drug data created for use in the first computer exercise of Chapter 10:

Drug (1)	Non-Drug (2)
12, 9, 13, 6, 11, 11, 14, 10, 10, 12, 9, 7, 13, 12	7, 4, 8, 9, 5, 7, 10, 6, 6, 8, 9, 7, 7, 6, 9

Since the example involves two independent groups and $\sigma_{\bar{x}_1 - \bar{x}_2}$ is not known, the *Independent-Samples T Test* command will be used. A 95% confidence interval for the mean difference will be determined.

Recall that SPSS requires "stacked" data entry consisting of two variables: a treatment variable with a code for drug and non-drug groups (*Trt*), and the measurements of memory (*Meas*). Retrieve the SPSS Save file for the drug data of chapter 10 as follows:

> *File>Open>Data*
>   (Select the saved drug data file.)
>   Open
>   OK

If the drug data were not saved, refer to Chapter 10 regarding "stacked" data entry for SPSS.

A confidence interval may be now be computed as follows:

> *Analyze>Compare Means>Independent-Samples T Test*
>   Test Variable(s): Meas   [highlight and transfer]
>   Grouping Variable: Trt
>   Define Groups: Use specified values
>   Group 1: 1
>   Group 2: 2
>   Continue
>   Options: Confidence Interval: 95%
>   Continue
>   OK

The 95% confidence level listed under "Options" is the default for this command. The row labeled "Equal variances assumed" shows the results for the confidence limits computation in boldface type. For the drug data, the difference between sample means is shown to be 3.4429 with 95% confidence limits from 1.9206 to 4.9651. The output shown below is truncated horizontally somewhat to emphasize the sample mean difference and confidence limits. Highlight the desired output and print in landscape orientation:

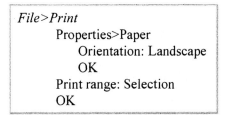

File>Print
    Properties>Paper
        Orientation: Landscape
        OK
    Print range: Selection
    OK

Exit SPSS:

File>Exit

SPSS Program Output

T-Test

Independent Samples Test

	Levene's Test for Equality of Variances		t-test for Equality of Means						
	F	Sig.	t	df	Sig. (2-tailed)	Mean Difference	Std. Error Difference	95% Confidence Interval of the Difference	
								Lower	Upper
Equal variances assumed	1.58	.220	4.64	27	.000	**3.4429**	.7419	**1.9206**	**4.9651**
Equal variances not assumed			4.59	23.5	.000	3.4429	.7504	1.8922	4.9935

● ● ● ● ●

CHAPTER 12

INTRODUCTION TO RESEARCH DESIGN • • • • •

CONCEPT GOALS

Be sure that you thoroughly understand the following concepts and how to use them.

- ◆ Steps in conducting research
- ◆ Experimental and observational research, causal and noncausal relationships
- ◆ Independent and dependent variables
- ◆ Operational definitions
- ◆ Reliability and validity
- ◆ Control groups, extraneous variables, confounding
- ◆ Participant and observer bias, single and double blind designs

• • • • • GUIDE TO MAJOR CONCEPTS

Introduction

Research design consists of the methods scientists use to make observations that will produce **empirical** information, usually about the relationship between two or more things called **variables**. Science relies heavily on systematic observation, which is why science is called [1]_____ . Typically, researchers observe the relationship between two or more [2]_____ according to systematic methods which collectively are called [3]_____ .

The "things" scientists study are [4]_____ , and there are two general kinds, **independent** and **dependent**. The variable thought to influence the other is the [5]_____ variable, while the variable thought to be influenced is the [6]_____ variable. The methods of [7]_____ then, describe the [8]_____ relationship between the [9]_____ and [10]_____ .

Such relationships may be **causal** or **noncausal**. For example, the independent variable might actually influence or determine the value of the dependent variable in some direct way. In this case, the relationship is [11]_____ . Alternatively, the two variables might be related, but the [12]_____ variable does not directly produce the values of the [13]_____ variable, in which case the relationship is [14]_____ .

Observational and **experimental** research methods differ in the kind of relationship that can be described. If the purpose of the research is to describe a relationship between two or more variables, regardless of whether that relationship is or is not [15]_____ , then [16]_____ methods might be used. However, if the purpose of the research is to describe a [17]_____ relationship, then [18]_____ methods would be preferred.

Regardless of which approach is taken, the process of conducting research typically consists of five steps. The first is to **formulate a scientific question**. Because science relies on systematic observations, that is, it is [19]_____ , a proper scientific question usually involves a relationship between at least two observable [20]_____ . Therefore, the first step in conducting research is to [21]_____ about two observable variables.

The next step is to **operationalize** the variables and their relationship. When a variable is defined in terms of the actions required to measure it, the result is an [22]_____ definition.

The third step is **data collection**. Making the actual observations and recording the measurements constitutes [23]_____ .

The next step is to **analyze the data**. It is in this phase that the numerical information is described, relationships quantified, and inferences drawn. Typically, statistics are used to [24]_____ .

The fifth step consists of **drawing conclusions and interpretations**. As a result of the data analysis, the researcher attempts to answer the scientific question by [25]_____ .

Suppose a scientist wanted to study the effects of viewing violent television on the aggressive behavior of children. The first step would be to [26]_____ . That might be: Does viewing violent television increase aggressive social behavior in nursery school children?

The next step is to [27]_____ the variables and their relationships. That is, "watching violent television" might be defined to be having the children watch 30 minutes of Road Runner cartoons each day at 9 am for two weeks during nursery school. Similarly, "aggressive behavior" and all the other procedures of the research must be [28]_____ .

Then comes the actual [29]_____ followed by the [30]_____ . As a result of these steps, the researcher will [31]_____ about the answer to the original question.

The skill in designing research is to create conditions so that the scientific question can be answered with some degree of certainty. For example, one requirement is that the variables of interest are measured accurately, that is, that those measurements have **reliability** and **validity**. When the measurement procedures assign the same value to a characteristic each time that it is measured under essentially the same circumstances, the measurement has [32]_____ . If the procedures produce measurements that accurately reflect the conceptual variable being measured, they have [33]_____ .

For example, if two trained observers both rate the aggressiveness of children after observing them for several days and the ratings of the two observers correlate highly across the sample of children, then the measurement of aggressiveness has [34]_____ between observers. If the ratings also correlate highly with the number of times each child verbally or physically attacks other children, then the ratings might be said to have [35]_____ .

A requirement of experimental research is that the study be designed so that it is reasonable to conclude that the independent variable caused or influenced the dependent variable. To do this, a simple experiment might consist of two groups, the **experimental** and the **control** groups. The treatment of interest is given to the [36]_____ group. For example, the group of nursery school children shown Road Runner cartoons might be the [37]_____ group. In contrast, another group of children would be given an experience as similar as possible to that of the experimental group except for the treatment of interest. It would be the [38]_____ group.

It is necessary to define the control group in such a way as to minimize **confounding** by an **extraneous variable**. For example, if the control group watched no television in nursery school at all and if the experimental children were more aggressive than the control children, one would not know if they were more aggressive because they saw television—any television—or because they saw violent television in particular. In this case, the independent variable of violent television would be [39]_____ with the [40]_____ of viewing television in general.

Sometimes the extraneous variable resides in the participants or in the observers. When the participants in the research influence its outcome because they know, or think they know, something about the study, it is called **participant bias**. Sometimes, for example, parents know the researcher is studying parental behavior so they try to be "good" parents while being observed. They are introducing [41]_____ into the results. At other times, however, the observers might be the source of bias. For example, the raters might know that children who watched violent television "should" be more aggressive, so they might tend to rate them as being more aggressive. Then one has a case of [42]_____ .

To minimize these possibilities, research is sometimes designed to be **single** or **double blind**. When both participants and observers do not know the research conditions, it is called a [43]_____ design. If one or the other, but not both, are ignorant about the research conditions, it is called a [44]_____ design.

Finally, an important procedural method used in experimental studies is to **randomly assign** participants to the experimental and control groups. Nursery school children, for example, differ in how aggressive they are before the scientific observations begin. If children are asked whether they want to watch Road Runner cartoons or Mister Rogers' Neighborhood, the aggressive children might all choose the cartoons. Any differences between the two groups would then be [45]_____ with the fact that the children in the experimental group were more aggressive to begin with. To minimize this possibility, the researcher would [46]_____ children to the two groups.

Throughout the design, conduct, and reporting of research, certain ethical principles must be followed. After the research is planned but before it is actually performed, a description of the proposed research must be reviewed by the institution's [47]_____ .

   The Board will decide issues of **risk/benefit, informed consent,** and **confidentiality.** For example, does the information to be gained from the proposed research outweigh any dangers to the participants? This is a question of [48]_____/_____ . The Board will also decide if the participants, who must read, understand, and sign a [49]_____ or [50]_____ form, will be given accurate and comprehensive information about the purpose, procedures, and possible risks and benefits of the research; that is, will the participants give truly [51]_____ ? Also, will the procedures protect the privacy of the participants and guarantee them [52]_____ of information?

   Researchers are also expected to report their procedures and results **honestly and forthrightly.** If an allegation is made that a researcher has not [53]_____ and [54]_____ reported the study, the institution's **scientific integrity procedures** may dictate a thorough review of the work. If the [55]_____ result in a judgment of guilt, the consequence of committing [56]_____ can be severe, effectively ending a research or academic career.

Answer Key to Introduction

[1]	empirical	[16]	observational	[28]	operationalized
[2]	variables	[17]	causal	[29]	data collection
[3]	research design	[18]	experimental	[30]	analysis of the data
[4]	variables	[19]	empirical	[31]	draw conclusions and
[5]	independent	[20]	variables		interpretations
[6]	dependent	[21]	formulate a scientific	[32]	reliabilty
[7]	research design		question	[33]	validity
[8]	empirical	[22]	operational	[34]	reliability
[9]	independent	[23]	data collection	[35]	validity
[10]	dependent variables	[24]	analyze the data	[36]	experimental
[11]	causal	[25]	drawing conclusions	[37]	experimental
[12]	independent		and interpretations	[38]	control
[13]	dependent	[26]	formulate a scientific	[39]	confounded
[14]	noncausal		question	[40]	extraneous variable
[15]	causal	[27]	operationalize	[41]	participant bias

[42]	observer bias	[48]	risk/benefit	[54]	forthrightly
[43]	double blind	[49]	consent	[55]	scientific integrity
[44]	single blind	[50]	release		procedures
[45]	confounded	[51]	informed consent	[56]	scientific misconduct
[46]	randomly assign	[52]	confidentiality		
[47]	Internal Review Board	[53]	honestly		

● ● ● ● ●   SELF-TEST

1. Methods that rely on direct systematic observations are called
    a. operational   c. empirical
    b. confounded   d. parametric

2. Research design consists of
    a. drawing a table of the groups to be studied
    b. the methods scientists use to make observations that will produce empirical information
    c. asking a scientific question
    d. analyzing the data with statistics

3. The "things" of scientific relationships are often called
    a. empirical concepts
    b. constants
    c. parameters
    d. variables

4. The variable whose values are thought to be influenced by another variable is called
    a. dependent   c. parametric
    b. independent   d. extraneous

5. If a researcher wants to describe a causal relationship, the research design should be
    a. observational   c. descriptive
    b. nonparametric   d. experimental

6.* A careful review of the research literature is likely to help in
    a. formulating the scientific question
    b. specifying parameters
    c. selecting control groups
    d. all of these

7.* A factor that influences a given behavior is a
    a. parameter
    b. extraneous variable
    c. independent variable
    d. all of these

8.* Factors in the research situation, but ones that are not related to the participants, that influence a given behavior are sometimes called
    a. exogenous parameters
    b. endogenous parameters
    c. extraneous variables
    d. dependent variables

9.   Specifying the actions required to measure a variable
      a.   makes it an independent variable
      b.   is its operational definition
      c.   constitutes its parameters
      d.   creates confounding

10.   When the measurements accurately reflect the conceptual variable being measured, they are said to be
      a.   reliable   c.   confounded
      b.   valid   d.   parametric

11.   When two observers tend to agree on the value of a variable for each member of a sample, the measurements are said to be
      a.   endogenous   c.   reliable
      b.   exogenous   d.   value

12.   The group of participants receiving the treatment of interest is called the
      a.   experimental group
      b.   endogenous group
      c.   pilot group
      d.   control group

13.   A procedure that minimizes participant bias is
      a.   random assignment of participants to groups
      b.   the double blind technique

      c.   using a control group that consists of participants selected in precisely the same way as those in the experimental group
      d.   all of the above

14.   The influence of an extraneous variable makes the design
      a.   a single blind   c.   confounded
      b.   a double blind   d.   experimental

15.* Placebos are sometimes used to control for
      a.   exogenous confounds
      b.   participant bias
      c.   nonrandom assignment of participants to groups
      d.   sampling error

16.   Generally, ethics in research is referred to as
      a.   honesty and forthrightness
      b.   informed consent
      c.   scientific integrity
      d.   confidentiality

17.   Ethical procedures that typically transpire before the research is actually carried out are
      a.   Internal Review Board approval
      b.   obtaining informed consent
      c.   deciding risk/benefit
      d.   all of these

*Questions preceded by an asterisk can be answered on the basis of the discussion in the text, but the discussion in this Study Guide does not answer them.

● ● ● ● ●   EXERCISES

1. Suppose a researcher was interested in determining the possible influence on children's aggressive social behavior of viewing violent television programs. The following experiment was designed. Two nursery schools agreed to participate. In Hillrise Nursery School, Mr. Gregory agreed to show Roadrunner cartoons for an hour each day beginning at 9 am to the 12 children ages 4–5 years in his class. At Greenbriar Nursery School, Mrs. Abernathy taught a class of 11 children ranging from 3 to 5 years of age. She said that she could not show cartoons to her children, but agreed to have the social behavior of her pupils observed.

    Cartoons were shown each weekday to Mr. Gregory's class for two weeks. On the last day, the cartoons were shown and then an observer came to watch the children play between 10 am and 11:30 am. The observer then ranked each child according to how aggressive he or she was during the observation period, with the rank of 1 going to the most aggressive child and the rank of 12 going to the least aggressive child. After lunch, the observer went to the Greenbriar school and observed the children there for an hour before their nap, and ranked those children in the same way as the children at Hillrise. The researcher then attempted to determine if watching violent television made the Hillrise children more aggressive than the Greenbriar children by comparing the average ranking for the two groups.

    Criticize this experiment. List and label all confounds and other problems that prevent the researcher from drawing a firm conclusion about the potential of watching violent television to produce aggressive social behavior in nursery school children.

2. Design a better experiment that would address the same research question posed above. Follow the steps of conducting a research project outlined in the text, and pay special attention to minimizing possible extraneous variables.

● ● ● ● ●   ANSWERS

Self-Test. (1) c. **(2)** b. **(3)** d. **(4)** a. **(5)** d. **(6)** d. **(7)** d. **(8)** a. **(9)** b. **(10)** b. **(11)** c. **(12)** a. **(13)** d. **(14)** c. **(15)** b. **(16)** c. **(17)** d.

Exercises. (1) The operational definition of watching violent television includes only watching cartoons and only Roadrunner cartoons. Therefore, the conclusion should be specific to Roadrunner cartoons, not all cartoons or violent television. Further, the operational definition of the control group involves not watching any kind of television. Therefore, it is possible that watching any kind of television might influence social aggressiveness. A number of extraneous variables confound the possible results. For example, participant bias might be involved because neither the schools nor the children were randomly assigned to experimental and control groups. Notice also that the teachers volunteered to show cartoons or not show them. Further, observer bias could occur because the observer knew which group saw the cartoons. A number of exogenous extraneous variables were present as well. For example, experimental and control groups were confounded with specific preschools, classrooms, teachers, sex of teacher, time of day, and the time since eating or before a nap at which the assessment of aggressiveness was conducted. Finally, ranking the children within a class will not produce data that will reflect the relative amount of aggressiveness the children in the two groups displayed. The mean rankings will be different only because there was a different number of children in each group. **(2)** Discuss your proposed research design with your teacher or classmates.

● ● ● ● ●

CHAPTER 13

TOPICS IN PROBABILITY ● ● ● ● ●

CONCEPT GOALS

Be sure that you thoroughly understand the following concepts and how to use them in statistical applications.

- ◆ Set, element, subset, disjoint sets, union of sets, intersection of sets
- ◆ Classical probability, sample space, elementary event, mutually exclusive events
- ◆ Conditional probability, independent and dependent events
- ◆ Permutations, combinations

● ● ● ● ● GUIDE TO MAJOR CONCEPTS

Introduction

The cornerstone of inferential statistics is the concept of **probability**. A mathematical way of quantifying the likelihood of a given event is [1]_____ .

Answer Key to Introduction

[1]   probability

Set Theory

The study of probability is made much easier by a knowledge of the terms of set theory. Objects or events can be thought of as being **elements** of **sets** or **subsets**.

A well-defined collection of things is called a [1]___ , and any member of the collection is an [2]_____ of that set. If we have two sets, *A* and *B*, and every element of set *A* is also an element of set *B*, then *A* is a [3]_____ of *B*. A population is an example of a [4]___ , a sample from that population constitutes a [5]_____ , and a particular subject in the sample is an [6]_____ .

Sets may have various relationships to one another. For example, they may be **equal** or **disjoint**. If every element of set *A* is also an element of set *B* and every element of *B* is also an element of *A*, then set *A* [7]_____ set *B*; they are the same set. On the other hand, if *no* element of *A* is also in *B* and *no* element of *B* is also in *A*, then the sets are totally different from each other, and we say that they are [8]_____ .

Sets may also share some, but perhaps not all, elements. For example, given two sets *A* and *B*, the set of all elements that are either in *A* or in *B* (and possibly in both *A* and *B*) is called the **union** of *A* and *B*, which is symbolized $A \cup B$. If set *A* includes all children aged 3 to 5 and set *B* includes all children aged 4 to 6, all children aged 3 to 6 constitutes the [9]_____ of *A* and *B*, or in symbols, [10]_____ . In ordinary language, we frequently use the word *or* instead of *union*, as when we mention children age 3 to 5 [11]___ 4 to 6. In the space provided in Figure 13–1, draw two intersecting circles *A* and *B* and shade the area representing the concept of union.

Figure 13–1. Graphic representation of $A \cup B$.
See Figure 13–3 in the text for the completed drawing.

Another important relationship is the **intersection** of two sets, symbolized by $A \cap B$. Given two sets, A and B, elements that are in both A and B (but not those in A or B alone) make up the [12]_____ of A and B, which is written [13]_____ . The intersection of the two sets of children age 3 to 5 and 4 to 6 would include children age [14]_____ . In ordinary language we often use the word *and* rather than [15]_____ , as when we designate that we want children who are in the group aged 3 to 5 [16]___ also in the group aged 4 to 6. In Figure 13–2, draw two intersecting circles A and B and shade the area representing the intersection of $A \cap B$.　　.

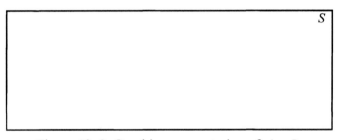

Figure 13–2. Graphic representation of $A \cap B$.

See Figure 13–4 in the text for the completed drawing.

A special case arises when the intersection of two sets contains no elements at all, which set is called **empty** or the **null set** symbolized by $\varnothing$. When [17]$A \cap B =$ _____ , or the [18]_____ set, A and B are said to be [19]_____ . Also, if A is a set, then all elements not in A are said to be in the **complement** of A, written A' and said "not A." Therefore, [20]$A \cap A' =$ ___ , or a set and its [21]_____ are [22]_____ . The set of all things being considered in any one discussion is the **universal set,** symbolized by S. Any set A within S is a subset of the [23]_____ and [24]$A \cup A' =$ ___ .

To review, let us start with people as the [25]_____ , and then let us divide the set *people* into two subsets, *men* and *women*. Mr. Jones is thus an [26]_____ of the [27]___ of men, which in turn is a [28]_____ of the set *people*. A group composed of either men (M) or women (W) is the [29]_____ of those sets, which is symbolized by [30]_____ . However, since no person is both a man and a woman, the [31]_____ of the groups men

The *probability* of Johnny's getting the car is said to be **conditional** upon whether the first child does, but the two *events* themselves are said to be **dependent events**. The events of drawing an ace from a deck of cards on both the first and second draws when cards are not replaced into the deck after drawing are two [5]_____ events, because the probability for the second draw is [6]_____ upon the outcome of the first draw. When the probability of a particular event is *not* conditional on the outcome of some other event, the two events are said to be **independent**. If cards are replaced into the deck after a draw, then the probability of an ace on the second draw does not depend on whether an ace was drawn on the first. These two events are said to be [7]_____ because the probability of the second is not [8]_____ upon the outcome of the first.

Answer Key to Conditional Probability					
[1]	1/10	[4]	0	[7]	independent
[2]	conditional probability	[5]	dependent	[8]	conditional
[3]	1/9	[6]	conditional		

Probability of $A \cap B$

Suppose we want to know the probability that two events will both occur, such as drawing 2 kings in row without replacement from a small deck of 12 cards containing the 4 kings, 4 queens, and 4 jacks. The event of drawing two consecutive kings is a complex one, consisting of the event A (obtaining a king on the first draw) *and* event B (obtaining a king on the second draw given a king was drawn on the first). The required probability is that both A *and* B occur, which in set theory is called their [1]_____ , symbolized by [2]_____ . The probability of the intersection of two events A and B is $P(A \cap B) = P(A)P(B|A)$. The probability that two events A and B both occur is the probability of A *times* the conditional probability of B given that A has already occurred. Applied to this example, the probability of drawing two consecutive kings without replacement is the probability of obtaining a king on the first draw (times/plus) [3]_____ the probability of obtaining a king on the second draw given that a king has already been drawn. The probability of drawing the first king is [4]$P(A) =$ ___ ; the probability of drawing the second king given that a king was obtained on the first draw, symbolized by [5]_____ , equals [6]__ . Therefore, the probability fo both events (of the [7]_____ of A and B) equals [8]$P(\_\_) =$ _____ = _____ = _____ = __ .

Similarly, winning a four-team, single-elimination basketball tournament (*single elimination* means that a team is eliminated when it loses one game) requires a team to win two consecutive games. Thus, event A is winning the first game; event B is winning the second game given that you've won the first. The probability of winning the first game is [9]$P(A) =$ ___ . The probability of winning the second game given that you win the first (you don't get to play the second without winning the first) is [10]$P(B|A) =$ ___ . Thus, the probability of winning the tournament is symbolized by [11]_____ and equals [12]_____ = _____ = __ .

When the probability of the intersection of two events is 0, the events are said to be **mutually exclusive**. If M includes male newborn infants and F includes female newborns, the two sets have no common elements and are said to be **disjoint**. Since no baby is born both male and female, the probability of $M \cap F$ is [13]__ , the sets are [14]_____ and the events of giving birth to a male and giving birth to a female are [15]_____ .

Answer Key to Probability of $A \cap B$

[1]	intersection	[7]	intersection	[11]	$P(A \cap B)$
[2]	$A \cap B$	[8]	$A \cap B = P(A)P(B|A) =$	[12]	$P(A)P(B|A) =$
[3]	times		$(4/12)(3/11) = 12/132$		$(1/2)(1/2) = 1/4$
[4]	4/12		$= 1/11$	[13]	0
[5]	$P(B|A)$	[9]	1/2	[14]	disjoint
[6]	3/11	[10]	1/2	[15]	mutually exclusive

Probability of $A \cup B$

Suppose that we want to know the probability that either one *or* the other of two events will occur. For example, what is the probability of selecting either a queen or a red card from a deck composed of 12 face cards (i.e., the 4 jacks, queens, and kings)? Again this is a complex event involving two simple events: event A, which is [1]_____ , and event B, which is

[2]_____ . The desired probability is for either one or the other (or both) events to

occur, which in set theory is known as the [3]_____ of A and B, symbolized by

[4]_____ . The probability is given by $P(A \cup B) = P(A) + P(B) - P(A \cap B)$. The probability

of A or B occurring is the probability of A *plus* the probability of B *minus* the probability of A

and B both occurring. In the present problem, the probability of A is [5]__ and the probability of B

is [6]__ . One more quantity is needed to solve the problem— the probability that both A and B

occur, which is that of drawing a red queen. There are two red queens in the deck of 12 cards, so

[7] $P(A \cap B) = $ __ .

Thus the probability of selecting either a queen or a red card from the special deck, which

can be found by the formula [8]_____ = _____ – _____ , is

[9] _____ = _____ = __ .

Similarly, the probability of getting an even number or a 1 in a single roll of a die equals the

probability of the [10]_____ of the events A (which is [11]_____) and B

(which is [12]_____). In this case there is no possibility of getting both an even number

and a 1 (events A and B are [13]_____), so [14]_____ $= 0$. Therefore, the

required probability is given by the formula

[15]_____ = _____ – _____ , which equals

[16]_____ = _____ = _____

Answer Key to Probability of $A \cup B$

[1]	selecting a queen	[8]	$P(A \cup B) = P(A) + P(B)$	[12]	obtaining a 1
[2]	selecting a red card		$-P(A \cap B)$	[13]	mutually exclusive
[3]	union	[9]	$(1/3) + (1/2) - (2/12)$	[14]	$P(A \cap B)$
[4]	$A \cup B$		$= 8/12 = 2/3$	[15]	$P(A \cup B) = P(A) + P(B)$
[5]	1/3	[10]	union		$-P(A \cap B)$
[6]	1/2	[11]	obtaining an even	[16]	$(1/2) + (1/6) - 0 = 4/6$
[7]	2/12		number		$= 2/3$

Counting

To determine the probability of an event, it is necessary to count both the total number of events in the sample space and the number of events that would qualify as the desired outcome (i.e., to know the values of #S and #A in the formula $P(A) = \#A/\#S$). Sometimes this process can be tedious. An *ordered* set of objects or events is called a **permutation**, and the number of [1]_____ of r objects that can be selected from a total of n objects is symbolized by $_nP_r$, which is read "the number of permutations of n things taken r at a time." Suppose there are ten dishes on a menu and you are interested in the number of different sequences of two dishes that you could have for dinner. Since you are concerned with the sequence in which you are to eat the dishes, you are interested in the number of [2]_____ of [3]__ things taken [4]__ at a time, which can be symbolized [5]__ .

The number of permutations of n things taken r at a time equals $_nP_r = n!/(n-r)!$.

Recall that n!, read "n factorial," means the product $n(n-1)(n-2)\ldots(1)$. In the present example, the number of permutations of ten things taken two at a time is

[6] __ = _____ = _____ = _____ = __ . Similarly, the number of sequences in which one could discard the first three cards of a seven-card rummy hand would be

[7] __ = _____ = _____ = _____ = __ . However, suppose one is interested in the number of groups of r elements taken from a set of n, but that the order of elements within a group is not at all important. Such a group is called a **combination**, symbolized $_nC_r$. For instance, suppose a store has ten postcards depicting scenes from the local area, and you want to pick two of them. How many two-card combinations can be selected? The order in which you pick the two cards does not matter. The number of [8]_____ of n things taken r at a time is $_nC_r = n!/[(n-r)!r!]$.

Applied to the problem of selecting two postcards from a set of ten, one has

[9] __ = _____ = _____ = _____ = __ possible combinations. Similarly, the number of different committees of three people that could be selected from a group of five is given by [10] __ = _____ = _____ = _____ = __ .

To review, the difference between permutations and combinations is one of sequence or order. When the order of events is important, the number of [11]_____ is required; but when order is unimportant, the number of [12]_____ is needed. Thus, if the first three runners in a six-person preliminary heat of the hurdles will qualify for the final race, finding the number of different groups of finalists that are possible is a question involving [13]_____ , but finding the number of win, place, and show (first, second, and third place) possibilities in a horse race is a problem involving [14]_____ .

These methods of counting can be used to determine the probability of certain events. For example, what is the probability of randomly guessing which horse will finish first, which second, and which third in a six-horse race? First, because the order of finish is important, this is a problem involving [15]_____ . Second, how many ways are there to pick the first three horses? Only one sequence of three horses will occur. Therefore, #(A) equals [16]__ . Third, the sample space consists of all possible permutations of [17]__ horses taken [18]__ at a time. Therefore, the #(S) is symbolized by [19]__ .

The required probability is

[20] $P(A) = \#(A)/\#(S) =$ __ = _____ = _____ = _____ = __ .

What is the probability of being dealt all hearts in a five-card poker hand? The event A is receiving [21]_____ , but there is more than one way to accomplish that feat. Since the order of dealing is irrelevant, you need to determine the number of [22]_____ of [23]__ hearts taken [24]__ at a time. Thus #(A) is symbolized by [25]__ and equals

[26] __ = _____ = _____ = _____ = _____ = __ .

However, the number of possible five-card hands constitutes the [27]_____ in this problem, and the actual number can be symbolized by [28]__ , which equals

[29] __ = _____ = _____ = _____ = _____ = ____ .

Thus, the required probability in this case is

$$[30] \quad P(A) = \#(A)/\#(S) = \underline{\hspace{3cm}} = \underline{\hspace{3cm}}.$$

A special application of determining the number of combinations occurs when there are only two possible outcomes — for example, success/failure, win/lose, rain/no rain — for each of several trials or occasions. This situation often calls for **binomial probability**. For example, flipping a coin five consecutive times is a case in which there are only two outcomes on a given flip, heads or tails, and a series of five trials or occasions, thus calling for [31]_____.

Suppose at a carnival, you are given three tries to make a basket with a basketball. You must get at least two baskets to receive a prize, and your shooting percentage is 60%. What is the likelihood you win a prize? This probability is the union of getting two out of three and three out of three baskets. To calculate the probability of getting exactly two out of three, one needs to use [32]_____.

Specifically, in a sequence of n independent trials that have only two possible outcomes (success/ failure) with the probability p of success and the probability q of failure ($q = 1 - p$), the probability of exactly r successes in n trials is $P(r, n; p) = {}_nC_r p^r q^{n-r}$ or

$P(r, n; p) = \dfrac{n!}{r!(n-r)!} p^r q^{n-r}$. So, to get exactly two out of three baskets, [33] $n = \underline{\ \ }$,

[34] $r = \underline{\ \ }$, [35] $p = \underline{\ \ }$, and [36] $q = \underline{\ \ }$ and the probability is given by

[37] $\underline{\hspace{3cm}} = \underline{\hspace{3cm}} = \underline{\hspace{3cm}} = \underline{\ \ }$. Similarly, the probability

of getting exactly three out of three baskets requires setting [38] $n = \underline{\ \ }$, [39] $r = \underline{\ \ }$, [40] $p = \underline{\ \ }$,

and [41] $q = \underline{\ \ }$ and solving (note that $0! = 1$ and $x^0 = 1$):

[42] $\underline{\hspace{2.5cm}} = \underline{\hspace{4cm}} = \underline{\hspace{2.5cm}} = \underline{\ \ }$. Therefore, the

probability of getting at least two out of three is the union of two out of three (A) and three out of three (B) or $P(A \cup B) = P(A) + P(B) = .432 + .216 = .648$. Perhaps the game is worth a try — if you like the prize.

Table 13–1 presents a summary and guide for the probability concepts discussed in this chapter. Do these problems now, and follow the same format in working the exercises.

Table 13–1 Guided Computational Examples

1. Probability

What is the probability of rolling a 4 or higher in one toss of a fair die?

$A =$ _____ $\#(A) =$ __

$S =$ _____ $\#(S) =$ __

$P(A) = \#(A)/\#(S) =$ _____ $=$ _____

2. Probability of the Intersection of Two Events

What is the probability of drawing 2 aces in a row without replacement from a deck of 52 cards?

$A =$ _____ $P(A) =$ _____

$B|A =$ _____ $P(B|A) =$ _____

$P(A \cap B) = P(A)P(B|A) =$ _____ $=$ _____ $=$ _____

3. Probability of the Union of Two Events

What is the probability of rolling an even number or obtaining a value greater than 4 with a single roll of a fair die?

$A =$ _____ $P(A) =$ _____

$B =$ _____ $P(B) =$ _____

$A \cap B =$ _____ $P(A \cap B) =$ _____

$P(A \cup B) = P(A) + P(B) - P(A \cap B) =$ _____ $=$ _____

4. Permutations

How many seating arrangements are possible for seven people in a room containing four chairs?

$n =$ __ $r =$ __ $_nP_r = n!/(n-r)! =$ _____ $=$ __

5. Combinations

How many different groups from among nine people can sit in six chairs?

$n =$ __ $r =$ __ $_nC_r = n!/[(n-r)!r!] =$ _____ $=$ __

6. Binomial Probability

If the likelihood of rain is 40% on each of the next four days, what is the probability that it rains on two of the four days? $n =$ __ $r =$ __ $p =$ __ $q =$ __

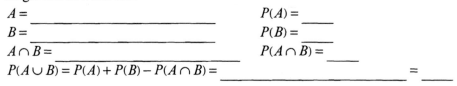

$P(r, n; p) = {_nC_r}p^r q^{n-r} = \dfrac{n!}{r!(n-r)!} / p^r q^{n-r} =$ _____ $=$ _____ $=$ __

Answer Key to Counting

[1]   permutations

[2]   permutations

[3]   10

[4]   2

[5] $_{10}P_2$

[6] $_nP_r = n!/(n-r)! = 10!/(10-2)! =$

$\dfrac{10 \cdot 9 \cdot 8!}{8!} = 90$

[7] $_nP_r = n!/(n-r)! = 7!/(7-3)! =$

$\dfrac{7 \cdot 6 \cdot 5 \cdot 4!}{4!} = 210$

[8]   combinations

[9] $_nC_r = n!/[(n-r)!r!] = 10!/[(10-2)!2!] =$

$\dfrac{\overset{5}{\cancel{10}} \cdot 9 \cdot 8!}{8! \cdot \cancel{2} \cdot 1} = 45$

[10] $_nC_r = n!/[(n-r)!r!] = 5!/[(5-3)!3!] =$

$\dfrac{5 \cdot \overset{2}{\cancel{4}} \cdot 3!}{\cancel{2} \cdot 1 \cdot 3!} = 10$

[11] permutations

[12] combinations

[13] combinations

[14] permutations

[15] permutations

[16] 1

[17] 6

[18] 3

[19] $_6P_3$

[20] $1/_6P_3 = 1/[n!/(n-r)!] = 1/[6!/(6-3)!] =$

$\dfrac{1}{\frac{6 \cdot 5 \cdot 4 \cdot 3!}{3!}} = \dfrac{1}{120}$

[21] all hearts

[22] combinations

[23] 13

[24] 5

[25] $_{13}C_5$

[26] $_{13}C_5 = n!/[(n-r)!r!] = 13!/[(13-5)!5!] =$

$\dfrac{13 \cdot \cancel{12} \cdot 11 \cdot \cancel{10} \cdot 9 \cdot 8!}{8! \cdot \cancel{5} \cdot \cancel{4} \cdot \cancel{3} \cdot \cancel{2} \cdot 1} = 13 \cdot 11 \cdot 9 = 1287$

[27] sample space

[28] $_{52}C_5$

[29] $_{52}C_5 = n!/[(n-r)!r!] = 52!/[(52-5)!5!]$

$= \dfrac{52 \cdot 51 \cdot \overset{10}{\cancel{50}} \cdot 49 \cdot \overset{2}{\cancel{48}} \cdot 47!}{47! \cdot \cancel{5} \cdot \cancel{4} \cdot \cancel{3} \cdot \cancel{2} \cdot 1} =$

$52 \cdot 51 \cdot 10 \cdot 49 \cdot 2 = 2{,}598{,}960$

[30] $1287/2{,}598{,}960 = .0005$

[31] binomial probability

[32] binomial probability

[33] 3

[34] 2

[35] .60

[36] .40

[37] $P(2, 3; 60) = \dfrac{3!}{2!(3-2)!}(.60)^2(.40)^{3-2} =$

$\dfrac{3 \cdot 2 \cdot 1}{2 \cdot 1 \cdot 1}(.60)^2(.40)^1 = .432$

[38] 3

[39]   3

[40]   .60

[41]   .40

[42] $P(3,\ 3;\ 60) = \dfrac{3!}{3!(3-3)!}(.60)^3(.40)^{3-3} =$

$1(.60)^3(.40)^0 = .216$

●●●●●   SELF-TEST

1.   In an introductory statistics class, 10 of the students, including Mary Smith, are psychology majors. Of these, 7 are also taking a course in learning. None of the students are taking experimental psychology. The three psychology majors who are not taking learning are studying clinical psychology. Two of the students taking clinical and three of the students taking learning are also enrolled in personality theory. Below are some set-theoretical concepts. Give an example of each from the situation described above.
   a.   the null set
   b.   disjoint sets
   c.   a set and a subset of it
   d.   the union of two sets
   e.   the intersection of two sets
   f.   the complement of a set
   g.   an element of a set

2.   Define the simple probability of an event A.

3.   What is the probability of the union of five mutually exclusive events if the complement of that union is the null set?

4.   Are the following pairs of events mutually exclusive?
   a.   rolling an even number, and rolling less than a 5 with a fair die
   b.   rolling an even number, and rolling less than 2 with a fair die
   c.   drawing a heart and drawing a face card from a deck of 52 cards

5.   Which pairs of events are dependent and which are independent?
   a.   You select the chocolate cream pie from a cart containing one each of eight different desserts; you let your date pick a dessert first.
   b.   After drawing a king on your first draw, obtaining one ace in the next four draws without replacement.
   c.   Rolling a six after rolling four consecutive sixes with a fair die.
   d.   The baby is female in each of two consecutive births in a family.

6.*   What is the relationship between conditional probability and independence?

7.   Indicate whether each of the following illustrates the intersection or the union of two events.
   a.   rolling either 2 or 4 in a single roll of a die
   b.   drawing a card that is both red and even numbered
   c.   becoming a pilot in either the Army or the Air Force
   d.   answering each of 10 questions correctly

●●●●● **EXERCISES**

1. In a special deck consisting of four aces, four kings, four queens, four jacks, and four jokers, determine the probability of drawing:
   a. an ace
   b. a red queen or a joker
   c. a club (jokers are not considered to be members of any of the four suits)
   d. the king of hearts followed by a joker with replacement after the first draw
   e. the king of hearts followed by the king of spades without replacement
   f. two kings in a row with replacement
   g. two kings in a row without replacement

2. There are two baseball games being played this weekend. There is a forecast of 40% chance of rain for the Friday night game and a 30% chance for the Saturday contest.
   a. What is the probability that both games are rained out?
   b. What is the probability that they play both games?
   c.* What is the probability that one or no games are rained out?
   d.* What is the probability that exactly one game is rained out?

3. A teacher divides the class into two teams. Team *A* has three students, and team *B* has four. Each team member must work on a mathematics problem independently. A team wins if all members of the team complete the problem successfully. Suppose that the students in team *A* have probabilities of .65, .80, and .90 of solving the problem, whereas for team *B* these probabilities are .70, .75, .85, and .90.
   a. Which team would you bet on?
   b. What is the probability that neither team wins?

4. Since 10 of the applicants in the Campus Trivia-Talent Search Contest tie for the top score, a random drawing is conducted to determine who among the six men and four women will become the three people who will make up the team to be sent to the Collegiate Trivia Nationals.
   a. If the first person chosen for the team is a male, what is the probability that the second person will also be a male?
   b. If the first two team members are female, what is the probability that the third person drawn is a male?
   c. What is the probability that an all female team will be drawn?

5. Suppose Las Vegas bookies estimate the probability to be .20 that the horse named By-the-Nose will win the Triple Crown. The same bookies are estimating the probability of By-the-Nose winning both the first two races in the three-race Triple Crown sequence to be .50. Assuming that the three races are independent events, what is the probability that By-the-Nose will win the third race?

6. Suppose that you apply for two summer jobs and that you know that you are one of a total of five applicants for the first and one of three for the second job. On a purely chance basis, what is the likelihood that you'll be unemployed this summer?

7. In a league of eight teams, how many different groups of teams could there be in a playoff tournament if the playoffs involved:
   a. four teams?   b. two teams?

8. In joining a book club, you can choose any three books from a group of 12 titles. How many groups of books are possible?

9. How many orders of finish (first place through last) are possible in a six-horse race?

10. If there are 10 cars in a Grand Prix race, how many possible orders of finish for the first, second, and third place cars are there?

11. What is the probability of being dealt a five-card poker hand in which all cards are spades? In which all cards are of one suit? (No jokers are in the deck.)

12. If a basketball coach has six guards, five forwards, and two centers, how many teams could be composed? (A basketball team has two guards, two forwards, and a center.)

13. Suppose that on a test of extra sensory perception a "receiving" subject is required to guess which of four geometric patterns a "transmitting" subject is viewing. The patterns are on four cards that are shuffled between each trial to obtain randomness. What is the probability that a receiver will be correct on at least three of four trials by chance alone?

14. Suppose a very long multiple-choice test contains questions with four alternative answers each, and your score will be the number right minus one-third the number wrong.
   a. If you know absolutely nothing about the answer to a question, should you guess?
   b. If you can eliminate one alternative as being definitely wrong, is it to your advantage to guess?

Questions preceded by an asterisk can be answered on the basis of the discussion in the text, but the discussion in this Study Guide does not answer them.

• • • • • ANSWERS

Table 13–1. (1) A = rolling a 4, 5, or 6; $\#(A) =$ 3; S = rolling a 1, 2, 3, 4, 5, or 6; $\#(S) = 6$; $P(A) = 3/6 = 1/2$. **(2)** A = an ace on the first draw; $P(A) = 4/52$; $B|A$ = an ace on the second draw given that an ace was obtained on the first draw; $P(B|A) = 3/51$; $P(A \cap B) = (4/52)(3/51) = 1/221$.
(3) A = rolling a 2, 4, or 6; $P(A) = 3/6$; B = rolling a 5 or 6; $P(B) = 2/6$; $A \cap B$ = rolling a 6; $P(A \cap B) = 1/6$; $P(A \cup B) = (3/6) + (2/6) - (1/6) = 2/3$.
(4) $n = 7$; $r = 4$, $7!/(7-4)! = 840$. **(5)** $n = 9$; $r = 6$; $9!/[(9-6)!6!] = 84$. **(6)** $n = 4$, $r = 3$, $p = .40$, $q = .60$; $\dfrac{4!}{3!(4-3)!}(.40)^3(.60)^{4-3} =$
$= \dfrac{4 \cdot 3!}{3!1!}(.40)^3(.60)^1 = .1536$.

Self-Test. (la) Students in the sample taking experimental psychology; **(1b)** students taking learning and students taking clinical; **(1c)** the two students enrolled in personality are a subset of the set of students taking clinical; **(1d)** students taking learning or clinical; **(1e)** students taking learning and personality; **(1f)** students not taking personality; **(1g)** Mary Smith. **(2)** $P(A) = \#(A)/\#(S)$. **(3)** 1.00. **(4a)** No;

(4b) yes; **(4c)** no. **(5a)** Dependent; **(5b)** dependent; **(5c)** independent; **(5d)** independent. **(6)** A and B are independent if the conditional $P(B|A) = P(B)$. **(7a)** Union; **(7b)** intersection; **(7c)** union; **(7d)** intersection.

Exercises. (la) $1/5$; **(1b)** $3/10$; **(1c)** $1/5$; **(1d)** $1/100$; **(1e)** $1/380$; **(1f)** $1/25$; **(1g)** $3/95$. **(2a)** $(.4)(.3) = .12$; **(2b)** $(1-.4)(1-.3) = .42$; **(2c)** $1 - .12 = .88$ or $[P(\text{play both}) = (.6)(.7) = .42]$ plus $[P(\text{rain, play}) = (.4)(.7) = .28]$ plus $[P(\text{play, rain}) = (.6)(.3) = .18] = .88$; **(2d)** $.4(.7) + .6(.3) = .46$. **(3a)** $P(A) = .468$, $P(B) = .402$, bet on A; **(3b)** $P(A' \cap B') = (1 - .468)(1 - .402) = .32$. **(4a)** $5/9$; **(4b)** $6/8$; **(4c)** $(4/10)(3/9)(2/8) = 1/30$. **(5)** $P(A)$ = win first two races = .50; B = win third race; $P(A \cup B) = P(A)P(B|A) = .20$; $P(B|A) = .40$. **(6)** $P(\text{unemployed}) = P(A')P(B')$ $= (4/5)(2/3) = 8/15$. **(7a)** $_8C_4 = 70$; $_8C_2 = 28$. **(8)** $_{12}C_3 = 220$. **(9)** $_6P_6 = 720$. **(10)** $_{10}P_3 = 720$. **(11)** $_{13}C_5/_{52}C_5 = 33/66640$; $4(33/66640) = 33/16660$. **(12)** $(_6C_2)(_5C_2)(_2C_1) = 300$.

(13) $\dfrac{n!}{(n-r)!\,r!}\,p^r q^{n-r} = 3\,/\,64$. **(14a)** For every four such questions on which you guess, you will get one correct and three wrong, yielding a score of $1-(1\,/\,3)(3)=0$, so there is no advantage or disadvantage in the long run to guessing; **(14b)** For every six such questions, you will get two correct and four wrong, yielding a score of $2-(1\,/\,3)(4)=2\,/\,3$, so there is some advantage in the long run to guessing under these circumstances.

● ● ● ● ●

CHAPTER 14

SIMPLE ANALYSIS OF VARIANCE •••••

CONCEPT GOALS

Be sure that you thoroughly understand the following concepts and how to use them in statistical applications.

- ◆ Notation: $X_{ij}, p, n_j, N, T_j, \overline{X}_j, T, \overline{X}$
- ◆ Sum of squares (SS), degrees of freedom (df), mean square (MS)
- ◆ Between-groups and within-groups variance estimates
- ◆ Treatment variability and error variability
- ◆ F distribution and F ratio
- ◆ Assumptions of the analysis of variance

••••• GUIDE TO MAJOR CONCEPTS

Introduction

In Chapter 10 you learned how to test the hypothesis that the means of two groups of scores differed from each other only because of [1]_____ . But suppose you have more than two groups. What is the probability that the means of these several groups differ from one another by sampling error alone? A problem of this type often requires the statistical technique known as the [2]_____ .

[1]   sampling error   [2]   analysis of variance

Notation

It will be helpful to review the notation and terminology presented in the text. The data for a simple analysis of variance can be cast into a form similar to that presented in Table 14–1. The scores are clustered into p groups. Each score is designated by X_{ij}, meaning the ith case in the jth group. So X_{42} is the [1]_____ case in the [2]_____ group. The symbol n_j denotes the number of cases in the jth group: Thus n_2 is the number of cases in the [3]_____ group. N stands for the total number of cases in the entire data set: [4] $n_1 + n_2 + \cdots + n_p = $ ___ . There are p groups, so the score for the third case in the last group is [5]___ , and the number of cases in the last group is [6]___ . Sometimes it is convenient to talk about some case in some group without specifying any particular one. In this event, one uses the subscripts i and j rather than specific numbers; the score of some unspecified case is thus denoted [7]___ , and the number of cases in some unspecified group can be expressed by [8]___ .

The mean of the jth group is written $\overline{X}_j$; the mean of the first group is thus [9]___ . The mean over all cases in the data set, called the **grand mean**, is written without subscripts, simply as [10]___ . Notice that the formula for the grand mean involves two summation signs: $\sum_{j=1}^{p} \sum_{i=1}^{n_j} X_{ij} / N$. This is a symbolic way of directing you to sum the scores of all the cases within each group ($\sum_{i=1}^{n_j}$) and over all groups ($\sum_{j=1}^{p}$) . One must also be careful to note which subscript, i or j, is being summed. For example, the sum of all the scores in the second group is written [11]_____ , whereas the sum of the p group means would be designated [12]_____ . By analogy, the formula for the mean of the third group would be [13]_____ .

Table 14–1 General Notation for Simple Analysis of Variance

	Group 1	Group 2	...	Group p	
	X_{11}	X_{12}	...	X_{1p}	
	X_{21}	X_{22}	...	X_{2p}	
	X_{31}	X_{32}	...	X_{3p}	
	X_{41}	X_{42}	...	X_{4p}	
	.	.	.	.	
	.	.	.	.	
	.	.	.	.	
	$X_{n_1 1}$	$X_{n_2 2}$	...	$X_{n_p p}$	
					Grand Total
Group Totals	T_1	T_2	...	T_p	T
					Grand Mean
Group Means	$\overline{X}_1 = T_1 / n_1$	$\overline{X}_2 = T_2 / n_2$	...	$\overline{X}_p = T_p / n_p$	$\overline{X}$

X_{ij} = score for the ith case in the jth group

p = number of groups

n_j = number of cases in the jth group

N = $n_1 + n_2 + \cdots + n_p = \sum_{j=1}^{p} n_j$ = total number of cases over all groups

T_j = total of all scores in group j

$\overline{X}_j$ = mean for group $j = T_j / n_j$

T = grand total over all cases

$\overline{X}$ = grand mean $= T / N$

The analysis of variance also uses some special terminology for discussing variances. In the formula for a sample variance, $s^2 = \sum(X_i - \overline{X})^2 / (N-1)$, the numerator is **a sum of squares (SS)**—the sum of the squared deviations of scores about their mean. In the context of the analysis of variance, the sum of these squared deviations is called a [14]_____ , abbreviated [15]__ . The denominator of the formula, $N-1$, is the number of **degrees of freedom (*df*)** corresponding to that *SS*. Therefore, in the formula for the variance, one divides the

[16]_____ by its [17]_____ . Finally, variance estimates are called **mean**

squares (*MS*), because they are roughly the mean of the squared deviations. So in the context of

the analysis of variance, a variance estimate consists of a [18]_____ divided by its

[19]_____ ; this quantity is called a [20]_____ . In symbols,

[21]__ = _____ .

Answer Key to Notation

[1]	fourth	[7]	X_{ij}	[13]	$\sum_{i=1}^{n_3} X_{i3} / n_3$	[18]	sum of squares
[2]	second	[8]	n_j	[14]	sum of squares	[19]	degrees of
[3]	second	[9]	$\overline{X}_1$	[15]	*SS*		freedom
[4]	N	[10]	$\overline{X}$	[16]	sum of squares	[20]	mean square
[5]	X_{3p}	[11]	$\sum_{i=1}^{n_2} X_{i2}$	[17]	degrees of	[21]	$MS = SS / df$
[6]	n_p	[12]	$\sum_{j=1}^{p} \overline{X}_j$		freedom		

Rationale

Now let us consider the rationale of simple analysis of variance. Two estimates of the population

variance are needed, one based upon the deviation of scores about their own group mean (the

within-groups mean square), and the other based upon the deviations of the group means about

the grand mean (the **between-groups mean square**). Thus, the basic strategy of the analysis of

variance is to derive two variance estimates, or [1]_____ , from the data—one that is

sensitive to differences between groups, called the [2]_____ mean square, and one that

is not sensitive to group differences, called the [3]_____ mean square.

Suppose a scientist is interested in the conservative or liberal character of political opinions

of people in four age groups — 20–29, 30–39, 40–49, and 50–59. A questionnaire provides a

measure of political opinion. First, consider why two individuals in *different age groups* do not

score the same value. Obviously, political opinion may vary with the difference between

groups—age. This is called variability due to **treatment effects**. But it is also true that political opinion is not completely determined by the treatment group; people will have different political attitudes even if they are the same age. Moreover, the measurement itself is not precisely the same from person to person. These other sources of variability are collectively called **error**. The mean square that reflects both variability due to [4]_____ and variability due to [5]_____ is the [6]_____ mean square.

Second, consider why individuals *within a single age group* differ from one another. Since these people all belong to the same age group, their scores do not vary because of [7]_____ effects. Variation within a group is caused only by [8]_____ , and such variability is reflected in the [9]_____ mean square.

To summarize, the between-groups mean square reflects variability associated with [10]_____ and with participant and measurement [11]_____ , whereas the within-groups mean square reflects variability associated only with such [12]_____ . But the null hypothesis for the analysis of variance states that there are no group differences—no treatment effects—in the population. According to the null hypothesis, then, both the between-groups and the within-groups mean square reflect variability associated only with [13]_____ . Consequently, under the null hypothesis the two mean squares should be equal except for [14]_____ .

The ratio of two independent variance estimates is a statistic called [15]__ . In the case of the analysis of variance, this is expressed: $F_{obs} = MS_{between} / MS_{within}$. Under the null hypothesis, the value of F_{obs} will vary only due to sampling error. The F distribution presented in Table E in Appendix 2 of your text states how much variability due to sampling error should occur in the value of F_{obs} if $\mu_1 = \mu_2 = \cdots = \mu_p = \mu$, that is, under the [16]_____ . If it is not too improbable that the actual value of F_{obs} is a product only of sampling error, then [17]_____ . Since group differences influence the size of the [18]_____ mean square but not the [19]_____ mean square, as group differences increase, the value of F_{obs} will become (larger/smaller) [20]_____ . When the value of F_{obs} is too large to be explained on the basis of [21]_____ alone, one [22]_____ .

Consider the example of age and political opinion mentioned above. Table 14–2 lists the hypothetical political opinion scores of five participants in each of the four age groups. The column means $(\overline{X}_j)$ and the grand mean $(\overline{X})$ are given. The sum of squares between groups (SS_{between}) is the number of cases in each group $(n_j = 5)$ times the sum of squared differences between each group mean and the grand mean. For the first group (ages 20–29) compute [23] $n_1(\overline{X}_1 - \overline{X})^2 =$ _____ = __ . Adding this quantity for all groups gives [24] $SS_{\text{between}} =$ __ . Now, within each group determine the sum of squared deviations (SS), that is, the sum of squared differences between each score and its group mean. You should have found the SS_{within} for the four age groups to be [25]__ , [26]__ , [27]__ and [28]__ . Adding these gives the sum of squares within groups (SS_{within}), which in this case equals [29]__ . To determine the mean square, divide the [30]_____ by its [31]_____ . Since [32] $df_{\text{between}} = p - 1 =$ __ and [33] $df_{\text{within}} = N - p =$ __ , [34] $MS_{\text{between}} =$ _____ = __ , [35] $MS_{\text{within}} =$ _____ = __ , and their ratio [36] $F_{\text{obs}} =$ __ .

Now let us consider what happens to MS_{between} and MS_{within} if the null hypothesis, $\mu_1 = \mu_2 = \cdots = \mu_p = \mu$, is not true. The scores in the bottom of Table 14–2 are the same as those at the top, except that 0, 2, 4, or 6 has been added to all the scores in a column respectively to simulate treatment differences between age groups in the population. Now compute MS_{within}, MS_{between}, and F_{obs} at the bottom of the table in the same manner as above. You should have found that while MS_{within} retains the value [37]__ , MS_{between} now equals [38]__ . Thus, differences between groups are reflected in the value of [39]_____ but not in the value of [40]_____ . F_{obs} now equals [41]__ .

The critical values of the theoretical sampling distribution of the ratio of two independent variance estimates, called [42]__ , are presented in Table E in Appendix 2 of your text. Turn to it now. The columns of the table correspond to the number of [43]_____ for the mean square in the [44]_____ of the F ratio, while the rows correspond to the number of [45]_____ for the mean square in the [46]_____ of this fraction. For this particular example, the df for MS_{between} is [47] $p - 1 =$ __ , while MS_{within} has [48] $df = N - p =$ __ . The values in the table at the intersection of the column for 3 df and the row for 16 df are [49]__ and [50]__ . These represent the critical values of F for a test at the .05 and the .01 [51]_____ levels, respectively. Thus, the critical value of F at the .05 level is [52]__ . Since $F_{\text{obs}} \geq F_{\text{crit}}$ at the bottom of Table 14–2, [53]_____ H_0.

Table 14–2 How $MS_{between}$ Is Changed by a Treatment Effect

	Age Groups 20–29	30–39	40–49	50–59	
	7	2	9	6	
	5	6	3	2	
	3	9	5	11	
	4	9	6	1	
	1	4	2	5	
Total: $\sum_{i=1}^{n_j} X_{ij}$	20	30	25	25	Grand Total: $\sum_{j=1}^{p} \sum_{i=1}^{n_j} X_{ij} = 100$
Mean: $\overline{X}_j$	4	6	5	5	Grand Mean: $\overline{X} = 5.0$
SS_{within}: $\sum_{i=1}^{n_j}(X_{ij} - \overline{X}_j)^2$					$SS_{within} = \sum_{j=1}^{p} \sum_{i=1}^{n_j}(X_{ij} - \overline{X}_j)^2 = \underline{\quad}$
					$SS_{between} = n_j \sum_{j=1}^{p}(\overline{X}_j - \overline{X})^2 = \underline{\quad}$

$MS_{between} = SS_{between} / df_{between} = SS_{between} / (p-1) = \underline{\quad} = \underline{\quad}$; $F_{obs} = MS_{between} / MS_{within} = \underline{\quad} = \underline{\quad}$

$MS_{within} = SS_{within} / df_{within} = SS_{within} / (N-p) = \underline{\qquad\qquad} = \underline{\qquad}$

	Age Groups 20–29 +0	30–39 +2	40–49 +4	50–59 +6	
Treatment Effects					
	7	4	13	12	
	5	8	7	8	
	3	11	9	17	
	4	11	10	7	
	1	6	6	11	
Total: $\sum_{i=1}^{n_j} X_{ij}$					Grand Total: $\sum_{j=1}^{p} \sum_{i=1}^{n_j} X_{ij} = 160$
Mean: $\overline{X}_j$					Grand Mean: $\overline{X} = 8.0$
SS_{within}: $\sum_{i=1}^{n_j}(X_{ij} - \overline{X}_j)^2$					$SS_{within} = \sum_{j=1}^{p} \sum_{i=1}^{n_j}(X_{ij} - \overline{X}_j)^2 = \underline{\quad}$
					$SS_{between} = n_j \sum_{j=1}^{p}(\overline{X}_j - \overline{X})^2 = \underline{\quad}$

$MS_{between} = SS_{between} / df_{between} = SS_{between} / (p-1) = \underline{\quad} = \underline{\quad}$; $F_{obs} = MS_{between} / MS_{within} = \underline{\quad} = \underline{\quad}$

$MS_{within} = SS_{within} / df_{within} = SS_{within} / (N-p) = \underline{\qquad\qquad} = \underline{\qquad}$

Answer Key to Rationale

[1]	mean squares	[19]	within-groups	[37]	9.38
[2]	between-groups	[20]	larger	[38]	43.33
[3]	within-groups	[21]	sampling error	[39]	$MS_{between}$
[4]	treatment effects	[22]	rejects H_0	[40]	MS_{within}
[5]	error	[23]	$5(4-5)^2 = 5$	[41]	4.62
[6]	between-groups	[24]	10	[42]	F
[7]	treatment	[25]	20	[43]	degrees of freedom
[8]	error	[26]	38	[44]	numerator
[9]	within-groups	[27]	30	[45]	degrees of freedom
[10]	treatment effects	[28]	62	[46]	denominator
[11]	error	[29]	150	[47]	3
[12]	error	[30]	sum of squares	[48]	16
[13]	error	[31]	degrees of freedom	[49]	3.24
[14]	sampling error	[32]	3	[50]	5.29
[15]	F	[33]	16	[51]	significance
[16]	null hypothesis	[34]	$10/3 = 3.33$	[52]	3.24
[17]	do not reject H_0	[35]	$150/16 = 9.38$	[53]	reject
[18]	between-groups	[36]	.36		

Computation

The example above used definitional formulas for calculations. This approach helps us under-stand how the analysis of variance works, but other formulas that give the same numerical result are much more convenient for most applications. Suppose a study of how parents discipline their 10-year-old children identifies three groups of parents. One group is very controlling, restrictive, and strict. Another is quite permissive and laissez-faire, while a third group is between these extremes, combining firmly enforced rules with provisions for independence. The children are then observed in a special situation in which they are given 10 opportunities to obey an adult. The number of times the children are obedient is recorded.[1] A guided computational example of this study is given in Tables 14–3 and 14–4.

Table 14–3 Guided Computational Example: Formal Summary

Hypotheses H_0: _____

H_1: _____ (non-directional)

Assumptions and Conditions

1. The participants are _____ and _____ sampled.

2. The groups are _____ .

3. The population variances are _____ .

4. The population distributions are _____ in form.

Decision Rules (from Table E of Appendix 2 in the text)

Given a significance level of _____ and $df = p - 1 = $ __ and $N - p = $ __ :

If _____ , _____ .

If _____ , _____ .

Computation

See Table 14–4. $F_{\text{obs}} = $ _____

Decision

_____ H_0.

The null hypothesis that all the population means are equal can be stated in symbols as [1] H_0: __ = __ = ··· = __ = __ . The alternative is best expressed as the negation of H_0. Thus, [2] H_1: _____ . The assumptions are that the participants are [3]_____ and [4]_____ sampled, the groups are [5]_____ of one another, the variances in the populations are the same from group to group (i.e., they are [6]_____), and the population

---

[1]   Inspired by, but not identical to, research reported by D. Baumrind, "Current Patterns of Parental Authority," *Developmental Psychology Monographs*, vol. 4. no. 1. pt. 2 (1971).

distributions are [7]_____ in form. As found in Table E in Appendix 2 of your text, for $df = 2$ and 13 at the .05 level, [8] $F_{crit} =$ ___ . The decision rules are stated as if a one-tailed test is being performed because only large F_{obs} values will lead to rejection of H_0. However, the alternative hypothesis is not considered directional because the direction of differences between means is not specified. All tests in the analysis of variance in this text will be nondirectional. Thus, if F_{obs} is greater than or equal to F_{crit}, H_0 is rejected. Formally:

If [9]_____ , [10]_____ .

If [11]_____ , [12]_____ .

Table 14–4 Guided Computational Example: Calculations

A. Data

	Discipline Group			
	Controlling	Combination	Permissive	
	3	6	4	
	5	9	7	
	2	5	3	
	1	8	5	
	4	7	6	
			5	
Totals, T_j				$T = \sum_{j=1}^{p} T_j =$ ___
n_j				$N = \sum_{j=1}^{p} n_j =$ ___
Group Means, $\overline{X}_j$				
Sum of squared scores, $\sum_{i=1}^{n_j} X_{ij}^2$				$\sum_{j=1}^{p}(\sum_{i=1}^{n_j} X_{ij}^2) =$ ___
Squared sum of scores divided by n_j, T_j^2 / n_j				$\sum_{j=1}^{p}(T_j^2 / n_j) =$ ___

B. Intermediate Quantities

$(\mathbf{I}) = T^2 / N =$ _____ $(\mathbf{II}) \sum_{j=1}^{p}(\sum_{i=1}^{n_j} X_{ij}^2) =$ _____ $(\mathbf{III}) \sum_{j=1}^{p}(T_j^2 / n_j) =$ _____

C. Summary Table

Source	df	SS	MS	F_{obs}
Between groups	$p - 1 =$ ___	$(\mathbf{III}) - (\mathbf{I}) =$ ___	$SS_{between} / df =$ ___	$MS_{between} / MS_{within} =$ ___
Within groups	$N - p =$ ___	$(\mathbf{II}) - (\mathbf{III}) =$ ___	$SS_{within} / df =$ ___	
Total	$N - 1 =$ ___	$(\mathbf{II}) - (\mathbf{I}) =$ ___		

The computational routine is presented in Table 14–4. For each group, first total the scores to obtain [13]___ , which when divided by n_j gives the group [14]_____ . Next, sum each squared score within a group to obtain [15]_____ , and then square the group total and divide by n_j to compute [16]_____ . At the right, add up these values over the groups. Then calculate the three intermediate quantities in part B of Table 14–4. Notice that these intermediate quantities are defined differently than they were in the regression and correlation chapters. Then calculate the *SS*, *df*, *MS*, and F_{obs} in the summary table of part C. The numerical results are given at the end of this chapter.

Answer Key to Introduction

[1]	$\mu_1 = \mu_2 = \mu_p$	[5]	independent	[10]	do not reject H_0	[15]	$\sum_{i=1}^{n_j} X_{ij}^2$
	$= \mu$	[6]	homogeneous	[11]	$F_{obs} \geq 3.80$	[16]	T_j^2 / n_j
[2]	not H_0	[7]	normal	[12]	reject H_0		
[3]	randomly	[8]	3.80	[13]	T_j		
[4]	independently	[9]	$F_{obs} < 3.80$	[14]	mean		

• • • • •   SELF-TEST

1.* Explain why the analysis of variance is preferable to a series of *t* tests of the differences between pairs of means as a method of evaluating
$H_0: \mu_1 = \mu_2 = \cdots = \mu_p = \mu.$

2. Define the *F* ratio (as used in this type of analysis of variance). Does the ratio increase or decrease if the values within each group become more variable?

3.* Explain how the partition of variability in the analysis of variance is analogous to the partition of variability in regression and correlation.

4. In the context of an experiment, $MS_{between}$ is sometimes referred to as $MS_{treatment}$ while MS_{within} is sometimes referred to as MS_{error}. Explain.

5. What are the assumptions of the analysis of variance, and why is each necessary?

Questions preceded by an asterisk can be answered on the basis of the discussion in the text, but the discussion in this Study Guide does not answer them.

• • • • •   EXERCISES

1. A developmental psychologist was interested in testing the popular notion that breast-feeding one's infant increases the warmth and intimacy of the mother-child relationship and serves as a good foundation for this relationship for years to come. The psychologist sent observers to the homes of a sample of three-year-old children who had been breast-fed for 0, 1–2, 2–5, or more than 5 months. These observers spent an entire day in the home and rated the degree of closeness and intimacy in the relationship between mother and child. The data are given in the accompanying table; a high score means a close mother-child relationship. Evaluate these hypothetical data by following the procedures outlined in Tables 14–3 and 14–4.

Months of Breast Feeding			
0	1–2	2–5	5+
5	7	1	4
7	6	3	2
2	3	6	7
3	9	5	4
4	7	6	
2			

2. Various claims have been made for the merits of different kinds of nursery schools. One of the most frequently heard arguments is that less structured schools foster more creativity and intellectual curiosity than traditional, structured programs. To test these claims, an educator located three nursery schools that received children from approximately equal educational and socioeconomic levels of the community. The schools were a traditional school, a Montessori school, and a Summerhill-type "free" school. The children in these schools were given a nonverbal creativity test. The data are presented in the accompanying table. Statistically evaluate the observed differences between these schools.[2]

Creativity		
Traditional	Montessori	Free
6	2	1
9	5	3
7	4	3
5	4	5
8	6	
8		

---

[2]   Based on, but not identical to, a study by A. S. Dreyer and D. Rigler, "Cognitive Performance in Montessori and Nursery School Children," *Journal of Educational Research* 62 (1969): 411–16.

• • • • • **ANSWERS**

Table l4–4. $T_j = 15, 35, 30$; $T = 80$; $n_j = 5, 5,$
6; $N = 16$; $\sum X_j^2 = 55, 255, 160$; $\sum X^2 = 470$;
$T_j^2 / n_j = 45, 245, 150$; $T^2 / N = 440$;
(I) = 400, **(II)** = 470, **(III)** = 440; between
groups: 2, 40, 20; within groups: 13, 30,
2.3077; Total: 15, 70; $F_{\text{obs}} = 8.67^{**}$.

Self-Test. (1) The statistical question
addressed by the analysis of variance has to do
with the set of group means, not with pairs of
means; the probability estimate based on
numerous t tests would be ambiguous because
the several tests would not be independent.
(2) $F = MS_{\text{between}} / MS_{\text{within}}$, decrease. **(3)** See
the text, pages 356–359. In regression and
correlation, one partitions the variability of the
predicted variable into a portion associated
with the predictor variable and a portion not so
associated (i.e., error). In the analysis of
variance, one partitions the variability in the
dependent variable into a portion associated
with group membership (i.e., with the
independent variable) and a portion associated
with error. **(4)** In an experiment, different

groups receive different treatments (for
example, different drug levels). Differences
between the group means are due to differential
effects of the treatments plus uncontrolled
random effects. Differences within groups are
due only to uncontrolled random effects (i.e.,
error). **(5)** See pages 365–367 of the text.

Exercises. (1) Follow the format given in
Tables 14–3 and 14–4. **(I)** = 432.4500,
(II) = 523, **(III)** = 453.4167; $df_{\text{between}} = 3$,
$SS_{\text{between}} = 20.9667$, $MS_{\text{between}} = 6.9889$,
$df_{\text{within}} = 16$, $SS_{\text{within}} = 69.5833$,
$MS_{\text{within}} = 4.3490$, $df_{\text{total}} = 19$,
$SS_{\text{total}} = 90.5500$; $F_{\text{obs}} = 1.61$, F_{crit} (significance
level .05, $df = 3, 16$) = 3.24, do not reject H_0.
(2) (I) = 385.0667, **(II)** = 460,
(III) = 432.3667; $df_{\text{between}} = 2$,
$SS_{\text{between}} = 47.3000$, $MS_{\text{between}} = 23.6500$,
$df_{\text{within}} = 12$, $SS_{\text{within}} = 27.6333$,
$MS_{\text{within}} = 2.3028$, $df_{\text{total}} = 14$,
$SS_{\text{total}} = 74.9333$; $F_{\text{obs}} = 10.27$, F_{crit}
(significance level .05, $df = 2, 12$) = 3.88,
reject H_0.

• • • • • STATISTICAL PACKAGES • • • • •

• • • • •   MINITAB

(To accompany the guided computational example in Table 14–4.)

MINITAB will compute a simple one-way analysis of variance for independent groups on data such as that presented in Table 14–4. The purpose of the analysis is to compare the means of the three groups being measured. MINITAB will compute the mean and standard deviation of each group, carry out a one-factor analysis of variance, and plot group means and error bars (i.e., confidence intervals). Two methods of data entry are possible in MINITAB, "stacked" and "unstacked."

To enter data directly from Table 14–4, the simplest method is to place the outcome data into three columns, each of which corresponds to a discipline group. This is the method MINITAB refers to as "unstacked" data entry.

Start the MINITAB program. Click on the Data window. Enter the values for the three discipline groups into the first three columns of the spreadsheet. Label these columns *Control*, *Combin*, and *Permiss*. The spreadsheet should now appear as follows:

Control	Combin	Permiss
3	6	4
5	9	7
2	5	3
1	8	5
4	7	6
		5

To save the data as a MINITAB worksheet:

> *File>Save Worksheet As*
>   (Enter folder and name for the Worksheet file.)
>   OK

To carry out the one-way (one factor) analysis of variance, use the *One-way Unstacked* command:

> *Stat>ANOVA>One-way (Unstacked)*
>   Responses (in separate columns):
>   Control Combin Permiss   [double-click each to transfer]
>   OK

The output gives more information than we do currently need, but it includes the entire analysis of variance table as well as group means and standard deviations. Notice that confidence intervals for each mean are based upon the standard deviation that is pooled across all groups, not the individual standard deviation for each group.

To print the results of the Analysis of Variance, print the Session window:

> *File>Print Session Window*
> Print Range: All
> OK

The same result can be produced using the "stacked" method of data entry, in which a treatment variable, or factor, is used to indicate group membership. To enter data for the analysis using the "stacked" method of data entry, enter the factor, *Discip* (coded 1=Control, 2=Combination, 3=Permissive), in one column and the dependent variable, *Obed*, in a second column. Label the two columns with the variable names. The data in the spreadsheet should appear as follows:

Discip	Obed
1	3
1	5
1	2
1	1
1	4
2	6
2	9
2	5
2	8
2	7
3	4
3	7
3	3
3	5
3	6
3	5

Then the analysis may be carried out using the One-way command:

> *Stat>ANOVA>One-way*
> Response: Obed   [double-click to transfer]
> Factor: Discip
> OK

The computer output for the "stacked" method appears essentially the same except for the variable names. To exit MINITAB:

> *File>Exit*

MINITAB Program Output

```
One-way ANOVA: Control, Combin, Permiss
Analysis of Variance
Source     DF         SS         MS        F        P
Factor      2      40.00      20.00     8.67    0.004
Error      13      30.00       2.31
Total      15      70.00
                                    Individual 95% CIs For Mean
                                    Based on Pooled StDev
Level      N       Mean      StDev   ---+---------+---------+---------+---
Control     5      3.000      1.581   (------*------)
Combin      5      7.000      1.581                        (------*------)
Permiss     6      5.000      1.414               (------*------)
                                    ---+---------+---------+---------+---
Pooled StDev =     1.519            2.0       4.0       6.0       8.0
```

●●●●●   SPSS

(To accompany the guided computational example in Table 14–4.)

To have SPSS compute the simple analysis of variance given in Table 14–4, you need to identify the independent variable, also known as the treatment variable, and the dependent variable or outcome measure. The treatment variable is called a *factor*, and the simple analysis of variance becomes a one-factor design. In this example the factor is the level of discipline (1=Control, 2=Combination, 3=Permissive); the dependent variable is the measure of obedience. The purpose of the analysis is to compare the means of the three groups being measured.

Start the SPSS program. The Data Editor window will fill the screen.

Enter the level of discipline, *Discip*, in the first column of the spreadsheet, and the corresponding measure of obedience, *Obed*, in the second column. To enter the variable names, click on the bottom tab labeled "Variable View" and label the variables. Go back to the Data View. The data in the spreadsheet should appear as follows:

Discip	Obed
1	3
1	5
1	2
1	1
1	4
2	6
2	9
2	5
2	8
2	7
3	4
3	7
3	3
3	5
3	6
3	5

To carry out the simple (one-factor) analysis of variance:

> *Analyze>Compare Means>One-Way ANOVA*
> 　　　Dependent List: Obed　　　　[highlight and transfer]
> 　　　Factor: Discip
> 　　　Options:　Statistics: Descriptive
> 　　　　　　　　　Continue
> 　　OK

The output appears on the next page. It includes the group means and standard deviations and the ANOVA table. The group means table requires landscape orientation to fit easily across a page.
　　To print the output:

> *File>Print*
> 　　　　Properties: Paper:
> 　　　　　　Orientation: Landscape
> 　　　　　　OK
> 　　　　Print range: All visible output.
> 　　　　OK

To save the data that you entered:

> *Window>SPSS Data Editor*
> *File>Save As*
> (Enter folder and file name for SPSS Save file.)
> Save

Exit SPSS:

> *File>Exit*

SPSS Program Output

Oneway

Descriptives

OBED

	N	Mean	Std. Deviation	Std. Error	95% Confidence Interval for Mean		Minimum	Maximum
					Lower Bound	Upper Bound		
1.00	5	3.0000	1.5811	.7071	1.0368	4.9632	1.00	5.00
2.00	5	7.0000	1.5811	.7071	5.0368	8.9632	5.00	9.00
3.00	6	5.0000	1.4142	.5774	3.5159	6.4841	3.00	7.00
Total	16	5.0000	2.1602	.5401	3.8489	6.1511	1.00	9.00

ANOVA

OBED

	Sum of Squares	df	Mean Square	F	Sig.
Between Groups	40.000	2	20.000	8.667	.004
Within Groups	30.000	13	2.308		
Total	70.000	15			

● ● ● ● ●

CHAPTER 15

TWO-FACTOR ANALYSIS OF VARIANCE •••••

CONCEPT GOALS

Be sure that you thoroughly understand the following concepts and how to use them in statistical applications.

- ◆ Factor, level, cell
- ◆ Main effect, interaction
- ◆ Partitioning of variability
- ◆ Notation: X_{ijk}, N, n, p, q, T_{jk}, $T_{j\cdot}$, $T_{\cdot k}$, $T_{\cdot\cdot}$, $\overline{X}_{j\cdot}$, $\overline{X}_{\cdot k}$, $\overline{X}_{\cdot\cdot}$

••••• GUIDE TO MAJOR CONCEPTS

Introduction

In Chapter 14 you learned how to test the significance of the difference between a set of means for groups distinguished from one another by a single classification scheme. This is done by partitioning the total [1]_____ in the sample into a component associated with differences [2]_____ groups and a component associated with differences among individuals [3]_____ groups. Both the between-groups and within-groups variance estimates, called [4]_____ , estimate the same population variance, assuming that [5]__ is true. Their ratio is distributed as the theoretical relative frequency distribution [6]__ , with degrees

307

of freedom corresponding to the *df* associated with the *MS* in the [7]_____ and in the
[8]_____ of the *F* ratio. Under H_0, *F* should vary only by sampling error, but if H_0 is
wrong and the groups come from populations whose means differ from one another, *F* will
probably be so (large/small) [9]_____ that such a ratio is very unlikely to occur by
[10]_____ alone. In that case, H_0 is [11]_____ .

Answer Key to Introduction

[1]	variability	[4]	mean squares	[7]	numerator	[10]	sampling error
[2]	between	[5]	H_0	[8]	denominator	[11]	rejected
[3]	within	[6]	*F*	[9]	large		

Two-Factor Design

Suppose, however, that the participants in the experiment can be simultaneously categorized
according to two classification schemes, which in the analysis of variance are called **factors**. For
example, suppose both males and females are shown either an athletic, violent, or sensual film
episode and the researcher is interested in the amount of the viewer's emotional involvement as
measured by heart-rate levels. In this case, participants can be classified as male or female, which
defines the gender [1]_____ . In addition, the particular film episode they view defines
the film [2]_____ . A participant is located in one and only one subgroup of each factor,
called a **level** of the factor. Thus *male* and *female* are the [3]_____ of the gender
[4]_____ ; the athletic, violent, and sensual film episodes constitute the
[5]_____ of the film [6]_____ . Factors are usually abbreviated with capital
letters, such as *G* and *F* for [7]_____ and [8]_____ (or *A* and *B* for unspecified
factors), and the levels within a film factor are designated by the corresponding lower-case letter
with subscripts (e.g., a_1, a_2). Thus, the two genders might be labeled [9]_____
and [10]_____ , while the three kinds of film would be labeled [11]_____ ,
[12]_____ , and [13]_____ .

What kinds of results might be obtained from such an experiment? The average heart rate for
males and females might be different, or the heart rate for the three levels of the film factor might

be significantly different from one another. If so, we say that there is a **main effect** for Factor G or for Factor F. Population mean differences between the levels of one factor, ignoring the levels of the other factor, constitute a [14]_____ . In a two-factor design such as this, one or both of the factors may exhibit a [15]_____ .

However, suppose that the difference between levels of Factor A is not the same within one level of Factor B as it is within another level of Factor B. This is called an **interaction**; that is, the nature of the effects of one factor interact with or depend on the levels of the other factor. Suppose males have higher heart rates than females during the athletic film but lower heart rates during the violent episode, while the genders do not differ when watching sensual material. In this case there would be an [16]_____ between Factors G and F. In a two-factor design, then, there are three possible effects: two [17]_____ and one [18]_____ .

It is helpful to graph some of these possible results. In Figure 15–1 are six sets of axes. On each graph draw two lines, one for males and one for females, which reflect the mean heart rates for these groups under each film condition. Graph A is drawn for you, and it represents a [19]_____ for gender, no [20]_____ for film, and no [21]_____ .

In the same manner, in graph B draw a result in which there is a significant main effect for film, no main effect for gender, and no interaction. In C, plot a situation in which both main effects are significant but there is no interaction; in D, a case in which both main effects and the interaction are significant; in E, a case in which only the interaction is significant; and in F, a case in which neither the main effects nor the interaction is significant.

Answer Key to Two-Factor Design

[1]	factor	[7]	gender	[13]	f_3	[19]	main effect
[2]	factor	[8]	film	[14]	main effect	[20]	main effect
[3]	levels	[9]	g_1	[15]	main effect	[21]	interaction
[4]	factor	[10]	g_2	[16]	interaction		
[5]	levels	[11]	f_1	[17]	main effects		
[6]	factor	[12]	f_2	[18]	interaction		

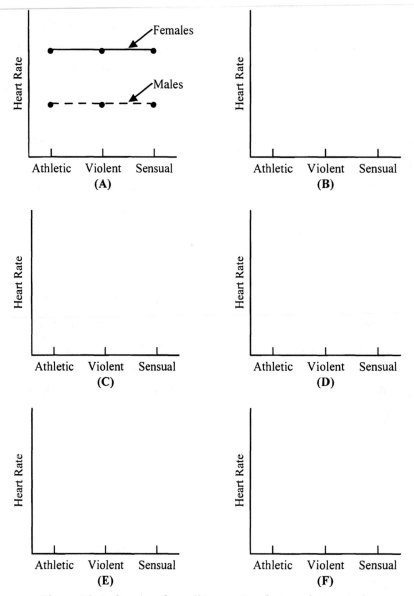

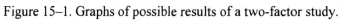

Figure 15–1. Graphs of possible results of a two-factor study.

Rationale

The rationale of two-factor analysis of variance is an extension of the logic of simple analysis of variance. Suppose that the score of a particular female watching the athletic film deviates 16 points from the grand mean over all participants. What accounts for this? The deviation can be partitioned into four parts; the sum of the four parts equals the total deviation. First, suppose that the heart rate for females averages 10 points higher than the grand mean. One source of variability is thus the difference associated with being female, that is, with [1]_____ . But this person also watched the athletic film, and on the average people who saw the athletic film were 5 points lower than the grand mean; so a second source of variability is associated with the film condition or [2]_____ . Third, females watching the athletic events had heart rates that averaged 7 points above the grand mean even after general differences between the genders and film conditions were considered. So a third source of variability is the [3]_____ between G and F. Finally, 4 points separate this person's score from the mean of her particular group. This variability about a group mean is known as [4]_____ variability or error. The particular person scored 16 points above the grand mean: +10 because she was a female, −5 because she watched the athletic film, +7 because of the unique interaction of the gender and film factors for that group and +4 because of individual differences and measurement error (within-group variation or error). Note that $16 = 10 - 5 + 7 + 4$.

When all these deviations are squared and summed over all participants to produce **sums of squares**, we have that $SS_{total} = SS_{gender} + SS_{film} + SS_{gender \times film} + SS_{within}$. The sum of squares of all deviations about the grand mean (SS_{total}) is equal to the sum of squares due to gender plus the sum of squares due to film plus the sum of squares due to the interaction between gender and film plus the sum of squares due to within-group variation. This is what is meant by **partitioning of variability**. In short, the [5]_____ variability in the sample can be [6]_____ into four sources: one part attributable to [7]_____ , another to [8]_____ , another to their [9]_____ , and the remaining part to [10]_____ variation. These sums of squares add to equal the total variability:

[11]_____ = _____ + _____ + _____ + _____ .

As in the case of simple analysis of variance, the null hypotheses for the main effects and the interaction are that these groups come from populations having the same means. Under these conditions, the four mean squares all estimate the same population variance. Restated in symbols, when [12]__ is true, [13]_____ , [14]_____ , [15]_____ and [16]_____ all estimate the same population variance. But while MS_{gender}, MS_{film}, and $MS_{gender \times film}$ are all influenced by treatment effects, MS_{within} is not. Therefore, MS_{gender}, MS_{film}, and $MS_{gender \times film}$ can each serve as the numerator in an F ratio in which MS_{within} is the [17]_____ . When compared to the F distribution, such ratios allow us to determine the likelihood that the observed differences between means are a result of [18]_____ alone.

Answer Key to Rationale

[1]	Factor G	[8]	Factor F	[13]	MS_{gender}
[2]	Factor F	[9]	interaction	[14]	MS_{film}
[3]	interaction	[10]	within-group	[15]	$MS_{gender \times film}$
[4]	within-group	[11]	$SS_{total} = SS_{gender} +$	[16]	MS_{within}
[5]	total		$SS_{film} + SS_{gender \times film} +$	[17]	denominator
[6]	partitioned		SS_{within}	[18]	sampling error
[7]	Factor G	[12]	H_0		

Notation

We will consider the notation used for a two-factor analysis of variance and then give a numerical illustration of these points. The mathematical notation for a score and the several formulas for an analysis of variance often appear frighteningly complex at first, but they are actually rather simple. Consider Table 15–1, which outlines the notation used in two-factor analysis of variance. Notice first that the data are arranged into rows and columns, with the levels of Factor A constituting the rows and the levels of Factor B the columns. A score is designated with three subscripts: X_{ijk} stands for the score of the ith participant in the jth level of Factor A and the kth level of Factor B. Thus X_{312} would represent the score of the [1]_____ person in the [2]_____ level of A and the [3]_____ level of B. Each group of scores is called a **cell** of the design, and ab_{23} is the notation for [4]_____ 23 (read "cell

two three"), which is the cell found at the intersection of the [5]_____ row and

[6]_____ column. If there are p levels of Factor A and q levels of Factor B with n cases per

cell, the total number of cells in the design is [7]__ and the total number of participants is [8]__ , or

simply N. While the number of cases in a cell is [9]__ , the total number of participants in the

entire analysis is [10]__ . Notice that the number of cases is the same in each [11]_____ .

The total of the scores in a single cell is symbolized by T_{jk}. Thus, the total of the scores in

cell 23 is labeled [12]__ , and T_{31} is the total of the scores in the group representing the

[13]_____ level of Factor A and the [14]_____ level of Factor B. Similarly, the

mean of the jkth cell is represented by $\overline{X}_{jk} = T_{jk} / n$, since there are n scores per cell. The mean for

cell 45 is written [15]__ = _____ . The total of all scores in all cells in the jth row is $T_{j.}$, in

which the dot signifies that the scores have been summed over all columns. The same kind of nota-

tion is used for the mean of a row. Therefore, the total of all scores in row 3 is written [16]__ , so the

mean of the scores over all cells in that row is symbolized by [17]__ . Since there are n cases per

group and q groups within a row, the formula for the mean of row 2 is [18]_____ . By analogy,

the total and mean of column 4 are written respectively as [19]__ and [20]__ . Since the number of

cases per group is [21]__ and there are p groups per column, the formula for the mean of column 1 is

[22]_____ . The grand total and grand mean of all participants in the design are written with a

subscript of two dots, which indicate that the scores for participants have been summed over all

rows and columns. The grand total is represented by [23]__ , and the grand mean is [24]__ .

Answer Key to Notation

[1]	third	[7]	pq	[13]	third	[19]	$T_{.4}$
[2]	first	[8]	npq	[14]	first	[20]	$\overline{X}_{.4}$
[3]	second	[9]	n	[15]	$\overline{X}_{45} = T_{45} / n$	[21]	n
[4]	cell	[10]	N	[16]	$T_{3.}$	[22]	$\overline{X}_{1} = T_{1} / np$
[5]	second	[11]	cell	[17]	$\overline{X}_{3.}$	[23]	$T_{..}$
[6]	third	[12]	T_{23}	[18]	$\overline{X}_{2.} = T_{2.} / nq$	[24]	$\overline{X}_{..}$

Table 15–1 Summary of Raw-Score Notation for the Two-Factor Analysis of Variance

		Factor B			
		b_1	b_2	$\ldots$	b_q	Row Means
	a_1	X_{111}	X_{112}	$\ldots$	X_{11q}	
		X_{211}	X_{212}	$\ldots$	X_{21q}	
		X_{311}	X_{312}	$\ldots$	X_{31q}	
		$\cdot$	$\cdot$		$\cdot$	
		$\cdot$	$\cdot$		$\cdot$	
		$\cdot$	$\cdot$		$\cdot$	
		X_{n11}	X_{n12}	$\ldots$	X_{n1q}	
		$\overline{X}_{11}=T_{11}/n$	$\overline{X}_{12}=T_{12}/n$	$\ldots$	$\overline{X}_{1q}=T_{1q}/n$	$\overline{X}_{1.}=T_1/nq$
	a_2	X_{121}	X_{122}	$\ldots$	X_{12q}	
		X_{221}	X_{222}	$\ldots$	X_{22q}	
		X_{321}	X_{322}	$\ldots$	X_{32q}	
		$\cdot$	$\cdot$		$\cdot$	
		$\cdot$	$\cdot$		$\cdot$	
Factor A		X_{n21}	X_{n22}	$\ldots$	X_{n2q}	
		$\overline{X}_{21}=T_{21}/n$	$\overline{X}_{22}=T_{22}/n$	$\ldots$	$\overline{X}_{2q}=T_{2q}/n$	$\overline{X}_{2.}=T_2/nq$
		$\cdot$	$\cdot$	$\ldots$	$\cdot$	$\cdot$
		$\cdot$	$\cdot$		$\cdot$	$\cdot$
	a_p	X_{1p1}	X_{1p2}	$\ldots$	X_{1pq}	
		X_{2p1}	X_{2p2}	$\ldots$	X_{2pq}	
		X_{3p1}	X_{3p2}	$\ldots$	X_{3pq}	
		$\cdot$	$\cdot$		$\cdot$	
		$\cdot$	$\cdot$		$\cdot$	
		$\cdot$	$\cdot$		$\cdot$	
		X_{np1}	X_{np2}	$\ldots$	X_{npq}	
		$\overline{X}_{p1}=T_{p1}/n$	$\overline{X}_{p2}=T_{p2}/n$	$\ldots$	$\overline{X}_{pq}=T_{pq}/n$	$\overline{X}_{p.}=T_p/nq$
Column Means		$\overline{X}_{.1}=T_{.1}/n$	$\overline{X}_{.2}=T_{.2}/n$	$\ldots$	$\overline{X}_{.q}=T_{.q}/n$	Grand Mean $\overline{X}_{..}=T_{..}/npq$

n = the number of subjects in each group

a_j = the jth level of factor A

b_k = the kth level of factor B

p = the number of levels of factor A

q = the number of levels of factor B

X_{ijk} = the ith score in the jkth group

T_{jk} = the total of all scores in the jkth group

$\overline{X}_{jk}$ = the mean of the jkth group

$T_{..}$ = the total of all scores

$\overline{X}_{..}$ = the grand mean

Illustration

Now consider a numerical illustration of how the four mean squares respond to different treatment effects. The data in Table 15–2 are similar to a set of randomly selected numbers drawn from a single population, except that they have been picked to make the computations as easy as possible. Since they are random-like, all the means estimate the same population mean and all the mean squares estimate the same population variance. First, determine the means of each cell, row, and column as well as the grand mean. Then calculate SS_A, SS_B, SS_{AB}, and SS_{within} according to the formulas presented. You should have found that [1]$SS_A = $ ___ , [2]$SS_B = $ ___ , [3]$SS_{AB} = $ ___ (very unusual), and [4]$SS_{within} = $ ___ .

Now suppose that there is a population difference between the levels of Factor A. Table 15–3 presents the same data as in the previous example, but 10 points have been added to each score in row a_2 to reflect the population difference. Now recompute the analysis of variance.

As one might expect, the sum of squares for Factor A increased over the first analysis. SS_A is now [5]___ , compared to the previous value of [6]___ . Clearly, a population difference between levels of A causes an (increase/decrease) [7]_____ in [8]___ . In contrast, the sums of squares for Factor B and the AB interaction (did/did not) [9]_____ change. Observe also that SS_{within} (is/is not) [10]_____ the same as before. Thus, SS_{within} (is/is not) [11]_____ sensitive to treatment effects. In short, a treatment effect in which the means for the levels of Factor A are different from each other will influence only the size of the SS for [12]_____ , whereas the SS for [13]___ , [14]___ , and [15]_____ remain unchanged.

Suppose an interaction exists in the population that can be represented in the data by adding 10 points only to cell ab_{21}. This has been done in Table 15–4. Complete this analysis of variance. Notice again that no charge occurred for the SS for [16]_____ . However, not only did the interaction sum of squares rise from a former value of [17]___ to [18]___ , but SS_A and SS_B both (increased/decreased) [19]_____ . The main effects changed, because adding 10 points to a single cell changes not only the mean of that cell but also the means of the respective row and column, whose values enter into the calculation of the [20]_____ . Because of this, when an analysis reveals a significant interaction, statisticians must be careful when interpreting a significant main effect.

Table 15–2 Numerical Illustration of Two-Factor Analysis of Variance with No Effects

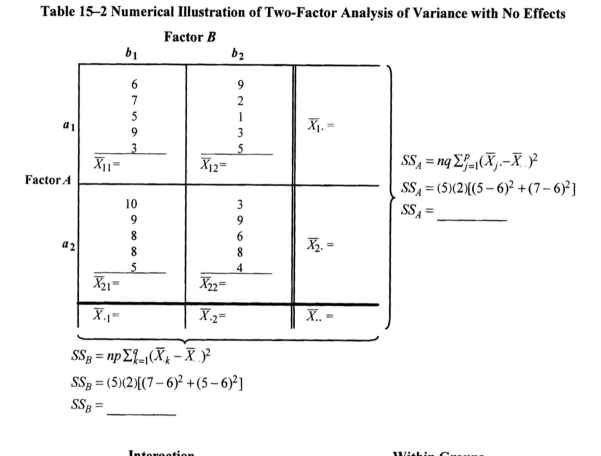

$$SS_A = nq \sum_{j=1}^{p} (\overline{X}_{j\cdot} - \overline{X}_{\cdot\cdot})^2$$

$$SS_A = (5)(2)[(5-6)^2 + (7-6)^2]$$

$$SS_A = \underline{\hspace{2cm}}$$

$$SS_B = np \sum_{k=1}^{q} (\overline{X}_{\cdot k} - \overline{X}_{\cdot\cdot})^2$$

$$SS_B = (5)(2)[(7-6)^2 + (5-6)^2]$$

$$SS_B = \underline{\hspace{2cm}}$$

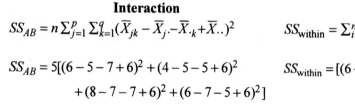

Interaction

$$SS_{AB} = n \sum_{j=1}^{p} \sum_{k=1}^{q} (\overline{X}_{jk} - \overline{X}_{j\cdot} - \overline{X}_{\cdot k} + \overline{X}_{\cdot\cdot})^2$$

$$SS_{AB} = 5[(6-5-7+6)^2 + (4-5-5+6)^2$$
$$+ (8-7-7+6)^2 + (6-7-5+6)^2]$$

$$SS_{AB} = \underline{\hspace{2cm}}$$

Within Groups

$$SS_{\text{within}} = \sum_{i=1}^{n} \sum_{j=1}^{p} \sum_{k=1}^{q} (X_{ijk} - \overline{X}_{jk})^2$$

$$SS_{\text{within}} = [(6-6)^2 + (7-6)^2 + (5-6)^2 + \cdots + (4-6)^2]$$

$$SS_{\text{within}} = \underline{\hspace{2cm}}$$

Table 15–3 Numerical Illustration of Two-Factor Analysis of Variance
with an Effect for Factor A

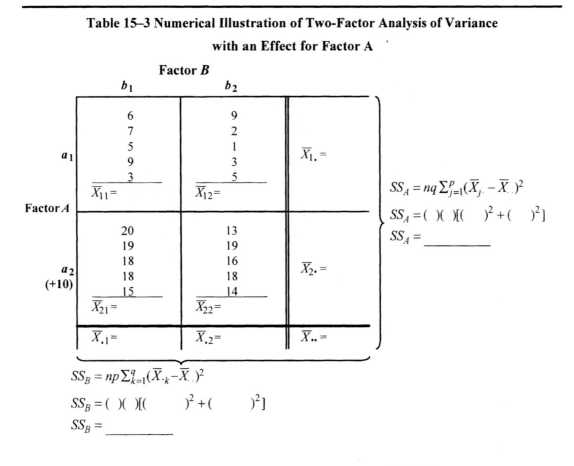

$$SS_A = nq \sum_{j=1}^{p} (\overline{X}_{j.} - \overline{X}_{..})^2$$

$$SS_A = (\quad)(\quad)[(\quad)^2 + (\quad)^2]$$

$$SS_A = \underline{\hspace{2cm}}$$

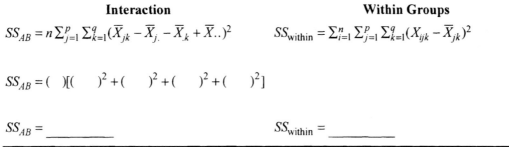

$$SS_B = np \sum_{k=1}^{q} (\overline{X}_{.k} - \overline{X}_{..})^2$$

$$SS_B = (\quad)(\quad)[(\quad)^2 + (\quad)^2]$$

$$SS_B = \underline{\hspace{2cm}}$$

Interaction

$$SS_{AB} = n \sum_{j=1}^{p} \sum_{k=1}^{q} (\overline{X}_{jk} - \overline{X}_{j.} - \overline{X}_{.k} + \overline{X}..)^2$$

Within Groups

$$SS_{\text{within}} = \sum_{i=1}^{n} \sum_{j=1}^{p} \sum_{k=1}^{q} (X_{ijk} - \overline{X}_{jk})^2$$

$$SS_{AB} = (\quad)[(\quad)^2 + (\quad)^2 + (\quad)^2 + (\quad)^2]$$

$$SS_{AB} = \underline{\hspace{2cm}} \qquad\qquad SS_{\text{within}} = \underline{\hspace{2cm}}$$

Table 15–4 Numerical Illustration of a Two-Factor Analysis of Variance with an Interaction Effect

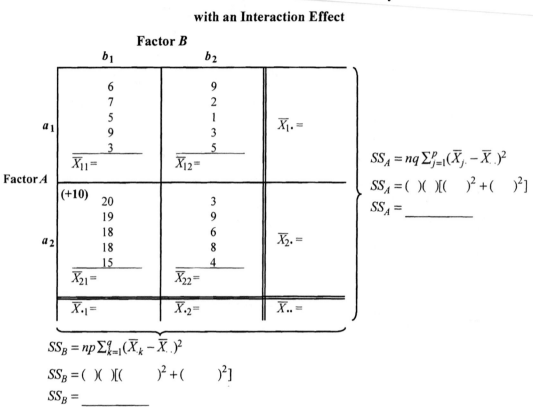

Factor B

	b_1	b_2	
a_1	6 7 5 9 3 $\overline{X}_{11} =$	9 2 1 3 5 $\overline{X}_{12} =$	$\overline{X}_{1.} =$
a_2	(+10) 20 19 18 18 15 $\overline{X}_{21} =$	3 9 6 8 4 $\overline{X}_{22} =$	$\overline{X}_{2.} =$
	$\overline{X}_{.1} =$	$\overline{X}_{.2} =$	$\overline{X}_{..} =$

$$SS_A = nq \sum_{j=1}^{p} (\overline{X}_{j.} - \overline{X}_{..})^2$$

$$SS_A = (\ )(\ )[(\quad)^2 + (\quad)^2]$$

$$SS_A = \underline{\qquad}$$

$$SS_B = np \sum_{k=1}^{q} (\overline{X}_{.k} - \overline{X}_{..})^2$$

$$SS_B = (\ )(\ )[(\qquad)^2 + (\qquad)^2]$$

$$SS_B = \underline{\qquad}$$

Interaction

$$SS_{AB} = n \sum_{j=1}^{p} \sum_{k=1}^{q} (\overline{X}_{jk} - \overline{X}_{j.} - \overline{X}_{.k} + \overline{X}..)^2$$

$$SS_{AB} = (\ )[(\quad)^2 + (\quad)^2 + (\quad)^2 + (\quad)^2]$$

$$SS_{AB} = \underline{\qquad}$$

Within Groups

$$SS_{\text{within}} = \sum_{i=1}^{n} \sum_{j=1}^{p} \sum_{k=1}^{q} (X_{ijk} - \overline{X}_{jk})^2$$

$$SS_{\text{within}} = \underline{\qquad}$$

Answer Key to Illustration

[1]	20	[6]	20	[11]	is not	[16]	within
[2]	20	[7]	increase	[12]	Factor A	[17]	0
[3]	0	[8]	SS_A	[13]	B	[18]	125
[4]	100	[9]	did not	[14]	AB	[19]	increased
[5]	720	[10]	is	[15]	within	[20]	main effects

Computation

The computational procedures, which differ from the definitional formulas used above, are outlined in Table 15–5, which presents a guided computational example on another set of data. The data are presented in part A; determine the values of p, q, n, and N. Then in part B, form a table of totals, T_{jk}, which are the sums within cells, rows, and columns as well as the grand total. (You can also calculate a table of means with which you can interpret and graph the nature of any significant effects.) In part C, you must calculate five intermediate quantities. The first **(I)** is the grand total squared divided by the total number of scores in the sample, which is symbolized by [1]_____ . The second quantity **(II)** is the sum of all the squared scores, or [2]_____ . The third **(III)** is found by summing the squared row totals and dividing the sum by nq, which is written [3]_____ ; the fourth **(IV)** is found by summing the squared column totals and dividing the sum by np, which is symbolized by [4]_____ ; and the fifth **(V)** is found by summing the squared cell totals and dividing the sum by n, which can be expressed as [5]_____ . The degrees of freedom and sums of squares are computed in part D, and the summary table is outlined in part E with each $MS = SS/df$ for that source and each F equal to the MS for that source divided by MS_{within}. The degrees of freedom are then used to determine the critical values from Table E in Appendix 2.

Answer Key to Computation

[1]	$T_{..}^2/N$	[3]	$\sum_{j=1}^{p} T_{j\cdot}^2/nq$	[5]	$\sum_{j=1}^{p}\sum_{k=1}^{q} T_{jk}^2/n$
[2]	$\sum_{i=1}^{n}\sum_{j=1}^{p}\sum_{k=1}^{q} X_{ijk}^2$	[4]	$\sum_{k=1}^{q} T_{\cdot k}^2/np$		

Table 15–5 Guided Computational Example for Two-Factor Analysis of Variance

A. Data

		Factor B			
		b_1	b_2	b_3	b_4
	a_1	1 4 3 1	7 10 9 8	6 9 7 8	9 7 10 8
Factor A	a_2	4 1 2 3	9 10 5 8	1 0 3 2	3 4 5 3

$p =$ ___ $\qquad$ $q =$ ___ $\qquad$ $n =$ ___ $\qquad$ $N =$ ___

B. Table of Totals

		Factor B				
		b_1	b_2	b_3	b_4	
	a_1	$T_{11}=$	$T_{12}=$	$T_{13}=$	$T_{14}=$	$T_{1\bullet}=$
Factor A	a_2	$T_{21}=$	$T_{22}=$	$T_{23}=$	$T_{24}=$	$T_{2\bullet}=$
	a_2	$T_{\bullet 1}=$	$T_{\bullet 2}=$	$T_{\bullet 3}=$	$T_{\bullet 4}=$	$T_{\bullet\bullet}=$

C. Intermediate Quantities

$(\mathbf{I}) = T_{\bullet\bullet}^2 \,/\, N =$ _____

$(\mathbf{II}) = \sum_{i=1}^{n} \sum_{j=1}^{p} \sum_{k=1}^{q} X_{ijk}^2 =$ _____

$(\mathbf{III}) = \sum_{j=1}^{p} T_{j\bullet}^2 \,/\, nq =$ _____

$(\mathbf{IV}) = \sum_{k=1}^{q} T_{\bullet k}^2 \,/\, np =$ _____

$(\mathbf{V}) = \sum_{j=1}^{p} \sum_{k=1}^{q} T_{jk}^2 \,/\, n =$ _____

D. Degrees of Freedom and Sums of Squares

$df_A = p-1 =$ _____ $\qquad$ $df_B = q-1 =$ _____ $\qquad$ $df_{AB} = (p-1)(q-1) =$ _____

$df_{within} = N - pq =$ _____ $\qquad$ $df_{total} = N-1 =$ _____ $\qquad$ $SS_A = (\mathbf{III}) - (\mathbf{I}) =$ _____

$SS_B = (\mathbf{IV}) - (\mathbf{I}) =$ _____ $\qquad$ $SS_{AB} = (\mathbf{V}) + (\mathbf{I}) - (\mathbf{III}) - (\mathbf{IV}) =$ _____

$SS_{within} = (\mathbf{II}) - (\mathbf{V}) =$ _____ $\qquad$ $SS_{total} = (\mathbf{II}) - (\mathbf{I}) =$ _____

E. Summary Table

Source	df	SS	MS	F
A				
B				
AB				
Within				
Total				

For a significance level of .05 (from Table E, Appendix 2 of the text)

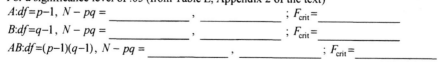

$A: df = p-1,\ N-pq =$ _____ , _____ ; $F_{crit} =$ _____

$B: df = q-1,\ N-pq =$ _____ , _____ ; $F_{crit} =$ _____

$AB: df = (p-1)(q-1),\ N-pq =$ _____ , _____ ; $F_{crit} =$ _____

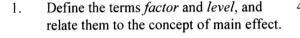

SELF-TEST

1. Define the terms *factor* and *level*, and relate them to the concept of main effect.

2. Name the three sources of variation in a two-factor analysis of variance that are associated with treatment effects.

3. Define *interaction*.

4.* In a two-factor analysis of variance, what implication does a significant interaction have for any significant main effects?

5.* What are the assumptions of the two-factor analysis of variance, and why is each necessary?

6.* State the three sets of hypotheses in a two-factor analysis of variance.

Questions preceded by an asterisk can be answered on the basis of the discussion in the text, but the discussion in this Study Guide does not answer them.

EXERCISES

1. A physiological psychologist was studying the hormonal and genetic basis of gender differences in rough-and-tumble play among monkeys. Three groups of monkeys were observed for several days during their first year and another three groups during their second year of life. The three groups were normal males, normal females, and animals that were genetically female but whose mothers had been treated with the male hormone testosterone while pregnant, thus producing a pseudomale. The time each animal spent in rough-and-tumble play is given below.[1] Evaluate these data.

	Factor *B* (Gender)		
		Pseudo-	
	Males	**males**	**Females**
	10	9	2
First Year	13	8	5
	14	8	4
Factor A (Age)	12	11	5
	11	7	4
Second Year	8	10	3
	14	7	6
	10	9	7

2. A developmental psychologist who was interested in the effects of social

rhesus monkeys," in R. P. Michael, ed., *Endocrinology and Human Behavior* (Oxford: Oxford University Press, 1968).

---

[1] Based on, but not identical to, a study by R. W. Goy, "Organizing effects of androgen on the behavior of

stimulation and rearing circumstances on the smiling behavior of young babies observed infants in Israel of several different ages who were being reared either in a usual family environment, in a kibbutz, or in an orphanage. The number of smiles in an hour-long observation is given below for each infant in the study.[2] Evaluate the data.

		Factor B (Age in Months)			
		2	4	8	16
	Family	3	5	7	6
		4	9	6	7
		3	8	3	6
Factor A (Rearing Condition)	Kibbutz	4	6	7	3
		6	7	5	4
		2	5	3	5
	Orphanage	6	7	5	4
		2	8	3	5
		3	5	6	4

● ● ● ● ●

ANSWERS

Figure 15–1. See Figure 15–1 in your text. Your Graph B should be like the text's C, C like D, D like E, E like F, and F like A — but with three levels of film rather than two levels of vicarious reinforcement.

Table 15–5. (I) = 903.125, **(II)** = 1218.000, **(III)** = 963.625, **(IV)** = 1051.750, **(V)** = 1169.500; summary table, for Factor A:$df = 1$, $SS = 60.500$, $MS = 60.500$, $F = 29.94**$; Factor B:$df = 3$, $SS = 148.6250$, $MS = 49.5417$, $F = 24.52**$; interaction $A \times B$:$df = 3$, $SS = 57.2500$, $MS = 19.0833$, $F = 9.44**$; within: $df = 24$, $SS = 48.5000$, $MS = 2.0208$;

total: $df = 31$, $SS = 314.8750$; $F_{crit}(1, 24) = 4.26$, $F_{crit}(3, 24) = 3.01$.

Self-Test. (1) A factor is a basis of classification that includes two or more subgroups called levels. When there are significant differences in the population means for these levels, a main effect for this factor exists. **(2)** Main effect for Factor A, main effect for Factor B, $A \times B$ interaction effect. **(3)** An interaction exists when the nature of the effect for one factor is not the same under all levels of another factor. **(4)** A significant interaction indicates that any significant main effect probably should be qualified in its interpreta-

---

2   Based on, but not identical to, a study by J. L Gewirtz, "The Cause of Infant Smiling in Four Child-Rearing Environments in Israel," in B. M. Foss, ed., *Determinants of Infant Behavior*, vol. 3 (London: Methuen, 1965).

tion. **(5)** See discussion of *Assumptions of Two-Factor Analysis of Variance* in the text.

(6) $H_0: \alpha_1 = \alpha_2 = \cdots = \alpha_j$; H_1: not H_0;

$H_0: \beta_1 = \beta_2 = \cdots = \beta_k$; H_2: not H_0;

$H_0: \alpha\beta_{11} = \alpha\beta_{12} = \alpha\beta_{21} = \cdots = \alpha\beta_{jk}$; H_1: not H_0.

Exercises. (1) (I) = 1617.0417, **(II)** = 1879, **(III)** = 1618.0833, **(IV)** = 1815.1250, **(V)** = 1822.7500; summary table, for age factor: $df = 1$, $SS = 1.0416$, $MS = 1.0416$, $F = .33$; gender factor: $df = 2$, $SS = 198.0833$, $MS = 99.0417$, $F = 31.6931**$; age × gender interaction: $df = 2$, $SS = 6.5834$, $MS = 3.2917$, $F = 1.0533$; within: $df = 18$, $SS = 56.2500$, $MS = 3.1250$; total: $df = 23$, $SS = 261.9583$. The amount of rough-and-tumble play seems to be related to testosterone level during and after the prenatal period. **(2) (I)** = 920.1111, **(II)** = 1032, **(III)** = 925.1667, **(IV)** = 961.1111, **(V)** = 974.6667; summary table, for rearing condition factor: $df = 2$, $SS = 5.0556$, $MS = 2.5278$, $F = 1.06$; age factor: $df = 3$, $SS = 41.0000$, $MS = 13.6667$, $F = 5.72**$; rearing × age interaction: $df = 6$, $SS = 8.5000$, $MS = 1.4167$, $F = .59$; within: $df = 24$, $SS = 57.3333$, $MS = 2.3889$; total: $df = 35$, $SS = 111.8889$. Age, but not rearing environment, was associated with smiling rates.

●●●●● STATISTICAL PACKAGES ●●●●●

●●●●● MINITAB

(To accompany the guided computational example in Table 15–5.)

MINITAB will perform a two-factor independent-groups analysis of variance using the General Linear Model command. The data must be presented in a "stacked" format. This approach requires entering the dependent variable value and the levels of the two factors for that value on a separate line for each score in the dataset. In this example, the dependent variable, or *response* variable, is Y, and the factors are A and B.

Start the MINITAB program and click on the Data window. Using the data from Table 15–5, enter the values of the Y variable in the first column of the spreadsheet, followed by the levels of the two factors A and B in the second and third columns, respectively. Enter the variable names at the head of the three columns.

The data you have entered should appear on the spreadsheet as follows:

Y	A	B	Y	A	B	Y	A	B
1	1	1	8	1	3	5	2	2
4	1	1	9	1	4	8	2	2
3	1	1	7	1	4	1	2	3
1	1	1	10	1	4	0	2	3
7	1	2	8	1	4	3	2	3
10	1	2	4	2	1	2	2	3
9	1	2	1	2	1	3	2	4
8	1	2	2	2	1	4	2	4
6	1	3	3	2	1	5	2	4
9	1	3	9	2	2	3	2	4
7	1	3	10	2	2			

To save the data as a MINITAB Worksheet:

File>Save Worksheet As
    (Enter folder and file name.)
    OK

To carry out a two-factor analysis of variance, the *General Linear Model* command is the most flexible. Note that you must enter both factors and the interaction term exactly as shown below:

Stat>ANOVA>General Linear Model
    Responses: Y   [double-click to transfer]
    Model: A B A*B   [type in both factors and the interaction term]
    OK

Then use the *Cross Tabulation* command to compute cell means:

Stat>Tables>Cross Tabulation
    Classification variables: A B   [double-click each to transfer]
    Display: Counts
    Summaries
        Associated variables: Y   [double-click to transfer]
        Display: Means, Standard deviations
        OK
    OK

On the General Linear Model output, the ANOVA table for Y shows "Seq SS" and "Adj SS" which will be equal and simply the SS, "Adj MS" is the MS, and "Error" is Within. On the Tabulated Statistics output, the count n, mean, and standard deviation for each cell and for the marginals ("All") are shown.

Alternatively, for this example, a two-factor analysis of variance can be carried out using the simpler *Two-way* command. To carry out the analysis using the *Two-way* command:

> *Stat>ANOVA>Two-way*
> Response: Y [double-click to transfer]
> Row factor: A Display means: Yes
> Column factor: B Display means: Yes
> OK

The *Two-way* command has the advantage that it plots means and 95% confidence intervals for the levels of each factor, and it is available on the student version of MINITAB. Note, however, that use of the *Two-way* command requires both factors to be "fixed" (i.e., predetermined), and also for all cells to have equal numbers of observations. This example fulfills both requirements.

The output, illustrated below, shows output first from the *Two-way* and then from the *General Linear Model* commands.

To obtain a copy of the program output, print the Session window:

> *File>Print Session Window*
> Print Range: All
> OK

Exit MINITAB:

> *File>Exit*

MINITAB Program Output

```
Two-way ANOVA: Y versus A, B

Analysis of Variance for Y
Source      DF        SS        MS        F        P
A            1      60.50     60.50    29.94    0.000
B            3     148.63     49.54    24.52    0.000
Interaction  3      57.25     19.08     9.44    0.000
Error       24      48.50      2.02
Total       31     314.88
                        Individual 95% CI
  A          Mean   ----+---------+---------+---------+-------
  1          6.69                               (-----*-----)
  2          3.94    (-----*-----)
                     ----+---------+---------+---------+-------
                     3.60      4.80      6.00      7.20

                        Individual 95% CI
  B          Mean   ----+---------+---------+---------+-------
  1          2.38    (----*----)
  2          8.25                               (----*----)
  3          4.50              (----*-----)
  4          6.12                     (-----*----)
                     ----+---------+---------+---------+-------
                     2.00      4.00      6.00      8.00

General Linear Model: Y versus A, B

Factor      Type Levels Values
A           fixed     2  1 2
B           fixed     4  1 2 3 4

Analysis of Variance for Y, using Adjusted SS for Tests

Source      DF     Seq SS     Adj SS     Adj MS       F        P
A            1     60.500     60.500     60.500    29.94    0.000
B            3    148.625    148.625     49.542    24.52    0.000
A*B          3     57.250     57.250     19.083     9.44    0.000
Error       24     48.500     48.500      2.021
Total       31    314.875

Unusual Observations for Y

Obs       Y       Fit   StDev Fit   Residual   St Resid
 23   5.0000    8.0000     0.7108    -3.0000     -2.44R

R denotes an observation with a large standardized residual
```

```
Tabulated Statistics: A, B
 Rows: A      Columns: B

            1         2         3         4        All
 1          4         4         4         4         16
       2.2500    8.5000    7.5000    8.5000    6.6875
       1.5000    1.2910    1.2910    1.2910    2.9375

 2          4         4         4         4         16
       2.5000    8.0000    1.5000    3.7500    3.9375
       1.2910    2.1602    1.2910    0.9574    2.8860

 All        8         8         8         8         32
       2.3750    8.2500    4.5000    6.1250    5.3125
       1.3025    1.6690    3.4226    2.7484    3.1870

 Cell Contents --
                Count
              Y:Mean
                StDev
```

• • • • •   SPSS

(To accompany the guided computational example in Table 15–5.)

To compute a two-factor analysis of variance like the one shown in Table 15–5, you must first identify the dependent variable (the outcome measure) and the independent variables (factors). In this example the dependent variable is Y, and the factors are A and B. Both factors are "fixed."

Start the SPSS program. The Data Editor window will fill the screen.

Enter the dependent measure Y in the first column of the spreadsheet, followed by the coded factor values for A and B in the second and third columns, respectively. The levels for factor A run from 1 to 2 and for factor B from 1 to 4. Select the "Variable View" tab to label the columns with the variable names Y, A, and B, respectively.

The data you have entered should appear on the spreadsheet as follows:

Y	A	B	Y	A	B	Y	A	B
1	1	1	8	1	3	5	2	2
4	1	1	9	1	4	8	2	2
3	1	1	7	1	4	1	2	3
1	1	1	10	1	4	0	2	3
7	1	2	8	1	4	3	2	3
10	1	2	4	2	1	2	2	3
9	1	2	1	2	1	3	2	3
8	1	2	2	2	1	3	2	4
6	1	3	3	2	1	4	2	4
9	1	3	9	2	2	5	2	4
7	1	3	10	2	2	3	2	4

To carry out the two-factor analysis of variance:

> *Analyze>General Linear Model>Univariate*
>   Dependent Variable: Y   [highlight and transfer]
>   Fixed Factor(s): A, B
>   Options: Display Means for: A, B, A*B   [highlight and transfer]
>   Continue
>   OK

The SPSS program outputs appear on the following two pages. The ANOVA table for this analysis gives more information than you need. By comparison, the analysis of variance summary table given in the text is composed only of the headings and lines *A*, *B*, *AB*, Residual (that is, Within), and Total.

Means and standard deviations for each cell and for the marginals were obtained with the *Display Means* option in the *Univariate* command. The second page of the output shows the tables of means for this example.

To print the ANOVA table and the tables of means:

> *File>Print*
>   Print range: All visible output
>   OK

To save the data that you entered:

> *Window>SPSS Data Editor*
> *File>Save As*
> (Enter folder and file name for SPSS Save file.)
> Save

Exit SPSS:

> *File>Exit*

SPSS Program Output

Univariate Analysis of Variance

Between-Subjects Factors

		N
A	1.00	16
	2.00	16
B	1.00	8
	2.00	8
	3.00	8
	4.00	8

Tests of Between-Subjects Effects

Dependent Variable: Y

Source	Type III Sum of Squares	df	Mean Square	F	Sig.
Corrected Model	266.375[a]	7	38.054	18.831	.000
Intercept	903.125	1	903.125	446.907	.000
A	60.500	1	60.500	29.938	.000
B	148.625	3	49.542	24.515	.000
A * B	57.250	3	19.083	9.443	.000
Error	48.500	24	2.021		
Total	1218.000	32			
Corrected Total	314.875	31			

a. R Squared = .846 (Adjusted R Squared = .801)

Estimated Marginal Means

1. A

Dependent Variable: Y

A	Mean	Std. Error	95% Confidence Interval	
			Lower Bound	Upper Bound
1.00	6.688	.355	5.954	7.421
2.00	3.938	.355	3.204	4.671

2. B

Dependent Variable: Y

B	Mean	Std. Error	95% Confidence Interval	
			Lower Bound	Upper Bound
1.00	2.375	.503	1.338	3.412
2.00	8.250	.503	7.213	9.287
3.00	4.500	.503	3.463	5.537
4.00	6.125	.503	5.088	7.162

3. A * B

Dependent Variable: Y

A	B	Mean	Std. Error	95% Confidence Interval	
				Lower Bound	Upper Bound
1.00	1.00	2.250	.711	.783	3.717
	2.00	8.500	.711	7.033	9.967
	3.00	7.500	.711	6.033	8.967
	4.00	8.500	.711	7.033	9.967
2.00	1.00	2.500	.711	1.033	3.967
	2.00	8.000	.711	6.533	9.467
	3.00	1.500	.711	3.302E-02	2.967
	4.00	3.750	.711	2.283	5.217

● ● ● ● ●

CHAPTER 16

NONPARAMETRIC TECHNIQUES •••••

CONCEPT GOALS

Be sure that you thoroughly understand the following concepts and how to use them in statistical applications.

- ◆ Parametric vs. nonparametric tests
- ◆ Pearson chi-square test
- ◆ Mann-Whitney U test for two independent samples
- ◆ Kruskal-Wallis test for k independent samples
- ◆ Wilcoxon test for two correlated samples
- ◆ Spearman rank-order correlation

 ••••• GUIDE TO MAJOR CONCEPTS

Introduction

The statistical techniques described in the previous chapters have represented tests on parameters, such as μ or ρ. Such tests often assume that the data consist of measurements made on at least an interval scale, that the population distributions are normal, and that homogeneity of variance prevails. Sometimes one cannot make such assumptions about population parameters. Then it is helpful to have some **nonparametric** statistical techniques available as alternatives to the **parametric** ones discussed in previous chapters. The t test between two means and the analysis of variance are

[1]_____ tests, whereas techniques that do not test the values of parameters and that make different assumptions about the nature of the populations involved are called [2]_____ tests.

It is not always clear when to use nonparametric rather than parametric techniques. If the data consist of percentages of participants who did one thing or another or if participants are ranked, then one would probably choose [3]_____ methods. However, if the measurements are made with interval scales but the distributions are skewed or variances differ from group to group, the decision is not so clear. Generally, if the data are only mildly deviant from the assumptions of [4]_____ distributions and [5]_____ variances, one can still use [6]_____ tests; however, if departures from these assumptions are severe, it may be best to use a [7]_____ technique.

Answer Key to Introduction

| [1] | parametric | [3] | nonparametric | [5] | homogeneous | [7] | nonparametric |
| [2] | nonparametric | [4] | normal | [6] | parametric | | |

Pearson Chi-Square Test

Almost three decades ago, an opinion pollster wanted to know where people placed the blame for the Watergate scandal. After President Nixon held his first press conference following the beginning of the Senate hearings in 1973, the pollster drew a sample and offered each person five choices of where the blame should be put: (1) a plot against the President, (2) the President himself, (3) usual dirty politics, (4) the men around the President, or (5) no opinion. The result of such a survey is the number (or percentage) of people questioned who responded with each of the five alternatives. These data are on a [1]_____ scale of measurement and require a [2]_____ analysis, in this case the **Pearson chi-square test**.

The pollster suspects that opinion might depend or be **contingent** upon whether the person answering the question is a Republican, Democrat, or an Independent. For example, Democrats may be more likely to blame the Republican President than other groups. Statistically, one would like to determine the probability that the distribution of responses over the five categories is the same for each of the three samples of respondents (Republican, Democrats, Independents). That is, what is the probability that these distributions are not [3]_____ upon group membership? The statistical question is addressed by the [4]_____ test.

Suppose that the results of this survey are those presented under "Computation" in Table 16–1. The row sums in the rightmost column and the column sums in the last row are called **marginals** (because they are in the margins of this table of data). They indicate how many Republicans, Democrats, and Independents were sampled and how many people, regardless of political affiliation, sided with each alternative.[1] Thus, the total sample included [5]__ people of whom Republicans numbered [6]__ , Democrats [7]__ , and Independents [8]__ . Regardless of political affiliation, [9]__ people blamed the President as indicated by the [10]_____ of the table. The numbers within each cell of the table indicate the observed number of people with a particular affiliation who placed the blame on the circumstance indicated in that column. Thus, the President was blamed by [11]__ of the Democrats, while only [12]__ Republicans blamed him.

The results of the statistical technique can be used only to make inferences about a population whose characteristics are distributed in the proportions specified by the marginals in the table of sample data. Thus, the null hypothesis states: Given the observed [13]_____ , the distribution of responses is identical for the three populations sampled (i.e., political affiliations). The alternative hypothesis states: [14]_____

_____ .

The statistical technique assumes that people were [15]_____ and [16]_____ sampled and that the groups are [17]_____ of one another. Moreover, any single participant may qualify for **one and only one cell** or category. Thus, each person must have one political group affiliation and must choose only one of the five alternatives: Participants must be in [18]_____ and only one [19]_____ . A final assumption of this test is that no expected frequency can be less than [20]__ , and in a 2 X 2 table, not less than [21]__ .

----

1   The distribution of response to these five categories regardless of political affiliation was reported by Daniel Yankelovitch, Inc., and published in *Time* (International Edition), 10 September 1973. The breakdown according to political affiliation is fictitious.

Table 16–1 Guided Computational Example for the $r \times c$ Chi-Square Test

Hypotheses

H_0: Given the observed _____ , the distributions of frequencies in the population are not different for the groups.

H_1: Given the observed marginals, these _____ are different for these groups (nondirectional/directional).

Assumptions and Conditions

1. The participants are _____ and _____ sampled.

2. The groups are _____ .

3. Each observation qualifies for one and only one _____ .

4. No _____ frequency is less than _____ (if $r=c=2$, not less than _____).

Decision Rules

Given a significance level of _____ , a _____ test, and $df = (r-1)(c-1) =$ _____ :

If _____ : _____ .

If _____ : _____ .

Computation

1. Place data into an $r \times c$ table.

2. Calculate the expected frequencies (if necessary) for each cell by taking the product of the _____ and _____ marginal frequencies and dividing by _____ .

	Plot	President	Response Category Politics	Appointees	No Opinion	Total
Republicans	O=60	O=20	O=130	O=110	O=30	350
	E=	E=	E=	E=	E=	
Democrats	O=40	O=70	O=115	O=200	O=25	450
	E=	E=	E=	E=	E=	
Independents	O=10	O=40	O=55	O=60	O=35	200
	E=	E=	E=	E=	E=	
	110	130	300	370	90	1000

3. Check: Do expected frequencies add to equal the marginals?

4. Calculate χ^2_{obs}:

$$\chi^2_{obs} = \Sigma^r_{j=1} \Sigma^c_{k=1}(O_{jk} - E_{jk})^2 / E_{jk}$$

$$\chi^2_{obs} = \text{_____} = \text{_____}$$

where O_{jk} is the _____ frequency for the jkth cell and E_{jk} is the _____ frequency for the jkth cell

Decision: _____ H_0 .

The decision rules are stated in terms of the statistic that will be calculated, χ^2, read "chi square." Critical values of the [22]_____ distribution are presented in Table G in Appendix 2 of your text. Look at that table now. The degrees of freedom are listed at the left, and critical values are given as a function of significance level and whether a directional or nondirectional test is appropriate. The degrees of freedom are given by $df = (r-1)(c-1)$ where r and c represent the number of rows and columns of the data table, respectively. For the polling example, [23] $df = ($_____$)($_____$) =$ ___ . The critical value for a nondirectional test at .05 is [24]___ . The chi-square distribution, like the F, is not symmetrical, and the computation is set up so that the null hypothesis is rejected if $\chi^2_{obs} \geq \chi^2_{crit}$. Therefore, the decision rules for this example are

If [25]_____ , [26]_____ .

If [27]_____ , [28]_____ .

The computation of $\chi_{obs}{}^2$ proceeds according to the outline in Table 16–1. First calculate the **expected** frequency for each score. The obtained or **observed** frequency for the jkth cell is symbolized by O_{jk}, while E_{jk} represents the [29]_____ frequency. The E_{jk} for each cell is the product of the row and column marginals for that cell divided by the total number of cases, N. Thus, for the first cell (Republicans who attributed the Watergate scandal to a plot against the President), the [30]_____ frequency, symbolized for this cell by [31]___ , equals [32]( )( ) / ( ) = ___ . Similarly, the value of E_{23} equals [33]( )( ) / ( ) = ___ . You can check the accuracy of your expected frequencies by determining whether they add up to the observed marginal totals.

Once these expected frequencies are determined for each cell, χ^2_{obs} is given by

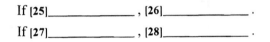

$\chi^2_{obs} = \sum_{j=1}^{r} \sum_{k=1}^{c} (O_{jk} - E_{jk})^2 / E_{jk}$ which directs one to take the difference between the [34]_____ and [35]_____ frequencies in a cell, [36]_____ it, divide it by the [37]_____ frequency for that cell, and [38]_____ these quantities over all cells. For the first cell, [39] $O_{11} =$ ___ , [40] $E_{11} =$ ___ , [41] $(O_{11} - E_{11}) =$ ___ , [42] $(O_{11} - E_{11})^2 =$ _____ , and [43] $(O_{11} - E_{11})^2 / E_{11} =$ _____ ; and so on for each cell. The total of such values over all cells equals [44] $\chi^2_{obs} =$ _____ , which conforms to the (first/second) [45]_____ decision rule to [46]_____ H_0. In this case, we conclude that the [47]_____ of responses concerning Watergate are (the same/different) [48]_____ for people having the three political affiliations. You might want to make a table of the percentage of each group responding to each of the five alternatives to see this more clearly. Now complete all parts of the guided computational example in Table 16–1.

Answer Key to Pearson Chi-Square Test

[1]	nominal	[15]	randomly	[32]	$(350)(110)/1000^2 = 38.5$		
[2]	nonparametric	[16]	independently	[33]	$(450)(300)/1000 = 135$		
[3]	contingent	[17]	independent	[34]	observed		
[4]	Pearson chi-square	[18]	one	[35]	expected		
[5]	1000	[19]	cell	[36]	square		
[6]	350	[20]	5	[37]	expected		
[7]	450	[21]	10	[38]	sum		
[8]	200	[22]	chi-square	[39]	60		
[9]	130	[23]	$(3-1)(5-1) = 8$	[40]	38.5		
[10]	marginals	[24]	15.51	[41]	21.5		
[11]	70	[25]	$\chi_{obs}^2 < 15.15$	[42]	462.25		
[12]	20	[26]	do not reject H_0	[43]	12.0065		
[13]	marginals	[27]	$\chi_{obs}^2 \geq 15.51$	[44]	88.18		
[14]	Given the observed	[28]	reject H_0	[45]	second		
	marginals, these	[29]	expected	[46]	reject		
	population distributions	[30]	expected	[47]	distributions		
	are not identical	[31]	E_{11}	[48]	different		

Mann-Whitney *U* Test for Two Independent Samples

Suppose that an experiment is conducted in which two independent groups of measurements are to be compared. Ordinarily, you would test the difference between the means of these groups with a [1]_____ for [2]_____ groups. But suppose that the measurements have been made on an ordinal scale or that the necessary assumptions regarding the population distributions cannot be met. In this case one might consider using a nonparametric analogue to the *t* test, such as the [3]_____ test.

Consider the following experiment.[2] Suppose that some social scientists are interested in the effects of viewing different types of television programs on the behavior of preschool children. Two groups of children (from 3 1/2 to 5 1/2 years old) from low-income families are enrolled in a preschool for six weeks. One group spends part of each school period watching such violent programs as *Batman* and *Superman*, while the other children view episodes from the program *Mister Rogers' Neighborhood*, which emphasizes sharing, cooperation, adaptive coping with frustration, and other forms of positive social behavior (which psychologists call *prosocial* behavior). The behavior of these children in the preschool setting is observed for a fixed period of time, and a panel of judges rates each child's prosocial behavior from 1 (minimum) to 10 (maximum). The data are presented under "Computation" in Table 16–2. The scores are presented in one row with each child's television group affiliation (*A* for violent or *B* for prosocial) shown above it. Notice that the scale of measurement is probably [4]_____ in nature. Thus, a [5]_____ statistical test, the [6]_____ test, is selected.

The rationale of the *U* test is simple. One ranks the scores, ignoring group affiliation. If there are no differences between groups, the average rank for each of the two groups should vary only by [7]_____ . If they differ more than could be expected by sampling error, then the null hypothesis (that the groups are from identical [8]_____) should be [9]_____ .

The wording of the hypotheses for the *U* test is slightly different than for the parametric *t* test. For the *t* test, the null hypothesis H_0 is stated directly in terms of the population means: [10]_____ . However, in the *U* test, no assumptions are made about the population variances, and consequently the null hypothesis must be stated with respect to the entire form of the two **population distributions**, not simply the means. Thus,

H_0: The population [11]_____ from which the two samples are drawn are

    [12]_____ .

H_1: The [13]_____ distributions are different in some way.

---

2   The data in this example are based upon, but not identical to, the results of a study conducted by L. K. Friedrich and A. H. Stein, "Aggressive and Prosocial Television Programs and the Natural Behavior of Preschool Children," *Monographs of the Society for Research in Child Development*, vol. 38, no. 151 (1973).

Table 16–2 Guided Computational Example for the Mann-Whitney U Test for Two Independent Samples

Hypotheses

H_0: The population _____ from which the two samples are drawn are _____ .

H_1: These _____ are different in some way (nondirectional/directional).

Assumptions and Conditions

1. The participants are _____ and _____ sampled.

2. The two groups are _____ .

3. The variable is _____ and the measurement scale is at least _____ .

Decision Rules

If n_A and $n_B \leq 20$	**If n_A or $n_B \geq 20$**
Values of U_{obs} are found in Table H, Appendix 2.	U_{obs} is translated into a z_{obs} and the standard
Given $n_A =$ __ , $n_B =$ __ , a significance level of _____ , and a	normal distribution (Table A, Appendix 2) is
_____ test:	used with
If __ $< U_{obs} <$ __ , _____ H_0.	
If $U_{obs} \leq$ _____ or $U_{obs} \geq$ _____ ,	
_____ H_0.	

$$z_{obs} = \frac{U_{obs} - n_A n_B/2}{\sqrt{[(n_A)(n_B)(n_A + n_B + 1)]/12}}$$

Computation (A = violent, B = prosocial)

Group	A	A	A	A	B	A	A	A	B	A	A	B	B	B	B	A	B	B
Score	1	2	2	4	5	5	5	6	6	6	7	8	9	9	9	9	10	10
Rank																		

Checks

$n_A =$ _____ $\left.\right\} N =$ _____ $T_A =$ _____ $\left.\right\} T_A + T_B =$ _____
$n_B =$ _____

Does $T_A + T_B$ equal $N(N+1)/2 =$ _____ ?

$U_{obs} = n_A n_B + [n_A(n_A+1)]/2 - T_A =$ _____ = _____

Decision: _____ H_0.

The assumptions are that the subjects (or observations) are [14]_____ and
[15]_____ sampled and the two groups are [16]_____ . In addition, it is
necessary to assume that the variable underlying the scale of measurement is **continuous** and that
the measurement scale has at least **ordinal** properties. In the present case, the ratings of prosocial
behavior do form a scale with [17]_____ characteristics, and we can assume that they
reflect a continuous dimension of prosocial tendency in the children. Thus, the dependent
variable is [18]_____ and the measurement scale is at least [19]_____ in nature.

The decision rules are stated somewhat differently, depending upon whether the number of
subjects in each group (n_A and n_B) is more than 20. *If n_A and $n_B \leq 20$*, then you can determine
the critical values of U by consulting Table H in Appendix 2 of your text. Look at this table now.
Notice first that there is a different page for each significance level. Therefore, you must locate
the correct page depending upon the chosen [20]_____ and upon whether the test is
directional or nondirectional. The rows and columns represent the number of observations in each
group. Simply find the intersection of the row and column corresponding to n_A and n_B. The two
numbers located there are the upper and lower critical values for U. Thus, in the present example,
[21]$n_A =$ ___ and [22]$n_B =$ ___ ; for a nondirectional test at significance level .05, [23]$U_{crit} =$ ___ and
[24]___ . These critical values are similar to a confidence interval, so if U_{obs} falls *between* these
values, then H_0 is [25]_____ ; if U_{obs} is *equal to or outside these limits*, then we
[26]_____ H_0 . Formally,

If [27]___ $< U_{obs} <$ ___ , [28]_____ .
If [29]_____ or [30]_____ , [31]_____ .

If either n_A or n_B is greater than 20, Table H cannot be used. Instead, one would compute a z_{obs}
with the formula given in Table 16–2 and use Table A in Appendix 2 of your text.

The computational procedures for U_{obs} (see Table 16–2) begin with placing the scores in
order of increasing size regardless of group affiliation. Then they are ranked, the rank 1 being
given to the lowest score. When scores are duplicated, all scores with the same value are given a
rank equal to the average of the ranks these scores would have received if they had not been tied.
Rank the scores in Table 16–2; when you get to the two scores of 2 you will see that these two

scores, if not tied, would have received the ranks of [32]__ and [33]__ . Since they are tied, they are both assigned the average of these two ranks, which is [34]__ . But what rank is given to the next score, which is 4? Had the two scores of 2 not been tied, they would have occupied ranks 2 and 3, so the next assignable rank would be [35]__ . The score of 4 receives this rank. Rank the rest of the scores. You should have given the three scores of 6 the rank [36]__ and each of the scores of 9 the rank [37]__ .

You will need the values of n_A, n_B, N, T_A, and T_B. Calculate these in Table 16–2. The total number of cases, N, equals the sum of the numbers in group A and group B, in this case [38]__ + __ = __ . T_A and T_B are the sum of the ranks for groups A and B. [39]$T_A = $__ and [40]$T_B = $__ .

Many errors are made in ranking in this and other nonparametric procedures. You can check your ranking accuracy with two tests. First, the highest score should receive, or share with a tied score, a rank equal to the total number of scores being ranked. In this case, the total number of scores is [41]$N = $__ . The two scores of 10 share ranks [42]__ and [43]__ and thus fulfill this check. Second, the total of all ranks of N scores should equal $N(N+1)/2$, in this case, [44]__(_____)/ __ = __ , and $T_A + T_B$ should equal this same value: [45]$T_A + T_B = $__ + __ = __ .

Now you are ready to calculate U_{obs}. Use the formula $U_{obs} = (n_A)(n_B) + [n_A(n_A+1)]/2 - T_A$ which for the present example equals [46]$U_{obs} = $__ + (_____ / __) − __ = __ .

In this case, U_{obs} conforms to the (first/second) [47]_____ decision rule, and H_0 is [48]_____ . We conclude that the scores of children who saw violent television and of those who saw prosocial television are probably from population distributions that are different in some way. Now complete the guided computational example for this problem given in Table 16–2.

Answer Key to Mann-Whitney U Test for Two Independent Samples

[1]	t test	[4]	ordinal	[7]	sampling error	[11]	distributions
[2]	independent	[5]	nonparametric	[8]	populations	[12]	identical
[3]	Mann-Whitney U	[6]	Mann-Whitney U	[9]	rejected	[13]	population
				[10]	$\mu_1 = \mu_2$	[14]	randomly

[15]	independently	[24]	63	[33]	3	[43]	18
[16]	independent	[25]	not rejected	[34]	2.5	[44]	$18(18+1)/2$
[17]	ordinal	[26]	reject	[35]	4		$=171$
[18]	continuous	[27]	17, 63	[36]	9	[45]	$65.5+105.5=$
[19]	ordinal	[28]	do not reject	[37]	14.5		171
[20]	significance		H_0	[38]	$10+8=18$	[46]	$10(8)+10(11)/2$
	level	[29]	$U_{obs} \leq 17$	[39]	65.5		$-65.5=69.5$
[21]	10	[30]	$U_{obs} \geq 63$	[40]	105.5	[47]	second
[22]	8	[31]	reject H_0	[41]	18	[48]	rejected
[23]	17	[32]	2	[42]	17		

Kruskal-Wallis Test for *k* Independent Samples

Suppose that one cannot meet the assumptions of the simple analysis of variance, perhaps because the distributions are not at all [1]_____ in form or the variances of the several groups are decidedly not [2]_____ . An alternative is the [3]_____ test. In the experiment on television viewing and preschool behavior described above, there were actually three groups of children involved in the entire experiment: children who viewed the prosocial "Mister Rogers' Neighborhood," those who saw the violent programs, and those who saw neutral programs consisting of travelogues and nature shows. The scientists observed not only prosocial behavior but also aggressive actions among peers in the nursery school. Does this television fare influence the amount of verbal and physical aggression as expressed in a single aggression index? The data are presented under "Computation" in Table 16–3.

The nonparametric test to be illustrated is the [4]_____ test. The hypotheses and assumptions are similar to those for the Mann-Whitney *U* test.

H_0: The population [5]_____ from which the groups are sampled are

[6]_____ .

H_0: The [7]_____ distributions are different in some way.

Table 16–3 Guided Computational Example for the Kruskal-Wallis for *k* Independent Samples

Hypotheses

H_0: The population _____ from which the groups are sampled are _____ .

H_1: These _____ are different in some way (nondirectional/directional).

Assumptions and Conditions

1. The participants are _____ and _____ sampled.

2. The *k* groups are _____ and all $n_j \geq$ _____ .

3. The variable is _____ and the measurement scale is at least _____ .

Decision Rules

Given a significance level of _____ , a _____ test, and the fact that H is distributed as χ^2 (Table G) with $df = k-1 =$ _____ :

If _____ , _____ .

If _____ , _____ .

Computation

Prosocial		Neutral		Violent	
Score	Rank	Score	Rank	Score	Rank
7		9		3	
3		2		8	
8		4		8	
5		4		5	
6		7		6	
		7		1	
$n_1 =$ $T_1 =$		$n_2 =$ $T_2 =$		$n_3 =$ $T_3 =$	
$T_1^2 / n_1 =$		$T_2^2 / n_2 =$		$T_3^2 / n_3 =$	

$N = \sum_{j=1}^{k} n_j =$ _____ , $\sum_{j=1}^{k} [T_j^2 / n_j] =$ _____ .

$H_{obs} = \dfrac{12}{N(N+1)} \left[\sum_{j=1}^{k} \dfrac{T_j^2}{n_j} \right] - 3(N+1) =$ _____ $=$ ___

Check:

Does $\sum T_j =$ _____

equal $[N(N+1)]/2 =$ _____ ?

Decision: _____ H_0 .

Again, notice that the hypotheses are stated in terms of population [8]_____ , not specifically in terms of their [9]_____ . It is necessary to assume that the participants are [10]_____ and [11]_____ sampled; that the k groups are [12]_____ of one another; that the variable is [13]_____ ; and that the scale of measurement has at least [14]_____ properties. The number of cases in each group (n_j) must be at least five (in symbols, [15]_____) to have an accurate result.

The statistic to be calculated is called H, but H is distributed as χ^2 with $df = k-1$ where k is the number of groups. For this example, [16]$df =$ _____ $=$ __ . Given the .05 level of significance and a nondirectional test, the critical value of χ^2 (which is also H_{crit} for this problem) given in Table G of Appendix 2 is [17]$H_{crit} =$ __ . Therefore,

If [18]_____ , [19]_____ .
If [20]_____ , [21]_____ .

The computation of H_{obs} begins by ranking the scores without regard to group membership, assigning the rank 1 to the lowest score and treating ties as described above. Do this for the data in Table 16–3. It is most easily done by relisting in ascending order the scores in each group and then ranking across groups. Then determine the n_j and the total of the ranks (labeled [22]__) separately for each each group. As before, check the accuracy of your ranking. Does the largest score (9) have a rank equal to N, the total number of cases, in this instance [23]_____ ? And is the sum of the ranks for the three groups, [24]$T_1 + T_2 + T_3 =$ __ + __ + __ = __ equal to $N(N+1)/2$, which is [25] __ (_____) / __ = __ ?

The value of H_{obs} is determined by obtaining the square of the total rankings of each group divided by its n_j and summing over all k groups. This value is symbolized by $\sum_{j=1}(T_j^2 / n_j)$ and equals [26]_____ . N, the total number of participants, equals [27]__ . These values may be substituted into the formula

$$[28]\, H_{obs} = \frac{12}{N(N+1)} \left[\sum_{j=1}^{k} \frac{T_j^2}{n_j} \right] - 3(N+1) = (\underline{\hspace{3cm}})(\underline{\hspace{3cm}}) - \underline{\hspace{1cm}}$$

which yields an H_{obs} of [29]___ . In this case, H_{obs} (is/is not) [30]_____ large enough to reject H_0. We conclude that the observed differences in aggressive behavior between television groups could have resulted from [31]_____ . The different programs had no demonstrable effects on aggressive behavior.

Answer Key to Kruskal-Wallis Test for k Independent Samples

[1]	normal	[11]	independently	[20]	$H_{obs} \geq 5.99$	[26]	1379.2917
[2]	homogeneous	[12]	independent	[21]	reject H_0	[27]	17
[3]	Kruskal-Wallis	[13]	continuous	[22]	T_j	[28]	$12/[17(18)]\cdot$
[4]	Kruskal-Wallis	[14]	ordinal	[23]	17		$[1379.2917] -$
[5]	distributions	[15]	$n_j \geq 5$	[24]	$47.5 + 54 +$		$3(18)$
[6]	identical	[16]	$3 - 1 = 2$		$51.5 = 153$	[29]	.09
[7]	population	[17]	5.99	[25]	$17(17+1)/2$	[30]	is not
[8]	distributions	[18]	$H_{obs} < 5.99$		$= 153$	[31]	sampling error
[9]	means	[19]	do not reject				
[10]	randomly		H_0				

Wilcoxon Test for Two Correlated Samples

Suppose that nine amateur springboard divers enroll in a special clinic designed to improve their form. The instructor rates them before and after the course. If we want to know whether the course has been effective in improving their diving form, we might use the parametric [1]_____ for [2]_____ samples. However, if we cannot meet the required assumptions, we might choose a nonparametric test such as the [3]_____ test for two [4]_____ samples. The data and format for this test are given in Table 16–4.

The hypotheses for the Wilcoxon test are similar to those of previous tests.

H_0: The population [5]_____ for the two correlated groups of observations are
[6]_____ .

H_1: The [7]_____ distributions are [8]_____ in some way.

Table 16–4 Guided Computational Example for the Wilcoxon Test
for Two Correlated Samples

Hypotheses

H_0: The population _____ for the two correlated groups of observations are _____ .

H_1: These _____ are different in some way (nondirectional/directional).

Assumptions

1. The pairs of observations are _____ and _____ sampled, but the two observations of a pair are made on the _____ or _____ participants.

2. The measurement scale is _____ both for individual scores and for d_i, the differences between the scores in each pair.

Decision Rules

If $N < 50$	If $N > 50$
The critical values of W_{obs} are found in Table I. Given $N=$__ , a significance level of _____ and a _____ test: If _____ > __ : _____ . If _____ ≤ __ : _____ .	W_{obs} is translated into a z_{obs}, and the standard normal distribution (Table A) is used with $$z_{obs} = \frac{W_{obs} - [N(N+1)/4]}{\sqrt{[N(N+1)(2N+1)]/24}}$$

Computation

Before	After	d_i	$|d_i|$	Rank of $|d_i|$	Signed Rank of $|d_i|$
4.5	5.2				
3.0	4.5				
6.2	5.9				
4.9	5.2				
5.5	5.8				
5.8	6.1				
6.1	7.2				
7.0	7.1				
5.0	5.6				

$N =$ original number of pairs minus
the number of pairs for which $d_i = 0$

$N =$ _____

$W_{obs} =$ _____

$T_+ =$ _____

$T_- =$ _____

Check: Does $T_+ + T_- =$ _____ equal $N(N+1)/2$?

Decision: _____ H_0 .

It is necessary to assume that the pairs of observations are [9]_____ and [10]_____ sampled; a pair consists of observations made either on the [11]_____ participant or on closely [12]_____ participants. In this example, a pair consists of one diver's scores before and after instruction. Finally, the scale of measurement must be at least [13]_____ in nature; this applies not only to the scores within a pair, but also to the differences between scores in a pair.

The test statistic for the [14]_____ test is W. If N is 50 or less, then the critical value of W is given in Table I in Appendix 2 of your text. Look at this table now. It gives the value of W_{crit} for various N, for different significance levels, and for directional and nondirectional tests. In contrast to other tables, if W_{obs} is *less than or equal to* the tabled value of W_{crit}, then the null hypothesis is rejected. Thus, for $N = 9$ and a directional test (training programs rarely lead to poorer performance) at the .05 level, the critical value of W_{crit} would be [15]___ . If W_{obs} is larger than this value, [16]_____ H_0; if W_{obs} is less than or equal to this value, [17]_____ H_0. However, if N is greater than 50, Table I in your text cannot be used. In this case, a z_{obs} can be calculated (see Table 16–4) and the critical values obtained from Table A in Appendix 2.

The computation of W_{obs} follows the outline under "Computation" in Table 16–4. First, compute d_i, the difference in value between the two scores in each pair. In the next column, write the absolute value of the d_i. Then rank these $|d_i|$, giving the smallest $|d_i|$ rank 1; finally, in the last column, affix the sign of the original d_i to this ranking. For the first participant, [18]$d_i =$ ___ , [19]$|d_i| =$ ___ , the rank in the total sample will be 7, and since the original d_i was negative, the signed rank will be [20]___ . However, ranking for the Wilcoxon test is slightly different from ranking for other tests. If the difference between a pair of measurements is zero, then that pair is eliminated, is not given a ranking, and is not counted in the total N, which is the original number of pairs minus the number of pairs for which $d_i = 0$. Complete the ranking of the scores in Table 16–4 now. The total of the positive ranks is symbolized by T_+ and equals [21]___ ; the total of the negative rankings (without the minus signs) is called T_- and equals [22]___ . Again, you should check the accuracy of your rankings by determining that $T_+ + T_-$ equals $N(N+1)/2$. In this case, these two quantities should both be [23]___ .

If there is no difference between the two populations of measurements, T_+ and T_- should be nearly equal. But if the populations differ from one another, then there will be a difference between T_+ and T_-. As this difference becomes greater, one of the T's will grow large and the other quite small. W_{obs} is the smaller of T_+ and T_-; in this case, [24] $W_{obs} = $ ___ . To reject H_0 and conclude that the clinic produced improvement, this value must be [25]_____ than or [26]_____ to W_{crit}; otherwise, do not reject H_0. Since W_{crit} is 8, the decision is to [27]_____ H_0; that is, the clinic has helped. Complete Table 16–4 now.

Answer Key to Wilcoxon Test for Two Correlated Samples

[1]	t test	[8]	different	[15]	8	[22]	41.5
[2]	correlated	[9]	randomly	[16]	do not reject	[23]	45
[3]	Wilcoxon	[10]	independently	[17]	reject	[24]	3.5
[4]	correlated	[11]	same	[18]	−.7	[25]	less
[5]	distributions	[12]	matched	[19]	.7	[26]	equal
[6]	identical	[13]	ordinal	[20]	−7	[27]	reject
[7]	population	[14]	Wilcoxon	[21]	3.5		

Spearman Rank-Order Correlation

It is sometimes preferable to use a nonparametric index of correlation rather than the Pearson product-moment correlation coefficient presented in Chapter 7. Such a nonparametric index is the [1]_____ correlation coefficient, symbolized by r_S. Perhaps the distributions of scores are not normal or the measurements are so crude that you trust only the ordinal properties of the scale. In these cases, you might want to use the [2]_____ correlation coefficient, or [3]__ .

In the study of television programming and aggressive behavior described previously, one might be interested in whether there is a relationship between the aggression of the child when he or she comes to the preschool and the amount of increase in aggressive behavior which occurs after seeing the violent TV programs. Suppose trained raters rank order 10 preschool children on general aggressiveness before the experiment begins. Then, the number of aggressive acts committed by each child is counted before and after the two-week period in which violent television programs are shown in the school. Table 16–5 presents the general aggressiveness ranking (1 = least aggressive) and the amount of *increase* in aggressive behavior over the two-week period.

Table 16–5 Guided Computational Example for the
Spearman Rank-Order Correlation Coefficient

Hypotheses

H_0: _____

H_1: _____ (nondirectional/directional)

Assumptions and Conditions

1. The participants are _____ and _____ sampled.

2. The scales of measurement have at least _____ properties.

Decision Rules

Given a significance level of _____ , $N=$ _____ pairs of scores, and a _____ test (see Table J, Appendix 2 of the text):

If _____ , _____ .

If _____ , _____ .

Computation

Participant	General Aggression Rank	Increment in Aggression	Rank of Aggression	Rank of Increment	d_i	d_i^2
A	6	−1				
B	2	−3				
C	3	8				
D	8	10				
E	9	17				
F	1	7				
G	4	5				
H	7	16				
I	10	14				
J	5	8				

N = number of pairs of measurements including zero differences = _____ $\sum_{i=1}^{N} d_i^2 =$ _____

$$r_S = 1 - 6\left[\frac{\sum_{i=1}^{N} d_i^2}{N^3 - N}\right] = \text{_____} = \text{_____}$$

$r_S =$ _____

Decision: _____ H_0.

To compute r_S you must rank the scores in each column separately. In this case, the scores under "general aggression" are already ranked, so these rankings need only be repeated under "rank aggression." However, the scores under "increment in aggression" must be ranked. The ranking is done in the same manner as for the Mann-Whitney U test, and ties are given average ranks. Complete this ranking in Table 16–5 now. In the next columns, the differences in the ranks for each pair of measures (d_i) is calculated, and then this value is squared (d_i^2) in the final column. Sum these squared differences in ranks to obtain $\sum_{i=1}^{N} d_i^2$, which equals [4]___ . N is the number of pairs *including* those having no difference in their rankings; in this case, [5]$N =$ ___ . The value of r_S is given by the formula

$$r_S = 1 - (6)\left[\frac{\sum_{i=1}^{N} d_i^2}{N^3 - N}\right]$$

[6] $r_S =$ ___ $-$ _____ $=$ _____

which yields a value of [7]$r_S =$ ___ . This rank-order correlation coefficient can be interpreted in the same manner as the Pearson r. Thus, r_S can take on values between [8]___ and [9]___ , the absence of any linear relationship between the measures is indicated by [10]$r_S =$ ___ , and the proportion of variability shared by the two variables is given by [11]___ .

To test whether the observed value of r_S is really from a population in which $\rho_S = .00$, one need only to consult Table J in Appendix 2 of the text, which gives the critical values of r_S for specified N, various significance levels, and directional and nondirectional tests. For this example, the critical value of r_S with $N = 10$ for a nondirectional test at significance level .05 is [12]___ . Therefore, we [13]_____ H_0. Complete Table 16–5 at this time.

Answer Key to Spearman Rank-Order Correlation

[1]	Spearman rank-order	[6]	$1 - 6(43.5)/(1000 - 10)$	[10]	0
[2]	Spearman rank-order		$= 1 - .26$	[11]	r_S^2
[3]	r_S	[7]	.74	[12]	.649
[4]	43.5	[8]	-1.00	[13]	reject
[5]	10	[9]	$+1.00$		

• • • • •   **SELF-TEST**

1. Under what circumstances might a nonparametric test be preferred over a parametric test?

2.* If a sample is relatively small and contains one very extreme score, why might you prefer to use a nonparametric test?

3. In general, how do null hypotheses in parametric tests of the differences between groups differ from those in nonparametric tests?

4. Which nonparametric statistical test would be appropriate in the following situations?

   a. A sampling of 25 graduate students and 24 professors participated in a blind taste test, trying to distinguish between an American lager beer and an imported lager after a skeptical student asked why the professor always paid twice as much for imported beer when the difference in taste is not detectable anyway. Are students and professors different in their ability to identify the two beers? (One professor participated in the experiment but claimed that the results were irrelevant, since people never drink beer blindfolded.)

   b. To examine the relationship between creativity and need for affiliation, the art projects of 30 eighth-grade students were ranked on creativity by a panel of artists. The same students were given a Need-for-Affiliation test which contained items such as "I like to spend several hours each day by myself."

   c. A group of 25 15-day-old rats are given a diet that contains a small amount of lead. Another group of 25 rats are given the same diet without the lead. Each infant rat in the lead group is matched to a littermate of the same sex and weight in the non-lead group. As adults, each animal is tested for number of errors in a visual discrimination task.

   d. To test the common belief that boys initiate aggressive behavior more often than girls do, 16 boys and 14 girls were observed in a nursery school for a week. Each child's aggressive instigations were counted, and the groups were compared.

   e. It is predicted on the basis of brain hemisphere dominance that left-handed students are more likely to major in a "quantitative" as opposed to "verbal" area than right-handed students. One hundred left-handed and 100 right-handed students are polled as to their majors. The major areas of study are divided into "strongly quantitative," "strongly verbal," and "mixed."

   f. People are said to differ in social assertiveness as a function of their general body build. Three groups of 10 men were selected according to their general physique (endomorph, mesomorph, ectomorph) and then given a test of social assertiveness to assess this notion.

5.   Given a nondirectional alternative, the .05 level of significance, and the tables in Appendix 2 of the text, specify the critical values and decision rules for each of the situations in question 4 above. (Check your answers to question 4 first, and assume that there are no rank differences of 0.)

6.* The Mann-Whitney U test is sometimes said to be the nonparametric version of the t test. However, the two statistical tests are different in some ways. Discuss the important differences.

7.   In what test are participants eliminated from the analysis if their data do not help to discriminate between groups?

Questions preceded by an asterisk can be answered on the basis of the discussion in the text, but the discussion in the Study Guide does not answer them.

EXERCISES

1.   When scores originally measured on interval or ratio scales are converted to ranks, some information is lost. When the distributions of the raw scores are skewed or have different variability, these characteristics are modified by the ranking process; therefore, a parametric test and nonparametric test on the same data may yield different results. Below is a small set of data from two independent groups of participants. Perform both a parametric t test and a Mann-Whitney U test on these data. Note how the extreme scores and skewness of the original measurements are altered when the data are ranked. Contrast the results of the two statistical tests, compare this difference with the difference between the mean and median of a distribution, and discuss the importance of this characteristic for the choice a researcher

sometimes must make between parametric and nonparametric tests.

Original Data		Ranking of Data	
A	**B**	**A**	**B**
1	4		
2	6		
2	6		
3	9		
3	10		
5	12		
5	12		
8	14		
15	46		

2.   Ethnologists report that there seems to be a nearly universal tendency for women to smile more frequently than men. To examine this tendency among American teenagers, the photographs in a junior high school yearbook were classified as smiling (with teeth showing) or not smiling (no

teeth showing).[3] Are the differences shown in the following data significant?

	Smiling	Not Smiling
Boys	118	28
Girls	112	5

3. A social scientist was concerned about the accuracy of feedback that students in urban schools receive from teachers concerning their academic performance. Two high schools were selected, one in which the students have a good record of academic performance and one in which they do not. Twelve juniors are randomly selected from the good school and 14 from the poor school. They are given a standardized test of academic achievement and are then asked to rate on a 10-point scale how well they are doing in school (10 is very good). The results are given below.[4] Using nonparametric techniques first test the hypothesis that there is no difference in test performance in the two samples. Then determine if there is no difference in the students' perceptions of how well they are doing in school. What is the relationship between test performance and judgment of school performance for each of these two groups? Are these values different from zero? What do

these results seem to be saying about the feedback these students are receiving about their school performance?

Good School	
Achievement Test	Performance Rating
92	2
97	3
84	6
122	7
113	5
99	4
102	5
128	6
114	7
109	5
117	4

Poor School	
Achievement Test	Performance Rating
87	7
99	10
103	10
84	7
90	6
78	4
81	6
95	9
76	5
85	5
95	7
93	8
78	5

---

[3] Data based on the 1985 yearbook of Valley View Junior High, Omaha, Nebraska.

[4] Based on, but not identical to, research reported by Sanford M. Dornbush, "Racism Without Racists: Institutional Racism in Urban Schools." *The Black Scholar* 7 (November 1975); also appears in Stanford Center for Research and Development in Teaching, occasional paper no. 8 (November 1975).

4. In a special summer tutoring program, teenagers who are from low-income families and who do not have summer jobs are assigned to tutor grade-school youngsters three times per week. Since it was hoped that the program would

provide benefits to the tutors as well as to the youngsters, the class rankings of the tutors on a standardized academic achievement test for the school year prior to the tutoring experience were compared to the class rankings in the school year after the experience. Suppose the following data were obtained. Did the tutors increase their own academic performance relative to their peers?

Class Rankings		
Tutor	Before	After
A	34	29
B	54	54
C	82	86
D	17	9
E	23	19
F	36	12
G	66	57
H	7	5
I	119	95

5. For more than 60 years the Fels Research Institute has conducted a study of children from birth through adulthood. As part of this study, IQ tests were given periodically throughout each child's life, and the child's parents were rated on a variety of dimensions. Children could be classified as showing an increase, no change, or a decrease in IQ from ages 3 to 17. Below are the ratings made on the children's parents with respect to how much they attempted to accelerate the mental development of their children.[5] Determine whether there is any association between pattern of IQ change and parental attempts at acceleration.

Decline in IQ	No Change in IQ	Increase in IQ
75	81	91
78	86	95
86	89	89
79	85	99
85	88	98
78	89	86
87	80	84

6. At a casino, a given die showed over 120 rolls the following pattern of scores from 1 to 6: 17, 21, 28, 15, 19, 20. Test whether the die is fair.

---

5 Inspired by R. B. McCall, M. I. Appelbaum, and P. S. Hogarty, "Developmental Changes in Mental Performance," *Monographs of the Society for Research in Child Development* vol. 38, no. 150 (1973).

● ● ● ● ●   ANSWERS

Tables 16–1 to 16–5. See corresponding tables in text.

Self-Test. (1) When the assumptions made by parametric tests cannot be met, a nonparametric alternative may be appropriate. Typically this occurs when the scale of measurement is nominal or ordinal or when the assumptions of normality or homogeneity of variance cannot be met. **(2)** Nonparametric tests usually use only the ordinal characteristics of the scale of measurement and would therefore minimize the influence of an extreme score on the result. The extreme score is also likely to make the distributions deviate from normality and the variances not be homogeneous. **(3)** In a parametric test, the nature of the null hypothesis is: population value = population value. In a nonparametric test the null states: population distribution = population distribution. **(4a)** 2×2 chi square contingency table; **(4b)** Spearman rank-order correlation; **(4c)** Wilcoxon; **(4d)** Mann-Whitney U; **(4e)** 2×3 chi square contingency table; **(4f)** Kruskal-Wallis. **(5a)** If $\chi^2_{obs} < 3.84$, do not reject H_0; if $\chi^2_{obs} \geq 3.84$, reject H_0; **(5b)** If $r_S < .363$, do not reject H_0; if $r_S \geq .363$, reject H_0; **(5c)** If $W_{obs} > 89$, do not reject H_0; if $W_{obs} \leq 89$, reject H_0; **(5d)** If $64 < U_{obs} < 160$, do not reject H_0; if $U_{obs} \leq 64$ or $U_{obs} \geq 160$, reject H_0; **(5e)** If $\chi^2_{obs} < 5.99$, do not reject H_0; if $\chi^2_{obs} \geq 5.99$, reject H_0; **(5f)** If $H_{obs} < 5.99$, do not reject H_0, if $H_{obs} \geq 5.99$, reject H_0. **(6)** The t test examines the difference between means directly, uses measurement information higher than the

ordinal level, and has somewhat more power-efficiency; the U test compares all aspects of the two distributions, considers only ordinal information from the measurement scale, and has good power efficiency, although somewhat less than t. **(7)** The Wilcoxon test.

Exercises. (1) $t_{obs} = 1.86$ (or 1.87 with rounding), t_{crit} (significance level = .05, $df = 16$) = 2.120, do not reject H_0. $U_{obs} = 68$, U_{obs} (significance level = .05, $n_1 = n_2 = 9$) = 17, 64; reject H_0. The ranking reduces the influence of an extreme score (46) on the estimate of the variance of the sampling distribution (the denominator in the t formula) and reduces skewness and heterogeneity of variance in this example. Thus, when there are a few extreme scores, nonparametric tests may be more sensitive to group differences than parametric tests. **(2)** $\chi^2_{obs} = 13.15$, $\chi^2_{crit} = 3.84$ for .05 level, $df = 1$; reject H_0. **(3)** For achievement test performance: $U_{obs} = 18$, $U_{crit} = 37$, 106 for .05 level, nondirectional, $n = 11$, 13; reject H_0. For performance ratings: $U_{obs} = 109.5$, $U_{crit} = 37$, 106 for .05 level, nondirectional, $n = 11$, 13 reject H_0. For the good school: $r_S = .53$; critical value = .619 for .05 level, nondirectional, $N = 11$; do not reject H_0. For the poor school: $r_S = .88$, critical value

=.561 for .05 level, nondirectional, $N = 13$; reject H_0. It appears that students in poor schools are actually doing more poorly but they think they are doing well. Maybe their teachers are telling them they are doing well, and/or maybe they think they are doing well because they are doing well enough relative to other students in their school. Their performance ratings do correlate well with their achievement scores. **(4)** $W_{obs} = 2.5$, $W_{crit} = 3$, .05 level, nondirectional, $N = 8$; reject H_0. **(5)** $H_{obs} = 8.96$ (rounding errors can be large, maintain at least three significant digits), $H_{crit} = 5.99$, .05 level, nondirectional, $df = 2$; reject H_0. **(6)** $\chi^2_{obs} = 5.00$; $\chi^2_{crit} = 11.07$, .05 level, nondirectional, $df = 4$; do not reject H_0, the evidence is not sufficient to question the fairness of the die.

• • • • • STATISTICAL PACKAGES • • • • •

• • • • •   MINITAB

(To accompany the guided computational examples in
Tables 16–1, 16–2, 16–3, 16–4, and 16–5.)

Chi-Square Test (Table 16–1)

MINITAB will compute expected frequencies, the observed chi-square, and its associated probability value directly from an $r \times c$ contingency table. The data for this example are given in Table 16–1. There are three rows and five columns in the table of observed frequencies.

     Start the MINITAB program. In the Data window enter the observed frequencies directly into the first five columns of the spreadsheet. Do not label the column headings. The frequencies you have entered should appear on the spreadsheet as follows:

C1	C2	C3	C4	C5
60	20	130	110	30
40	70	115	200	25
10	40	55	60	35

Save the data that you entered as a MINITAB Worksheet:

> *File>Save Worksheet As*
>   (Enter folder and file name for the Worksheet file.)
> OK

The chi-square analysis may be carried out using the *Chi-Square Test* command. This command will process a contingency table of observed frequencies up to seven columns wide. (If you have raw data instead of frequencies and need to form the contingency table, use the *Cross Tabulation* command instead.)

> *Stat>Tables>Chi-Square Test*
> Columns containing the table: C1–C5   [highlight all five columns]
> Select
> OK

On the output for this analysis, the expected frequencies are printed below the observed frequencies for each cell. Note that the observed chi-square value (88.182) is so large that the *p* value, at the bottom, is listed as 0.000. Therefore the probability that such a value should occur by chance is $p < .001$.

Print the MINITAB output and open a new spreadsheet for the next example:

> *File<Print Session Window*
> Print Range: All
> OK
> *File>New Worksheet*

MINITAB Program Output

```
Chi-Square Test

Expected counts are printed below observed counts

              C1        C2        C3        C4        C5     Total
    1         60        20       130       110        30       350
           38.50     45.50    105.00    129.50     31.50

    2         40        70       115       200        25       450
           49.50     58.50    135.00    166.50     40.50

    3         10        40        55        60        35       200
           22.00     26.00     60.00     74.00     18.00

Total        110       130       300       370        90      1000

Chi-Sq = 12.006 + 14.291 +  5.952 +  2.936 +  0.071 +
          1.823 +  2.261 +  2.963 +  6.740 +  5.932 +
          6.545 +  7.538 +  0.417 +  2.649 + 16.056 =  88.182

DF = 8,  P-Value = 0.000
```

Mann-Whitney *U* Test (Table 16–2)

MINITAB will calculate a Mann-Whitney *U* Test for two independent samples, but it does not report the observed *U*. However, it does give the probability of the observed *U* with and without adjustment for tied ranks. In the example in Table 16–2, observers rated children's positive behavior after watching one of two different television program types, violent or prosocial. The dependent variable is the behavior rating. There are two program groups to be compared, Prosocial and Violent.

For this analysis, MINITAB requires that the data be entered in "unstacked" form, with the data for the two program groups in separate columns. In the Data window spreadsheet, enter the behavior ratings for the two program groups in the first two columns of the spreadsheet. Label the two columns *Psocial* and *Violent*. The data in the spreadsheet should now appear as follows:

Psocial	Violent
1	5
2	6
2	8
4	9
5	9
5	9
6	10
6	10
7	
9	

Save the data in a MINITAB Worksheet:

> *File>Save Worksheet As*
> (Enter folder and file name for the Worksheet file.)
> OK

To carry out the analysis which will calculate a table and test statistic for the sample:

> *Stat>Nonparametrics>Mann-Whitney*
> First Sample: Psocial   [double-click to transfer]
> Second Sample: Violent
> Alternative: not equal
> OK

In the output for this analysis, $W = 65.5$ is the sum of the ranks for *Psocial,* which we call T_A (It is *not* U_{obs}, which must be calculated by hand using the formula in Table 14–2). The next-to-last line of the output gives the unadjusted probability (which is used in this text), and the last line adjusts this probability for ties. These values differ slightly from those used in the other programs because of the way the correction is made.

Select the new portion of the Session window and print the output. Then open a new spreadsheet for the next example:

> *File<Print Session Window*
>   Print Range: Selection
>   OK
> *File>New Worksheet*

MINITAB Program Output

```
Mann-Whitney Test and CI: Psocial, Violent

Psocial    N =  10     Median =        5.000
Violent    N =   8     Median =        9.000
Point estimate for ETA1-ETA2 is      -4.000
95.4 Percent CI for ETA1-ETA2 is (-6.000,-0.999)
W = 65.5
Test of ETA1 = ETA2   vs   ETA1 not = ETA2 is significant at 0.0100
The test is significant at 0.0092 (adjusted for ties)
```

Kruskal-Wallis Test for *k* Independent Samples (Table 16–3)

The Kruskal-Wallis test is used when the number of groups being compared is greater than two. MINITAB will compute a Kruskal-Wallis Test for *k* independent samples and requires that the data be entered using the "stacked" method. For each participant in Table 16–3, values of *Behavior*, the dependent or response variable, must be entered, followed by the kind of TV programs they viewed (1=Prosocial, 2=Neutral, 3=Violent).

In the Data window, enter the values for *Behavior* in the first column of the spreadsheet, and the *Program* code in the second column. Label the two columns *Behavior* and *Program*.

The spreadsheet data should appear as follows:

Behavior	Program
7	1
3	1
8	1
5	1
6	1
9	2
2	2
4	2
4	2
7	2
7	2
3	3
8	3
8	3
5	3
6	3
1	3

To save the data as a MINITAB Worksheet:

> *File>Save Worksheet As*
>   (Enter folder and file name for the Worksheet file.)
>   OK

Calculate the test statistic for the Kruskal-Wallis analysis:

> *Stat>Nonparametrics>Kruskal-Wallis*
>   Response: Behavior   [double-click to transfer]
>   Factor: Program   [double-click to transfer]
>   OK

The output reports the value of H, df, and p without (which is used in this text) and with adjustment for ties. Note that the Student Version of MINITAB gives only the H adjusted for ties (but no probability level), so you must use the H with Table G in your text to obtain the probability level.

Select the new portion of the output to print. Then open a new spreadsheet for the next example:

> *File<Print Session Window*
>   Print Range: Selection
>   OK
> *File>New Worksheet*

MINITAB Program Output

```
Kruskal-Wallis Test: Behavior versus Program

Kruskal-Wallis Test on Behavior

Program     N     Median    Ave Rank          Z
1           5      6.000         9.5       0.26
2           6      5.500         9.0       0.00
3           6      5.500         8.6      -0.25
Overall    17                    9.0

H = 0.09  DF = 2  P = 0.956
H = 0.09  DF = 2  P = 0.955 (adjusted for ties)
```

Wilcoxon Test for Two Correlated Samples (Table 16–4)

MINITAB can be used to carry out the Wilcoxon test on the difference between two correlated (for example, before and after values) samples. Data must be entered as paired variables on the spreadsheet and a difference score calculated.

Enter the values from Table 16–4 for the two measures, *Before* and *After*, in the first two columns of the Data window spreadsheet, and label the columns accordingly. A difference score (*Diff*) must be calculated by subtracting the value of *Before* from the value of *After*. Define a new variable *Diff* by typing its name at the top of the third column of the spreadsheet. Then use the *Calculator* command to fill in the values of *Diff*:

> *Calc>Calculator*
>   Store result in variable: Diff   [double-click to transfer]
>   Expression: After - Before   [double-click, or type in]
>   OK

The spreadsheet, with the new variable, should appear as follows:

Before	After	Diff
4.5	5.2	0.7
3.0	4.5	1.5
6.2	5.9	−0.3
4.9	5.2	0.3
5.5	5.8	0.3
5.8	6.1	0.3
6.1	7.2	1.1
7.0	7.1	0.1
5.0	5.6	0.6

To save the data as a MINITAB Worksheet file:

> *File>Save Worksheet As*
> (Enter folder and file name for the Worksheet file.)
> OK

Calculate the table and test statistic for the Wilcoxon Signed Rank test on the variable *Diff*:

> *Stat>Nonparametrics>1-Sample Wilcoxon*
> Variables: Diff   [double-click to transfer]
> Test median: Yes   Value: 0.0
> Alternative: not equal
> OK

The output reports N, the number of pairs, and the Wilcoxon statistic, in this case T_+, and its associated p value. Notice that the "Wilcoxon Statistic" on the output may or may not be the smaller of T_+ and T_- (in this case it is *not* the smaller value) which is taken to be W_{obs} in the text and used to enter Table I in the textbook to determine the probability. The probability on the output, however, should be accurate.

Select the new portion of the output to print. Then open a new spreadsheet for the next example:

> *File<Print Session Window*
> Print Range: Selection
> OK
> *File>New Worksheet*

MINITAB Program Output

Wilcoxon Signed Rank Test: Diff

Test of median = 0.000000 versus median not = 0.000000

	N	N for Test	Wilcoxon Statistic	P	Estimated Median
Diff	9	9	41.5	0.028	0.4500

Spearman Rank-Order Correlation (Table 16–5)

The Spearman rank-order correlation coefficient is equivalent to applying the Pearson correlation to ranked data. It is a nonparametric measure of association to be used when the data are ordinal in nature. MINITAB does not calculate directly a Spearman rank-order correlation, but you can get the program to compute it by entering the data, ranking them, and then computing a Pearson correlation on the ranks.

Enter the pairs of aggressiveness ratings from Table 16–5 into the first two columns of the spreadsheet. Label the two columns *Before* and *After*. Define two new variables by typing the names *Brank* and *Arank* at the top of empty columns three and four in preparation for determining rankings. Calculate the rankings using the *Rank* command:

Manip>Rank
     Rank data in: Before   [double-click to transfer]
     Store ranks in: Brank
     OK

Manip>Rank
     Rank data in: After   [double-click to transfer]
     Store ranks in: Arank
     OK

The spreadsheet, with the rankings for *Before* and *After* stored in the new variables, should appear as follows:

Before	After	Brank	Arank
6	−1	6	2.0
2	−3	2	1.0
3	8	3	5.5
8	10	8	7.0
9	17	9	10.0
1	7	1	4.0
4	5	4	3.0
7	16	7	9.0
10	14	10	8.0
5	8	5	5.5

Save the spreadsheet data in a MINITAB Worksheet file:

> *File>Save Worksheet As*
> 　　(Enter folder and file name for the Worksheet file.)
> 　　OK

Finally, obtain the correlation coefficient, Spearman's *rho*, by correlating the two rankings:

> *Stat>Basic Statistics>Correlation*
> 　　Variables: Brank Arank　　[double-click to transfer]
> 　　Display p-values: Yes
> 　　OK

The output shown below reports the Pearson correlation between the two rankings. That is in fact the Spearman correlation between the raw scores. MINITAB also reports a *p* value for the correlation.

　　Select the new portion of the output to print.

> *File<Print Session Window*
> 　　Print Range: Selection
> 　　OK

　　To obtain the results for all five of the nonparametric analyses, specify "All" for the print range.

Exit MINITAB:

> *File>Exit*

MINITAB Program Output

```
Correlations: Brank, Arank
Pearson Correlation of Brank and Arank = 0.736
P-Value = 0.015
```

• • • • •   SPSS

(To accompany the guided computational examples in
Tables 16–1, 16–2, 16–3, 16–4, and 16–5.)

Chi-Square Test (Table 16–1)

To compute the Pearson chi-square for a row-by-column set of independent frequencies such as
in Table 16–1, SPSS requires three input variables: one that contains the frequencies for each
cell, one for the row number, and one for the column number. In this example, there are three
rows and five columns in the table of frequencies.

Start the SPSS program to bring up the Data Editor window. Enter the frequency data from
Table 16–1 for each of the 15 cells, one cell at a time. The cell frequency, *Freq*, goes in the first
variable on the spreadsheet. The row number, *Row*, goes in the second variable, and the column
number, *Col*, goes in the third variable. Label the columns with the variable names *Freq*, *Row*,
and *Col*. The data you have entered should appear on the spreadsheet as follows:

Freq	Row	Col
60	1	1
20	1	2
130	1	3
110	1	4
30	1	5
40	2	1
70	2	2
115	2	3
200	2	4
25	2	5
10	3	1
40	3	2
55	3	3
60	3	4
35	3	5

SPSS requires the *Weight Cases* command to multiply each cell by its frequency, so in effect it is
reading information for 1000 cases (the total number of persons sampled) rather than the 15 cells
that are entered on the spreadsheet. The *Crosstabs* command sets up the contingency table and
calculates the chi-square statistic to test for independence between the table variables.

Weight the cases by cell frequency:

> *Data>Weight Cases*
>   Weight cases by: Yes
>   Frequency Variable: Freq   [highlight and transfer]
>   OK

Set up the contingency table and calculate the chi-square statistic:

> *Analyze>Descriptive Statistics>Crosstabs*
>   Row(s): Row   [highlight and transfer]
>   Column(s): Col
>   Statistics: Chi-square: Yes
>   Continue
>   Cells: Counts: Observed; Expected
>   Percentages: None (Row, Column or Totals can be specified.)
>   Continue
>   OK

The program output appears on the next page. The Crosstabulation table contains the frequencies (Counts) and the expected frequencies in each cell, and the Pearson Chi-square value and associated probability value appear on the first line of the Chi-square Tests table.

To print the output, make sure the SPSS Viewer window is on the screen. Click on the yellow box next to the heading "Crosstabs" on the *left* side of the SPSS view window. This will highlight the portion of the output to be printed:

> *File>Print*
>   Print range: Selection
>   OK

To save the data that you entered and clear the spreadsheet for the next analysis:

> *Window>SPSS Data Editor*
> *File>Save As*
>   (Enter folder and file name for SPSS Save file.)
>   Save
> *File>New>Data*

SPSS Program Output

Crosstabs

Case Processing Summary

	Cases					
	Valid		Missing		Total	
	N	Percent	N	Percent	N	Percent
ROW * COL	1000	100.0%	0	.0%	1000	100.0%

ROW * COL Crosstabulation

			COL					Total
			1.00	2.00	3.00	4.00	5.00	
ROW	1.00	Count	60	20	130	110	30	350
		Expected Count	38.5	45.5	105.0	129.5	31.5	350.0
	2.00	Count	40	70	115	200	25	450
		Expected Count	49.5	58.5	135.0	166.5	40.5	450.0
	3.00	Count	10	40	55	60	35	200
		Expected Count	22.0	26.0	60.0	74.0	18.0	200.0
Total		Count	110	130	300	370	90	1000
		Expected Count	110.0	130.0	300.0	370.0	90.0	1000.0

Chi-Square Tests

	Value	df	Asymp. Sig. (2-sided)
Pearson Chi-Square	88.182[a]	8	.000
Likelihood Ratio	87.972	8	.000
Linear-by-Linear Association	7.365	1	.007
N of Valid Cases	1000		

a. 0 cells (.0%) have expected count less than 5. The minimum expected count is 18.00.

Mann-Whitney U Test (Table 16-2)

The Mann-Whitney U Test compares two independent samples. In the case of Table 16–2, observers rated children's positive behavior after watching one of two different television programs, violent or prosocial. The dependent or test variable is the behavior rating, *Behavior;* the coded treatment or grouping variable is the program type, *Program* (1=Prosocial; 2=Violent).

The SPSS Data Editor will fill the screen. Enter the values from Table 16–2 for the behavior ratings in the first column and the code for the type of programming in the second column. Label the two columns with the variable names *Behavior* and *Program*. The data in the spreadsheet should now appear as follows:

Behavior	Program
1	1
2	1
2	1
4	1
5	1
5	1
6	1
6	1
7	1
9	1
5	2
6	2
8	2
9	2
9	2
9	2
10	2
10	2

Calculate the test statistics and tables for the analysis:

Analyze>Nonparametric Tests>2 Independent Samples
    Test Variable List: Behavior   [highlight and transfer]
    Grouping Variable: Program
    Define Groups: Group 1: 1
                Group 2: 2
                Continue
    Test Type: Mann-Whitney U
    OK

SPSS program output for this example appears below. The value of U reported on the Test Statistics table is 10.5. This may or may not be the one you obtain by other methods because there are two possible values of U, 10.5 and 69.5, depending on which group is designated A for the formula given in the text. The asymptotic probability corrected for ties is reported in the second to last line of the output, followed by the exact probability for a non-directional (2-tailed) test, which is not corrected for ties and is the one used in this text.

To print the output, make sure the SPSS Viewer window is on the screen. Click on the yellow box next to the heading "Mann-Whitney Test" on the *left* side of the SPSS view window. This will highlight the portion of the output to be printed:

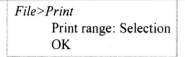

File>Print
>   Print range: Selection
>   OK

To save the data that you entered and clear the spreadsheet:

Window>SPSS Data Editor
File>Save As
>   (Enter folder and file name for SPSS Save file.)
>   Save
File>New>Data

SPSS Program Output

Mann–Whitney Test

Ranks

	PROGRAM	N	Mean Rank	Sum of Ranks
BEHAVIOR	1.00	10	6.55	65.50
	2.00	8	13.19	105.50
	Total	18		

Test Statistics

	BEHAVIOR
Mann-Whitney U	10.500
Wilcoxon W	65.500
Z	-2.649
Asymp. Sig. (2-tailed)	.008
Exact Sig. [2*(1-tailed Sig.)]	.006[a]

a. Not corrected for ties.

Kruskal-Wallis Test for *k* Independent Samples (Table 16–3)

The Kruskal-Wallis Test for *k* Independent Samples follows the same procedure as the Mann-Whitney Test but is for three or more independent samples. In the example in Table 16–3, there are three program types, so the coding for the variable *Program* ranges from 1 to 3.

Enter the values for *Behavior* from Table 16–3 in the first column of the SPSS Data Editor and the codes for *Program* (1 = Prosocial, 2 = Neutral, 3 = Violent) in the second column. The spreadsheet data should appear as follows:

Behavior	Program
7	1
3	1
8	1
5	1
6	1
9	2
2	2
4	2
4	2
7	2
7	2
3	3
8	3
8	3
5	3
6	3
1	3

Calculate the test statistics and tables for the analysis:

Analyze>Nonparametric Tests>k Independent Samples
      Test Variable List: Behavior   [highlight and transfer]
      Grouping Variable: Program
      Define Range: Minimum: 1
                    Maximum: 3
                    Continue
      Test Type: Kruskal-Wallis H
      OK

The program output for this example is shown on the next page. On the Test Statistics table, the chi-square statistic, degrees of freedom (df), and associated probability value (Asymp. Sig.) are reported. Only results corrected for ties are given, which may be different from your text, which does not make this correction.

To print the output, make sure the SPSS Viewer window is on the screen. Click on the yellow box next to the heading "Kruskal-Wallis Test" on the *left* side of the SPSS view window. This will highlight the portion of the output to be printed:

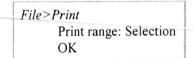

To save the data that you entered and clear the spreadsheet for the next analysis:

Window>SPSS Data Editor
File>Save As
            (Enter folder and file name for SPSS Save file.)
            Save
File>New>Data

SPSS Program Output

Kruskal-Wallis Test

Ranks

	PROGRAM	N	Mean Rank
BEHAVIOR	1.00	5	9.50
	2.00	6	9.00
	3.00	6	8.58
	Total	17	

Test Statistics

	BEHAVIOR
Chi-Square	.091
df	2
Asymp. Sig.	.955

Wilcoxon Test for Two Correlated Samples (Table 16–4)

To calculate a Wilcoxon Test for two correlated samples, two paired measures are entered on a separate line for each individual.

Call up the SPSS Data Editor spreadsheet and enter the values for the two measures, *Before* and *After*, in the first two columns of the spreadsheet. Label the columns accordingly. The spreadsheet should appear as follows:

Before	After
4.5	5.2
3.0	4.5
6.2	5.9
4.9	5.2
5.5	5.8
5.8	6.1
6.1	7.2
7.0	7.1
5.0	5.6

Calculate the tables and test statistics for the analysis:

Analyze>Nonparametric Tests>2 Related Samples
      Test Pair(s) List: Before — After   [select both variables, then transfer]
      Test Type: Wilcoxon
      OK

SPSS program output is illustrated on the following page. The program may rank the differences in a way different from your text, producing a different sum of ranks. Also, the Wilcoxon W statistic is not given on the output; only a z score and its associated p value (Asymp. Sig.) is reported.

    To print the output, make sure the SPSS Viewer window is on the screen. Click on the yellow box next to the heading "Wilcoxon Signed Ranks Test" on the *left* side of the SPSS view window. This will highlight the portion of the output to be printed:

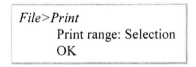

File>Print
      Print range: Selection
      OK

To save the data that you entered and clear the spreadsheet for the next analysis:

Window>SPSS Data Editor
File>Save As
      (Enter folder and file name for SPSS Save file.)
      Save
File>New>Data

SPSS Program Output

Wilcoxon Signed Ranks Test

Ranks

		N	Mean Rank	Sum of Ranks
AFTER - BEFORE	Negative Ranks	1[a]	3.00	3.00
	Positive Ranks	8[b]	5.25	42.00
	Ties	0[c]		
	Total	9		

a. AFTER < BEFORE
b. AFTER > BEFORE
c. BEFORE = AFTER

Test Statistics

	AFTER - BEFORE
Z	-2.318[a]
Asymp. Sig. (2-tailed)	.020

a. Based on negative ranks.

Spearman Rank-Order Correlation (Table 16–5)

The Spearman coefficient is equivalent to the Pearson correlation coefficient applied to ranks. As a nonparametric measure of association, it is used when the data are ordinal. SPSS will calculate the ranks and carry out the calculation directly as part of the *Bivariate* command.

Enter the values of the before and after aggressiveness ratings from Table 16–5 into the first two columns of the SPSS Data Editor and label the columns *Before* and *After*. The spreadsheet should appear as follows:

Before	After
6	−1
2	−3
3	8
8	10
9	17
1	7
4	5
7	16
10	14
5	8

Use the following to calculate the value of the nonparametric correlation coefficient:

> *Analyze>Correlate>Bivariate*
>   Variables: Before, After   [highlight and transfer]
>   Correlation Coefficients:
>   Pearson: No
>   Spearman: Yes
>   Test of Significance: Two-tailed
>   Flag significant correlations: No
>   OK

The output table shows Spearman's *rho* to be 0.736 and the associated two-tailed *p* value (Sig.) as .015.

To print the output, make sure the SPSS Viewer window is on the screen. Click on the yellow box next to the heading "Nonparametric Correlations" on the *left* side of the SPSS view window. This will highlight the portion of the output to be printed:

> *File>Print*
>   Print range: Selection
>   OK

To save the data that you entered:

> *Window>SPSS Data Editor*
> *File>Save As*
>   (Enter folder and file name for SPSS Save file.)
>   Save

Exit SPSS:

> *File>Exit*

SPSS Program Output

Nonparametric Correlations

Correlations

			BEFORE	AFTER
Spearman's rho	BEFORE	Correlation Coefficient	1.000	.736
		Sig. (2-tailed)	.	.015
		N	10	10
	AFTER	Correlation Coefficient	.736	1.000
		Sig. (2-tailed)	.015	.
		N	10	10

● ● ● ● ●

APPENDIX

REVIEW OF BASIC MATHEMATICS
AND ALGEBRA • • • • •

• • • • • SYMBOLS AND SIGNS

Introduction

Relationships between quantities can be expressed by symbols. If a and b are numerically identical, we write [1]_____ . However, if a and b are not equal, this fact can be expressed by [2]_____ . We use > to mean "is greater than" and < to mean "is less than." Thus [3]5__3 and [4]3__5. You can remember the difference between the two symbols by noting that the open end (larger end) of the symbols is always on the side of the larger number. Therefore, if a is greater than b, we write [5]a__b or [6]b__a.

If one quantity is greater than or equal to another, we use a combination of the equality and greater than symbols, $\geq$. If c is greater than or equal to d, we write [7]c__d or [8]d__c. If t is a positive number or zero, we can write [9]t__0. If t is negative or zero, [10]_____ . If t falls between 10 and 20, we can say that 10 is less than t, in symbols, [11]_____ , and that t is less than 20, [12]_____ . These two statements can be combined into $10 < t < 20$. If t can either equal 10 or 20 or fall somewhere between them, we write [13]_____ .

Some numbers are negative (i.e., below 0); that introduces the problem of signs when we perform elementary mathematical operations: [14]$7 + (-4) =$ __ , [15]$7 - (-4) =$ __ , and [16]$-a - (-b) =$ _____ .

The sign of the product obtained by multiplying several quantities together depends upon the number of negative values to be multiplied. If there is an even number of negative values among the values to be multiplied, the product is positive. For example, [17] $(2)(4) = $ ___ , [18] $(-2)(-4) = $ ___ , [19] $(2)(-1)(-3) = $ ___ , [20] $(1)(-2)(4)(-3) = $ ___ , [21] $(-x)y(-z) = $ ___ . If there is an odd number of negative values to be multiplied, the product is negative: [22] $(-1)(4) = $ ___ , [23] $(3)(-2) = $ ___ , [24] $(-2)(-3)(-1)(2) = $ ___ , and [25] $(a)(-b)(c) = $ ___ .

The same rule applies to division. If there is an even number of negative values, the result is positive: [26] $6/2 = $ ___ , [27] $-14/-7 = $ ___ , [28] $(-2)(-3)/(-1)(-4) = $ _____ , and [29] $-a/b(-c) = $ _____ . If there is an odd number of negative values in the division, the result is negative: [30] $-8/2 = $ ___ , [31] $12/-4 = $ ___ , [32] $(-2)(4)/(3) = $ _____ , and [33] $(-a)(-b)/c(-d) = $ _____ .

At times we want to disregard the algebraic sign of a quantity and consider only its absolute value. The absolute value of a is written $|a|$. To disregard the sign of d we write [34] ___ , and the absolute value of $(X - Y)$ is symbolized [35] _____ . For example, [36] $|-4| = $ ___ , and [37] $|6| = $ ___ .

Answer Key to Introduction

[1]	$a = b$	[11]	$10 < t$	[21]	xyz	[31]	-3
[2]	$a \neq b$	[12]	$t < 20$	[22]	-4	[32]	$-8/3$
[3]	$>$	[13]	$10 \leq t \leq 20$	[23]	-6	[33]	$-ab/cd$
[4]	$<$	[14]	3	[24]	-12	[34]	$|d|$
[5]	$>$	[15]	11	[25]	$-abc$	[35]	$|X - Y|$
[6]	$<$	[16]	$-a + b$	[26]	3	[36]	4
[7]	$\geq$	[17]	8	[27]	2	[37]	6
[8]	$\leq$	[18]	8	[28]	$3/2$		
[9]	$\geq$	[19]	6	[29]	a/bc		
[10]	$t \leq 0$	[20]	24	[30]	-4		

OPERATIONS

● ● ● ● ●

Fractions

The product of two or more fractions equals the product of the numerators divided by the product of the denominators: [1]$(1/2)(3/5) =$ _____ , [2]$(1/3)(1/5)(2/7) =$ _____ , and [3]$(a/c)(b/d) =$ _____ . To divide one fraction by another, invert the divisor (the fraction you want to divide *by*) and multiply. To divide $1/2$ by $3/5$, invert the divisor to obtain [4]_____ and then multiply, [5]_____ $=$ __ . Similarly, [6]$(x/y) \div (a/b) =$ _____ $=$ _____ .

Fractions often can be simplified by **factoring** and **cancellation**. Factoring involves determining the simplest set of numbers which, when multiplied together, will yield the original number. The number 12 can be factored into $(3)(4)$, and the 4 can be further factored into $(2)(2)$, yielding $(3)(2)(2)$ as the simplest factored equivalent of 12. In the same way, 18 can be factored into [7]_____ , 24 into [8]_____ , and 64 into [9]_____ .

To simplify fractions, factor the numerator and the denominator and cancel numbers that appear in both the numerator and denominator:

$$\frac{6}{9} = \frac{(2)(3)}{(3)(3)} = \frac{2}{3} .$$

Thus [10]$12/36 =$ _____ $=$ __ and [11]$64/72 =$ _____ $=$ __ .

The multiplication of fractions can be simplified by factoring and canceling any terms that occur in both the numerators and denominators: [12]$(2/3)(3/4) =$ _____ $=$ __ and [13]$(3/5)(2/3)(5/6) =$ _____ $=$ __ .

Two fractions can be added or subtracted only if they both have the same denominator. Therefore, fractions that do not have the same denominator must be converted to ones having the same denominator. This is done by multiplying the numerator and denominator of a fraction by the same number, often the denominator of the other fraction. To add 1/2 and 1/3, change them both into fractions with denominators 6. The fraction $1/2$ can be changed by multiplying it by

3 / 3 to produce [14]_____ , and 1 / 3 can be changed by multiplying it by 2 / 2 to produce

[15]_____ . Then their numerators are simply added and their sum divided by the common

denominator: [16]$(3 / 6) + (2 / 6) =$ _____ . To add a / b and c / d convert both fractions

to ones having a common denominator [17]_____ . Then add the numerators and divide

by the common denominator, [18]_____ . Subtraction follows a similar process:

[19]$(1 / 4) - (1 / 5) =$ _____ = _____ .

Answer Key to Fractions

[1]	3 / 10	[9]	(2)(2)(2)(2)(2)(2)	[15]	2 / 6	
[2]	2 / 105	[10]	$\dfrac{(2)(2)(3)}{(2)(2)(3)(3)} = \dfrac{1}{3}$	[16]	5 / 6	
[3]	ab / cd			[17]	$(ad / bd) + (cd / bd)$	
[4]	5 / 3	[11]	$\dfrac{(2)(2)(2)(2)(2)(2)}{(2)(2)(2)(3)(3)} = \dfrac{8}{9}$	[18]	$(ad + cd) / bd$	
[5]	$(1 / 2)(5 / 3) = 5 / 6$	[12]	$\left(\dfrac{2}{3}\right)\left(\dfrac{3}{2 \cdot 2}\right) = \dfrac{1}{2}$	[19]	$(5 / 20) - (4 / 20) =$	
[6]	$(x / y)(b / a) = xb / ya$				1 / 20	
[7]	(2)(3)(3)	[13]	$\left(\dfrac{3}{3}\right)\left(\dfrac{2}{3}\right)\left(\dfrac{3}{3 \cdot 2}\right) = \dfrac{1}{3}$			
[8]	(3)(2)(2)(2)	[14]	3 / 6			

Factorials

When you calculate certain formulas, it will be necessary to use factorials. For example, 3!, read

"three factorial," is a simplified way of writing (3)(2)(1). In the same way,

[1]$5! =$ _____ = __ . [2]$(5 - 3)! =$ _____ = __ , and

[3]$5! / 3! =$ _____ = __ . It is important to know that $0! = 1$; thus,

[4]$3! / 0! =$ _____ = __ .

Answer Key to Factorials

[1]	(5)(4)(3)(2)(1) = 120	[3]	$\dfrac{(5)(4)(3)(2)(1)}{(3)(2)(1)} = 20$
[2]	2! = (2)(1) = 2	[4]	$[(3)(2)(1)] / (1) = 6$

Exponents

Exponents, small numbers written after and above a base number, signify that the base number is to be multiplied by itself as many times as the exponent states. Thus, $3^2 = (3)(3) = 9$ and [1] $3^3 = $ _____ $= $ __ . It is important to distinguish between [2] $(2 + 3 + 5)^2 = $ __ $= $ __ and [3] $2^2 + 3^2 + 5^2 = $ _____ $= $ __ . For the following set of scores, then,

1

6

2

4

the sum is [4] __ , the squared sum is [5] __ , and the sum of squared scores is [6] __ .

Note that $n^1 = n$ and that $n^0 = 1$.

Generally, numbers with exponents cannot be added except by carrying out the exponentiation and then adding. Thus, $2^2 + 2^3 = (2)(2) + (2)(2)(2) = 4 + 8 = 12$ and [7] $2^4 - 3^2 = $ _____ $= $ _____ $= $ __ . However, the *product* of two exponential quantities *having the same base number* is equal to that same number raised to the *sum* of the exponents, as [8] $(2^3)(2^4) = 2^{3+4} = 2^7$, $(3^2)(3^3) = $ _____ $= $ __ , and [9] $(r^s)(r^t) = $ __ . To divide two exponential quantities *having the same base number,* subtract their exponents. For example, [10] $2^5 / 2^4 = 2^{5-4} = 2$, $3^6 / 3^2 = $ _____ $= $ __ , and [11] $r^s / r^t = $ __ .Remember: to perform these multiplication and division operations on exponential quantities, the two quantities must have the [12]_____ . A fraction like $2^2 / 3^2$, in which the base numbers in the numerator and denominator are different, is simplified by carrying out the exponentiation separately within the numerator and denominator, [13]_____ $= $ __ .

To raise a fraction to a power, raise the numerator and the denominator to that same power. Thus, $(2/3)^2 = (2^2/3^2)$, [14] $(3/4)^2 = $ _____ , and [15] $(s/t)^r = $ _____ .

Answer Key to Exponents

[1]	$(3)(3)(3) = 27$	[7]	$(2)(2)(2)(2) - (3)(3) =$	[12]	same base number
[2]	$10^2 = 100$		$16 - 9 = 7$	[13]	$[(2)(2)] / [(3)(3)] = 4/9$
[3]	$4 + 9 + 25 = 38$	[8]	$3^{2+3} = 3^5$	[14]	$3^2 / 4^2$
[4]	13	[9]	r^{s+t}	[15]	s^r / t^r
[5]	169	[10]	$3^{6-2} = 3^4$		
[6]	57	[11]	r^{s-t}		

Binomial Expansion

It will sometimes be necessary to square a binomial, which is an expression involving the addition or subtraction of two quantities, such as $(a + b)^2$. The result is the square of the first term, plus two times the product of the two terms, plus the square of the second term. Thus, [1]$(a + b)^2 = $ _____ . If a negative term is involved, the process is the same, but greater attention must be paid to the signs: [2]$(a - b)^2 = $ _____ . This technique is quite general and can be applied to any binomial. For example, [3]$(X - \overline{X})^2 = $ _____ and [4]$98^2 = (100 - 2)^2 = $ _____ = __ .

Answer Key to Binomial Expansion

[1]	$a^2 + 2ab + b^2$	[3]	$X^2 - 2X\overline{X} + \overline{X}^2$
[2]	$a^2 - 2ab + b^2$	[4]	$10,000 - 400 + 4 = 9604$

Square Roots

Although most square roots can be determined on a hand calculator, it is helpful to know some simple algebra pertaining to square roots. The [1]$\sqrt{25} = $ __ and [2]$\sqrt{.25} = $ __ ,but $\sqrt{2.5}$ is 1.58. Notice that [3]$\sqrt{4x} = \sqrt{4}\sqrt{x} = $ _____ , [4]$\sqrt{16x^2} = \sqrt{16}\sqrt{x^2} = $ __ , and [5]$\sqrt{4/11} = \sqrt{4} / \sqrt{11} = $ _____ . On the other hand, $\sqrt{9 + x^2}$ cannot be reduced further, and $\sqrt{a^2 - b^2}$ does *not* equal $a - b$.

Answer Key to Square Roots

| [1] | 5 | [2] | .5 | [3] | $2\sqrt{x}$ | [4] | $4x$ | [5] | $2/\sqrt{11}$ |

Factoring and Simplification

As explained in the text, the process of breaking down a number into parts which, when multiplied together, equal the number is called [1]_____ . The process of reducing the number of quantities in an expression is called [2]_____ .

Occasionally, algebraic expressions may be simplified by removing parentheses. When no multiplication or division is involved, remove parentheses and perform any addition or subtraction necessary: $4 + (-2) = 4 - 2 = 2$, [3]$-5 - (-4) + (-1) =$ _____ $=$ ___ , and [4]$(a) - (-b) - (c + d) =$ _____ . When several different operations are required, it is best to simplify the expression by following a specific sequence of operations. Suppose you are required to simplify $700 - 2(4 + 6)^2$. First, perform any additions or subtractions within terms or parentheses. Thus, the expression becomes [5]$700 - 2(\_\_)^2$. Second, perform any exponentiations or square roots: [6]$700 - 2(\_\_)$. Third, calculate any multiplications or divisions: [7]$700 - \_\_$. Finally, perform any addition or subtraction between terms: [8]$700 - 200 = \_\_$. Following the same sequence, the expression $(4 + 2) - 2\sqrt{2 + 7}$ can be simplified by

first,	[9]$(\_\_) - 2\sqrt{\_\_}$
second,	[10]$6 - 2(\_\_)$
third	[11]$6 - \_\_$
and fourth,	[12]$= \_\_$

Sometimes it is helpful to transpose terms from one side of an expression to the other. The simplest method is to add (or subtract) the same term on both sides of the equation. For example, to get b on one side of the following equation, subtract a from each side:

$$a - b = c$$
$$\underline{-a = -a}$$
$$a - b - a = c - a$$
$$-b = c - a$$

and to solve for X in $2X - 3 = 1$,

$$2X - 3 = 1$$

[13]_____

[14]_____

This last expression can be solved for X by dividing each side of the equation by 2:

$$(2X)/2 = 4/2$$

[15] $X =$ ___

Similarly, if you want to solve for a in $a/b = c$, multiply both sides of the equation by [16]__ giving [17]_____ . Then cancel, giving [18]_____ .

To *factor* an algebraic expression, break it down into a set of components that, when multiplied, equal the original expression. For example, $ab + ac = a(b + c)$; [19] $ab - ac =$ _____ ; [20] $-ab - ac =$ _____ ; and [21] $ab + ac + db + dc =$ _____ = _____ .

Sometimes in the course of simplifying an expression it helps to divide each term in the numerator by the denominator: $(a - b)/c = (a/c) - (b/c)$, and [22] $(ac - b)/b =$ _____ = _____ . Be careful not to make the following mistake: $a/(b + c)$ is *not* equal to $a/b + a/c$.

Answer Key to Factoring and Simplification

[1]	factoring	[3]	$-5 + 4 - 1 = -2$	[5]	10
[2]	simplification	[4]	$a + b - c - d$	[6]	100

[7]	200	[13]	$3+3$	[19]	$a(b-c)$
[8]	500	[14]	$2X=4$	[20]	$-a(b+c)$
[9]	$(6)-2\sqrt{9}$	[15]	2	[21]	$a(b+c)+d(b+c)=$
[10]	3	[16]	b		$(a+d)(b+c)$
[11]	6	[17]	$b(a/b)=bc$	[22]	$(ac/b)-b/b=$
[12]	0	[18]	$a=bc$		$(ac/b)-1$

●●●●●   SELF-TEST

1. Using the less than and greater than symbols, express the unequal relationship between 2 and 4 in two ways.

2. State symbolically the fact that *X:*
    a. falls between 10 and 20
    b. is negative
    c. is greater than or equal to 0
    d. is less than or equal to 0 and greater than -10

3. Simplify
    a. $(-3)(-2)$
    b. $(-a)(b)(-c)$
    c. $-12/6$
    d. $-10+5$
    e. $5-[(-23)(-5)/(-23)]$

4. Simplify and solve the following:
    a. $(2/3)\cdot(1/4)$
    b. $(2/3)\div(1/4)$
    c. $(2/3)+(1/4)$
    d. $(1/2+7/10)(2/3-1/4)$
    e. $6!/4!$

5. Simplify.
    a. $28/32$
    b. $(3/5)(2/3)(15/16)$

6. Simplify
    a. 3^4 c. $(2/3)^4$ e. $(2-b)^2$
    b. 2^{5-3} d. $(a+b)^2$

7. Simplify.
    a. $5-3(2)+(3+4)$
    b. $5X-10=20$
    c. $(ab+bc)/[b(a+c)]$
    d. $[a(b-c)+(ab-ac)]/[-a(c-b)]$
    e. $x(y+z)=xy+2$
    f. $[-1(-ab)-ac+a^2]/a+c$

8. Determine the sum, the square of the sum, and the sum of the squared scores for:

5
-3
2
2
-5
1

● ● ● ● ●   ANSWERS

Self-Test. (1) $2 < 4$, $4 > 2$. **(2a)** $10 < X < 20$;   **(4e)** 30. **(5a)** $7/8$; **(5b)** $3/8$. **(6a)** 81; **(6b)** 4;
(2b) $X < 0$; **(2c)** $X \geq 0$; **(2d)** $-10 < X \leq 0$.   **(6c)** $16/81$; **(6d)** $a^2 + 2ab + b^2$;
(3a) 6; **(3b)** abc; **(3c)** -2; **(3d)** -5; **(3e)** 10.   **(6e)** $4 - 4b + b^2$. **(7a)** 6; **(7b)** $X = 6$; **(7c)** 1;
(4a) $1/6$; **(4b)** $8/3$; **(4c)** $11/12$; **(4d)** $1/2$;   **(7d)** 2; **(7e)** $xz = 2$; **(7f)** $a + b$. **(8)** 2, 4, 68.

● ● ● ● ●

CPSIA information can be obtained
at www.ICGtesting.com
Printed in the USA
FFOW03n2220130415
12603FF